VISUAL QUICKSTART

Microsoft Office 2013

STEVE SCHWARTZ

Peachpit Press

Visual QuickStart Guide

Microsoft Office 2013

Steve Schwartz

Peachpit Press
www.peachpit.com
To report errors, please send a note to errata@peachpit.com
Peachpit Press is a division of Pearson Education

Copyright © 2013 by Steve Schwartz

Editor: Clifford Colby
Copyeditor: Valerie Haynes Perry
Production editor: David Van Ness
Compositor: Steve Schwartz
Indexer: Valerie Haynes Perry
Cover design: RHDG / Riezebos Holzbaur Design Group, Peachpit Press
Interior design: Peachpit Press
Logo design: MINE™ www.minesf.com

ISBN-13: 978-0-321-89749-7
ISBN-10: 0-321-89749-8

9 8 7 6 5 4 3 2 1

Printed and bound in the United States of America

Contents at a Glance

Table of Contents

PART II   Microsoft Word

Introduction

Welcome to *Microsoft Office 2013: Visual QuickStart Guide*. In the pages that follow, you'll find the information and instructions needed to quickly become productive with the key applications in Microsoft Office.

Like other titles in the Visual QuickStart series, this book was written primarily as a reference. Unlike a book on a single program, however, this one covers four major applications: Word, PowerPoint, Excel, and Outlook. Rather than discuss every command and procedure in excruciating detail (as you'd expect in a one-program book), this book focuses on the commands and procedures that you're most likely to actually use.

How This Book Is Organized

To make it easy for you to find the information you need at any given moment, the book is divided into major sections called parts.

- Part I describes the changes you'll find in Office 2013 and provides an introduction to essential Office procedures. Certain tools and features (such as using the Backstage, working with graphics, and creating charts and tables) work the same regardless of the Office program you're using at the moment. Rather than repeat this material for each application, it's presented in Chapters 2 and 3.

- Parts II through V are devoted to the individual Office applications—one part for each application.

- Part VI shows some ways that you can use the applications together, combining elements from one application with another (such as incorporating Word tables in Excel worksheets).

Which Suites Are Covered?

Microsoft Office 2013 is available in four configurations (or *suites*), each with a different combination of applications (**Table I.1**). With the exception of the Home & Student suite, each includes the four core applications discussed in this book: Word, Excel, PowerPoint, and Outlook.

TIP For a solid, inexpensive primer about an earlier version of Microsoft Access, you might want to pick up a copy of *Microsoft Office Access 2003 for Windows: Visual QuickStart Guide*, written by yours truly.

The Office Applications

If you're unfamiliar with any of the applications covered in this book, the following pages provide a quick overview of the tasks for which each one is best suited.

Microsoft Office Word 2013

Word is a word-processing program. You can use it to write letters, memos, contracts, reports, or the Great American Novel. Because Word is so commonly used in the business world, you'll find that most word-processing documents you receive from others will be Word files or ones that can be opened using Word.

Like other word-processing programs of the past twenty years, Word uses a *WYSIWYG* (What You See Is What You Get) approach to document formatting, layout, and display. That is, the fonts, paragraph formats, margins, and page breaks you see onscreen will precisely match those in the printout.

If your needs go beyond simple text documents, you can embellish them with tables, clip art, and photos. You can also apply stylish 3-D effects called WordArt to text and important titles or insert bulleted lists as eye-catching SmartArt.

In addition to allowing you to create new documents from scratch, Word provides an array of templates for useful documents and forms. Many can be used as-is or with only minor modification. And if you want to generate personalized mailings, Word has a mail merge feature.

Microsoft Office Excel 2013

As popular as Word, Excel is the most widely used spreadsheet application around. You can use a spreadsheet to enter, analyze, and summarize large amounts of numerical and text data on a row-and-column grid.

Excel is an excellent tool for performing calculations (via formulas and its built-in functions), as well as for creating colorful, informative graphs. And because so many

TABLE I.1 Microsoft Office 2013 Suites

Applications	Home & Student	Home & Business	Professional	Office 365 Home Premium
Word, Excel, PowerPoint, OneNote	√	√	√	√
Outlook		√	√	√
Publisher, Access			√	√

people use worksheets to record lists, Excel also includes list-management features.

The days of the drab, colorless, single-font worksheet are over. Excel supports mixed fonts, styles, colors, and rotated text, as well as cell backgrounds and conditional formatting. To further embellish any worksheet, you can add clip art, photos, predefined shapes (such as arrows and text balloons), WordArt, and SmartArt.

Microsoft Office PowerPoint 2013

PowerPoint is Office's "best in class" application for creating presentations: slide shows with between-slide transition effects, within-slide animations, recorded audio narration, presenter notes, and handouts.

To give your slides a consistent, professional look, you can select one of the included themes or download others from Office.com. You can also create and save templates that include designs and other key elements, such as a company logo or address information.

After you've rehearsed and set the timing for your presentation, it can be played on a computer, professionally output to slides, or used to broadcast a web-based presentation.

Microsoft Office Outlook 2013

Outlook's primary function is that of a mail client. Outlook can send, receive, and manage email for all types of accounts (including certain web-based ones, such as Hotmail and Windows Live). Outlook 2013 can also be configured to receive Really Simple Syndication (RSS) message feeds.

In addition to providing email capabilities, Outlook can serve as your business and home calendar (allowing you to record and schedule reminders for upcoming appointments, meetings, and other events), handle your to-do list, and manage work and personal contacts.

How to Use This Book

This is a book for beginning to intermediate users of Microsoft Office 2013 for Windows. If you're using Office for the first time or already know the basics but want to get more out of your investment in Office, this book is for you. If you learn better from step-by-step instructions and graphic examples than from reference manuals that just describe what the commands do, this book is also for you. Most of all, if you know what you want to do and want to get started in the shortest possible time, this book is definitely for you.

I've worked hard to create a book that will let you turn to the directions for any procedure, learn what it does, and then do it yourself. Color screen shots illustrate significant steps. The goal is to give you all the information you need and little that you don't, making you productive as quickly as possible. Along the way, you'll find many tips that offer helpful information about the procedures.

Command Conventions

Office's implementation of the Ribbon provides a new place where you can find and execute Office commands—in addition to toolbars, floating windows, panels and panes, dialog boxes, context menus, and keyboard shortcuts.

Ribbon Commands

Ribbon components are separated by a colon (:). When choosing a command from a drop-down menu on the Ribbon, the menu-specific components are separated by the **>** symbol.

Ribbon tab : group : command

Example: "To format selected text as bold-face, click Home:Font:Bold."

Explanation: In the Font group on the Home tab, click the Bold icon.

Ribbon tab : group : icon > menu item

Example: "To set 1" margins for a document, choose Page Layout:Page Setup:Margins > Normal."

Explanation: Switch to the Page Layout tab. In the tab's Page Setup group, click the Margins icon and choose Normal from the drop-down menu.

Note that whenever a Ribbon command is described, the components are always presented in their proper order.

Toolbars, Panes, Palettes, Dialog Boxes, and Context Menus

To prevent commands for these elements from being confused with Ribbon commands, the commands are generally written out in plain English, such as this: "On the Indents and Spacing tab of the Paragraph dialog box, choose a paragraph alignment from the Alignment drop-down menu."

Keyboard Shortcuts

A command may also have an associated keyboard shortcut that executes the command as though it had been chosen from the Ribbon or elsewhere. Keyboard shortcuts are written out in plain text, such as "Press Ctrl-V to paste the most recently copied or cut item."

Too Many Commands, Too Little Space

Over the years, many programs have expanded to offer users multiple ways of performing a command or procedure. With this flexibility, however, can come confusion. In previous editions of this book (as well as my other Peachpit titles), I've prided myself on detailing all the possible ways you might execute a particular command. Knowledge is power, right?

But with the addition of the Ribbon, task panes, and object buttons, it occurs to me that:

- There may now be as many as half a dozen ways to execute some commands.

- Rather than helping you by allowing you to pick the most convenient method from all possible command-execution methods, I may inadvertently be adding to the confusion.

- Presenting every imaginable option takes up a lot of page space and may, in fact, detract from the presentation.

Based on my new assumption that you don't want or need to know *every* way to issue each command, this book will try to limit the presented options to two or three. At a minimum, I'll list the Ribbon command. Keep in mind that you should still explore the available toolbars, dialog boxes, and panes/panels to see if there's a more convenient method of executing a particular command.

TIP Be sure to try right-clicking selected text and objects. Microsoft provides many context menus that appear in response to a right-click. You may find right-clicking to be more expedient than scouring Ribbon tabs and memorizing keyboard shortcuts.

About the Author

Since modern man shoved aside the typewriter in favor of the keyboard, I've been writing computer articles and books. (I was going to say "Since the dawn of time…," but thought it would be a bit much. Thirty-five years of computer-industry writing *is* a long time, though!) My first computer book was published in 1984, and I've written more than 60 additional titles since then. This may not make me the first computer book author or the most prolific, but I must be close on both counts.

My background includes Editor-In-Chief of a computer periodical/book, as well as Technical Services Director for a software company. I also have a Ph.D. in psychology that I don't use, but the diploma does make a nifty wall hanging.

What's New in Office 2013?

In this chapter, you'll receive a brief overview of the new features and changes introduced in Office 2013—changes in each application, as well as changes that affect all applications.

As mentioned in the Introduction, not all new features mentioned in this chapter will be covered in the book—although many will. Changes that affect typical users will be found in the application chapters.

In This Chapter

Office-wide Changes

In addition to the many new application-specific features and enhancements, Office 2013 includes changes that apply to the entire suite or to multiple programs.

Another New Look

Launch any Office 2013 application and you'll immediately see how it differs from past versions 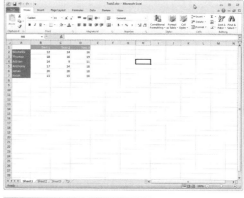. Forsaking the more colorful interfaces of Office 2003–2010, the new interface is unassuming, unobtrusive, and somewhat stark by comparison. If you like, you can optionally apply an Office background to all title bars, such as tree rings or calligraphy. This new look also appears in the Office Web Apps.

The Well-lubricated Office

Selecting and moving items employs a frictionless style of animation. Whether moving cells in Excel or text within Word, material glides effortlessly around the page. On Android cell phones and tablets, this type of animation has been described as *buttery*. While it doesn't change how these same operations have always worked, they *feel* different.

Office in the Cloud

SkyDrive support is built into Office 2013, allowing you to open and save your Office documents to Microsoft servers as easily as to your own hard drive . When you store files in the cloud, you can access them from any computer or device, as well as share them with colleagues and friends. And if Office isn't available on your current computer, you can view and edit your Sky-Drive documents using a browser and the Office Web Apps.

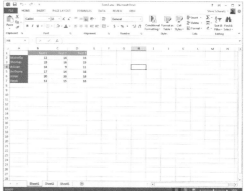

Ⓐ Excel 2010 (top) and Excel 2013 (bottom).

SkyDrive account

Ⓑ Whenever you open or save an Office 2013 document, you can use your computer's hard drive or your SkyDrive account.

Format Picture
task pane

Online Pictures and Videos

In addition to inserting photos and videos from your computer into Office documents, you can insert them from the Internet **C**. Online image sources include clip art and royalty-free photos from Office.com, images found in a Bing web search, and material in your SkyDrive account. Online video can come from Bing searches, YouTube, or web site videos that provide an *embed code*.

C If you're looking for a photo, a Bing search can usually suggest some suitable ones.

Task Panes

In addition to the familiar dialog boxes, context menus, and Ribbon controls, Office 2013 makes it easier to perform related commands by opening a *task pane* on the right side of the document window. For example, when designing a PivotTable in Excel, the PivotTable Fields task pane automatically appears. When you're editing a photo in Word and click the Format Shape dialog box launcher, the Format Picture task pane opens **D** rather than a tabbed dialog box.

The purpose of each task pane is to simplify the process of issuing related commands without requiring multiple trips to the Ribbon. To dismiss an open task pane, click its close box.

D It's often more convenient to use a task pane than to use the Ribbon or context menus.

Buttons

In various places in Office, *buttons* appear beside selected objects. Chart buttons in Excel enable you to easily modify chart elements, the chart style, or apply filters. When a photo or other object is selected in Word, you can click the Layout button to set word wrap for the item **E**. Like the task panes, buttons enable you to bypass the Ribbon when performing basic edits and changing properties.

Button

E When selected, some items display a button that you can click to access a pop-out menu or gallery.

Apps for Office

Free and paid add-ins for Office **F** can be downloaded from the Office Store and run from within your documents. After downloading an app, you can run it by choosing it from the Insert:Apps:Apps for Office menu.

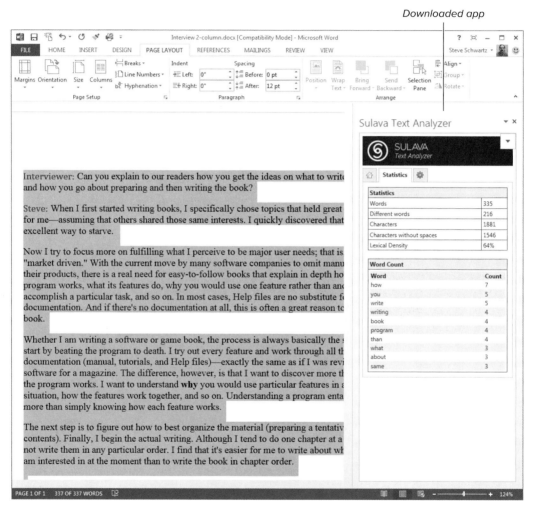

Downloaded app

F Downloaded apps for Office can add new capabilities to Office 2013. For example, the Sulava Text Analyzer returns statistics about selected text in any Word document or Excel worksheet.

Selected range (A1:D7)　　　Quick Analysis icon

Quick Analysis categories　　　　Commands

A Use the Quick Analysis tools to quickly issue commands, while avoiding the Ribbon.

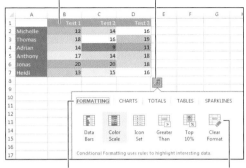

B When you reopen a PowerPoint or Word document, you can optionally jump to the last active slide or page.

Eyedropper　Selected color

Object to be colored

C Pick a color to apply to the selected object.

Application Changes

In this section, you'll learn about significant application-specific features and changes introduced in Office 2013.

New in Microsoft Excel 2013

- Use the *Quick Analysis* tools **A** on a selected range to apply conditional formatting, create a chart, add column or row summary statistics, convert the range to a table or PivotTable, or add sparklines.

- When creating a chart, click *Recommended Charts* to view chart types that are appropriate for the selected data.

- *Chart buttons* appear when you're editing a chart, enabling you to easily add or remove elements, change the style or colors, and apply data filters.

- Use *Flash Fill* to intelligently parse a column of data into its component elements, such as extracting the first and last names from a full name.

New in Microsoft PowerPoint 2013

- When you reopen a presentation in PowerPoint, a *resume reading* icon **B** appears on the document's edge. Click it to jump to the last slide viewed in the previous session.

- *Wide-screen (16:9) layouts* are provided.

- *Smart Guides* simplify the process of aligning and spacing objects.

- Use the *eyedropper tool* **C** to pick an existing color on a slide and apply it to a selected object.

- *Presenter view* has been revised to provide an automatic setup that's based on your "sensed" equipment. It now works with a single monitor, too.

New in Microsoft Word 2013

- When you reopen a Word document, a *resume reading* icon appears . Click the icon to jump to the last page viewed in the previous session.

- Office 2010's Full Screen Reading view has been replaced by *Read Mode* . It displays the document in magazine style and operates within the confines of the document window. In Read Mode, you can temporarily zoom in on a table, chart, or image by double-clicking it.

- You can *expand or collapse document sections* by clicking their headings  (similar to the way that you can expand and collapse parts of an outline).

- You can *open and edit the content of PDF files*.

- If you enable Format : Arrange : Align Objects > Use Alignment Guides, green *alignment guides* appear as you drag an object—showing when it's aligned with a margin or the center of the page. *Live preview* continuously shows how surrounding text will wrap around an object as you drag it.

- *Simple Markup* is a new, uncluttered revision view that displays a red vertical bar in the margin to indicate any tracked change (see ⓓ for examples). Click a change bar to view or hide the specific changes.

- Using the File : Share : Present Online command, you can *broadcast Word documents* on the web ⓕ. Invited participants open their browsers to a special address and can follow along as you scroll through the document pages.

Read Mode menus

Previous page   *Next page*

ⓓ Word 2013's new Read Mode.

ⓔ Any text that Word recognizes as a heading can be collapsed or expanded.

ⓕ You can present Word documents online.

Lundin Dental

Itemized statement for 2012   3/21/2012
Steve, Attached is the
itemizted statement for 2012.

G Each message in the message list can display the first 1–3 lines of the message body—making it easier to spot any messages that you should read immediately.

Pick up o-ring at Neat Pools   All day

Mail Calendar Peop

FILTER APPLIED

H Rest the cursor on Calendar to display a pop-up calendar and list of scheduled events for any date.

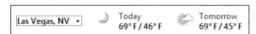

Las Vegas, NV ▾   🌙   Today   ☁ Tomorrow
                        69° F / 46° F   69° F / 45° F

I The weather bar helps keep you abreast of the current and forecasted weather.

New in Microsoft Outlook 2013

- You can *preview message content* by electing to display the first 1–3 lines of each message in the message list **G**. Choose an option from the View: Arrangement: Message Preview menu.

- After setting a preference in Mail Options, you can type *Inline comments* in replies. Each time you enter text in the quoted section of a person's message, the new material is preceded by your name in brackets. Text typed above the original message, on the other hand, is handled normally—without the attribution text and brackets.

- Use *Calendar peek* **H** to check your schedule without leaving Mail. Hover the cursor over Calendar in the navigation bar to view a pop-up calendar with your scheduled events and appointments. Peek works for tasks in the same way.

- You can display a *weather bar* **I** at the top of Calendar, showing the current and upcoming weather for up to five cities.

2

Office Basics

Although the applications in the various Office suites aren't heavily integrated with one another, they do have some similarities. For example, saving files, working with windows, printing, and other basic operations vary little from one Office application to the next. In this chapter, you'll become acquainted with these *Office essentials*.

In This Chapter

Launching Office Applications

You launch Office applications in the same manner as other Windows applications.

To launch an Office application in Windows 7 and earlier:

1. Click the Start button, All Programs, and the Microsoft Office 2013 folder **Ⓐ**.

   The folder expands, showing the installed Office 2013 applications.

TIP To quickly open the Start menu, press the Windows logo key on your keyboard.

2. Click the application that you want to run.

   The selected application launches.

To launch an Office application in Windows 8:

1. Switch to the Start screen.

2. *Do either of the following:*

   ▸ Scroll until you see the tile of the Office application that you want to run. Click its tile.

   ▸ Search for the Office application by typing part of its name, such as **Exc** for Excel. Windows displays tiles for all matching applications. Click the Office application's tile.

   The Desktop appears and the application launches.

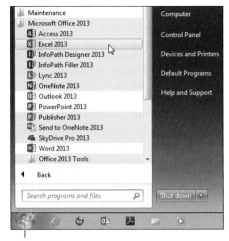

Start button

Ⓐ The most common way to launch a program in Windows 7 and earlier is to choose it from the Start menu.

Other Launch Methods

You can also launch an Office application in most versions of Windows by doing any of the following:

- If you recently ran the application, you can select its name from the list in the Start panel.

- If you've created them, you can click a Desktop or Quick Launch short-cut for the application or one of its documents.

- Open an Office document by clicking (or double-clicking) its file icon. The document opens in the appropriate Office application.

- In Windows Vista, you can choose a recently opened Office document from the Start > Recent Items sub-menu. In Windows 7, each recently used application provides its own recent document list. Choosing a document launches the Office application (if it isn't already running).

Back

A Click the Back button to exit the Backstage and continue working on the document.

Blank document thumbnail

B Click a thumbnail to create a new document.

Single- vs. Double-clicking

Whether it takes a single or double click to open a folder, document, or program depends on a control panel setting:

1. Click the Start button and select Control Panel.

2. Open the Folder Options control panel. (It's in the Appearance and Personalization group in Windows 7.)

3. In the Click items as follows section of the control panel, select the Single-click or Double-click radio button.

4. Click OK to save the new setting.

Using the Backstage

In Office 2007, core applications had a large, glowing icon in the upper-left corner of the document window called the *Office Button*. Clicking it revealed a page on which you could perform file and document-related tasks, such as opening, saving, and printing, In Office 2010, the Office Button was replaced by the File tab. When clicked, the *Backstage* appears.

In this section, I'll explain the basics of using the Backstage. Application-specific differences will be covered in application chapters.

To open or close the Backstage:

- To open the Backstage, click the File tab.

- To exit from the Backstage, click the Back button **A** or press Esc.

Creating a New Document

By default, previous versions of document-based Office programs (Word, Excel, and PowerPoint, for example) automatically created a new, blank document each time you launched the program. The procedure for creating a new document differs slightly in Office 2013 when you're launching the program or it's already running.

To create a new document at launch:

- At launch, the Backstage immediately appears. Click the thumbnail for a Blank document (Word) **B**, Blank worksheet (Excel), Blank presentation (PowerPoint), or a document template.

TIP You can also create a new, blank document by pressing Esc.

To create a new document when the program is running:

- *Do one of the following:*

  ▸ Press Ctrl-N to create a new, blank document.

  ▸ Click the File tab and select New in the Backstage **C**. Click the thumbnail of the type of document you want to create. If you select any thumbnail other than Blank document (Word), Blank worksheet (Excel). or Blank presentation (PowerPoint), a template description window appears **D**. Click the Create button.

TIP A few templates are created instantly—without displaying the template description and Create button.

  ▸ To search for a template at Office.com, enter search text **C** or click a Suggested search link beneath the search box. When the results thumbnails appear **E**, select one and click Create. The template is downloaded to your computer and opens as a new document.

TIP You can further focus an Office.com template search by selecting a category.

TIP A downloaded template can be used as the basis for other new documents by clicking the File tab, New, and the template thumbnail.

New category   Search online   Templates

C Click New and then click the thumbnail of the document you want to create.

Create button

D If you select a template, a description of it appears in a new window. Click Create to create the new document. (To cancel, click outside the window or press Esc.)

E Office.com downloadable templates.

Open options

F The Open section in the Backstage (Word).

G To open a file that's stored online in your SkyDrive account, select a SkyDrive folder you've recently accessed or click Browse. To learn more about SkyDrive, see the sidebar "SkyDrive: Office in the Cloud," later in this chapter.

H You can pin a frequently used file or folder to a list in the Open section of the Backstage.

Opening Documents

In addition to creating new documents, you can open existing documents—to view, print, or revise them. You can open documents from within Office applications or from the Desktop (simultaneously launching the creating program, if it isn't running).

To open an existing document from within an Office application:

1. Click the File tab and select the Open category (or press Ctrl-O).

   The Open section of the Backstage appears **F**.

2. Depending on the document's location, the options you'll typically use include:

   ▸ **Recent Documents.** If you've recently worked on the document, click its name in the Recent Documents list.

   ▸ **SkyDrive.** Click a folder in the Recent Folders list or click Browse **G**. In the Open dialog box, navigate to the folder that contains the document, select its filename, and click Open.

   ▸ **Computer.** Click a listed folder or click Browse. In the Open dialog box, navigate to the folder that contains the document, select its filename, and click Open.

   The document opens in a new window.

> **TIP** If Folder Options on your PC has been set to open items by single-clicking (see the sidebar "Single- vs. Double-clicking," earlier in this chapter), the document may open without having to click the Open button.

> **TIP** If you frequently work with a particular file or folder, you can *pin* the file or folder to the Recent Documents list or a Recent Folders list. Hover the cursor over the filename or folder and click the pushpin icon **H**. To later unpin the item, click the pushpin icon again.

To open an existing Office document from the Desktop:

1. Locate the document file on the Desktop or in the folder in which it's stored.

2. *Do either of the following:*

   ▸ Click (or double-click) the file icon.

   ▸ Right-click the file icon and choose Open from the context menu 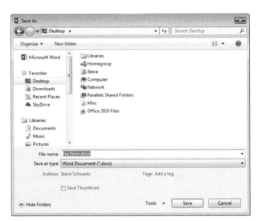.

   The appropriate Office program launches (if it isn't currently running) and the document opens.

Saving Documents

Until you save a document to disk, it exists only in your PC's memory. If you close a document or exit an application without saving, the document and changes are lost.

TIP Note that if AutoRecover is enabled for the Office program, you may be able to recover such unsaved documents. Refer to "AutoRecover Options," later in this chapter.

To save a new document:

1. *Do one of the following:*

   ▸ Click the Save icon on the Quick Access Toolbar  or press Ctrl-S.

   ▸ Click the File tab, and then click Save or Save As in the Backstage. Select a location, such as Computer or SkyDrive. Within the location, select a listed folder or click Browse.

   The Save As dialog box opens 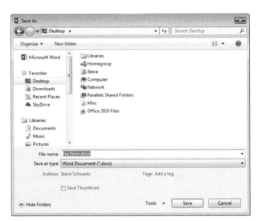.

2. Navigate to the destination disk and folder (if the current one isn't correct).

3. Enter a name in the File name box, select a format from the Save as type drop-down list, and click Save.

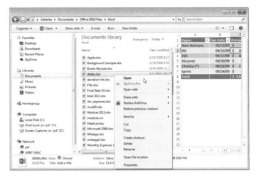

I In a folder or on the Desktop, you can also open an Office document by right-clicking its file icon or filename and choosing Open.

Save

J You can save a new or existing file by clicking the Save icon at the top of the document window.

K Use the Save As dialog box to save a new document. You can also use it to save an edited document with a new name, new file format, or in a different disk/folder.

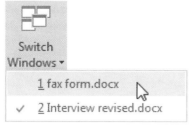

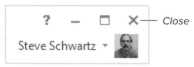

L You can switch to any open document by selecting its name from the Switch Windows drop-down list.

M You can close a document by clicking its close box.

Another Way to Save As

From the Backstage, you can quickly specify an alternate Save As format. Click Export, Change File Type, and the new format. A Save As dialog box appears with the selected format already set.

Sanitized for Your Protection

When you attempt to open a document that originated from a potentially unsafe source (such as an Internet email attachment), an Office 2013 application will automatically open the file in Protected View. Such documents can be read but not edited. If you trust the document's source and want to edit it, click the Enable Editing button in the Protected View yellow banner that appears at the top of the document.

To save an edited document:

- *Do either of the following:*

  ▸ To replace a current Word, Excel, or PowerPoint file with the edited version, click the Save icon in the Quick Access Toolbar **J**, click the File tab and choose Save, or press Ctrl-S. The previous version is replaced by the current version.

  ▸ You can save a copy of an edited document with a different name, in a different file format, or to a new location. Click the File tab, and then click Save As. The Save As dialog box appears **K**. Specify a filename, format, and location, and then click Save.

Closing Documents

It isn't necessary to quit an Office application just to work with another document. When you're done working with a document, you can close it.

To close a document:

1. Make the document *active* by doing one of the following:

   ▸ Click the document's icon on the taskbar.

   ▸ Choose the filename from the View: Window:Switch Windows menu **L**.

2. *Do one of the following:*

   ▸ Click the File tab and select Close in the Backstage (or press Ctrl-W).

   ▸ Click the close box (X) in the upper-right corner of the document **M**.

   If this is the application's *only* open document, the application quits. Otherwise, the document closes. If the document has never been saved or contains unsaved edits, you're given an opportunity to save.

TIP You can also close a document by right-clicking its taskbar icon and choosing the Close command.

TIP In Windows 7, open documents are grouped within an application's taskbar icon and each has its own close box (X). To reveal the application's open documents, hover the cursor over its taskbar icon 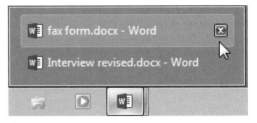.

 You can click a close box in an application's pop-up taskbar list.

Printing

The process of printing a document varies little from one Office application to another. The biggest difference lies in the options you can set. For details on application-specific Print options, see the application's chapters.

To print a document:

1. Open the document you want to print.

2. *Do either of the following:*

   ▶ Click the File tab. In the Backstage, click Print.

   ▶ Press Ctrl-P.

   The Print section appears 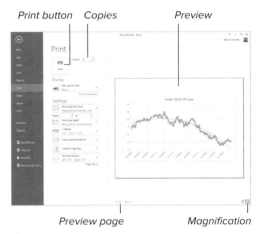.

3. Select the destination printer from the Printer drop-down list.

TIP Not only can you print to a printer that's directly connected to your PC, you may also be able to print to network printers (if you're on a network and have permission to use the printer).

TIP If the destination printer isn't listed, you can install it by choosing Add Printer from the Printer drop-down list 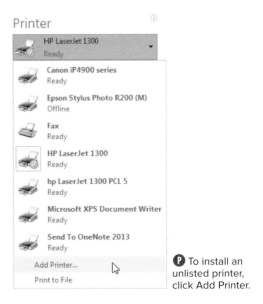.

Print button   *Copies*   *Preview*

Preview page   *Magnification*

 Select a printer, set options, and click Print.

 To install an unlisted printer, click Add Printer.

Identify Yourself

To automatically use your name as the author of your Office documents, you must personalize your copy of Office. This information is also used to identify edits and comments of contributors.

1. Open an Office document and click the File tab.

2. In the Backstage, click Options.

3. In the General section of the Options dialog box, enter your User name and click OK.

Personalize your copy of Microsoft Office	
User name:	Steve Schwartz

SkyDrive: Office in the Cloud

In January 2010, Microsoft launched Windows Live SkyDrive, providing 25 GB of online file storage to anyone with a free Windows Live/Hotmail account. In Office, when you're signed into your Microsoft account, you can access the SkyDrive servers to accomplish the following:

- Open, save, and share documents using Office 2013

- Use a browser on any computer to view and edit Office documents in the Office Web Apps

- Access your files on other devices, such as tablets and mobile phones

4. Specify the number of copies.

5. Indicate the pages to print by choosing an option from the first Settings menu, such as Print All Pages or Print Selection (to print only the currently selected pages or object).

TIP To print specific pages or a page range, enter the page numbers and range(s) in the Pages box. Separate pages and ranges with commas, such as 1,3,5–7,9.

6. Set other options in the Settings section, such as paper size, orientation, and collation.

   As you change settings, they're reflected in the preview.

TIP Use the controls at the bottom of the preview area to change the magnification or the page you're previewing.

7. *Optional:* To change the margins, layout, and similar settings, click Page Setup (below the Settings menus).

8. Ensure that the printer is on and ready to print, and click the Print button.

   The print job is sent to the selected printer.

TIP If you save a document after printing, the print settings are also saved.

Using the Ribbon

If the most recent version of Office you've used was Office 2003 or earlier (or if this is your first Office version), you're probably wondering what happened to the command menus. To provide easier access to all parts of the Office applications, Microsoft removed the menus from Word, Power-Point, and Excel 2007. In Office 2010, they finished modifying the core applications by removing Outlook's menus, too. In their place is a new interface known as the *Ribbon*.

The Ribbon Ⓐ is the interface for every Word, Excel, PowerPoint, and Outlook document, displayed across the top of the window. Within the Ribbon, similar commands and procedures are listed together on a *tab*, such as Insert or View. Within a tab, procedures are further divided into *groups*, based on similarity of function. To perform a command, you switch to the appropriate tab by clicking its name, locate the desired group, and then click the command icon or control.

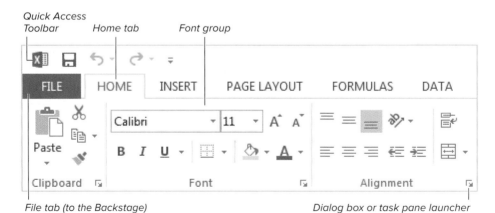

Ⓐ A section of the Ribbon interface in Excel 2013.

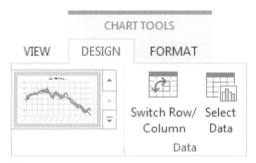

B When you select a chart in Excel, the Chart Tools contextual tab appears on the Ribbon. Click the Design or Format tab to set or edit the chart's properties.

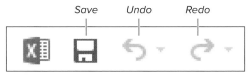

Collapse the Ribbon

C Click this icon to minimize the Ribbon.

Save Undo Redo

D The default Quick Access Toolbar contains only a few command icons.

Contextual Tabs

When working with certain kinds of items in a document, such as an image, table, or chart, a colored *contextual tab* appears above the other Ribbon tabs **B**. Click a new tab beneath it to view and use commands that are relevant to the selected material. Note that some contextual tabs, such as Chart Tools in Excel and Table Tools in Word, are split into multiple tabs.

When you're done using a contextual tab's tools, you can dismiss it by selecting a different object or clicking elsewhere in the document.

TIP If you like, you can hide the Ribbon so only the tab names are displayed. Click the Collapse the Ribbon control **C** or press Ctrl-F1. To access a tab's controls and temporarily reveal the Ribbon, click the tab's name. When you're done using the tab, the Ribbon automatically collapses again.

To restore the Ribbon, click a tab or press Ctrl-F1 to reveal the Ribbon, and then click the pushpin icon that appears in place of the Collapse the Ribbon control.

Quick Access Toolbar

In the upper-left corner of the document window is the *Quick Access Toolbar* **D**. It has icons for the most basic program procedures, such as saving the current document (Word, Excel, PowerPoint), performing a Send/Receive All (Outlook), and undoing and redoing commands. As discussed later in this chapter, you can add other commands to the Quick Access Toolbar.

Working with Windows

If you occasionally have several documents open, you can arrange and manipulate their windows using Office commands. Window management commands can be found in the View:Window group . Note that the availability, location, and implementation of these commands vary from one Office application to another.

New Window. The New Window command creates a new instance of the current document. Each new instance is named using the convention *filename:instance number*, such as `memo.docx:2`. Use the New Window command to view and work in two sections of a document at the same time.

Arrange All. This command simultaneously displays all open documents in an application. In Word, the documents are displayed one above the other. In PowerPoint, they're arranged side-by-side. In Excel, you can specify the arrangement in the dialog box that appears when you click View:Window: Arrange All Ⓑ.

Cascade. Arranging documents in cascade fashion displays the top edge of each one, enabling you to quickly switch documents by clicking any exposed edge Ⓒ. In PowerPoint, the Cascade icon is in the Window group. In Excel, this option can be selected in the Arrange Windows dialog box Ⓑ.

Ⓐ The View:Window group (Word).

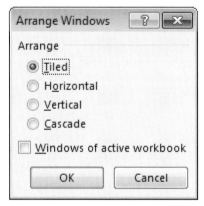

Ⓑ In Excel, you have great flexibility in arranging open workbook windows.

Ⓒ When you cascade documents, you can see the top edge and title of each one. Click any exposed edge to make a document active.

Split bar   Split bar

D You can split a Word or Excel document window to simultaneously work in multiple sections of the document.

Minimize Maximize

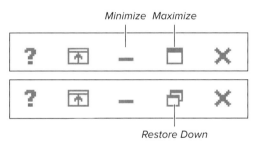

Restore Down

E The Maximize/Restore Down button changes, depending on the window's current state.

Split. Click the Split icon to split the current document into two (Word) or four parts (Excel) **D**, enabling you to work in two or four sections simultaneously. In Word, a split bar appears that you position by clicking. In Excel, the split appears above the current cell. You can reposition a split by clicking it and dragging. To remove splits, click the Split (or Remove Split) icon. You can also remove a split by dragging it off the document's edge.

Every Office application also supports standard Windows controls and techniques for manipulating windows (as explained below).

To use standard Windows controls:

- *Do any of the following:*
  - ▸ Click the Minimize button **E** to minimize a window to the taskbar. Click its taskbar icon to restore the window to its original onscreen position and size.
  - ▸ The Maximize/Restore Down button **E** has two states. When it's a box, click it to *maximize* the window, filling the screen. When a window is maximized, the button becomes a pair of boxes. Click it to restore the window to its original onscreen position and size.
  - ▸ To move a window, drag it by the title bar.
  - ▸ To manually resize a window, move the cursor over any edge or corner. When the cursor becomes a double arrow, click and drag to change the window's size.

Setting Magnification

If you're having difficulty reading a Word or Excel document because the type is too tiny or you want a bird's-eye view of a PowerPoint presentation, you can change the document's magnification (*zoom*).

To set the magnification in Word, Excel, or PowerPoint:

- Use the zoom control  in the bottom-right corner of the document window in any of these ways:

  - Drag the slider to a specific magnification percentage.

  - Click the – or + button to decrease or increase magnification by 10 percent.

  - Click the current zoom number to open the Zoom dialog box **B**.

- In the View:Zoom group **C**, *you can do any of the following:*

  - Click Zoom to open the Zoom dialog box **B** or 100% to zoom the document to its normal magnification.

  - If you've selected an object or other material in the document, you can click Zoom to Selection to fill the window with the selected material. When you're done, click View:Zoom:100% to return the magnification to normal.

> **TIP** You must set magnification separately for each open document in an application.

To set the magnification in Outlook:

- In the window for an existing email message or one you're composing, click the Message:Zoom:Zoom icon. Set a magnification level in the Zoom dialog box **D** and click OK.

A The zoom control provides three ways for you to set the current magnification.

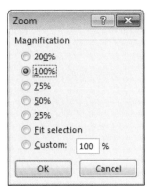

B Use the Zoom dialog box to set a specific or page-related magnification.

C Magnification commands can also be found in the View:Zoom group.

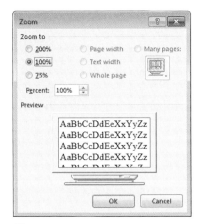

D You can also set the magnification for an Outlook email message.

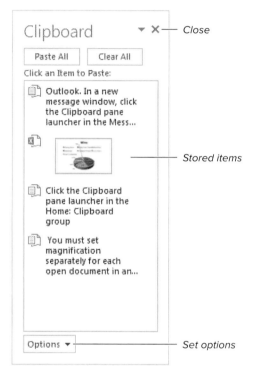

A Click here to open the Office Clipboard.

Clipboard ▼ × —— Close

—— Stored items

—— Set options

B The Office Clipboard.

C Each item in the Office Clipboard has its own Paste/Delete menu.

Using the Office Clipboard

The *Windows Clipboard* is an area in memory that stores the last item you cut or copied. When you paste an item, it's drawn from the Clipboard. If you copy or cut a new item, it takes the place of the current item stored in the Clipboard. Using the Clipboard, you can insert items into the current document, a different document, or even documents of other applications.

While working in Office, you can continue to use the Windows Clipboard as you've always done. In addition, you can use the *Office Clipboard*, a dedicated clipboard for sharing data among open Office documents. Unlike the Windows Clipboard, the Office Clipboard can store up to 24 items.

To open the Office Clipboard:

- **Word, Excel, PowerPoint.** Click the Clipboard task pane launcher in the Home : Clipboard group **A**.

- **Outlook.** In a new message window, click the Clipboard task pane launcher in the Message : Clipboard group.

  The Office Clipboard appears **B**.

To paste Office Clipboard items into a document:

1. Select the spot in the Office document where you want to paste the item(s).

2. *Do one of the following:*

   ▸ To paste an item, click the item in the Office Clipboard, or click the item's down arrow and choose Paste **C**.

   ▸ To simultaneously paste all items stored in the Office Clipboard, click the Paste All button **B**.

To clear items from the Office Clipboard:

- *Do either of the following:*
  - ▸ To remove a single item, move the cursor over the item, click the item's down arrow, and choose Delete from the drop-down menu **C**.
  - ▸ To remove all current items from the Office Clipboard, click the Clear All button **B**.

To set Office Clipboard options:

- Click the Options button **D** and set any of these options:
  - ▸ **Show Office Clipboard automatically.** Automatically display the Office Clipboard whenever you copy an item.
  - ▸ **Show Office Clipboard When Ctrl+C Pressed Twice.** Open the Office Clipboard by quickly pressing Ctrl-C twice.
  - ▸ **Collect Without Showing Office Clipboard.** Items are added to the Office Clipboard without displaying it.
  - ▸ **Show Office Clipboard on Taskbar.** Add a system tray icon for the Office Clipboard when it's active.
  - ▸ **Show Status Near Taskbar When Copying.** A status message appears when a new item is added to the Office Clipboard **E**.

To close the Office Clipboard:

- Click the Office Clipboard's close box (X) **B** or the Clipboard task pane launcher **A**.

D The Options menu for the Office Clipboard.

E A message like this can optionally appear to denote a newly added item.

Office Clipboard Tips

Here are some more facts you should know about the Office Clipboard:

- If you add more than 24 items to the Office Clipboard, the oldest item is automatically deleted to make room for the new item.

- To paste from the Windows Clipboard rather than from the Office Clipboard, use the normal Paste command (click the Paste icon or press Ctrl-V).

- The last item copied or cut also becomes the current item in the Windows Clipboard.

- Items remain in the Office Clipboard until you exit all Office programs.

The Mechanics of Copy, Cut, Paste, and Drag-and-Drop

Most Windows and Macintosh programs allow you to copy and cut text and objects to the Clipboard, and then paste the most recently copied or cut material to another location in the same document, a different document, or a document in another program. These procedures allow you to easily duplicate or move material. The last copied or cut item remains on the Clipboard and is available for pasting until a new copy or cut is performed.

Some programs also support the direct procedure of *drag-and-drop*, enabling you to accomplish a cut-and-paste by simply dragging the material to a new location. Unlike cutting, drag-and-drop doesn't use the Clipboard.

Surprisingly, many novice and seasoned computer users don't understand or take advantage of these marvelous time-saving techniques. Let's review how they work in Office. Note that these same commands and procedures are generally available in other Windows applications, too.

To perform a copy-and-paste:

1. Select the text or object(s) that you want to copy.

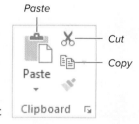

2. Click the Copy icon in the Home:Clipboard group or press Ctrl-C. The copied material is stored in the Windows Clipboard. If the Office Clipboard is active, the material is also stored there.

3. To select a destination for pasted text, position the text insertion mark at the spot in the document where you want to paste. To paste object(s), click the approximate location on the page where you want to paste the material.

4. Click the Paste icon in the Home:Clipboard group or press Ctrl-V. The material appears at the destination location.

To perform a cut-and-paste:

1. Select the text or object(s) you want to cut. Unlike copying, cutting is a destructive procedure and removes the selected material from its original location.

2. Click the Cut icon in the Home:Clipboard group or press Ctrl-X. The cut material is stored in the Windows Clipboard. If the Office Clipboard is active, the material is also stored there.

3. Select a destination for the cut material (as described for copying). Click the Paste icon in the Home:Clipboard group or press Ctrl-V to execute the paste.

To use drag-and-drop to perform a move:

1. Select the material to be moved.

2. Drag the selected material to the desired destination. Release the mouse button to complete the move.

Customizing Office

You can modify any Office program to make it easier to use and suit your working style by setting preferences, customizing the Quick Access Toolbar and Ribbon, and assigning keyboard shortcuts to commands.

Setting Preferences

Preference settings (called *options* in Office) determine how common procedures work in an Office application. Essentially, by modifying these settings, you're telling the application to "perform this action when I do this, rather than doing that." In Excel, for example, you can specify the direction that cell selection moves when you press Enter and whether to hide or show the formula bar. Although the default behaviors for commands and procedures are designed to meet the needs of most users, you can customize the way an application operates by changing its options settings.

To view or change preferences:

1. In a running Office application, click the File tab to go to the Backstage **A**.

2. Click Options.

   The *application name* Options dialog box appears **B**.

3. Select an options category from the list on the left side of the dialog box.

4. View and change options settings as desired.

5. *Optional:* To view or change settings in other categories, repeat Steps 3–4.

6. To enable all changes that you've made to the settings, click OK. Otherwise, to ignore changes (or if you've made no changes), click Cancel.

   The Options dialog box closes.

A The Backstage categories in Outlook.

Option categories (Outlook)

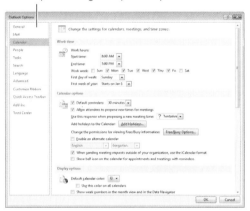

B Select an option category, view or change the settings, and click OK.

TIP Some option categories don't fit on a single screen. Use the scroll bar on the side of the dialog box to view the additional options.

TIP Most option settings apply to the application. A few, however, affect only the current *document*, such as the When calculating this workbook settings in the Advanced section of Excel Options.

Click to open list

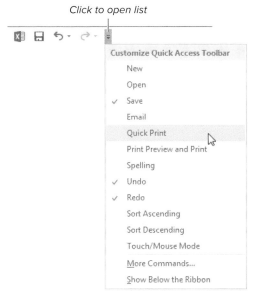

 Many common commands can be chosen from this drop-down list.

Select commands to add   *Add*

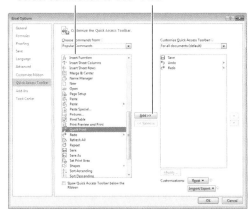

 Select a command from the left list and click Add to add it to the Quick Access Toolbar.

Customizing the Quick Access Toolbar

The Quick Access Toolbar in each Office application (see **D** in "Using the Ribbon") initially contains only a few command icons. However, you are free to expand it by adding commands for other procedures. The advantage of doing this is that commands on the Quick Access Toolbar are *always* available to you—regardless of the Ribbon tab you're currently using.

To add commands to the Quick Access Toolbar:

- *Do either of the following:*
  - ▸ Click the Customize Quick Access Toolbar icon at the right side of the toolbar and choose new commands from the list that appears **C**. Checked commands will appear in the toolbar.
  - ▸ Click the File tab, followed by Options. In the *application name* Options dialog box, select the Quick Access Toolbar category. To add a command to the toolbar, select it from the list on the left and click Add **D**. When you're done making changes, click OK.

TIP Another way to reach the Quick Access Toolbar section of the Options dialog box is to choose More Commands from the drop-down list **C**.

TIP To remove a command from the toolbar, choose it from the list **C** to remove its check mark. If the command isn't listed, open the Options dialog box **D**, select the command in the right-hand list, and click Remove.

Customizing the Ribbon

You aren't stuck with the standard Ribbon configuration for each program. If you want (although most users won't bother), you can customize the Ribbon by adding, removing, reordering, and renaming groups, tabs, and commands.

Keep the following in mind:

- Although you can remove any group from a tab or move it to a new position within the tab (or even to a different tab), you cannot remove or move command icons within the default tabs.

- Items that can't be modified are shown in gray text.

- You can add command icons to any tab or group, whether it's a default or custom tab or group.

To customize the Ribbon:

1. In the application you want to customize, click the File tab.

TIP To go directly to the Customize Ribbon section of the Backstage, right-click any Ribbon tab and choose Customize the Ribbon from the drop-down menu. Go to Step 4.

2. Click Options.

The *application name* Options dialog box opens.

3. Select the Customize Ribbon category **E**.

4. *Do any of the following:*

- **Show or hide a tab.** Add or remove the tab's check mark in the right-hand pane. For example, you can display the Developer tab in Excel, enabling you to record macros. Similarly, you can hide tabs you don't use.

Customize Ribbon   *Move Up/Move Down*

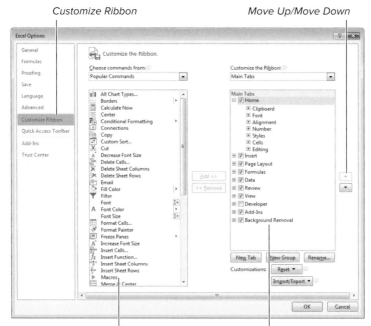

Command list   *Current tabs, groups, and commands*

E You can make changes to the Ribbon in this section of the application's Options dialog box.

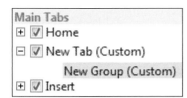

F When adding a tab, it appears under the currently selected tab (in this case, Home). Like other items, you can change its position.

G You can rename a tab, group, or command (top). When renaming a group or command, you can also select an icon to represent it (bottom).

▸ **Move a tab or group.** Select the tab or group in the right-hand pane and click a Move button.

TIP You can also change an item's position by dragging it up or down.

▸ **Create a new tab.** In the right-hand pane, select the tab beneath which the new tab will be added. Click New Tab. A tab named New Tab (Custom) is inserted into the list, as well as a placeholder for the tab's first group **F**. Rename them **G** by selecting each one and clicking Rename.

▸ **Create a new group.** In the right-hand pane, select the group beneath which the new group will be added. Click New Group. A group named New Group (Custom) is inserted into the list. Rename the group by selecting it and clicking Rename.

▸ **Add a command to a custom group.** Select a command set from the drop-down list above the left-hand pane. Select the group in the right-hand pane to which you want to add the command and click Add.

▸ **Remove a command.** Select the command in the right-hand pane and click Remove. (You can only remove commands previously added to a custom group; defaults are grayed out.)

▸ **Rename a tab, group, or command.** Select the item in the right-hand pane, click Rename, and rename the item **G**. Note that you can only rename items that aren't grayed out.

continues on next page

5. Click OK to accept the changes.

The document window appears, reflecting the Ribbon changes.

> **TIP** To restore the default Ribbon, click **Reset** and choose **Reset all customizations** from the drop-down menu. Click **Yes** in the confirmation dialog box that appears . Note that modifications you've made to the Quick Access Toolbar will also be reset.

> **TIP** To remove only the changes you've made to a specific tab, select the tab or any of its components in the right-hand pane, click **Reset**, and choose **Reset only selected Ribbon tab** from the drop-down menu.

Modifying Word Keyboard Shortcuts

To make it simpler to execute your favorite Word 2013 commands, you can assign keyboard shortcuts to them, as well as change existing shortcuts.

To view, change, or assign Word keyboard shortcuts:

1. In Word 2013, click the File tab, followed by Options.

The Word Options dialog box appears.

2. Select Customize Ribbon from the category list.

3. Click the Customize button beneath the left pane ❶.

The Customize Keyboard dialog box appears ❷.

❷ Confirm the Ribbon and Quick Access Toolbar reset by clicking Yes.

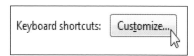

❶ Click this button to view or modify Word's keyboard shortcuts.

Categories   *Commands*

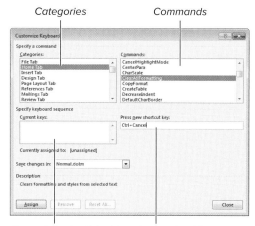

Current shortcut(s)   New shortcut key(s)

❷ View, change, or assign keyboard shortcuts in the Customize Keyboard dialog box.

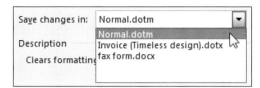

 You can save the keyboard shortcuts to the default template or to an open Word document.

4. Select a category from the Categories list and select a command to modify from the Commands list.

The current keyboard shortcuts (if any) assigned to the command are shown.

5. Press the keyboard shortcut that you want to assign to the command. If it's currently unassigned, click Assign.

Keyboard shortcuts normally consist of a letter or number key, plus one or more of these modifier keys: Shift, Ctrl, or Alt. Function keys, such as F7, can also be used as keyboard shortcuts—alone or in combination with other modifiers.

CAUTION **Be extremely careful when assigning or changing shortcuts. If the key combination you specify is currently assigned to another command, it is reassigned without warning to the selected command.**

6. If desired, repeat Steps 4 and 5 for other commands.

7. To accept all changes, click Close.

TIP **Shortcuts are either saved to the default Word template (Normal.dotm) or to a currently open document, depending on the selection for Save changes in . If you save to the former, the shortcuts will be available in all new documents. If you save to a specific document, the shortcuts will only work in that document.**

TIP **To remove a currently assigned shortcut, select it in the Current keys list for the command and click Remove.**

TIP **To restore all default Word shortcuts, click Reset All.**

Document Management Tools

Regardless of the core application you're running, you can use the following tools to safeguard your Office documents or prepare them to be shared:

- **AutoRecover options.** In Options, you can instruct an Office program to automatically save documents every so many minutes, protecting you from accidental data loss.

- **Document Inspector.** When sharing a document publicly or with a select set of users, the Document Inspector can be used to strip the document of embedded personal information, hidden text, invisible content, and the like.

- **Compatibility Checker.** Use this tool to quickly determine if there are compatibility issues with the current document that could affect users of earlier versions of this Office application.

- **Protect Document.** You can assign a password to any document to prevent unauthorized access to its contents.

- **Document Properties.** Every saved document has properties that you and others can view, such as author, size, pages, word count, and when it was last changed. There are also optional properties you can set, such as a title, tags, and comments.

A Set AutoRecover options in the Save category of each application's Options dialog box.

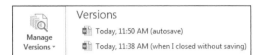

B Two drafts of the current document are listed. The first is a normal, period-based autosave. The second resulted from closing the changed document without saving.

More AutoRecover Information

You may find the following tips helpful:

- AutoRecover must be enabled separately for each Office application.

- Do not use AutoRecover as a substitute for regular manual Saves. If the interval is set to 10 minutes, you still risk losing that many minutes of document edits—depending on when you made your last edit and when the last autosave occurred.

- Frequent disk accesses drain laptop batteries. Laptop users may want to increase the AutoRecover interval.

- You can also examine unsaved versions of documents by going to the Backstage and choosing Manage Versions > Recover Unsaved Documents.

AutoRecover Options

As you work on a Word, Excel, or PowerPoint document, Office can automatically save a draft copy whenever changes are noted during a specified interval. Enabling AutoRecover options protects your work in the event of a crash, power outage, or failure to save. When you issue a normal Save, autosaved draft files created in prior intervals are automatically deleted. By default, AutoRecover options are enabled.

To enable document AutoRecover:

1. In an Office 2013 application, click the File tab, followed by Options.

   The Options dialog box opens.

2. Select the Save category.

   AutoRecover options can be found in the Save documents section **A**.

3. To enable AutoRecover, click the Save AutoRecover information every *X* minutes check box and specify an autosave frequency (in minutes).

   As you work on a document, Office will automatically save a copy in the designated location at the specified interval.

4. *Optional:* Check Keep the last autosaved version if I close without saving.

   If you close a document without saving your changes, a version will automatically be saved.

5. To accept the new settings, click OK.

> **TIP** To compare or revert to an autosaved version of the current document, click the FIle tab and select the Info category. To open a version, click its filename in the Versions area **B**.

> **TIP** Following a crash, a Document Recovery task pane appears, enabling you to save any recovered documents. Choose Save As from a listed file's drop-down menu.

Document Inspector

Before sharing an Office document with someone or openly posting it on the web, you should be aware that it can contain data you may not wish to share. Examples include comments and revision marks, as well as *invisible data*, such as personal information and text formatted as hidden. You can run the Document Inspector to find and remove this material.

To run the Document Inspector:

1. Open the Office document and click the File tab to go to the Backstage.

   The Info section is selected.

2. Click the Check for Issues icon and choose Inspect Document.

   The Document Inspector dialog box appears .

3. Remove check marks from elements you don't want to examine. Click Inspect.

   The document is examined and the results are presented **D**.

4. To eliminate a found element from the document, click its Remove All button.

5. Dismiss the Document Inspector by clicking Close.

6. If material has been removed, *do one of the following:*

   ▸ To incorporate Document Inspector changes into the original document, click the File tab and click Save, click the Save icon on the Quick Access Toolbar, or press Ctrl-S.

   ▸ Save the Document Inspector changes in a new file. Click the File tab, click Save As, and save the revised document with a new name. Send *this* copy to the recipient rather than the original document.

C Remove check marks from any items you want to ignore, and then click Inspect.

— *Issue*

D Found material is marked with an exclamation point (!). Click the Remove All button to eliminate the material from the document.

E You can view the essential issues in the Info section prior to running the Document Inspector.

TIP Basic issues are automatically listed to the right of the Check for Issues icon in the Info section of the Backstage **E**.

CAUTION Think carefully before saving the changes to the original document. You can't Undo a Save.

F Review the noted compatibility issues.

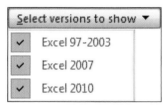

G Restrict the examination to only the checked versions.

H Click the Convert button to upgrade an older document so it can include Office 2013 features.

Compatibility Checker

With each new Office version, new features are introduced and older ones modified. As a result, although a current document can often be opened by a previous version of Office, the new and modified features may not be supported. Before sharing a document with someone who runs Office 2003, for example, you can run the Compatibility Checker to alert you to potential problems.

To run the Compatibility Checker:

1. Open the Office document. Click the File tab to go to the Backstage.

   The Info section is selected.

2. Click the Check for Issues icon and choose Check Compatibility.

   The Compatibility Checker launches and lists incompatibilities **F**.

3. *Optional:* To restrict the check to particular versions of Office, select them from the Select versions to show list **G**.

4. Examine each incompatibility and decide whether you want to correct it.

   To go directly to a listed incompatibility, click its Find text **F**.

5. *Optional:* If the document will regularly be shared with users of earlier Office versions, click the Check compatibility when saving... check box **F** to automatically alert you to new issues.

6. Close the dialog box by clicking OK.

TIP You can convert a file that's in an older Office format to an Office 2013 document by clicking the Convert icon in the Info section **H**. This option is only available when working on an older document, denoted by [Compatibility Mode] in the title bar.

Protecting Documents

Whether a document will be distributed to others in your office or school, sent around the world (via the web), or never leave your PC, Word provides ways for you to protect it. The two simplest options are:

- Mark the document as final, changing it to read-only to discourage additional changes.

- Encrypt the document, requiring a password to open and work with it.

To mark a document as final:

1. Open the Office document. Click the File tab to go to the Backstage.

   The Info section is selected.

2. Click the Protect Document (Word), Presentation (PowerPoint), or Workbook (Excel) icon and choose Mark as Final from the drop-down menu .

3. Click OK in the confirmation dialog box.

   The document is marked as final and saved. An explanatory dialog box appears.

4. Click OK to dismiss the dialog box.

   The document is now read-only. When opened, any user (including you) will be discouraged from editing the document.

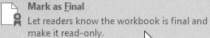

Protect Workbook

Mark as Final
Let readers know the workbook is final and make it read-only.

Encrypt with Password
Require a password to open this workbook.

Protect Current Sheet
Control what types of changes people can make to the current sheet.

Protect Workbook Structure
Prevent unwanted changes to the structure of the workbook, such as adding sheets.

Add a Digital Signature
Ensure the integrity of the workbook by adding an invisible digital signature.

A Choose Protect Workbook > Mark as Final.

Mark as Final Caveats

Mark as Final is not a secure means of protecting a document because:

- When opened in earlier Office versions, the document can be freely edited.

- To override Mark as Final, a user need only click the Edit Anyway button at the top of the document.

- To change it back to a normal Office 2013 document, anyone can open the document and reissue the Mark as Final command.

J Enter the password you will use to open this document.

K A password dialog box appears whenever anyone attempts to open the document.

L This dialog box appears when an incorrect password is entered. To try again, the user must reopen the document.

To encrypt a document:

1. With the document open in Office, click the File tab, select Info, and click the Protect Document (Word), Presentation (PowerPoint), or Workbook (Excel) icon. Choose Encrypt with Password from the drop-down menu **I**.

   The Encrypt Document dialog box **J** appears.

2. Enter the password you will use to open the file. Click OK.

3. Reenter the password in the Confirm Password dialog box. Click OK.

4. When you're done working with the document, save the changes. Saving enables the encryption and password protection.

   When you or another user attempt to open the document, a Password dialog box appears **K**. Unless the correct password is entered, the document will refuse to open **L**.

TIP To remove encryption and password protection from a document, choose Encrypt with Password again and delete the password that's shown. (You must first open the document by supplying the password before you can remove the password.)

TIP If you forget a document's password, you will not be able to open it. It's a good idea to either keep a record of the password in a secure place or retain an unencrypted copy of the document.

TIP Digital signatures and restricted permissions are other protection features supported by Office, but they require you to enroll in optional services.

Document Properties

As in previous versions of Office, there are a variety of *properties* you can set for a document to help identify, categorize, indicate its current status, and so on. Properties can be assigned to assist your own tracking needs or to provide additional information when you'll be sharing the document with others.

To set or view document properties:

1. Open the Office document and click the File tab.

   The Info section is selected. Property information is displayed on the right side of the document window 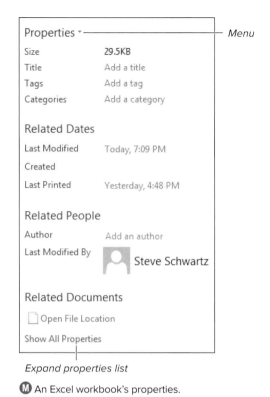.

2. *Do any of the following:*

   ▸ You can edit basic properties by typing directly into fields in the Properties pane. Most properties that you can edit are shown in light gray, such as Title, Tags, and Author.

   ▸ To display additional properties in the pane such as Status, Subject, and Company, click Show All Properties. Like the basic properties, many can be edited in the pane.

   ▸ You can use the Document Panel to view, add, or edit several key properties. Choose Show Document Panel from the Properties drop-down menu. When you're done, click the panel's close box.

   ▸ To view, add, or edit *all* properties, open the Properties dialog box by choosing Advanced Properties from the Properties pane's menu or from the Document Properties menu at the top of the Document Panel.

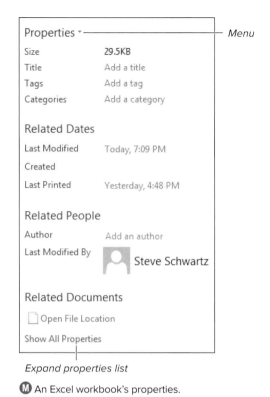

Ⓜ An Excel workbook's properties.

Ⓝ Document properties can be entered or edited in the Document Panel.

Featured Apps

Visit the Office Store

A The Apps for Office window.

B You can download apps in the Apps for Office window or your browser.

Close

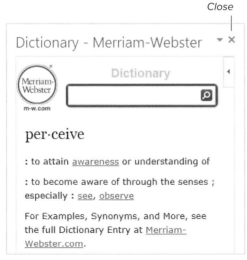

C You can use the Merriam-Webster Dictionary app to find the definition of a selected word.

Installing and Using Apps for Office

Office 2013 provides support for a class of add-ins known as *Apps for Office*. Available from the Office Store, these free and paid utilities add new features to Office.

To download and install apps:

1. In Word, Excel, or PowerPoint, choose Insert : Apps : Apps for Office > See All.

The Apps for Office window opens **A**.

2. *Do either of the following:*

- ▸ To see a subset of the apps available in the Office Store, click the Featured Apps link. App thumbnails appear in the window.

- ▸ To view the complete offerings of the Office Store, click Find more apps at the Office Store. Your default browser fetches the Office Store site.

3. If you see an app you want, click *Add* (free apps) **B** or *Trial* (paid apps).

The app downloads, installs, and opens in a task pane **C**.

To launch an installed app:

1. Open the Insert : Apps : Apps for Office menu, and *do one of the following:*

- ▸ Choose the app from the Recently Used Apps list.

- ▸ Choose See All, click My Apps **A**, select the app, and click Insert.

A task pane opens for the selected app.

2. When you're done using the app, click its close (X) box **C**.

Getting Help

Office applications can draw help information from files stored on your computer, as well as from Office.com (using an Internet connection). Simple help is provided by means of *ToolTips* (small pop-up windows).

To view a ToolTip:

■ Rest the cursor over a command or control. A ToolTip (including its keyboard shortcut, if any) appears Ⓐ.

To get help with an Office application:

■ Click the Microsoft Office Help icon Ⓑ or press F1.

The Help window appears Ⓒ.

To work in an Office Help window:

1. *Do any of the following:*

   ▸ To view the main Help page, click the Home (house) icon at the top of the Help window.

   ▸ To read information on a topic, click its blue link text. (When you move the cursor over link text, an underline appears beneath the text.)

   ▸ To search Help for a particular topic, type search text in the box and click the Search icon (or press Enter).

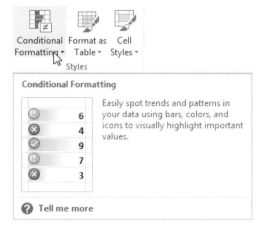

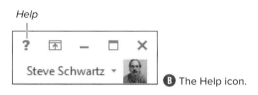

Ⓐ A ToolTip explains what a command icon does.

Ⓑ The Help icon.

Ⓒ An Office 2013 Help window (Excel shown).

If you preselect text prior to clicking the Print icon, you can restrict the printout to the selection.

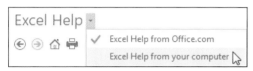

Click this menu icon to specify which help information to use.

- To go backward or forward among Help pages you've viewed, click the Back or Forward icon.
- To change the size of the Help text, click the Use Large Text icon.
- To print the current help topic, click the Print (printer) icon.
- To print a partial Help topic, select the desired text and click the Print icon. In the Print dialog box, set Page Range to Selection 🄳, and click OK.

2. When you're done using Help, click the Help window's close box (X).

TIP To switch between offline and online help information, click the menu 🄴 at the top of the Help window and choose an option.

TIP You can copy Help text and paste it into other applications' documents, such as Word or OneNote. Select the text (including images, if you like) and press Ctrl-C. The selected material is copied to the system Clipboard. If the Office Clipboard is active, it's also stored there.

TIP You can minimize Help to the taskbar by clicking its minimize icon. You can also resize the window by dragging any edge or corner.

TIP To make the Help window float on top of all other windows, click the pushpin icon beneath the close (X) box.

3

Tables, Charts, and Art

Although many documents consist solely of pages of text or numbers, you can make your Office documents more informative and attractive by adding tables, charts, and artwork, such as photos, clip art, WordArt, and SmartArt.

In this chapter, you'll learn how to insert these items into your documents; embellish artwork by adding color, 3-D effects, and rotation; and specify how surrounding text will wrap around them. You'll also learn about Office 2013's image-editing tools.

In This Chapter

Inserting Tables

The old way to add a table to a document mimicked using a typewriter. Using tabs, text and data were carefully aligned in columns. Word, PowerPoint, and Outlook avoid this rigmarole by letting you place a spreadsheet-style row-and-column table wherever you like.

You can insert or create a table in any of the following ways **Ⓐ**:

- Specify the number of rows and columns by dragging or entering numbers in a dialog box
- Manually draw the table grid
- Convert existing text to a table
- Insert an Excel worksheet
- Select a Quick Table template and replace its data with your own

Note that table-creation options differ somewhat among the three applications.

To insert a table:

1. Set the text insertion mark at the spot in the document where you want to insert the table.

2. Click Insert : Tables : Table to reveal the drop-down menu **Ⓑ**.

3. *Do one of the following:*

   ▸ **Insert table by highlighting.** In the top section of the menu, highlight squares to specify the table's dimensions, such as 4 x 4. To place the table, click the lower-right square of the highlighted selection.

   ▸ **Insert table via dialog box.** Choose Insert Table. In the Insert Table dialog box **Ⓑ**, specify the number of columns and rows, select an AutoFit behavior, and click OK.

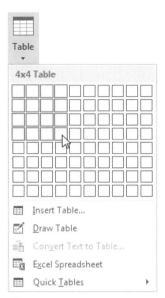

Ⓐ Open the Table menu and choose a table insertion method.

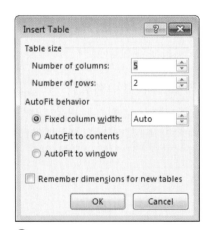

Ⓑ For additional precision when creating a table, use the Insert Table dialog box.

TIP When using the Insert Table dialog box, the default behavior is to create fixed-width columns. If you select AutoFit to contents, each column will automatically expand as needed to fully display the longest text string in the column.

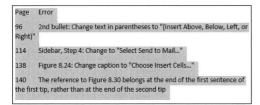

C These tools are available when drawing a table on a document page.

Page	Error
96	2nd bullet: Change text in parentheses to "(Insert Above, Below, Left, or Right)"
114	Sidebar, Step 4: Change to "Select Send to Mail..."
138	Figure 8.24: Change caption to "Choose Insert Cells..."
140	The reference to Figure 8.30 belongs at the end of the first sentence of the first tip, rather than at the end of the second tip

D Select the text to convert to a table. (For Office to determine how to arrange the text, it should be delimited with Returns, tabs, or commas.)

E Set conversion options and click OK to create the table.

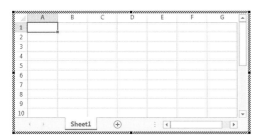

F If you need the full capabilities of Excel to manipulate your data, embed a worksheet in your document rather than use a table.

▸ **Draw a table.** Choose Draw Table and use the pencil tool to draw the table's line segments. While drawing the outline and cells, use tools in the Table Tools:Layout:Draw group to switch between drawing and erasing lines. Tools on the Design contextual tab **C** enable you to change the line style, width, or color; add or remove cell borders; and apply cell shading.

TIP If you switch to a Design tool while drawing, you leave drawing mode. To go back to drawing, click Layout:Draw:Draw Table again.

TIP Table Tools can be used to modify *any* table. Click Layout:Draw:Draw Table and click it again when you're done editing.

▸ **Convert existing text to a table**. In Word or Outlook, select the text to convert **D** and choose Convert Text to Table. In the Convert Text to Table dialog box **E**, verify the number of columns and rows, select an AutoFit behavior, ensure that the correct text separator is specified, and click OK.

▸ **Insert a worksheet.** Choose Excel Spreadsheet to embed a worksheet in the current document **F**. Use Excel procedures to enter data, create formulas, and format cells.

▸ **Insert a Quick Table.** In Word or Outlook, choose a table from the Quick Tables submenu to insert a formatted table into the document. Replace the sample labels and data with your own information.

Entering Data Into a Table

Unless you converted existing text to a table or inserted a Quick Table, you're now staring at an empty grid. Table cells can contain virtually anything that might be found in an Office document, such as text, numeric data, images, and charts.

To enter data into a table:

1. Click in the first cell in which you want to enter data.

2. *Do one of the following:*

   ▸ Type or paste text into the cell. If the cell is fixed width, text will wrap within the cell as needed. If an AutoFit option has been applied, the column expands to fit the longest character string in the cell.

   ▸ Select an item from the Insert: Illustrations (Word and Outlook)  or Images (PowerPoint) group to insert into the cell, such as a picture or shape.

     In Word and Outlook, objects are inserted into cells. In PowerPoint, on the other hand, objects float on the slide. They aren't inserted *into* cells.

   ▸ Paste a copied object or use drag-and-drop to move it into the cell.

3. To enter additional data, *do either of the following:*

   ▸ Press Tab to move to the next cell or Shift-Tab to move to the previous cell . (Note that if you tab out of the bottom-right cell, a new row is automatically created.)

   ▸ Click in the next cell into which you want to enter data.

A In addition to pasting, you can insert images and objects by choosing commands from the Insert: Illustrations or Images group.

B Tabbing from cell to cell (as indicated by the arrows) works as it does in a spreadsheet.

A If a table has to be a specific size, set the dimensions in the Table Size group.

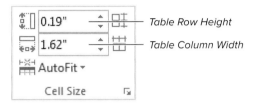

B To precisely set row or column sizes, enter numbers in these boxes.

Element-selection Assistance

When you need some help selecting table elements, you can choose commands from the Layout:Table:Select menu. (Note that PowerPoint lacks the Select Cell command.)

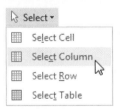

Modifying the Table Grid

Unless you plan very carefully when creating a table, you'll often find that the grid needs some modification in order to fit the data. For example, you may need to change the size of the entire table, modify row heights or column widths, change line colors or styles, or color individual cells or the entire table.

To change the size of table elements:

- *Do any of the following:*
  - ▸ To change the table size, move the cursor over the table's lower-right corner, and click and drag. To resize proportionately, hold down Shift as you drag.
  - ▸ To exactly set table dimensions, enter the table height and width in the Layout:Table Size group **A** (PowerPoint) or the Preferred Width on the Table tab of the Table Properties dialog box (Word and Outlook).
  - ▸ To manually change a column width, move the cursor over the column's right edge until it turns into a double arrow. Drag to the left or right to resize the column.
  - ▸ To manually change a row height, move the cursor over the row's bottom edge until it turns into a double arrow. Drag up or down to resize the row.
  - ▸ To precisely set column widths or row heights, select the columns or rows and click the Layout tab. Enter a number (in inches) into the Cell Size:Table Column Width or Table Row Height box **B**.

continues on next page

- ▸ To change a table in Word or Outlook from AutoFit to fixed-width columns (or vice versa), choose an option from the Layout:Cell Size:AutoFit menu **C**.

TIP You can evenly distribute the total width of several selected columns or total height of selected rows. Click the Distribute Columns or Distribute Rows icon in the Cell Size group **D**.

TIP If a row or column contains an object, neither the row height nor the column width can be made smaller than the object. To reduce such a row height or column width, you must first reduce the object's size.

To remove or add rows or columns:

- ■ *Do any of the following:*
  - ▸ To delete selected rows or columns, choose an option from the Layout: Rows & Columns:Delete menu **E**.
  - ▸ To insert rows or columns, select the cell above or below which you want to insert rows or to the right or left of which you want to insert columns. Click an Insert icon in the Layout: Rows & Columns group **F**.

TIP To insert more rows or columns, click the same icon. If one column or row is selected when you click the icon, one is inserted. If *multiple* rows or columns are selected, that number is inserted.

TIP You don't have to select *entire* rows or columns. Select sufficient cells so the application can determine what to do. For instance, when modifying one row or column, you can select a single cell in the row or column. To modify two columns, you can drag-select two adjacent cells.

TIP In Word, if you move the cursor over the right edge of a row, a plus symbol in a circle appears. You can click it to add a new row with the same formatting beneath the current row.

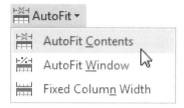

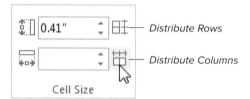

C Set the table to fixed column widths, AutoFit to match the cell contents, or AutoFit to the window.

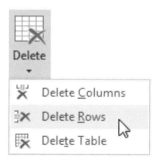

Distribute Rows

Distribute Columns

Cell Size

D To divide the total space allotted to several selected rows or columns, click one of these icons.

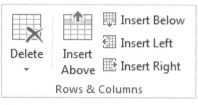

E You can delete selected rows, columns, or the entire table.

Insert Below
Insert Left
Delete   Insert   Insert Right
          Above
Rows & Columns

F Click an Insert command.

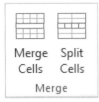

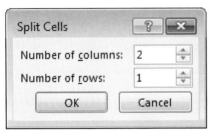

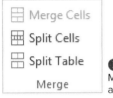

To merge or split cells:

1. Make the table active and select the Layout tab.

2. *Do one of the following:*

   ‣ To merge the selected cells into a single cell (to create a title row, for example), select the cells and click Merge:Merge Cells **G**.

   ‣ To reverse a merge or split a single cell into multiple cells, select the cell, click the Split Cells icon, and set options in the Split Cells dialog box **H**.

   ‣ *Word and Outlook only:* To divide a table into two tables, select a cell and click Merge:Split Table **I**. The rows above the selected cell become the first table; the selected row and the rows below become the second table.

G Click an icon in the Merge group to merge selected cells or split one cell into several.

H You can split a cell into two or more cells.

I In Word and Outlook, the Merge group also contains a Split Table command.

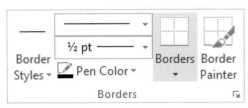

J Set line properties by choosing options in the Borders group.

Poor PowerPoint!

As you read about creating and modifying tables, you'll note that PowerPoint is missing some table features that are available in Word and Outlook. If the features are critical for the current table, create the table in Word or Outlook and then copy and paste it onto your PowerPoint slide.

To change border properties:

1. To modify one or more lines (*borders*) of one or more table cells, begin by selecting the cell(s).

2. Choose a border/line style, width, and pen color to apply from the drop-down menus in the Design:Borders group **J**.

3. *Do one of the following:*

   ‣ **Word and Outlook.** Open the Design:Borders:Borders menu and specify the border(s) to affect.

   ‣ **PowerPoint.** Click the Design:Draw Borders:Draw Table icon and click or draw the cell borders that you want to change.

   The chosen line style, width, and color are applied to the borders.

continues on next page

4. If desired, select other cells and repeat Step 3 to apply the current line properties to those cells.

TIP *Word and Outlook only:* **Similar to manually drawing a table, you can use the Border Painter tool** Ⓙ **to apply the current line properties to cell borders by clicking them.**

TIP **To selectively remove cell borders, click them with the Layout : Draw : Eraser (Word and Outlook) or the Design : Draw Borders : Eraser (PowerPoint).**

To apply cell shading:

1. Select the cells to which you want to apply a background color.

2. Open the Design : Table Styles : Shading menu and select a color Ⓚ. The menu provides a live preview of any color over which the cursor is hovered.

TIP *PowerPoint only:* **In addition to specifying a color, PowerPoint offers a variety of other background options** Ⓛ, **such as gradients, textures, and an Eyedropper tool to pick up a color from the background or another object.**

To apply a table style to a table:

1. Make the table active by clicking in a cell.

2. To format the entire table, choose a style from the Design : Table Styles gallery. A live preview is shown for any style over which the cursor is hovered. Click a style to apply it to the table.

CAUTION **Applying a table style overrides all manually applied borders and backgrounds.**

3. *Optional:* Modify the table style by checking options in the Design : Table Style Options group Ⓜ, such as formatting the bottom row differently because it contains totals.

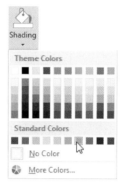

Ⓚ Select a background color in Word or Outlook.

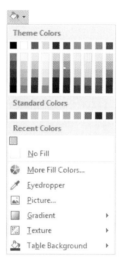

Ⓛ Select a background color in PowerPoint.

Ⓜ Click check boxes to add or remove other table-formatting options.

TIP *Word and Outlook only:* **To simultaneously apply multiple border and shading properties to selected cells, open the Borders and Shading dialog box by clicking the launcher at the bottom of the Design : Borders group.**

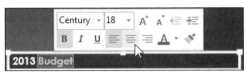

Alignment icons

Text Direction

Cell Margins

Alignment

Ⓐ Set paragraph alignment for selected cells by clicking an icon.

Century · 18 · A˄ A˅ ⇤ ⇥
B *I* U ≡ ≡ ≡ A · ✧
2013 Budget

Ⓑ The Mini toolbar.

More Data-formatting Tips

- If a cell contains several paragraphs, each one can have different paragraph formatting.

- You can also use keyboard shortcuts to apply character and paragraph formatting.

Formatting Table Data

Like other text in an Office document, table cells can have character and paragraph formatting applied to them.

To apply formatting to cell data:

1. Select the words, sentences, or cells to which the formatting will be applied.

2. To apply paragraph formatting to the selection, *do any of the following:*

   ▸ In the Layout : Alignment group **Ⓐ**, click an icon to set the paragraph alignment.

   ▸ In the Home : Paragraph group (Word and PowerPoint) or the Message : Basic Text group (Outlook), you can click icons to set alignment; decrease or increase the indent; or apply a bullet, number, or multilevel list format.

   ▸ Move the cursor up or right-click the selected text to reveal the Mini toolbar **Ⓑ**. By clicking its icons, you can align paragraphs, as well as decrease or increase the indent. (Note that Word provides few such options.)

3. To apply character formatting to the selection, *do any of the following:*

   ▸ In the Home : Font group (Word and PowerPoint) or the Message : Basic Text group (Outlook), you can change the font, size, style, color, and highlighting of the selected text.

   ▸ *Word only:* In the Home : Styles group, you can apply a defined style to the selected text.

   ▸ Move the cursor up or right-click the selected text to reveal the Mini toolbar **Ⓑ**. Apply formatting by clicking icons on the Mini toolbar.

Calculations in Tables

You can include simple row- or column-based formulas in tables to compute statistics, such as sums and averages. You can also sort a table numerically or alphabetically.

To enter a formula into a cell:

1. Click in the cell that will contain the formula.

   Generally, the cell will be in the bottom row or the rightmost column.

2. Click the Layout:Data:Formula icon .

   The Formula dialog box appears **B**.

3. Type an Excel-style formula in this form:

   =*function*(LEFT/RIGHT/ABOVE/BELOW)

   The word in parentheses specifies the cells included in the calculation. For example, to total the cells above the current cell, you'd use **=SUM(ABOVE)**.

4. *Optional:* Select a format for the result from the Number format drop-down list.

5. Click OK.

   The calculation is performed and the result is displayed.

TIP When performing complex calculations, it's easier to work in an inserted Excel worksheet than to create the formulas in a table.

TIP To copy a supported function into the Formula box, select the function name from the Paste function drop-down list.

CAUTION If the data on which a formula is based changes, the result does *not* automatically update. To force a recalculation, select the formula cell result, right-click it, and choose Update Field from the context menu **C**.

A The Layout:Data group.

B Create the formula in this dialog box.

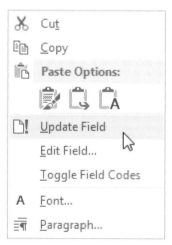

C Select the formula result, right-click it, and choose Update Field.

Original

Item	Jan	Feb	Mar	Apr	May	Totals
Paper Clips	120	147	96	77	185	596
Batteries	17	23	56	19	147	262
Blank DVDs	126	385	200	300	194	1205

Sorted

Item	Jan	Feb	Mar	Apr	May	Totals
Batteries	17	23	56	19	147	262
Blank DVDs	126	385	200	300	194	1205
Paper Clips	120	147	96	77	185	596

D To sort this table alphabetically by the first column, the options set were Sort by: Item column, Type: Text, Ascending, and Header row.

To sort a table:

1. Select the table that you want to sort **D**.

2. Click the Layout:Data:Sort icon **A**.

   The Sort dialog box appears **E**.

3. Select a sort field from the Sort by drop-down list, a data Type (Text, Number, or Date), and a sort order (Ascending or Descending).

4. *Optional:* To sort by more columns, repeat Step 3 for additional Then by sections in the Sort dialog box.

5. For My list has, click a radio button to indicate whether the table has column labels (*header row*).

6. Click OK to perform the sort **D**.

TIP Sorting a table works the same as sorting a range in Excel. Information in each table row is treated as a *record*. When you pick a column by which to sort, data in other columns of each record remains associated.

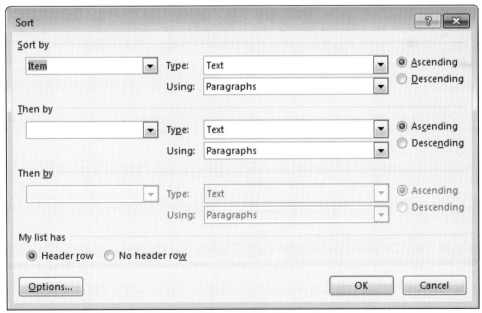

E Set options in the Sort dialog box and then click OK.

Creating Charts

Excel's charting tools also enable you to create charts in Word, PowerPoint, and Outlook. Each chart is embedded in the document and its data is stored in an Excel worksheet.

To create a chart:

1. Click Insert : Illustrations : Chart.

   The Insert Chart dialog box appears **A**.

2. Select the type of chart you want to create and click OK.

   An Excel worksheet appears, containing sample data **B**.

3. Replace the sample data with your data and labels by typing or pasting.

   The chart is constructed as you enter the data.

4. If your data's range doesn't match the sample range, drag the bounding box's lower-right corner **B** so the range matches that of your data. (In some cases, Excel will automatically adjust the bounding box for you.)

5. *Optional:* Embellish and modify the chart by choosing options from the Chart Tools : Design and Format contextual tabs. You can also set options by clicking the chart buttons.

   For more information on creating and modifying charts, see Chapter 12.

> **TIP** If you prefer, you can copy an Excel chart and paste it into Word, PowerPoint, or Outlook. Click the Paste Options icon that appears to determine whether the chart will be linked to the Excel data or treated as an embedded picture.

Chart types   Selected style

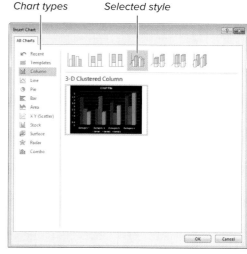

A Select a chart type from the left column, select a style icon, and then click OK.

Chart buttons

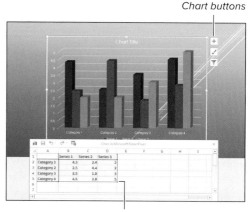

Drag here to change the range

B In the worksheet that appears, replace the sample data with your own data.

A You can click icons in the Insert:Illustrations, Images, or Text groups (PowerPoint shown) to add images, shapes, and text objects to a document.

B Using commands from the Picture Tools:Format contextual tab, you can change an image into impressive artwork.

About Adding Graphics and Objects

By clicking icons on the Insert tab **A**, you can add many common types of images and objects to Office documents. There are also features that help you create graphics, such as WordArt, SmartArt, and shapes.

An image can be placed *inline* with text or as a *floating object* that text wraps around. Images can be loaded from disk, copied from open documents in other programs, dragged directly into your document from an open document in certain other programs, or inserted from the web.

Office provides its own tools for modifying and embellishing graphics. For instance, you can do the following:

- Crop an image, removing unwanted parts
- Change the brightness or contrast
- Recolor a picture by adding a color cast
- Add a border in any combination of color, line width, and line style
- Apply special effects **B** (such as bevel, glow, 3-D rotation, and shadow) and artistic effects (such as texturizer, marker, and photocopy)
- Set text-wrap instructions for the image

Office 2013's image-editing tools are discussed at the end of this chapter.

TIP In Internet Explorer, many images are also clickable links. If you attempt to place such an image in your document via drag-and-drop, the link may appear rather than the image. You can, however, use copy-and-paste with such images or the Insert:Illustrations: Online Pictures command.

Adding Pictures

You can insert almost any photo or drawing from your hard disk into a PowerPoint, Excel, Word, or Outlook document. In Office 2013, picture insertion has been expanded to include *online pictures* (images from your SkyDrive account or the web).

To insert a picture from hard disk:

1. Click Insert : Illustrations : Pictures (Word, Excel, or Outlook) or Insert : Images : Pictures (PowerPoint).

   The Insert Picture dialog box appears .

2. Navigate to the drive and folder that contains the picture. Select the picture and click the Insert button.

   The picture appears in the document .

> **TIP** The Insert button also has a drop-down menu 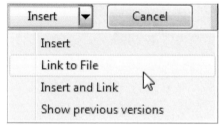. The menu choice determines whether a copy of the image is *embedded* in the document (Insert) or the image is *linked* to the file (Link to File) on your hard disk. Use Insert when a document will be shared with others who aren't on your network. Use Link when the image file will always be accessible to you and others who will have the document. (Linking helps reduce the file size.)

> **TIP** You can also insert a picture via copy-and-paste. Open the picture or the document in which it's embedded, select the picture, and choose Edit > Copy (Ctrl-C). Switch to the Office document, set the text insertion mark, and click Home : Clipboard : Paste (Ctrl-V).

> **TIP** You can click and drag a handle on any corner or edge of a placed or downloaded picture to change its size **B**. Drag a corner handle to resize the image proportionately.

A Select a picture and click the Insert button.

B The image appears in the document (in this instance, an Excel worksheet).

C Click the arrow beside the Insert button to specify file linking or embedding.

Insert from Facebook or Flickr

D Online pictures from a variety of sources can be inserted into your Office documents.

Perform search

E Enter search text and click the search icon.

F To insert an image from the web, use a Bing search to locate it—or, at least, something similar.

Live Layout in Word

Word 2013 introduces a feature known as *live layout* that simplifies the task of placing photos and other floating objects on the document page. As you drag the object, a green alignment guide appears whenever the object you're moving is aligned with a page edge, margin, top of a text block, center of the page or another object, and so on.

To insert a picture from SkyDrive:

1. Click Insert : Illustrations : Online Pictures (Word, Excel, or Outlook) or Insert : Images : Online Pictures (PowerPoint).

   The Insert Pictures window appears **D**.

2. Click SkyDrive or its Browse button.

3. Navigate to the folder that contains the picture. Select the picture's thumbnail and click the Insert button.

To insert clip art from Office.com:

1. Click Insert : Illustrations : Online Pictures (Word, Excel, or Outlook) or Insert : Images : Online Pictures (PowerPoint).

   The Insert Pictures window appears **D**.

2. Type a search term in the Office.com Clip Art box and click the search icon **E**.

3. Select the picture's thumbnail and click the Insert button.

To insert a picture from the web:

1. Click Insert : Illustrations : Online Pictures (Word, Excel, or Outlook) or Insert : Images : Online Pictures (PowerPoint).

   The Insert Pictures window appears **D**.

2. Type a search term in the Bing Image Search box and click the search icon **D**.

3. *Do one of the following:*

   ▸ If you see an image that you like **F**, select the picture's thumbnail and click Insert.

   ▸ Click Show all web results to perform a more thorough search. Select a picture's thumbnail and click Insert.

Adding Shapes

Office includes predefined shapes (such as arrows, callouts, and rectangles) that you can add to documents. Shapes can be assigned a color, shadow, and 3-D effects.

To insert a shape:

1. Select a shape from the Insert : Illustrations : Shapes gallery 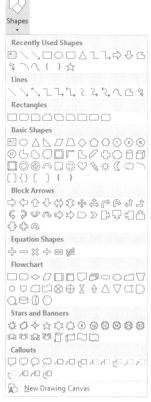.

2. Using the drawing cursor (+), click and drag in the document to create the shape.

> **TIP** To draw a *uniform* shape (a circle or square rather than an ellipse or rectangle, for example), press Shift as you draw.

3. Release the mouse button to complete the shape **B**.

4. *Optional:* Select the Format tab and format the selected shape by *doing any of the following:*

   ▸ **Apply a style.** Choose a style from the Shape Styles gallery.

   ▸ **Apply a solid, gradient, picture, or pattern fill.** Choose an option from the Shape Styles : Shape Fill menu.

   ▸ **Specify an outline.** Choose settings from the Shape Styles : Shape Outline and Shape Effects menus.

   ▸ **Apply a complex style.** Click the Format Shape task pane launcher (in the Shape Styles group). Use it to set color, line, size, rotation, and effects.

5. *Optional:* Change the shape's size or rotation by dragging its handles **B**.

> **TIP** Text can be added to many shapes. Some require only that you click in them and type. Right-click other shapes, and choose **Add Text** or **Edit Text** from the context menu. You can apply character and paragraph formatting to the added text.

A Select a shape from the gallery.

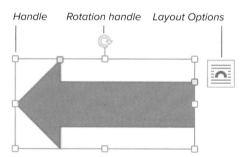

Handle   Rotation handle   Layout Options

B The completed shape is selected and surrounded by object handles.

Corner handle   Edge handle

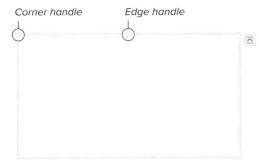

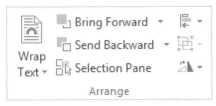

A A new drawing canvas.

B Commands in the Arrange group are useful for arranging and grouping drawing elements.

C Apply the Fit command to resize a drawing canvas to the smallest possible size that encloses all its elements.

The Little Yellow Dot

When you select an inserted shape, you may see a tiny yellow dot around the outside of or within the shape. You can click and drag the dot to modify a property of the shape. For example, when you drag the dot in the face's mouth **C**, you can switch from a smile to a frown.

Using a Drawing Canvas

If a drawing will require multiple shapes, you may find it easier to work in a special area called a *drawing canvas*. You can create as many drawing canvases as you need.

To create and use a drawing canvas (Word and Outlook only):

1. Each drawing canvas is created as an inline graphic. Position the text insertion mark where you want the drawing canvas to appear.

2. Choose Insert : Illustrations : Shapes > New Drawing Canvas (see **A** in "Adding Shapes").

   A drawing canvas appears **A**.

3. When working on the canvas, use tools on the Format and Insert tabs to add and modify shapes. Use the commands in the Format : Arrange group **B** to group objects, align objects with one another, and specify layering.

TIP To resize a drawing canvas, you can drag a corner or edge handle.

TIP Drawing canvases are *objects*. Using Format tab commands, you can set a text wrap for it, fill it with color or a gradient, add a shadow, or apply 3-D effects.

TIP When you're done drawing, you can resize the canvas to fit tightly around the drawn shapes. Right-click any edge and choose Fit from the context menu **C**.

TIP To delete a drawing canvas, right-click any edge and choose Cut from the context menu **C**.

Adding SmartArt

A *SmartArt* object is a ready-made combination of shapes and text. You can use SmartArt to create bullet lists and organizational charts, show processes, and illustrate relationships. SmartArt is available in all core Office applications.

To insert SmartArt:

1. Click Insert:Illustrations:SmartArt.

   The Choose a SmartArt Graphic dialog box appears 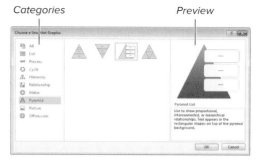.

2. Select a graphic category from the list on the left side of the dialog box.

   SmartArt graphics for the category are shown in the center of the dialog box.

3. Select a SmartArt graphic.

   A preview and explanation are shown.

4. To insert the selected SmartArt graphic into the document, click OK. Drag the graphic to the desired location 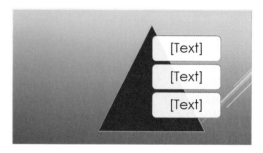.

5. To replace the text and picture placeholders with your own material, *do the following:*

   ▸ **Text.** Click a text placeholder and type. Or click the arrow icon on the left edge of the SmartArt graphic's border and enter text in the pop-out panel that appears 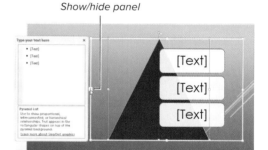.

   ▸ **Picture.** Click a picture placeholder. The Insert Picture dialog box appears. Select an image from disk and click Open.

Categories   *Preview*

A Select a SmartArt graphic from this dialog box. Click OK to insert it into the document.

B The SmartArt graphic with text placeholders appears on this PowerPoint slide.

Show/hide panel

C It's sometimes easier to type text in the pop-out panel than to enter it directly into the elements.

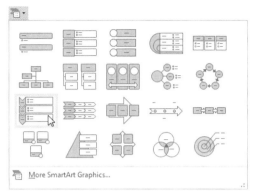

D If you already have text that would benefit from being presented as SmartArt, you can easily convert it.

About Layers

An Office document can have multiple layers. A page that contains only text or a single object has one layer. However, when you create or place additional objects on the page, each can either be on the same layer as the other material or on its own layer—on top of or beneath other objects and text.

To change a selected object's layer, choose a command from the Format: Arrange: Bring and Send menus. Ensure that In Line with Text is not the Wrap Text setting (see "Setting Text Wrap," later in this chapter).

6. You can format a selected element by choosing options from the Format tab. To change the SmartArt graphic's design or color scheme, add elements, or reorder or reorganize the elements, choose options from the Design tab.

TIP To format several objects the same way, select the objects (drag a selection rectangle around them or Ctrl-click each one) and apply the formatting.

TIP To delete an unneeded element, select it and press Delete, Del, or Backspace. To create more elements, select an element at the same level in the pop-out panel and press Enter. (Note, however, that not all SmartArt objects support additional elements.)

TIP In PowerPoint, you can convert a text object (such as a set of bullet points) to SmartArt by choosing a graphic from the Home : Paragraph : Convert to SmartArt Graphic gallery **D**.

Inserting Screenshots

Office 2010 introduced a feature that enabled you to capture an image of any open window or a selected portion of the screen and insert it as a picture into your document. If you don't have a Windows screenshot utility, you can use this feature to embellish a Word document with an image of the worksheet on which you're working or capture part of a web page for inclusion in an Outlook email message.

To insert a screenshot into an Office document:

1. To specify where you'd like to place the screenshot, *do the following:*

   ▸ **Word and Outlook.** Click to set the text insertion mark.

   ▸ **PowerPoint.** Click in a picture place-holder. If the target slide doesn't have one, it's sufficient to switch to the slide.

   ▸ **Excel.** No action is necessary; screen-shots are added as floating objects.

2. Click Insert : Illustrations : Screenshot or Insert : Images : Screenshot.

   A drop-down menu and gallery of open windows appears .

3. *Do one of the following:*

   ▸ To insert an image of an open window, select it in the Available Windows list.

   ▸ To capture part of the screen, choose Screen Clipping. The current Office document is hidden, exposing the screen and other windows beneath it. Drag to select an area of the screen.

   The window or clipping is inserted into the document. Move, resize, and format it as desired **B**.

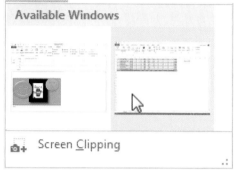

A The Available Windows list shows thumbnails of all open windows that are eligible to be used as screenshots.

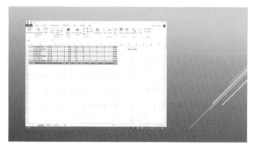

B The PowerPoint slide now has a screenshot of the open Excel workbook.

Screenshot Prep

You must prepare for the screenshot. First, because minimized windows aren't listed in the Available Windows list **A**, you must open any window you want to capture. Second, if you want to create a manual screen clipping, you must ensure that the area you want to capture isn't obscured by other windows.

(A) Select a style from the WordArt gallery.

(B) Replace this text placeholder with your text.

(C) An example of formatted WordArt.

Creating WordArt

WordArt is a decorative text object that you create by applying a special effect to text and optionally stylizing it using object-formatting commands. Although WordArt is too flashy for business and school documents, it's great for flyers, party invitations, brochures, and PowerPoint slide text.

To create WordArt:

1. *Optional:* Select text in the document that you want to convert to WordArt.

   WordArt can be created from existing text or typed in the WordArt placeholder.

2. Select a style from the Insert : Text : WordArt gallery (A).

   A placeholder appears (B) or the selected text is converted to WordArt.

3. If the WordArt text box contains a placeholder (**Your text here**), replace it with your own text by typing or pasting.

4. Using commands on the Format tab, other tabs (such as Home and Message), and the Mini toolbar, set the font, size, style, and alignment for the WordArt. Additional formatting options can be found in the Format : WordArt Styles group (C).

5. *Optional:* Resize the WordArt bounding box and, if necessary, reposition the WordArt by dragging it to another location.

TIP In Excel, WordArt is always created as placeholder text. It cannot be created by first selecting cell text. (Text in table cells, on the other hand, *can* become WordArt.)

TIP If you click the Layout Options icon beside the selected WordArt, you can specify a text-wrap setting for it (as described later in this chapter).

Adding a Text Box

A *text box* is a rectangular container object for text. Text boxes are commonly used to set off important snippets of text **A** (such as a quote) from the main text. Magazines often use text boxes (without the surrounding border or background) to print excerpts that summarize and draw attention to the article in which they're embedded.

To create a text box:

1. Choose Insert:Text:Text Box > Draw Text Box.

   A drawing cursor (+) appears.

2. Click and drag to draw the box.

   When you release the mouse button to complete the box, a text insertion mark appears inside the box.

3. Type or paste text into the box.

4. Format the text using commands on the Mini toolbar or the Home tab. If necessary, you can resize the box to fit the text by dragging a side or corner handle.

5. *Optional:* Format the bounding box using tools on the Format tab.

6. *Optional:* The default text-wrap setting for a text box is In Front of Text. You can choose a different setting by clicking the Layout Options icon that appears beside the selected text box **B**.

7. Click in the text box, move the cursor over any edge of the box, and then drag the box into the desired position.

TIP Word's Text Box drop-down menu contains a gallery of predefined boxes.

TIP To delete a text box, select it and press Delete, Del, or Backspace.

See a penny, pick it up, and all the day you'll have one cent.
—*Steve Schwartz, 1963*

A This text box has been formatted with a gradient fill.

B You can choose a text wrap setting from the Layout Options pop-out or the Format:Arrange: Wrap Text menu.

Linking Text Boxes

You can use text boxes to create complex documents (such as newsletters) that are normally handled with a desktop publishing program. To facilitate this use, text boxes in Word or Outlook can be *linked* to allow text to automatically flow from one box into the next.

1. Create the initial text box, and type or paste your text into it.

2. Create a second text box, but leave it empty. (You can only link to an empty text box.)

3. Select the first text box or set the text insertion mark inside it.

4. Click Format:Text:Create Link. Click the empty text box to set the link.

If you ever want to break the link, select the first text box and click Format:Text: Break Link.

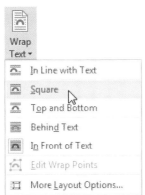

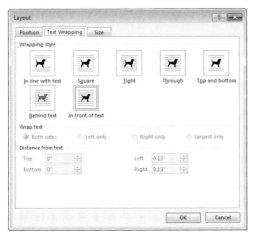

A The Wrap Text menu (Outlook).

B The Text Wrapping tab of the Layout dialog box.

Switching Between Floating and Inline Objects

The Layout Options pop-out and the Wrap Text menu can both be used to switch an object from inline to floating or vice versa.

- To convert a floating object to an inline object, choose In Line with Text.

- To convert an inline object to a floating object, choose any command other than In Line with Text.

Setting Text Wrap

Whether you're placing photos, charts, clip art, shapes, WordArt, SmartArt, text boxes, or another object type on document pages, each one must have a *text wrap* setting. It determines how surrounding text interacts with the object: whether it wraps around the object or enables the object to be placed beneath or on top of the text.

To set text wrap for an object:

1. Select the object.

2. *Do either of the following:*

   ► Choose an option from the Format: Arrange: Wrap Text menu **A**.

   ► Click the Layout Options icon that appears beside the selected object and choose a text wrap setting (see **B** in "Adding a Text Box").

3. Drag the object into position.

   The surrounding text wraps around the object as specified.

TIP Two additional wrap styles (Through and Tight), as well as specific position settings, can be set in the Layout dialog box **B**. To open the dialog box, choose More Layout Options from the Wrap Text menu **A** or click See More in the Layout Options pop-out (see **B** in "Adding a Text Box").

TIP You can add a watermark or stamp to a page, such as *Confidential* or *Not for Distribution*. Create a text box with large type (72 pt., for example), set the text color to a light gray, and then choose Behind Text as the Wrap Text setting. To learn about Word's watermark feature, see "Modifying the Background" in Chapter 5.

Resizing, Moving, and Rotating Objects

You can resize, move, and rotate most objects.

To change an object's size:

1. Select the object.

Handles appear around the object 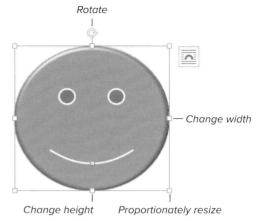.

2. *Do either of the following:*

- ▸ To change only an object's height or width, drag an edge handle. Resizing an object in this manner does not maintain its original proportions.

- ▸ To proportionately change both the object's height and width, hold down Shift while dragging a corner handle.

TIP To proportionately resize artwork such as a photo or clip art, it isn't necessary to hold down Shift as you drag a corner handle.

Rotate

Change width

Change height   *Proportionately resize*

A Every selected object is surrounded by handles.

Using the Selection Pane

Use the Selection pane when you have trouble selecting a placed object (so you can move it or alter its formatting, for example). Open the pane by clicking Format:Arrange:Selection Pane. All objects on the current page are listed in the pane; visible objects are marked with an eye symbol.

To select an object, click its name. If the object is obscured by another object, click the covering object's eye symbol to temporarily hide it and enable you to work directly with the obscured object.

Size and Rotation by the Numbers

You can also change the size or rotation of objects by specifying exact amounts.

Size. Type a number or click an arrow in the Format:Size:Shape Height or Shape Width box.

Dimensions entered in the Size group boxes resize only the selected dimension or proportionately resize the object, depending on a setting in the Layout dialog box. Click the icon at the bottom of the Size group. In the Layout dialog box, select the Size tab, add or remove the check mark from Lock aspect ratio, and click OK.

Rotation. Choose an option from the Format:Arrange:Rotate menu. To set a specific rotation angle, choose More Rotation Options.

Item	Jan	Feb
Batteries	17	23
Blank DVDs	126	385
Paper Clips	120	147

B To move a table, drag this icon.

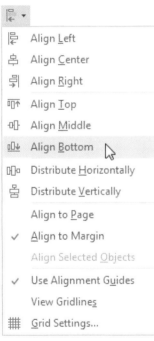

C To make it easier to move or format related objects, you can group them.

D Choose Align menu commands to align multiple objects to one another or distribute the distance between them.

To move an object:

1. Select the object.

2. Move the cursor over the object until the cursor changes to a stylized plus symbol.

   ▸ In drawn objects, photos, and clip art, click anywhere inside the item and drag.

   ▸ In a text box, drag any edge of the box.

   ▸ In a table, move the cursor over the upper-left corner and drag the plus icon that appears **B**.

3. Release the mouse button when the object is in the desired position.

TIP If you've carefully placed several objects and want to move them, it's easier if you *group* them first. Select the objects and choose **Format:Arrange:Group > Group C**. To later separate the objects (enabling you to work with them individually again), choose Ungroup from the menu.

To manually rotate an object:

1. Select the object.

   Handles appear around the object.

2. To rotate the object, click its rotate handle **A** and drag to the left or right.

TIP Some objects, such as tables, cannot be rotated.

TIP To *align* two or more selected objects with one another (making their bottom edges align, for example), choose a command from the **Format:Arrange:Align** menu **D**.

TIP In Word, the Format:Arrange group has a Position gallery that you can use to position a selected object relative to surrounding text.

Image-editing Tools

With Office 2013, you may find that it's no longer necessary to have a separate image-editing program to clean up, crop, or otherwise modify photos you want to include in documents. When you select an inserted photo, the Picture Tools contextual tab appears, providing a variety of image-editing tools and enhancement options.

As you'll learn in this section, you can do the following with photos placed in an Office document:

- Adjust the brightness, contrast, and sharpness
- Alter the color saturation or tone
- Apply artistic effects
- Apple style settings, such as a frame or border
- Turn a photo into a SmartArt object
- Crop an image to remove distracting elements or reform it to match a shape
- Remove the background, leaving only the photo's main subject
- Compress placed pictures to reduce the document's size
- Replace one picture with another, retaining the same size and applied formatting as the original
- Revert to the original photo, discarding all formatting changes

TIP When working with galleries on the Format tab, you may need to scroll the document to prevent the gallery from obscuring the photo you're editing.

TIP If you don't like the results, you can restore the image to its previous state by selecting the first gallery effect (labelled None or No *effect*). In the Format Picture task pane, click Reset.

General Image-editing Tips

Edits in Office only affect the way an image looks on the document page. The original photo on disk remains unchanged. To make *permanent* edits and corrections to a photo, *do either of the following:*

- Make your edits with a dedicated image-editing program, such as Adobe Photoshop.
- Right-click the image in your Office document, choose Save as Picture from the context menu that appears, and save the edited photo. You can overwrite the original file or save it using a new name, location, and/or file format.

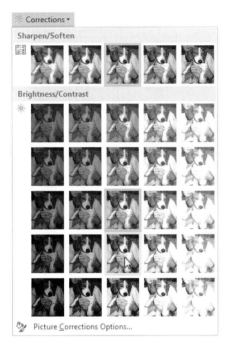

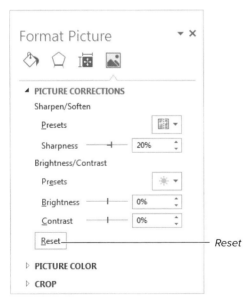

A Click to apply a new brightness/contrast or sharpness setting.

B One advantage of using the Format Picture task pane is that you can adjust brightness and contrast independently.

Reset

Adjusting Brightness, Contrast, and Sharpness

Because of lighting conditions or inappropriate use of a flash, it's not unusual for a photo to be too dark or bright, muddy looking (when shot with a web cam, for instance), or soft (a common problem with scanned photos). Depending on the degree of the problem, you may be able to salvage the photo by adjusting its brightness, contrast, and/or sharpness.

To adjust the brightness, contrast, or sharpness:

1. Select the inserted photo in the Office document.

   The Picture Tools contextual tab appears. Click the Format tab if it isn't automatically selected.

2. Open the Format:Adjust:Corrections gallery. It shows brightness/contrast combinations and sharpness settings you can apply **A**.

3. *Do either of the following:*

   ▸ As you hover the cursor over a thumbnail, a live preview of the setting is shown on the photo. Click the thumbnail to apply the setting.

   ▸ For more precise corrections, choose Picture Corrections Options. The Format Picture task pane opens. Use the controls in the Picture Corrections section **B** to adjust the brightness, contrast, and sharpness.

TIP When experimenting in the Picture Corrections section of the Format Picture task pane, you can discard your changes by clicking the Reset button **B**.

Setting Color Saturation and Tone

Office also has tools that enable you to adjust the overall color saturation (*density*) and color tone (*temperature*). Using these tools, you can brighten up a washed-out or faded shot, change a photo's mood, or create a *duotone*, for example.

To change the color saturation or tone:

1. Select the inserted photo in the Office document.

2. Open the Format:Adjust:Color gallery 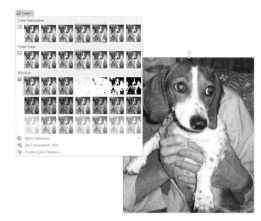 **C**.

3. *Do any of the following:*

   ▸ As you hover the cursor over a thumbnail, a live preview of the setting is shown on the photo. Click the thumbnail to apply that setting.

   ▸ To create a duotone from the photo, click an icon in the Recolor section of the gallery. To use a different recoloring shade, choose More Variations.

   TIP To change a color photo into a black-and-white image, select Grayscale in the Recolor area. Select Sepia or an orange/tan color to create a traditional duotone image.

   TIP The Black and White: 50% Recolor option provides an effect similar to Kodalith film—black and white only; no gray shades.

   ▸ For more precise corrections, choose Picture Color Options. Use controls in the Picture Color section of the Format Picture task pane to adjust saturation and tone **D**.

   TIP Another way to open the Format Picture task pane is to select the photo and click the launcher icon in the bottom-right corner of the Picture Styles group. You can also right-click the photo and choose Format Picture from the context menu.

C Select settings from the Color gallery to change a photo's color saturation or tone.

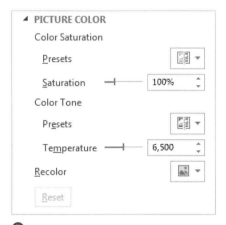

D Options in the Picture Color section of the Format Picture task pane enable you to simultaneously change multiple color settings.

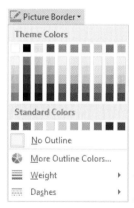

E Select an artistic effect from the gallery.

F To add a simple border, choose line options from the Picture Border drop-down menu.

G You can make certain photos stand out by adding a stylish frame.

Applying Artistic Effects

Occasionally, you may want to transform a photo into something artistic or funky. Office has almost two dozen artistic effects that you can apply to photos, such as Marker, Light Screen, and Glow Edges.

To add artistic effects:

1. Select the inserted photo in the Office document.

2. Open the Format : Adjust : Artistic Effects gallery **E**.

3. As you hover the cursor over a thumbnail, a live preview of the effect is shown on the photo. Click the thumbnail to apply the effect.

Adding a Border or Frame

When you insert a photo into a document, it's added unaltered. Other than its own natural colors, a photo has no frame or border. While this is fine—typical, in fact—for photos inserted into email messages, photos in Word documents often look better with a border.

To add a border or frame to a photo:

1. Select the inserted photo in the Office document.

2. In the Format : Picture Styles group, *do one of the following:*

   ▶ To apply a solid or dashed border to the photo, choose options from the Picture Border menu **F**. Revisit the menu for each additional line option that you want to apply.

   ▶ Choose a decorative frame from the Picture Styles gallery **G**.

continues on next page

- Choose an esoteric frame (such as a 3-D or reflection frame) from the Picture Effects submenus.

TIP You can remove a previously added line border by choosing **No Outline** from the Picture Border menu.

TIP To convert a selected image to a SmartArt object, select a SmartArt graphic from the Format : Picture Styles : Picture Layout gallery.

Cropping Photos

As framed in the camera, photos often contain extraneous material that you may wish to eliminate by judiciously *cropping* the photo. Picture Tools enables you to crop manually, crop to match an aspect ratio, or crop to conform to a particular shape.

To crop a photo manually:

1. Select the inserted photo in the Office document.

2. Click the Format : Size : Crop icon (or choose Format : Size : Crop > Crop).

    Black cropping handles appear around the picture 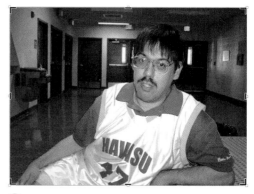. The photo's current height and width are shown in boxes in the Size group.

3. When the cursor is over a crop handle, its shape changes to match that of the handle. Drag handles to remove the unwanted portions of the picture.

    The area to be cropped out is shown in gray .

4. To complete the process, click anywhere else on the page or press Esc.

H Cropping handles appear at the photo's sides and corners.

I Drag one or more handles to select the part of the photo to retain.

J After choosing a shape, the photo is automatically cropped to match it.

K The Aspect Ratio submenu.

L Drag the cropping rectangle to select the area to retain.

TIP To crop proportionately from one corner, Shift-drag the corner handle. To crop equally from two edges, Ctrl-drag an edge handle. To crop equally from all edges, Ctrl-drag any corner handle.

TIP While cropping, you can also drag the image around while retaining the current crop dimensions.

TIP You can use the Compress Pictures tool to reduce the photo's size by discarding the cropped-out portions.

To crop to match a shape:

1. Select the inserted photo in the Office document.

2. Choose a shape from the Format : Size : Crop > Crop to Shape submenu.

   The photo is cropped to match the shape **J**.

To crop to an aspect ratio:

1. Select the inserted photo in the Office document.

2. Choose a setting from the Format : Size : Crop > Aspect Ratio submenu **K**.

   Crop dimensions that match the aspect ratio are overlaid on the photo.

3. If necessary, adjust the area that will be cropped by dragging the colored or gray area of the photo **L**.

4. To complete the process, click anywhere else on the page or press Esc.

Removing the Background

You can use the Remove Background command to isolate part of a photo, removing the material around it. The command's effect is similar to *masking* in Photoshop.

To remove the background:

1. Select the inserted photo in the Office document.

2. Click the Format : Adjust : Remove Background icon.

   The Background Removal tools appear and Office guesses the photo's subject.

3. *Optional:* Adjust the selection marquee by dragging its handles to include less or more material .

4. If necessary, adjust the selected material by *doing any of the following:*

   ▸ To expand the selection, click Background Removal : Refine : Mark Areas to Keep and draw lines to denote the new areas.

   ▸ If extraneous material is selected, click Refine : Mark Areas to Remove and draw lines to mark areas to be eliminated from the selection.

   ▸ If a drawn line doesn't have the desired effect, click the Delete Mark icon and then click the mark(s) you want to remove.

5. *Do one of the following:*

   ▸ To complete the background removal, click Keep Changes, press Esc, or press Enter .

   ▸ To abort the process, click Delete All Changes.

   TIP When adding and removing areas to keep, increasing the magnification can help.

Ⓜ The subject is displayed normally, while the material to be eliminated is shown in purple.

Ⓝ The photo with the background removed.

O Commands in the Adjust group.

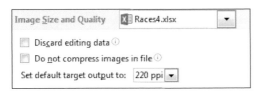

P The Compress Pictures dialog box.

Q Specify compression settings for the selected document.

TIP By default, the core Office applications compress photos placed in a document. To view or change the default setting, click the File tab and then Options. Select the Advanced category in the *application* Options dialog box. Make any desired changes in the Image Size and Quality section **Q**.

Compressing Pictures

Given the high megapixel cameras now available, digital photos can take up considerable space in documents, email messages, and presentations. Using the Compress Picture command, you can reduce the resolution of individual or all photos in an Office document in order to reduce the document's size.

To compress one or more pictures:

1. Select the inserted photo that you want to compress. (If you want to compress all photos in the document, it doesn't matter which photo you select.)

   The Picture Tools contextual tab appears. Click the Format tab if it isn't automatically selected.

2. Click the Format : Adjust : Compress Pictures icon **O**.

   The Compress Pictures dialog box appears **P**.

3. Review the following options:

   ▸ **Apply only to this picture.** To compress only the selected photo, check this option. To compress all photos in the document, clear the check mark.

   ▸ **Delete cropped areas of pictures.** If the selected photo(s) have been cropped, set this option to delete the cropped areas. (Cropping does not delete the cropped-out areas. It merely hides them.)

   ▸ **Target output.** This resolution setting determines the amount of compression applied to the photo(s).

4. Click OK to perform the compression.

   If the results are satisfactory, save the document. If not, click the Undo icon in the Quick Access Toolbar or press Ctrl-Z.

Replacing One Photo with Another

Use this command to replace a selected photo with a different one while retaining the size and formatting applied to the photo.

To replace a photo:

1. Select the inserted photo in the Office document.

2. Click the Format:Adjust:Change Picture icon **O**.

   The Insert Pictures dialog box appears **R**.

3. Select a replacement photo and click Insert.

   The new photo replaces the original in the document.

Resetting Edits

If you've been experimenting with formatting options for an photo, you can revert to the original image by issuing the Reset Picture command.

To reset edits for an image:

1. Select the inserted photo in the Office document.

2. Choose a command from the Format: Adjust:Reset Picture menu **S**.

   Choose Reset Picture to remove all edits and formatting changes or Reset Picture & Size to also restore the image to its original size.

R You can replace the current picture with one from your hard disk or an online image.

S Reset Picture options.

Getting Started with Word 2013

Microsoft Word is a word-processing application—perhaps the most widely used word-processing application in existence. You can use Word to write letters, memos, reports, and essays. Because it is so pervasive and allows you to save in a variety of file formats, there's an excellent chance you can create a version of a given Word document that can be opened by almost any recipient.

In this introductory chapter, you'll learn about the Word interface, working in different views, and entering and editing text. For information on launching and quitting Word, as well as performing basic document-related tasks, such as creating, opening, saving, and closing documents, see Chapter 2.

TIP Every Word document—whether new or opened from disk—opens in its own window. Clicking a document's close box (X) closes only that document. To close *all* documents and quit Word, you must close every open document.

The Word Interface

This section discusses the interface elements  you'll use when creating and editing Word documents. Many elements, such as the Ribbon and Quick Access Toolbar, can also be found in Excel, PowerPoint, and Outlook.

File tab. Click the File tab to perform file-related activities in the Backstage **B**, such as creating, opening, saving, and printing. Click Options to set Word preferences. To open a document on which you've recently worked, select Open and then click its filename in the Recent Documents list.

Quick Access Toolbar. Icons for common commands (such as Save and Undo) can be found on this customizable toolbar.

Back

B When printing the current document in the Backstage, print settings options and a preview are automatically displayed.

File tab Quick Access Toolbar Ruler Tab (Review) Group (Styles) Help

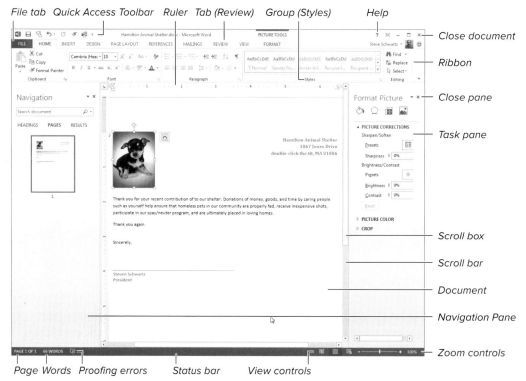

Close document
Ribbon
Close pane
Task pane

Scroll box
Scroll bar
Document
Navigation Pane
Zoom controls

Page Words Proofing errors Status bar View controls

A Elements of the Word 2013 interface.

Search box   *Close Help*

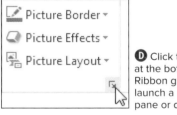

C Click text links and icons in Word Help to view help topics. Click the close box (X) to dismiss Word Help.

D Click this icon at the bottom of a Ribbon group to launch a related task pane or dialog box.

Help. Click this icon or press F1 to open the Word Help window **C**.

Ribbon. The Ribbon is Office's replacement for the program menus found in Word 2003 and earlier versions. Similar commands and procedures are listed together on a *tab*, such as Insert or View. Within each tab, procedures are further divided into *groups*, based on similarity of function. To perform a command, you switch to the appropriate tab by clicking it and then click the command's icon, menu, or control.

Rulers. Click the View:Show:Ruler check box to hide or show the horizontal and vertical rulers. Use the controls on the horizontal ruler to set or change tab stops and indents for the selected paragraph(s). The vertical ruler is visible only on the page that contains the text insertion mark.

Task panes. To make it easier to format and edit certain types of material, such as inserted charts and photos, you can open a task-related pane on the side of the document window. Many task panes are opened by clicking what was formerly a dialog box launcher on the Ribbon **D**.

Navigation Pane. When the Navigation Pane is displayed (View:Show:Navigation Pane), you can use it to go to a particular spot in a document by clicking a listed heading, page thumbnail, or search result.

Document. Most of Word's window is reserved for the current word-processing document. You can close panes or switch to Read Mode to increase the display area for the document.

Scroll bar and scroll box. You can drag the scroll box, click in the scroll bar, or click the arrow icons at either end of the scroll bar to navigate through a document's pages.

Page indicator. This indicator displays the current page number, as well as the total number of pages in the document. Click it to open or close the Navigation Pane.

Words indicator. This indicator shows the word count for the document. If text is selected, it shows the number of words in the selection. Click the indicator to open the Word Count dialog box **E**.

Proofing indicator. This indicator shows if there are proofing errors that need to be addressed, such as misspellings, repeated words, or extra spaces between words. Click the indicator to open a task pane in which you can view and optionally correct each suspected error.

View controls. Click an icon to switch views **F**. You can also switch views by clicking an icon in the View : Views group. The purpose of each view is explained in the following section.

Zoom controls. Change the current magnification by dragging the slider, clicking the + (increase) or – (decrease) button, or clicking the zoom percentage text.

Close. Click the close box (X) to close an open document or to quit Word. (When the current document is the *only* one that's open, clicking the close box quits Word.) You can also close the active document by clicking Close in the Backstage **B**.

> **TIP** Any docked pane, such as Navigation, can be turned into a floating palette by dragging the pane by its title area to a new location. To restore it to the original docked position, double-click in the pane's title area.

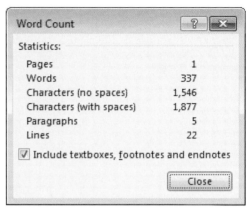

E For detailed word count information, open the Word Count dialog box.

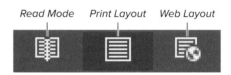

F You can switch to some views by clicking an icon in the status bar.

Resume Reading

When you reopen a Word document, the first page is displayed and the text insertion mark is set at the beginning of the document. In Word 2013, you can optionally jump to where you previously left off.

On opening, a Resume Reading icon appears in the right margin. Hover the cursor over it to learn the approximate jump point; click the icon if you want to scroll to that spot in the document.

The Views group has icons for each supported view. The current view is shown in blue.

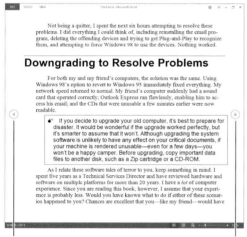

Previous page   *Next page*

Ⓑ In Read Mode, the document fills the window and is formatted in tablet/magazine-style. The view is especially useful for proofing documents, as well as reading ones that you've downloaded or received in email.

Working in Different Views

Depending on what you currently want to do with a document, you can work in any of Word's *views*: Read Mode, Print Layout, Web Layout, Outline, and Draft. Each view serves a particular purpose, as described below. To switch views, you can click an icon in the status bar (see Ⓐ and Ⓕ in "The Word Interface") or click an icon in the View:Views group Ⓐ.

Read Mode

If want to read or review a document, Read Mode Ⓑ can help simplify the task.

To control Read Mode:

1. *Do any of the following:*

   ▸ To switch pages, click the Previous page or Next page icon. You can also use your mouse's scroll wheel or press a supported navigation key, such as the arrow keys, Page Up/Page Down, and Spacebar/Shift-Spacebar.

   TIP Clicking *anywhere* in the left or right margin scrolls to the previous or next page.

   ▸ To change the magnification, use the zoom controls in the status bar.

   ▸ Choose commands from the menus. Use the Tools menu to perform a Find; use View menu commands to change display options.

2. To exit Read Mode, click the Print Layout icon on the status bar, choose View > Edit Document, or press Esc.

Print Layout View

Standard documents, such as memos, letters, and reports, are often written and edited in Print Layout view. One advantage of working in this view is its adherence to *WYSIWYG* (what you see is what you get). The margins, headers/footers, and formatting match the printed output. Pages are shown as equivalent pieces of paper with physical breaks between pages.

Web Layout View

Use Web Layout view to create, view, and edit pages as they'll appear online when opened in a browser. By choosing Save As in the Backstage, you can save pages in several web-compatible formats.

Outline View

Use Outline view to create, view, and edit outlines. (The table of contents for this book was created in Outline view .) For information about working in Outline view, see Chapter 6.

Draft View

Use Draft view when speed is of primary importance. In Print Layout view, physical pages and breaks are drawn. Draft view displays a document as continuous text; page breaks are denoted by dotted lines. Because repagination occurs almost instantly as you compose, this is an ideal view if you have an older, slower computer. Note that inserted graphics and other non-text objects are not shown in this view.

C Outline view is ideal for creating outlines. When working in this view, an Outlining tab with outline-related commands is added to the Ribbon.

Collapse and Expand Headings

In previous versions of Word, it was sometimes helpful to switch from Print Layout to Outline view simply because the latter enabled you to collapse and expand sections of the document. Word 2013 makes this unnecessary because this feature has been added to Read Mode, Print Layout, and Web Layout views.

You can collapse or expand any document section that begins with a paragraph that Word recognizes as a heading. To collapse a section, move the cursor to the left of the heading and click the downward pointing triangle. To expand the section, click the heading's triangle.

Collapsed section

> **(e)Directly Launching an App**
> **(e)Indirectly Launching an App**

Expanded section (normal)

A The View : Window group.

B You can make any open document active by choosing its name from the Switch Windows menu.

C Arrange All can make it simpler for you to work with multiple open documents. After selecting a document to edit or view, you can maximize or resize its window.

Managing Windows

When you create a new Word document or open an existing document, each one opens in a separate window. Because it's common to work with several documents at once, Word provides commands for managing windows in the View : Window group **A**.

To manage open document windows:

- *Do any of the following:*

  ▸ To create another instance of the current document, click View : Window : New Window. Edits made in any instance of a window affect the document.

  Each new instance has the same name as the original, followed by a colon and a number. For example, a new instance of **memo.docx** would be named **memo.docx:2**.

  ▸ To bring a document to the front and make it the *active document*, choose its name from the View : Window : Switch Windows menu **B**.

> **TIP** Every open Word document is represented by a taskbar entry. You can also switch documents by clicking or selecting their names on the taskbar.

  ▸ To view all open documents simultaneously, click View : Window : Arrange All. The documents are displayed in a stack **C**. To work with one of the documents, click anywhere in its window to make it active.

continues on next page

▶ To work with a pair of open documents, click View Side by Side. If more than two documents are open, the Compare Side by Side dialog box appears 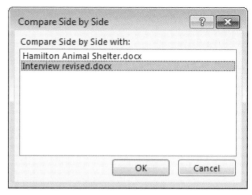. Select the second document and click OK.

TIP When working in View Side by Side mode, you can make the two documents scroll together by ensuring that the Synchronous Scrolling icon Ⓐ is enabled. This feature is useful for comparing two versions of the same document.

▶ To close the active Word document, click its close box (X), press Alt-F4 or Ctrl-W, or click the File tab and then click Close in the Backstage.

TIP To close a Word document, you can also right-click its taskbar button or right-click any blank spot in its title bar, and then choose Close from the context menu that appears Ⓔ.

TIP If you're running Windows 7 or 8, taskbar buttons are different from earlier versions of the operating system. If multiple Word documents are open, they are grouped together within a single Word taskbar button. To close one of the open documents, rest the cursor over the Word taskbar button, move up to highlight the document you want to close, and click its close box (X) Ⓕ.

Ⓓ After clicking the View Side by Side icon in the first document window, you'll be asked to select the comparison document—if more than two documents are open.

Ⓔ You can close a document by right-clicking its title bar and choosing Close from this pop-up menu.

Close the document

Taskbar button

Ⓕ In Windows 7 and 8, documents from the same application are grouped within a taskbar button.

☑ Ruler

☐ Gridlines

☐ Navigation Pane

Show

Ⓐ Click check boxes in the Show group to enable or disable display options.

Ⓑ Gridlines can make it easier to place objects.

Navigation Pane

Ⓒ Use the Navigation Pane to quickly move to a desired spot in a document.

Setting Display Options

In addition to using the zoom controls to change the magnification (see "Setting Magnification" in Chapter 2), you can show or hide the following elements in the document window by clicking check boxes in the View:Show group Ⓐ:

- **Ruler.** Use the ruler to position objects, set paragraph indents, and set tab stops.

- **Gridlines.** When enabled, each page is overlaid with a visible grid Ⓑ. Placed objects automatically snap to the nearest grid intersection.

- **Navigation Pane.** Use the Navigation Pane Ⓒ to move directly to a specific document page, heading, or search result. For instructions, see "Using the Navigation Pane," later in this chapter.

To show/hide rulers:

- Click the View:Show:Ruler check box.

To show/hide gridlines:

- Click the View:Show:Gridlines check box.

To show/hide the Navigation Pane:

- Click the View:Show:Navigation Pane check box. To switch among viewing document headings, page thumbnails, and search results, select a category beneath the pane's search box. To remove the pane, click its close box (X) or remove the Navigation Pane check mark from the Show group Ⓐ.

TIP You can also open and close the Navigation Pane by clicking the Page indicator on the left side of the status bar.

Entering Text

If you've previously used a word-processing program, you're already familiar with the basics of entering text. On the other hand, if you're new to word processing, you'll need to know the following information.

To enter text:

1. Create a new document or open an existing document.

2. *Do one of the following:*

   ▸ **New document.** The text insertion mark is automatically positioned at the top of the first document page 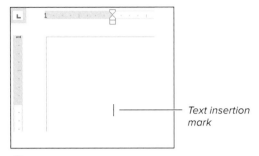.

   ▸ **Existing document.** The text insertion mark is set at the beginning of the document. Scroll to the page where you want to begin entering new text, such as the end of the last page. Click to set the text insertion mark.

3. Type your text.

   Entered text appears at the text insertion mark. In a new document, the text is formatted with the default font and the paragraphs are left-aligned. In an existing document, the formatting matches the text that it immediately follows.

4. As you type, text automatically wraps as needed to fit within the current paragraph's margins. When you want to begin a new paragraph, press Enter.

> **TIP** For information on changing character or paragraph formatting (such as applying a different font or centering a title), see Chapter 5.

> **TIP** You can add text copied from the document, other documents, or other applications to the current document by clicking the Home : Clipboard : Paste icon **B** or by pressing Ctrl-V.

Text insertion mark

A In a new or opened document, the text insertion mark is set at the beginning of the document.

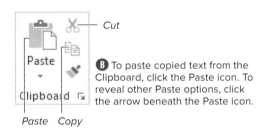

Cut

Paste Copy

B To paste copied text from the Clipboard, click the Paste icon. To reveal other Paste options, click the arrow beneath the Paste icon.

Using Click-and-Type

If you're more comfortable working with a typewriter than with a word-processing program, you can use Word's *click-and-type* feature to approximate a typewriter.

Instead of typing from the text insertion mark at the top of a new document or the current position in an opened document, you can double-click any blank spot below either of these points. Word sets the text insertion mark at the double-clicked spot and automatically adds sufficient paragraph returns to fill in the gap above.

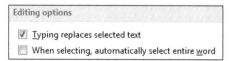

A Set the text insertion mark to the right or left of the text that you want to delete.

Selected text

B Selected text is highlighted like this.

Selecting Partial Words

If you find that you're frequently (and automatically) selecting entire words when trying to select partial words, a Word Options setting is interfering.

To change the setting, click the File tab. In the Backstage, click Options. In the Word Options dialog box, select the Advanced category and remove the check mark from When selecting, automatically select entire word **C**. Click OK to save the new setting.

Editing options

☑ Typing replaces selected text

☐ When selecting, automatically select entire word

C To simplify text selection, remove the check mark from the second check box in the Editing options section.

Basic Text Editing

You can use any of the following techniques to correct errors in a document and make other changes, such as adding new text. The techniques vary, depending on whether you're changing selected or unselected text.

To delete unselected text:

1. Position the text insertion mark immediately to the right or left of the text you want to correct or remove **A**.

2. *Do one of the following:*

   ▸ To delete the *previous* character (the one to the left), press Backspace.

   ▸ To delete the *next* character (the one to the right), press Del or Delete.

   To delete additional characters, continue pressing Backspace, Del, or Delete.

3. If necessary, replace the deleted text by typing new characters.

To delete or replace selected text:

1. To select the text **B** to be deleted or replaced, *do one of the following:*

   ▸ Set the text insertion mark at one end of the text to be selected, and then drag to or Shift-click the opposite end.

   ▸ Set the text insertion mark at one end of the text to be selected, and then— while holding down Shift—press arrow keys to move to the end of the text.

   ▸ Double-click to select a word or triple-click to select a paragraph.

continues on next page

2. *Do one of the following:*

▸ To *delete* the selected text, press Backspace, Del, or Delete.

▸ To *replace* the selected text, type the replacement text. When you begin typing, the selected text is deleted.

TIP You can also delete text by *cutting* it. Unlike a normal deletion, cut text is stored in the Clipboard (and the Office Clipboard), where it's available for pasting. To cut selected text, click the Home:Clipboard:Cut icon (see **B** in "Entering Text") or press Ctrl-X.

TIP You can use drag-and-drop to move selected text from one location to another— either within a document or between Word documents. This is equivalent to performing a cut-and-paste.

TIP If you want a drag-and-drop to leave the original text intact (working as a copy-and-paste rather than as a cut-and-paste), drag the selected text using the right mouse button. From the context menu that appears at the destination **D**, choose Copy Here.

To insert new text:

1. Position the text insertion mark where you want to add the new text.

You can insert new text anywhere in a document.

2. *Do either of the following:*

▸ Type the new text.

▸ Paste the new text by clicking the Home:Clipboard:Paste icon (see **B** in "Entering Text") or by pressing Ctrl-V.

TIP To undo the most recent edit, immediately click the Undo icon in the Quick Access Toolbar **E** or press Ctrl-Z. (Note that you can undo *multiple* actions—one by one—by clicking the Undo icon's down arrow.)

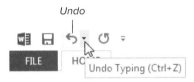

D When right-dragging text, you can elect to perform a copy rather than a move.

Undo

E You can often reverse your most recent action.

Controlling Paste Formatting

When you paste text into a Word document, its formatting is determined by settings in the Advanced section of the Word Options dialog box. Depending on the text's source and whether the styles conflict, either the original formatting is retained or the text is reformatted to match the surrounding text at the destination. However, you can override the default Paste formatting.

When pasting, the Paste Options icon appears at the end of or beneath the pasted text **F**. Click the icon to choose a formatting option. (You can also choose these formatting options from the Home:Clipboard:Paste icon's menu.)

Paste Options icon

F Choose a text-formatting method from the Paste Options drop-down menu.

A Select a dictionary to install and click Download.

Search box

Close pane

Execute search

Definition

B A dictionary's task pane.

C You can open the dictionary task pane by clicking Define.

Using the Proofing Tools

Word includes a spelling/grammar checker and a thesaurus that you can use to help with writing and editing. Spelling and grammar can be checked *on the fly* (as you type) or run as a traditional full-document or selected-text check. If you want to see a word's meaning, there are several free dictionaries that you can easily install.

To install a dictionary (to check word definitions):

1. Right-click any word in an open Word document and choose Define from the context menu that appears.

   The Dictionaries task pane appears **A**.

2. Click the Download button of the dictionary that you want to install.

   The dictionary downloads and installs. The definition for the selected word appears in the new task pane **B**.

> **TIP** After adding a dictionary, you can add others by downloading them from the Office Store. To use the additional dictionary, choose it from the Insert : Apps : Apps for Office menu.

To look up a word's definition:

- *Do either of the following:*
  - ▸ If the word is in the current document, select and right-click it. Choose Define from the context menu.
  - ▸ Click Review : Proofing : Define **C**, type or paste the word into the Search box **B**, and click the search icon (or press Enter).

  The word's definition is displayed in the task pane **B**.

To find a synonym for a word:

- *Do either of the following:*

  - ▸ If the word is in the current document, select and right-click it, and open the Synonyms submenu in the context menu. To replace the word, choose a synonym from the list. (If you'd rather use the Thesaurus task pane, choose Thesaurus.)

  - ▸ Click Review:Proofing:Thesaurus 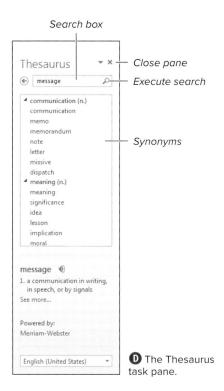. In the Thesaurus task pane **D**, type or paste the word into the search box. Click the search icon or press Enter. (If the word is preselected in the document, it will automatically appear in the search box.)

    To use a listed synonym, click the down arrow beside the word, and choose Insert or Copy **E**.

To check spelling and/or grammar as you type:

1. When Check spelling as you type is enabled in Word Options (see the Tip at the end of the next section), each suspected spelling or grammatical error is marked with a wavy, colored underline.

2. **Spelling.** To correct or dismiss a marked spelling error (red), right-click the underlined text and choose an option from the context menu **F**:

   - ▸ To accept a suggested correction (if any are listed), choose a replacement spelling from the listed words.

   - ▸ Choose Ignore or Ignore All to ignore this or every instance of the flagged spelling in the current document.

   - ▸ If the spelling is correct, choose Add to Dictionary to record the word and ensure that it's never flagged again.

D The Thesaurus task pane.

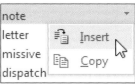

E To use a synonym, click its down arrow and choose Insert or Copy.

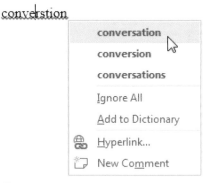

F Right-click a marked spelling error and choose an option from the context menu.

We is rock stars, isn't we? <u>Us</u> are going to Mandalay Bay to see the dolphins. I <u>seen</u> a good show <u>their</u>, but I were younger than.

there
Ignore
Hyperlink...
New Comment

G Right-click a blue grammatical error to view possible corrections.

H The Spelling and Grammar task panes. (Be sure to review the explanatory text under the list box.)

Correcting Letter Case Errors

Has this happened to you? You accidentally press Caps Lock instead of Shift and now your newly typed text reads **SUSAN JONES**. Or while entering mailing addresses, your assistant decides not to bother with capitalization. You can fix many such errors by selecting the text and choosing a correction from the Home:Font:Change Case menu.

3. Grammar. To correct or dismiss a marked grammatical error (blue), right-click the underlined text. Choose one of the following from the context menu **G**:

- ▸ Choose the suggested fix to let Word make the correction.

- ▸ Choose Ignore if you believe that the grammar is correct or if you want to manually make the correction.

To check spelling/grammar for selected text or the document:

1. *Optional:* To restrict the check to a specific portion of the document, select the text to be checked.

2. Click Review:Proofing:Spelling & Grammar (F7).

If suspected errors are identified, the Spelling or Grammar task pane opens.

TIP The task pane that appears depends on the first error. If spelling *and* grammar errors are found, the pane switches between Spelling and Grammar as needed to address each subsequent error.

3. Spelling. To handle a suspected spelling error **H**, *do one of the following:*

- ▸ To accept a suggested correction, select it in the list and click Change.

- ▸ To accept a suggested correction and apply it throughout the document, select it in the list and click Change All.

- ▸ To accept the flagged word as correct, click Ignore to skip this instance or Ignore All to ignore all instances of this word found in the document.

- ▸ To accept the flagged word as spelled correctly and add it to the Office user dictionary (so it isn't flagged in later checks), click Add.

continues on next page

4. Grammar. To handle a suspected grammar error , *do one of the following:*

▸ If you believe the grammar is correct or you intend to rewrite the text, click the Ignore or Ignore All button.

▸ Select the correction in the list box and then click the appropriate button, such as Change or Change All.

TIP To set spelling/grammar checking preferences, click the File tab to go to the Backstage and then click Options. In the Word Options dialog box, select the Proofing category **I**, make any desired changes, and click OK.

TIP Word 2013 can consider the *context* of words when performing spelling/grammar checks **J**, allowing it to flag words that are spelled properly but incorrect (distinguishing among *to, too,* and *two,* for example).

TIP If you choose Ignore or Ignore All for a suspected spelling or grammar error, the error will not reappear in subsequent spelling/grammar checks. To reconsider such errors, click the Recheck Document button in the Proofing section of the Word Options dialog box **I**.

TIP The AutoCorrect feature automatically corrects common typos and misspellings as you type. To view or edit the current AutoCorrect word list **K**, click the AutoCorrect Options button in the Proofing section of the Word Options dialog box **I**.

CAUTION Historically, Word's grammar checker has been only marginally useful. (Examine the error-laden paragraph in **G**, for example.) You shouldn't rely on it to identify and correct typical grammatical errors.

Proofing

I Set preferences for the proofing tools in the Proofing section of the Word Options dialog box.

I saw a good show their, but I was younger then.

J Although **their** is a proper word, Word flagged it as incorrect in the context of this sentence.

K Add words that you commonly misspell to the AutoCorrect list.

Find tab   Search string

Show additional options

A To perform a simple search, enter a search string in the Find what box and click Find Next.

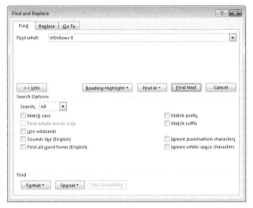

B Click More to expand the dialog box and set additional Find options.

Finding and Replacing Text

Using the Find and Replace dialog box, you can search for any text string and optionally replace it with another. In addition to performing standard text searches, you can search for and replace special items, such as paragraph characters (¶), graphics, or text formatted in a specific font. Note that simple searches are best performed in the Navigation Pane, described at the end of this chapter.

To perform a Find:

1. Click Home : Editing : Replace (Ctrl-H).

   The Find and Replace dialog box appears, open to the Replace tab.

2. Click the Find tab.

3. Enter a search string in the Find what box **A**.

4. *Optional:* To set additional options and criteria, click the More >> button. The dialog box expands **B**:

   ▸ To perform a more precise search, set options in the Search Options area. For instance, you can ensure that found text exactly matches the letter case of the search string (Match case) or specify the search direction (Search drop-down menu).

   ▸ To search for a special character such as a tab, insert it into the Find what box by choosing the character from the Special button's menu.

   ▸ To find only text with certain formatting (such as a particular font), choose an option from the Format button's menu.

   continues on next page

5. To begin the search, *do one of the following:*

- Click Find Next.

- Choose an option from the Find in button's menu to restrict the search to a particular document component.

Word highlights the first match, if any. Otherwise, a dialog box informs you that the search text wasn't found **C**.

6. *Do either of the following:*

- To search for the next match, click Find Next. Repeat as necessary.

- If you're finished, click Cancel or the close box (X).

To perform a Find/Replace:

1. Click Home : Editing : Replace (Ctrl-H).

The Find and Replace dialog box appears, open to the Replace tab.

2. Enter a search string in the Find what box and a replacement string in the Replace with box **D**.

3. *Optional:* To set additional options and criteria, click the More >> button. The dialog box expands **E**.

4. *Do either of the following:*

- To simultaneously replace every matching instance, click Replace All.

- To selectively replace text after examining each possible match, click Find Next. Word highlights the first match, if one is found. Click Replace if you want to make the replacement, or click Find Next to skip this instance and go to the next match. Repeat as necessary.

5. When you're finished, click Cancel or the close box (X).

C If the search string isn't found, this dialog box appears. A similar dialog box is presented after all matches have been found and viewed.

Show additional options

D Enter Find what and Replace with strings.

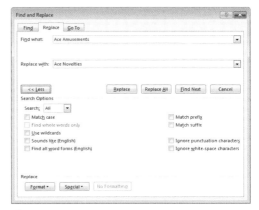

E You can expand the dialog box to enter more specific criteria.

Search Direction and Scope

The initial direction and scope of a search are determined by the location of the text insertion mark and your choice in the Search drop-down menu 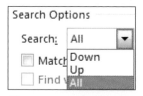 in the bottom half of the Find and Replace dialog box. Every search starts from the text insertion mark and proceeds in the direction specified in the Search menu:

- If Down or Up is chosen, the search proceeds to the bottom or top of the document or selection. When the bottom or top is reached, a dialog box asks if you'd like to search the rest of the document.

- If All is chosen from the Search menu, the search starts from the text insertion mark, continues downward until the end is reached, and then wraps around to the beginning in order to complete the search.

F You can control the search direction and scope.

TIP Regardless of the command you use to open the Find and Replace dialog box, you can switch between Finds and Replaces by clicking the appropriate tab.

TIP To restrict a Find or Replace to only *part* of a document, select the text before you execute the Find or Replace.

TIP When you replace text without checking Match case **E**, capitalization of the replacement text (Replace with) will match that of the replaced text (Find what).

TIP It's sometimes important to check Find whole words only **E** when performing a Replace. For example, when attempting to replace every instance of John with Mike, checking Find whole words only will prevent Johnson from being changed to Mikeson.

Entering Symbols and Special Characters

Some characters—especially symbols, such as copyright (©)—can be extremely difficult to type. Using the Symbol drop-down gallery or the Symbol dialog box, you can easily insert a symbol or other character from any font that's installed on your computer.

To insert a symbol or other character:

1. Set the text insertion mark at the spot in your text where you want to insert the symbol or character.

2. Open the Symbol gallery by clicking Insert : Symbols : Symbol.

3. *Do either of the following:*

   ▸ Choose the character . The character is inserted into the text.

   ▸ Choose More Symbols to open the Symbol dialog box **B**. To insert a character, double-click it or select it and click Insert. Click the Cancel button or the close box (X) to dismiss the dialog box.

TIP When inserting a character, Word uses the font at the text insertion mark. To use a different font (Webdings, for example, contains unusual characters not found in other fonts), choose it from the Font drop-down menu at the top of the Symbol dialog box **B**.

TIP To use a special character throughout a document, insert it once, select the character, copy it (Ctrl-C), and then paste the character (Ctrl-V) wherever it's needed.

TIP Many of the common symbols have a preassigned keyboard shortcut. Select the symbol **B** to see its shortcut. If a symbol doesn't have an accessible shortcut, you can click the Shortcut Key button to create one.

A Common symbols can be selected from this gallery.

Keyboard shortcut

B To insert a symbol that isn't in the Symbol gallery or one from a different font, open the Symbol dialog box.

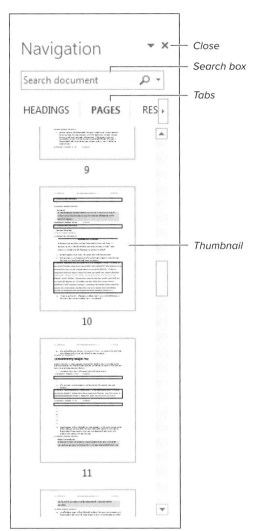

Navigation — Close

Search box

Tabs

HEADINGS | **PAGES** | RES ►

9

Thumbnail

10

11

A The Navigation Pane.

Using the Navigation Pane

In Office 2010, the Navigation Pane **A** replaced the Document Map. In addition to using it to quickly jump to important document sections by clicking a thumbnail or text heading, *you can do the following:*

- Rearrange document sections by dragging their headings

- Execute Finds to locate text in the document that marks the spot to which you want to go

- Search for other material, such as tables, graphics, equations, footnotes or endnotes, and reviewer comments

To open/close the Navigation Pane:

- To open the Navigation Pane, click the View : Show : Navigation Pane check box (see **A** in "Setting Display Options"), click the Home : Editing : Find icon, click the Page indicator on the status bar, or press Ctrl-F.

- To close the pane, click its close box (X), remove the check mark from the View : Show : Navigation Pane check box, or click the Page indicator again.

> **TIP** If the Navigation Pane fails to dock itself to the left side of the screen, double-click in its title area. To change the pane into a floating pane, drag it by the title area. To change the pane's width when docked, drag the divider between it and the document.

To go to a page or heading:

- To go to a page, click the Pages tab in the Navigation Pane. Click the thumbnail of the destination page **Ⓐ**.

- To go to a heading, click the Headings tab in the Navigation Pane. In the list that appears **Ⓑ**, click the desired heading.

  Only paragraphs that Word identifies as headings are listed in the pane. To learn about Word styles, see Chapter 5.

TIP You can expand and collapse headings in the Navigation Pane by clicking the triangle that precedes them.

To perform a text search:

1. *Optional:* To set specific search options (such as Match case or Find whole words only), click the arrow to the right of the search box **Ⓑ** and choose Options.

   The Find Options dialog box appears **Ⓒ**. Set options and click OK.

2. Type search text in the box at the top of the Navigation Pane. Word searches as you type and highlights matches in the document. The contents of the Navigation Pane depend on the selected tab:

   ▸ **Headings.** Any heading that contains a match is highlighted in yellow.

   ▸ **Pages.** Only pages that contain a match are shown; all others are hidden.

   ▸ **Results.** Matches are shown in context in the Navigation Pane **Ⓓ**.

Search menu

Ⓑ You can jump to any heading by clicking it.

Ⓒ You can set the same search options that appear in the expanded Find and Replace dialog box (see **Ⓑ** in "Finding and Replacing Text").

Next
Previous

Ⓓ Matches are presented in a scrolling list.

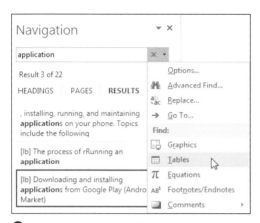

E You can also search for items other than text.

3. To go to a match, *do one of the following:*

  ▸ Click a heading, thumbnail, or text result in the Navigation Pane.

  ▸ Click the up (Previous) or down (Next) icons **D**.

  ▸ Choose Advanced Find, Replace, or Go To from the search box's menu **E** to open the normal Find and Replace dialog box.

  ▸ To find non-text items in the current document, choose a command from the Find section of the search box's menu **E**: Graphics, Tables, Equations, Footnotes/Endnotes, or Comments. To navigate among the found items, click the Previous and Next icons **D**.

  ▸ To clear the current search, click the close box (X) at the right end of the search box or press Esc.

Editing PDF Files

In addition to Office's ability to save and share documents as Adobe Acrobat PDF (*Portable Document Format*) files, Word 2013 can open and edit PDF files. When opened, they're automatically converted to Word format—enabling you to add and delete text, apply formatting, and so on.

To edit a PDF file in Word:

1. From within Word, open the PDF file that you want to edit by pressing Ctrl-O or clicking the File tab, followed by Open.

   The file is converted to Word format and opens in Word for editing.

2. Edit the document as desired.

3. To save the edited file, click the File tab, followed by Save; click the Save icon on the Quick Access Toolbar; or press Ctrl-S.

   A Save As dialog box appears **A**.

4. Select PDF (*.pdf) from the Save as type drop-down list.

5. Click the Save button.

   The document is converted back into PDF format and saved to disk.

> **TIP** To avoid overwriting the original PDF file, you may want to save it in a new location or with a different filename.

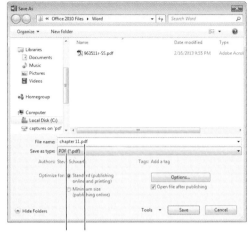

Save as type   File name

A Re-save the edited document as a PDF file.

Formatting Documents

If your main interest in Word is in generating a lot of text with as few interruptions as possible, you can probably do it faster using a simple text editor, such as Notepad or WordPad. In order to create documents that are attractive and pleasant to read, you must add *formatting*. Word supports three kinds of formatting:

- *Document formatting* affects the entire document and is primarily related to page settings, such as paper size, margins, orientation, sections, and columns. Other document-formatting commands enable you to insert page, section, and column breaks; add blank and cover pages; and insert headers and footers.

- *Paragraph formatting* applies to entire paragraphs and is used to set alignment, indents, and line spacing. You can also create numbered or bulleted lists.

- *Character formatting* can be applied to selected text and includes attributes such as font, size, color, and style.

To simplify the process of consistently applying paragraph and character formatting, you can define *styles*.

Specifying Page Settings

To set basic document formatting, you choose options from the menus in the Page Layout:Page Setup group **A**. These settings normally affect the entire document.

To set paper size and orientation:

- **Paper size.** Click the Size icon and choose a standard paper size.

  If you want to use a special paper size, choose More Paper Sizes. On the Paper tab of the Page Setup dialog box, select Custom size from the Paper size drop-down list, specify the paper's width and height, and click OK.

- **Orientation.** Pages can be laid out and printed in normal fashion (*portrait*) or sideways (*landscape*).

- **Columns.** Certain types of documents look better and are easier to read when arranged in multiple columns. To format a new document or reformat an existing one in this manner, choose the number of columns or a two-column layout (Left or Right) from the Columns menu **B**.

TIP To change a column's width, drag the right margin of the column in the horizontal ruler. If the ruler isn't visible, click the View:Show:Ruler check box.

TIP To restore a multi-column document to a single column, choose One from the Columns drop-down menu **B**.

Page Setup dialog box launcher

A Specify page settings by choosing options from the Page Layout:Page Setup group.

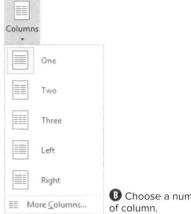

B Choose a number or type of column.

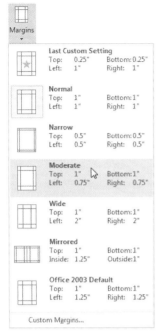

C Choose margin settings from this menu.

Tabs

Apply to menu

D You can also specify page settings on the tabs of the Page Setup dialog box.

■ **Margins.** Set margins for the document by choosing an option from the Margins menu **C**. To set margins that differ from the ones listed, choose Custom Margins and enter the desired settings on the Margins tab of the Page Setup dialog box.

TIP Although you may be tempted, it's usually inappropriate to set left or right margins of zero (0). First, many printers can't print from edge to edge. For instance, laser printers often have a *no-print zone* of 0.2–0.25" on each margin. Second, documents with tiny margins are often difficult to read because the lines are so long.

TIP Although it's uncommon, you can change page settings in mid-document—switching from portrait to landscape or setting new margins, for instance. Click the Page Setup dialog box launcher **A**. On the appropriate tab of the Page Setup dialog box **D**, set new options, choose This point forward from the Apply to drop-down menu, and click OK.

TIP You can also use the Page Setup dialog box to apply new settings to the entire document. Choose Whole document from the Apply to drop-down menu.

TIP You can specify page settings at any time: before you begin writing, after you've finished, or at any point in between.

Modifying the Background

You can choose options from the Design: Page Background group **A** to add color, a watermark/rubber stamp, or a border to every document page.

In general, you should apply background settings sparingly and only to special documents. Color and borders, for example, are best reserved for party invitations, ads, and flyers. On the other hand, a *watermark* can be extremely useful when applied to certain business documents, marking them as a Draft or Confidential, for example.

To add a background color to each page:

- Click the Page Color icon, and *do one of the following:*

  ▶ Click a color in the Theme Colors or Standard Colors palette **B**.

  ▶ To select from all possible colors, choose More Colors. Select a color in the Colors dialog box and click OK.

  ▶ To use a color gradient, texture, pattern, or picture as the background, choose Fill Effects. Select options from the tabs of the Fill Effects dialog box **C** and click OK.

  ▶ To remove a previously applied color, choose No Color.

TIP Document text may be easier to read on certain color, gradient, texture, pattern, and picture backgrounds than on others. For instance, if you choose a dark color, you may need to change the text color to one that contrasts better with the new background.

A You can change the page background by choosing options from this group.

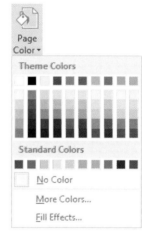

B The selected color will be applied to every document page.

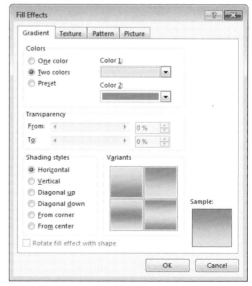

C The Fill Effects dialog box.

D Common text watermarks can be chosen from the gallery.

E To create a custom watermark or customize a gallery choice, set options in the Printed Watermark dialog box.

TIP You can apply a text watermark *or* a picture watermark—not both. If you switch types, the current watermark is replaced.

TIP Check the watermark's appearance with and without Semitransparent or Washout.

To apply a preset watermark:

- Click the Watermark icon and choose one of the preset watermarks from the gallery **D**.

  The watermark is applied to all pages.

To apply a custom watermark:

1. Click the Watermark icon and choose Custom Watermark from the gallery menu **D**.

   The Printed Watermark dialog box appears **E**.

2. *Do one of the following:*

   ▸ To use a text string as the watermark, select Text watermark; choose or type a text string; and choose settings for the language, font, size, color, and layout. For a fainter watermark, ensure that Semitransparent is checked.

   ▸ To use an image as the watermark, select Picture watermark. Click the Select Picture button to select an image file from your hard disk. You can choose a magnification for the image from the Scale menu or leave it set to Auto for the optimal size that will fit on the document page without cropping. Click the Washout check box for a fainter image.

   ▸ To remove an existing watermark from the document, select No watermark.

3. Click Apply to add the watermark to the document pages. If you don't like its appearance, you can change the settings and click Apply again.

4. When you're satisfied with the watermark, click OK to close the dialog box.

TIP You can also remove a watermark by choosing Remove Watermark from the Watermark gallery menu **D**.

To add borders around each page:

1. Click the Page Borders icon.

   The Borders and Shading dialog box appears 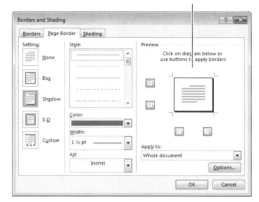. Select the Page Border tab.

2. Click an icon in the Setting list to specify the type of border you want to create.

3. Set line properties by choosing options from the Style, Color, Width, and Art drop-down menus.

   Your choices are reflected in the Preview area of the dialog box.

4. From the Apply to drop-down menu, indicate the document pages to which the border will be applied.

5. Click OK.

TIP To remove an existing page border or to begin designing one from scratch, select **None** in the Setting list.

TIP To remove individual lines from the border or to add a line, click that side of the box or the matching icon in the Preview area.

TIP Rather than create a line border, you can use artwork (such as pencils, scrollwork, or trees) as the border by choosing an image from the Art drop-down menu **G**.

Preview

F Select border settings on the Page Border tab of the Borders and Shading dialog box.

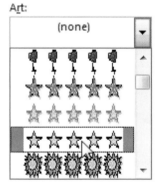

G Use artwork to add a festive or eye-catching border to a flyer or party invitation.

Automatic page break

simply knowing how each feature works.

The next step is to figure out how to best

In Draft view, automatic page breaks are shown as dotted lines.

Manual page break

book.¶

··········Page Break··········¶

When invisible characters are made visible in Draft view, manual page breaks are clearly marked.

Avoiding Widows and Orphans

In word processing, a single line at the end of a page is referred to as a *widow*; a single line at the beginning of a page (normally, the final line of a paragraph that began on the previous page) is an *orphan*. Layout rules suggest that both look amateurish and should be avoided.

If you carefully define and use paragraph styles (see "Working with Styles" in this chapter), you can automatically avoid widows and orphans. For example, when specifying the style for a header, you can enable a combination of Widow/Orphan control, Keep with next, and Keep lines together. For body-text paragraphs, Widow/Orphan control will suffice.

Inserting Breaks

Word adds an *automatic page break* wherever it's needed, based on the margins and the style setting of the paragraph that will be broken or moved to the next page. As you add or delete text, the automatic breaks are adjusted as needed; that is, Word repaginates as you type. In Print Layout and Read Mode views, breaks are shown as new physical pages. In Draft view, they're indicated by dotted lines .

Occasionally, breaks appear in spots where you'd prefer they not occur. For example, a key quote may be split between two pages. You can prevent this by inserting a *manual break* wherever it's needed. In addition to inserting manual page breaks, you can insert column and section breaks.

To insert a manual page break:

1. Set the text insertion mark at the start of the line on which you want to begin the new page.

2. *Do one of the following:*

   ▸ Click Insert : Pages : Page Break.

   ▸ Choose Page Layout : Page Setup : Breaks > Page.

   ▸ Press Ctrl-Enter.

   A page break is created at the text insertion mark.

TIP The safest time to insert most page breaks is after you've finished writing and editing.

TIP To remove a manual page break, select it and press Backspace, Delete, or Del. It's easiest to do when the breaks are visible . To display normally invisible characters, click the Home : Paragraph : Show/Hide ¶ icon.

To insert other types of manual breaks:

1. Set the text insertion mark at the start of the line where you want to insert the break.

2. Choose a command from the Page Layout:Page Setup:Breaks menu **C**:

    ▸ Choose Column to break the current column in a multi-column layout. The text following the text insertion mark will begin in the next column.

    ▸ Choose a command from the Section Breaks part of the menu to create or indicate the start of a new section.

    The column or section break is inserted.

TIP Unless you're writing a lengthy or complex report, you're unlikely to divide a document into sections. (I suspect that most Word users don't even know this feature exists.) Use sections when you need chapter-relative page numbering or want to dramatically change formatting in the middle of a document, such as switching between a single- and multi-column layout.

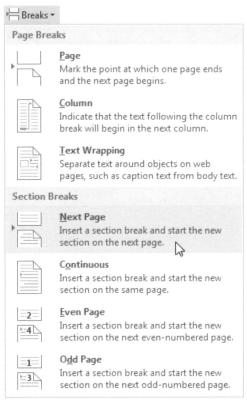

C You can insert manual breaks for new pages, columns, or sections by choosing a command from the Breaks menu.

A Choose a cover page from the gallery.

Placeholders

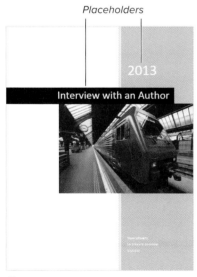

B To complete the cover page, replace the placeholder text.

Adding a Cover Page or Blank Page

You can add a pre-formatted *cover page* (or title page) to some documents. A cover page is especially useful for reports. The cover page is automatically placed at the beginning of the document and contains placeholders for important text elements such as the title, author, and date. Only one cover page is allowed per document. If you add another, it replaces the current one.

When writing a report or book that will be bound on the left edge, it's traditional to start each new section or chapter on a right-hand page. As such, if there's no material for the *facing page* (on the left), the page must be blank. You can insert blank pages wherever you like.

To add a cover page:

1. Choose a cover page from the Insert : Pages : Cover Page gallery **A**.

   The cover page is added as the first page.

2. Replace the placeholder text with your own text **B**.

TIP To view additional cover pages, move the cursor over the More Cover Pages from Office.com submenu **A** and wait for the cover thumbnails to appear.

TIP When you replace one cover page with another, placeholders that the cover pages have in common remain filled.

TIP To remove a cover page, choose Remove Current Cover Page from the Cover Page drop-down menu **A**.

To insert a blank page:

1. Set the text insertion mark where you want to add a blank page.

2. Click Insert:Pages:Blank Page **C**.

    A blank page is created at the text insertion mark by inserting two page breaks **D**. As required, text is reflowed around—but not into—the blank page.

    TIP You can leave the inserted page blank or type text on it.

    TIP To remove a blank page, delete the two manual page breaks and the blank paragraphs that were inserted. It's easiest to select and delete these items if you enable Home:Paragraph:Show/Hide ¶.

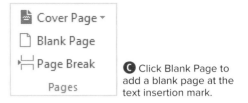

C Click Blank Page to add a blank page at the text insertion mark.

Blank page

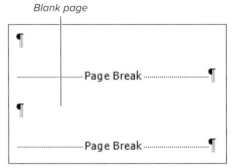

D To create a blank page, Word inserts a new paragraph surrounded by a pair of manual page breaks.

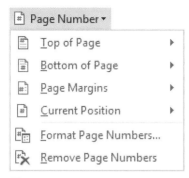

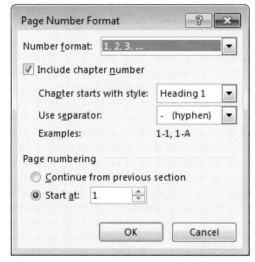

Adding Headers or Footers

Headers and *footers* are reserved areas at the top and bottom of each page, respectively, in which you can display important text, such as a page number, filename, or date. Header and footer styles can be chosen from a gallery or you can design them from scratch.

To add a header or footer that contains only a page number:

1. Open the Insert : Header & Footer : Page Number menu A and choose a number style from the appropriate position gallery: Top of Page (header), Bottom of Page (footer), or Page Margins (left or right margin).

2. *Optional:* To specify a numbering format (such as chapter-relative numbering) or a starting number, choose Page Number > Format Page Numbers A. Make changes in the Page Number Format dialog box B and click OK.

3. To resume editing the document, click Design : Close : Close Header and Footer C or double-click anywhere in the document body.

TIP To remove all inserted page numbers, choose Page Number > Remove Page Numbers A.

TIP Although the intent of the Page Number command is to add page numbering as the *sole* element in a header, footer, or margin, you can add other elements by following the instructions in "To add a pre-formatted header or footer" and "To create a custom header or footer."

A To insert only a page number into a header, footer, or margin, choose an option from these submenus.

B Use the Page Number Format dialog box to start numbering with a number other than 1, to select a different number format, or to apply chapter-relative numbering.

C Click this icon when you're ready to resume editing the document.

To add a pre-formatted header or footer:

1. Choose a style from the Insert : Header & Footer : Header or Footer gallery 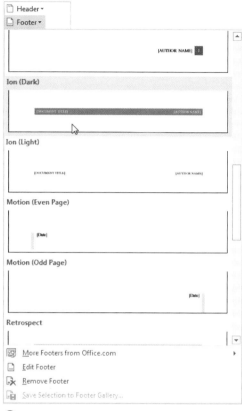.

   If you intend to show different header or footer text for odd and even pages, be sure to choose the correct one for the currently displayed page. If the *same* information will be shown on odd and even pages, it doesn't matter whether you choose an odd or even page style. The chosen style will be displayed on every page.

2. Make any necessary edits to the header or footer elements. For example, you can:

   ▸ Delete unwanted elements.

   ▸ Replace placeholder text by typing.

   ▸ Select an option, such as a date, from a placeholder's drop-down menu.

   ▸ Replace one element with another by deleting the original element and choosing Design : Insert : Quick Parts > Field. Common fields can also be chosen from the Quick Parts > Document Property submenu.

   ▸ Insert and position a new element. Add an alignment tab for the new element by clicking Design : Position : Insert Alignment Tab ⒺE.

3. If you want the header or footer to be different on odd and even pages, click the Design : Position : Different Odd & Even Pages check box. Then repeat Steps 1–2 with the opposite page type active—that is, odd or even.

4. To return to the body of the document, click Design : Close : Close Header and Footer ⒸC or double-click anywhere in the document body.

Ⓓ One of the most expedient ways to create a header or footer is to pick a style from the gallery.

Ⓔ You can add alignment tabs to position new elements.

To create a custom header or footer:

1. *Do either of the following:*

   ▸ In the Insert:Header & Footer group, open the Header or Footer menu and choose Edit Header or Edit Footer ⒟.

   ▸ In Print Layout view, double-click in the header or footer area.

   The text insertion mark appears in the header or footer ⒡.

continues on next page

Header area　　　Header & Footer Tools contextual tab　　　Close Header/Footer

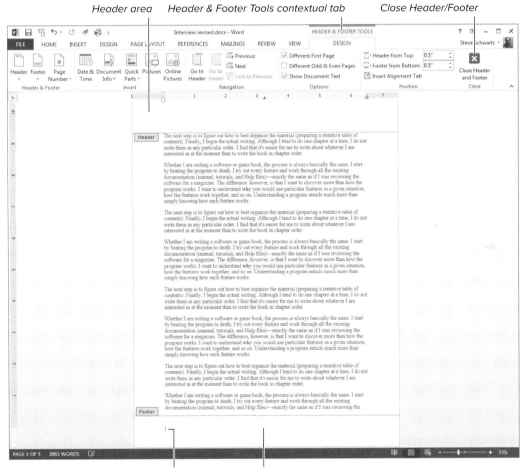

Text insertion mark　　Footer area

⒡ Creating or editing a header or footer is done in Print Layout view.

2. To insert header or footer elements, *do any of the following:*

   ▸ Type a text string, such as the project name, filename, or document title.

   ▸ To insert the current date, time, or both, click the Design:Insert:Date & Time icon. Select a format from the Date and Time dialog box . To show the current date and time each time you open the document, click Update automatically. Otherwise, the date/time entered at this moment will be treated as static text. Click OK.

   ▸ To insert a page number, choose Design:Insert: Quick Parts > Field. In the Field dialog box , select the Page field, select a number format from the Format list, and click OK.

TIP A Page field can be preceded by text, such as the word Page. Position the text insertion mark before the page number in the header or footer, and then type Page and a space.

3. To insert another element, click Design: Position: Insert Alignment Tab. In the Alignment Tab dialog box , select a position in the header or footer for the new element (Left, Center, or Right) and click OK. Repeat for a third element, if desired.

   By default, an element on the left side of the page is left-aligned with the left margin, a center element is center-aligned between the margins, and a right element is right-aligned with the right margin.

4. When you're done entering and editing elements in the header or footer area, *do either of the following:*

   ▸ Edit the other area by clicking in it.

   ▸ Click Design:Close:Close Header and Footer .

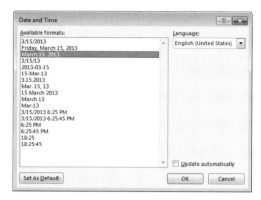

G Insert the date, time, or both by selecting a format from the Date and Time dialog box.

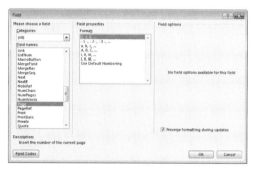

H To insert page numbers, select the Page field name and specify a display format.

I The Options group.

Header from Top:	0.5"
Footer from Bottom:	0.5"
Insert Alignment Tab	
Position	

J You can change the distance of the header or footer from the top or bottom of the page, respectively.

TIP If you base a document on a template, you should note that the template may contain a gallery from which you can choose other header and footer styles.

TIP If you find the body text distracting, you can temporarily hide it by removing the check mark from the Design : Options : Show Document Text check box **I**. When you finish working with the header and footer, the body text reappears.

TIP You can also add graphics to a header or footer, such as a logo or horizontal rule. To insert a graphic element, click the Design : Insert : Pictures icon.

TIP Text in a header or footer can be formatted as you like. Select a header or footer element or the entire header or footer. Choose formatting commands from the Mini toolbar or the Home : Font group.

TIP Page 1 of certain documents (such as a report with a title or cover page) often has no header/footer or it may need to contain special text. Click the Different First Page check box in the Options group **I**. You can then leave the page 1 header and footer blank or create a different page header and/or footer for it.

TIP To create different headers and footers on even/left and odd/right pages (as is often done for books and other publications with facing-page spreads), click the Different Odd & Even Pages check box **I**.

TIP You can reposition the header or footer by entering new settings in the Header from Top or Footer from Bottom boxes in the Design : Position group **J**.

TIP To edit a header or footer (whether it's gallery-based or one that you created from scratch), follow these same steps. Any element can be deleted or replaced.

Paragraph Formatting

In Word, a *paragraph*  is any amount of text (a word, line, sentence, or multiple sentences) that ends with a paragraph mark (¶). You finish a paragraph and begin a new one by pressing Enter. This action inserts a paragraph mark.

Generally, the new paragraph will have the same formatting as the previous one. The exception is when the *style* assigned to the current paragraph is designed to be followed by a paragraph of another style. For instance, a heading style is typically followed by a body text style.

Paragraph formatting, such as alignment or indents, can be applied to a selected paragraph by choosing options from the Home:Paragraph group **B** or Paragraph dialog box. You can also apply formatting by choosing a *paragraph style* (discussed later in this chapter).

Paragraph formatting has nothing to do with font, size, style, or color. It is concerned solely with alignment, spacing between lines, indents from one or both margins, and so on.

TIP Normally, paragraph marks are invisible, but you can show them by clicking Home:Paragraph:Show/Hide ¶ (Ctrl-*) **B**. Other normally hidden characters, such as tabs, spaces, and line breaks, also become visible.

TIP You can force certain characters (such as paragraph marks) to always display. Click the File tab and then click Options. In the Word Options dialog box, select the Display category, click the check boxes of items you always want to show **C**, and click OK.

> The next step is to figure out how to best organize the material (preparing a tentative table of contents). Finally, I begin the actual writing. Although I tend to do one chapter at a time, I do not write them in any particular order. I find that it's easier for me to write about whatever I am interested in at the moment than to write the book in chapter order.¶
>
> ¶
>
> Whether I am writing a software or game book, the process is always basically the same. I start by beating the program to death. I try out every feature and work through all the existing documentation (manual, tutorials, and Help files)—exactly the same as if I was reviewing the software for a magazine. The difference, however, is that I want to discover more than how the program works. I want to understand **why** you would use particular features in a given situation, how the features work together, and so on. Understanding a program entails much more than simply knowing how each feature works.¶

A Here are three paragraphs, each ending with a paragraph mark. The middle one is a blank paragraph.

Show/Hide ¶

Paragraph dialog box launcher

B The Paragraph group contains icons for common paragraph-formatting commands.

Always show these formatting marks on the screen

☐ Tab characters	→
☐ Spaces	•••
☐ Paragraph marks	¶
☐ Hidden text	abc
☐ Optional hyphens	¬
☑ Object anchors	⚓
☑ Show all formatting marks	

C Check the items that will always be shown, regardless of the status of Show/Hide ¶.

Left   *Center*

This paragraph is left-aligned. This paragraph is left-aligned. This paragraph is left-aligned. This paragraph is left-aligned. This paragraph is left-aligned. This paragraph is left-aligned. This paragraph is left-aligned. This paragraph is left-aligned.

This paragraph is center-aligned. This paragraph is center-aligned. This paragraph is center-aligned. This paragraph is center-aligned. This paragraph is center-aligned.

This paragraph is right-aligned. This paragraph is right-aligned. This paragraph is right-aligned. This paragraph is right-aligned. This paragraph is right-aligned. This paragraph is right-aligned. This paragraph is right-aligned.

This paragraph is fully justified between the left and right margins. This paragraph is fully justified between the left and right margins. This paragraph is fully justified between the left and right margins. This paragraph is fully justified between the left and right margins.

Justify   *Right*

D No matter how short or long, every paragraph has an alignment.

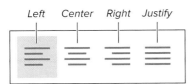

E Alignment icons.

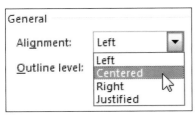

F In the Paragraph dialog box, choose an option from the Alignment menu.

Setting Alignment

A paragraph's *alignment* determines its position in relation to the margins. Every paragraph must have one of the following alignments **D**:

- **Left.** The left edge of the paragraph is flush with the left margin and the right edge is ragged. Body text of most documents is left-aligned.

- **Right.** The right edge of the paragraph is flush with the right margin and the left edge is ragged.

- **Center.** Each line of the paragraph is automatically centered between the margins. Center alignment is sometimes applied to titles and other headings.

- **Justify.** Both edges of the paragraph are flush with a margin. Word adjusts the spacing between words to enable each line to be flush with the margins. Magazine copy and block quotations are often justified.

To set paragraph alignment:

1. Select one or more paragraphs.

    To select a paragraph, it's sufficient to set the text insertion mark in it. To select multiple paragraphs, drag a selection through at least part of each one.

2. *Do one of the following:*

    ▸ Click an alignment icon in the Home: Paragraph group **E**.

    ▸ Press an alignment keyboard shortcut: Ctrl-L (Left), Ctrl-E (Center), Ctrl-R (Right), or Ctrl-J (Justify).

    ▸ In the Paragraph dialog box, click the Indents and Spacing tab, choose an alignment **F**, and click OK.

Setting Indents

Every paragraph has three indents that you can set to specify the distance between the text and the left/right margins:

- **Left.** Distance from the left margin.

- **Right.** Distance from the right margin.

- **First line.** Distance from the left margin that applies only to the paragraph's first line of text.

Indents are automatically set for bulleted and numbered lists (*hanging indents*). You can set equal left and right indents of 0.5" or 1" to format a block quote. Indents can be set on the horizontal ruler or in the Paragraph dialog box. Any or all indents can be set to 0.

To set indents:

- Select one or more paragraphs, and then *do any of the following:*

    - **Home:Paragraph group.** To increase or decrease the left indent in increments of 0.5", click the Increase or Decrease Indent icon **G**.

    - **Page Layout:Paragraph group.** Enter numbers (in inches) in the Left and/or Right box **H**.

    - **Paragraph dialog box.** You can also set exact indents on the Indents and Spacing tab **I**. To create a first line indent (similar to starting each paragraph by pressing Tab), choose First line from the Special drop-down menu and set the indent. To create a hanging indent for a bulleted or numbered list, choose Hanging from the Special drop-down menu.

    - **Horizontal ruler.** You can manually set indents by dragging markers on the horizontal ruler **J**.

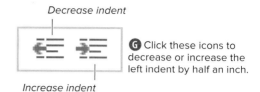

Decrease indent

Increase indent

G Click these icons to decrease or increase the left indent by half an inch.

H You can set precise left and right indents.

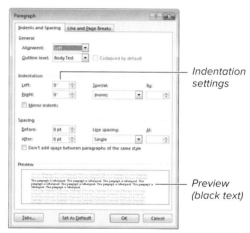

Indentation settings

Preview (black text)

I You can create any kind of indent in the Paragraph dialog box.

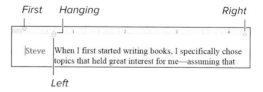

First   Hanging   *Right*

Left

J To create this outdent, I dragged the first line indent marker to the left.

TIP You can use the Paragraph dialog box to create an *outdent* (extending to the left of the left margin) by entering a negative number for the left indent **I**.

Ⓚ Enable the automatic creation of bulleted and numbered lists by clicking these check boxes.

Setting Indents with the Ruler

When setting indents on the ruler, you'll note the following behaviors:

- The first line and right indent markers move independently of other markers.

- The left and hanging indent markers move as a pair.

- When you drag the left indent marker, it and the hanging indent marker maintain their current distance from the first line indent marker.

- Drag the hanging indent marker to change its distance (and that of the left indent marker) from the first line indent marker.

Creating Lists

Bulleted and numbered lists are special kinds of hanging indent paragraphs. The hanging portion is either a bullet character (such as a filled or empty circle, diamond, or check mark) or a sequential number (or a letter). You can create such lists *automatically* (depending on settings in Word Options) or *manually* (by applying a bullet or number format to a set of paragraphs).

You can also create lists with multiple levels of indents. These *multilevel lists* can contain sub-lists beneath any list item.

To enable automatic bulleted and numbered lists:

1. Open the Word Options dialog box by clicking the File tab, followed by Options.

2. Select the Proofing category.

3. Click the AutoCorrect Options button near the top of the dialog box.

4. In the AutoCorrect dialog box, select the AutoFormat As You Type tab.

5. In the Apply as you type section of the dialog box **Ⓚ**, enable Automatic bulleted lists and Automatic numbered lists.

6. Click OK to close the AutoCorrect dialog box.

7. Click OK to close the Word Options dialog box.

TIP This is a one-time procedure. You'll have to revisit it only if you want to stop automatically creating one or both list types.

To automatically create a list:

1. At the beginning of a new paragraph, *do one of the following:*

   ▸ **Bulleted list.** To create the first item, type an asterisk (*) and a space. The asterisk is converted to a bullet.

   ▸ **Numbered list.** To create the first item, type **1.** and a space. This becomes the first item in a numbered list.

2. Finish the item paragraph and press Enter.

   Additional consecutive paragraphs you create by pressing Enter will continue the bullets or numbering.

3. To complete the final list item Ⓛ, press Enter twice.

To manually create a list:

1. *Do either of the following:*

   ▸ To create a bulleted or numbered list using the most recently applied bullet or number style, click the Home : Paragraph : Bullets or Numbering icon Ⓜ or these icons on the Mini toolbar.

   ▸ Select a specific bullet or numbering style from the Bullets or Numbering Library Ⓝ. When you hover the cursor over a gallery item, a live preview appears on the list.

2. Finish the item paragraph and press Enter.

   Additional consecutive paragraphs that you create by pressing Enter will continue the bullets or numbering.

3. To complete the final list item, press Enter twice.

> **TIP** You can also end a bullet or numbered list by clicking the Home : Paragraph : Bullets or Numbering icon Ⓜ.

Bulleted list

Buy the following fresh fruit:

- Bananas
- Pears
- Apples
- Pineapple

Prepare the fruit as follows:

1. Peel and chop the fresh fruit into tiny, bite-sized pieces.
2. Place in a large mixing bowl.
3. Call mom for other ingredients and instructions. ☺
4. Refrigerate

Numbered list

Ⓛ Examples of an automatic bulleted list and a numbered list.

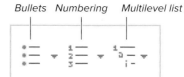

Bullets   Numbering   Multilevel list

Ⓜ You can create a list by clicking an icon or choosing a style from a drop-down gallery.

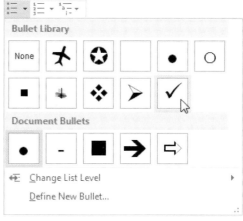

Ⓝ The Bullet Library.

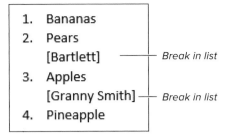

1. Bananas
2. Pears
   [Bartlett] —— *Break in list*
3. Apples
   [Granny Smith] —— *Break in list*
4. Pineapple

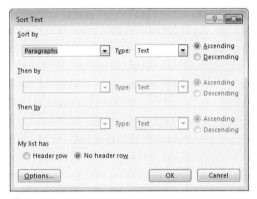

O Using line breaks, you can interrupt a list without ending it.

P These settings can be used to sort a bulleted list alphabetically.

TIP There are other characters that you can type (followed by a period and a space) to automatically start a numbered list with a different numbering format, such as a., A., i., and I.

TIP To type additional text directly beneath a bulleted or numbered point without interrupting the bullets or numbering **O**, end the previous line by pressing Shift-Enter to create a *line break*. Type the additional text on the new line. When you press Enter to end the line or paragraph, the bullets or numbering resumes.

TIP You can change the bullet or numbering style for an existing list. Select all bulleted or numbered points, and then select a different style from the Bullet or Numbering Library **N**.

TIP To change a list from bullets to numbers or vice versa, click the other icon in the Home: Paragraph group **M** or on the Mini toolbar.

TIP You can sort a bulleted list alphabetically, numerically, or in date order. Select the items, click the Home: Paragraph: Sort icon, and set options in the Sort Text dialog box **P**.

TIP You can change the formatting of all bullets and numbers in a list. Click one to select them all. Apply character formatting (such as a different font, boldface, or a color) by choosing options from the Home: Font group or from the Mini toolbar.

To create a multilevel list:

1. Begin an automatic or manual list by following the previous tasks' instructions.

2. To enter an item at a new level, click Home:Paragraph:Increase Indent ⓖ.

   Additional items created at the same indent level by pressing Enter will have the same bullet or number style.

3. To convert an item to a higher level, click Home:Paragraph:Decrease Indent ⓖ.

TIP You can also change levels by pressing Tab (increase) or Shift-Tab (decrease).

4. To specify the bullet or number format to be applied to each level, click Home:Paragraph:Multilevel List and choose a style from the List Library.

   The list is reformatted to match the library selection ⓠ.

TIP To select all items at a particular level in a bulleted or numbered list, click the bullet or number of any item at that level ⓡ.

TIP You can substitute other bullets for the ones in the gallery. Choose Home:Paragraph:Bullets > Define New Bullet. In the Define New Bullet dialog box ⓢ, click Symbol or Picture to select a character from a font (such as Symbol, Wingdings, or Webdings) or to use an image file, respectively.

❖ Pears
  ➤ Bartlett
  ➤ Anjou
    ▪ Red
    ▪ Green
❖ Apples
  ➤ Granny Smith
  ➤ Delicious
    ▪ Golden
    ▪ Red

ⓠ A multilevel bulleted list.

❖ Pears
  ➤ Bartlett
  ➤ Anjou
    ▪ Red
    ▪ Green
❖ Apples
  ➤ Granny Smith
  ➤ Delicious
    ▪ Golden
    ▪ Red

ⓡ You can select all items at the same level.

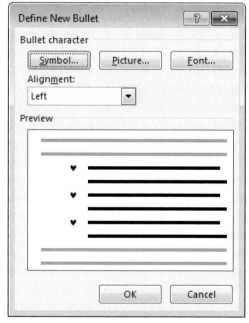

ⓢ You can create new bullets by choosing a symbol character or an image.

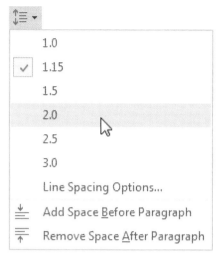

T The Line and Paragraph Spacing drop-down menu.

U You can select a line spacing option from this drop-down list.

WordArt and Text Effects

In Chapter 3, you learned how to create WordArt, a decorative text object. In Word, you can use Text Effects to apply the same decorative effects without changing the selected text into an object.

1. Select the text (such as a heading) that you want to format.

2. Choose an effect from the Home : Font : Text Effects and Typography gallery. Each effect provides a live preview.

You can modify other characteristics of the text (such as the font, size, or color) without losing the applied text effect.

Changing Paragraph and Line Spacing

Paragraph attributes also include the space between lines, as well as the space before and after a paragraph. Although line spacing and between-paragraph spacing are defined as part of every paragraph style, there are times when you'll want to change these settings. For instance, if a document is a few lines too long, you can make it fit in fewer pages by reducing the line spacing. Similarly, if an instructor insists on *double-spaced text* (a typewriter term), you can approximate it on a computer by increasing the line spacing of all paragraphs.

To change line spacing for paragraphs:

1. Select the paragraph(s) that will be affected by the new setting.

2. Click Home : Paragraph : Line and Paragraph Spacing **T**, and *do one of the following:*

   ▸ Choose a number, representing the space between each pair of lines. (Double spacing is 2.0, for example.) As you hover the cursor over an option, the line spacing is previewed on the selected text.

   ▸ Choose Line Spacing Options. The Paragraph dialog box opens. On the Indents and Spacing tab, set the Line spacing **U**, and click OK.

   The selected paragraphs are reformatted.

TIP To set line spacing in *points* (72 per inch), choose **Exactly** from the Line spacing drop-down menu **U**.

To change the before or after spacing for selected paragraphs:

1. Select the paragraph(s) that will be affected by the new settings.

2. *Do one of the following:*

   ▸ Enter numbers (in points) in the Page Layout:Paragraph:Spacing Before and/or Spacing After boxes 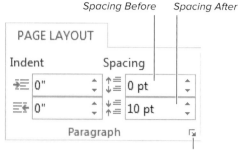.

   ▸ Click the Paragraph dialog box launcher **ⓥ**. On the Indents and Spacing tab, enter numbers (in points) in the Before and/or After boxes **ⓦ**. Click OK to close the dialog box.

   ▸ Choose Home:Paragraph:Line and Paragraph Spacing > Add (Remove) Space Before Paragraph or Add (Remove) Space After Paragraph **ⓣ** to add a 12-point space or remove the current space.

   The new before/after spacing is applied to the selected paragraphs.

TIP New line spacing and before/after settings affect only the selected paragraphs. To apply these settings to an entire document, set the text insertion mark and press Ctrl-A or choose Home:Editing:Select > Select All. Then set line or before/after spacing.

TIP If a paragraph or paragraph style is set for zero (0) space before and after, it may be hard to distinguish from surrounding paragraphs.

TIP In general, it's best to avoid applying new spacing settings directly to paragraphs. An inconsistently formatted document is the likely result. Instead, modify the document's *paragraph styles*. Doing so will ensure consistency because all paragraphs to which you've assigned a particular style will automatically update to reflect the new settings. Styles are discussed later in this chapter.

Spacing Before   *Spacing After*

Paragraph dialog box launcher

ⓥ Enter numbers in these boxes to set before and after spacing.

ⓦ Set the before and after spacing (in points), and then click OK.

Changing the Default Font

Whenever you create a new, blank Word document and begin typing, the font used is the *default font*. You can easily change this font, if you like.

1. Open the Font dialog box.

   The font, style, size, and other attributes of the currently selected text are shown.

2. To specify attributes other than those of the selected text, select a font and other attributes from the drop-down lists and check boxes.

3. Click the Set as Default button. In the new dialog box, select All documents based on the Normal.dotm template. Click OK.

4. Click OK to close the Font dialog box.

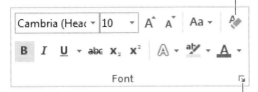

Clear All Formatting

Font dialog box launcher

A Common character-formatting attributes can be set by selecting commands from the Home:Font group.

B Every supported character-formatting attribute can be set in the Font dialog box.

Character Formatting

Character formatting is formatting that you selectively apply to words, phrases, lines, sentences, or paragraphs. To make a phrase stand out in its sentence, you might format it as italic, boldface, blue, or underlined. If the sentence containing the selected phrase was formatted with the Arial font, you might apply a variation of the font, such as Arial Narrow or Arial Black.

If you're applying a character format *as you type* (rather than by selecting existing text), you can think of the formatting as an on/off sequence. You turn the formatting feature on, type the new text, and then turn the feature off when you want to return to the original formatting.

If you want to easily reapply complex character formatting to other text in the document, you can use the Format Painter tool.

To apply formatting as you type:

1. To switch to a different character formatting, *do either of the following:*

   ▸ Choose character-formatting options from the Home:Font group **A**.

   ▸ Click the Font dialog box launcher **A** or press Ctrl-D. Choose new settings in the Font dialog box **B** and click OK.

2. Type the text that you want to format with the chosen attribute(s).

3. Disable the attributes applied in Step 1 by clicking their icons again.

TIP If you changed fonts, you can revert to the original font by choosing its name from any Font menu or list.

To apply formatting to existing text:

1. Select the text to which you want to apply a different character formatting.

2. *Do any of the following:*

   ▸ Choose character-formatting options from the Mini toolbar 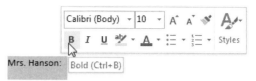. The Mini toolbar automatically appears whenever you select text.

   ▸ Choose character-formatting options from the Home:Font group Ⓐ.

     Rest the cursor over any icon to see a ToolTip description of its function.

   ▸ Click the Font dialog box launcher Ⓐ or press Ctrl-D. Choose settings in the Font dialog box Ⓑ and click OK.

> **TIP** Many character-formatting commands have keyboard shortcuts. You can apply or remove their formatting by pressing the keys listed in Table 5.1.

To remove character formatting:

1. Select the text from which you want to remove character formatting.

2. *Do any of the following:*

   ▸ To remove *all* character formatting (leaving only plain text), click Home: Font:Clear All Formatting Ⓐ.

   ▸ To selectively remove formatting (when you've applied multiple attributes to the selected text), click icons of the formats you want to remove on the Mini toolbar Ⓒ or in the Font group Ⓐ.

   ▸ Click the Font dialog box launcher Ⓐ or press Ctrl-D. Choose new settings in the Font dialog box Ⓑ and click OK.

Ⓒ Choose basic character-formatting commands from the Mini toolbar

TABLE 5.1 Character-formatting Keyboard Shortcuts

Keypress	Definition
Ctrl-B	Boldface
Ctrl-I	Italic
Ctrl-U	Underline (single)
Ctrl-Shift-D	Underline (double)
Ctrl-Shift-W	Underline words but not spaces
Ctrl-Shift-K	Small capital letters (caps)
Ctrl-=	Subscript
Ctrl-+	Superscript
Ctrl-<	Decrease font size
Ctrl->	Increase font size
Shift-F3	Change letter case
Ctrl-Spacebar	Remove manual character formatting

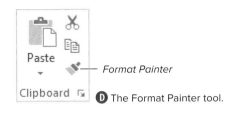

Format Painter

D The Format Painter tool.

Format Painter cursor

E Click in the word or drag-select the text to which you want to apply the copied formatting.

Before, During, or After?

It's important to understand that paragraph and character formatting can be applied at *any* time: before you begin typing a paragraph or text block, as you type it, or after it has been written and edited.

There's no single best approach—it depends on your writing style. For example, if you're making a numbered list, you can start a new paragraph, apply the number format, and then type the first item. For each additional paragraph you create, the numbering increments. On the other hand, it can be just as easy to write the entire list, select it, and then apply the numbered paragraph format.

To use the Format Painter to duplicate formatting:

1. Select the text whose formatting you want to duplicate or position the text insertion mark within that text.

2. Click the Home : Clipboard : Format Painter icon **D**, click the Format Painter icon on the Mini toolbar **C**, or press Ctrl-Shift-C.

   The Format Painter cursor appears.

3. Drag to select the target text **E**.

   The copied character formatting is applied to the target text.

> **TIP** To apply formatting to a single word, it's sufficient to click in the word with the Format Painter cursor.

> **TIP** You can use the Format Painter to duplicate character *and* paragraph formatting. Select the entire paragraph before selecting the Format Painter tool.

> **TIP** You can apply copied character attributes to multiple selections by double-clicking the Format Painter icon. One by one, drag-select each destination text string. When you're finished, click the Format Painter icon again.

> **TIP** You can easily apply new attributes to *multiple* text strings that have the same formatting. Begin by selecting one of the text strings. Choose Home : Editing : Select > Select All Text with Similar Formatting. As you choose new character formatting, it'll be applied to all the text selections.

Working with Styles

A *style* is a set of formatting instructions that you can apply to selected paragraphs or text. By applying styles rather than manually formatting a document, you can ensure consistent formatting throughout—resulting in a document with a professional appearance.

The Home:Styles:Styles gallery contains a subset of the defined styles for the current document. Designed to help you easily apply the most common paragraph and character styles to selected text, the Styles gallery encourages users who have previously ignored styles to start using them.

To apply a style:

1. Select a text string or paragraph to which you want to apply a style.

2. Open the Styles gallery. Move the cursor over a style icon **A**.

   A preview of the style is displayed on the selected text.

   TIP You can also select a style from the Styles pane (if it's open) or the Mini toolbar.

3. If it's the desired style, click it to apply the style to the text.

To create a new style for the current document:

1. You can create a new style from formatted text or paragraphs. Begin by applying the desired character formatting to some text or applying paragraph formatting to a paragraph.

2. Select the formatted word, text string, or paragraph.

A When you rest the cursor on a style, it is previewed on the selected text.

Give Your Document a Makeover

By applying a Word *theme* or *style set*, you can instantly change the look of your document. Found in the Design:Document Formatting group, each theme consists of complimentary fonts, colors, and effects. A style set contains defined styles.

You can preview the effect of a theme (in the Themes menu gallery) or a style set (in the Document Formatting gallery) by hovering the cursor over it. If you prefer, you can choose individual options from the Design tab's menus.

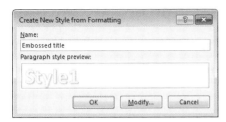

B Name the new style.

C Make any necessary changes and click OK.

D If the Styles pane isn't open, you can right-click the style in the Styles gallery.

3. Choose Create a Style from the Styles gallery menu **A**.

The Create New Style from Formatting dialog box appears **B**.

4. Name the new style and click Modify.

A new dialog box appears **C**.

5. Make any formatting changes that are required, and *do the following:*

▸ Ensure that the setting for Style type matches the kind of style you want to create: Character, Paragraph, or Linked (paragraph and character).

▸ If this style is routinely followed by a different style, specify it in the Style for following paragraph box.

6. Click OK.

An icon for the style appears in the Styles gallery. The style definition is added to the document's style list.

To modify a style by example:

1. Open the Styles pane by clicking the launcher icon at the bottom of the Styles gallery (Alt-Ctrl-Shift-S).

2. Make the desired changes to a text string or paragraph that is formatted with the style you want to modify.

3. Select the modified text or paragraph, move the cursor over the right edge of its selected style in the Styles pane, click the menu icon that appears, and choose Styles > Update *style name* to Match Selection.

TIP This command can also be chosen from the context menu that appears when you right-click the style's icon in the Styles gallery **D**.

To modify a style using a dialog box:

1. *Do either of the following:*

   ▸ Right-click the style icon in the Styles gallery and choose Modify 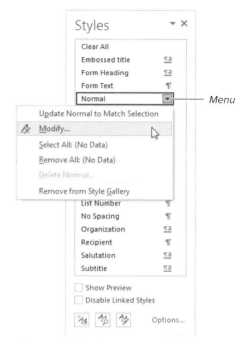.

   ▸ In the Styles pane, click the down-arrow beside the style name and choose Modify **E**.

   A Modify Style dialog box appears, identical to the one shown in **C**.

2. Make any desired changes and click OK.

   The modified style definition is stored. Current text or paragraphs formatted with the style automatically update to conform to the new definition.

> **TIP** To remove a style from the gallery, right-click its icon in the gallery **D** or open its menu in the Styles pane. Choose **Remove from Style Gallery.** (Note that this only removes the style from the gallery. It does not delete the style from the document's defined styles.)

> **TIP** To *delete* a style (permanently removing it from a document's style list), click the down-arrow beside the style name in the Styles pane and choose Delete *style name*. Text or paragraphs that are presently formatted with the style revert to the default formatting.

> **TIP** To remove all formatting applied by choosing a particular style, click the down-arrow beside the style's name in the Styles pane and choose **Clear Formatting of** *X* **Instance(s).**

> **TIP** To apply a different style to all text or paragraphs currently formatted with a given style, click the down-arrow beside the style in the Styles pane and choose **Select All.** Reformat the selected material by clicking a new style or by applying formatting from the Home tab.

E The Styles pane lists defined styles for the current document. Each style has its own menu.

Alternatives to the Styles Pane and Gallery

You can open a floating window from which you can choose styles to apply to selected text. Choose Apply Styles from the Styles gallery menu **D**.

If you've selected some text, you'll note that the Mini toolbar has a Styles icon. Click it to display the Styles gallery.

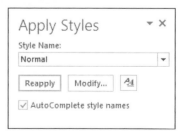

Merge Formatting

By adding specially formatted placeholder text called *merge fields* to a document and combining it with data from a second document created in Word, Excel 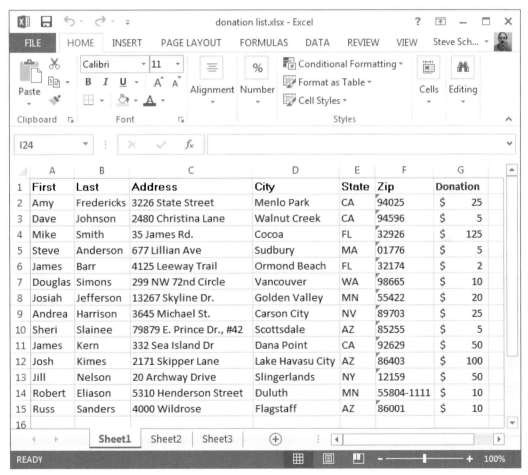, Outlook, or another application, you can *merge* the documents—creating a separate, customized document page for each data record.

For example, by inserting name and address placeholders in the main document, you could create a *mail merge*. A personalized letter containing their address and using their first name in the greeting line could be generated for each person.

The easiest way to learn how to perform a merge is to use the Mail Merge Wizard to step you through the process. As an example, you'll generate a series of personalized letters. To follow along, create an Excel worksheet similar to the one below. Each row is a data record. Be sure to create at least three or four records.

	First	Last	Address	City	State	Zip	Donation
1	First	Last	Address	City	State	Zip	Donation
2	Amy	Fredericks	3226 State Street	Menlo Park	CA	94025	$ 25
3	Dave	Johnson	2480 Christina Lane	Walnut Creek	CA	94596	$ 5
4	Mike	Smith	35 James Rd.	Cocoa	FL	32926	$ 125
5	Steve	Anderson	677 Lillian Ave	Sudbury	MA	01776	$ 5
6	James	Barr	4125 Leeway Trail	Ormond Beach	FL	32174	$ 2
7	Douglas	Simons	299 NW 72nd Circle	Vancouver	WA	98665	$ 10
8	Josiah	Jefferson	13267 Skyline Dr.	Golden Valley	MN	55422	$ 20
9	Andrea	Harrison	3645 Michael St.	Carson City	NV	89703	$ 25
10	Sheri	Slainee	79879 E. Prince Dr., #42	Scottsdale	AZ	85255	$ 5
11	James	Kern	332 Sea Island Dr	Dana Point	CA	92629	$ 50
12	Josh	Kimes	2171 Skipper Lane	Lake Havasu City	AZ	86403	$ 100
13	Jill	Nelson	20 Archway Drive	Slingerlands	NY	12159	$ 50
14	Robert	Eliason	5310 Henderson Street	Duluth	MN	55804-1111	$ 10
15	Russ	Sanders	4000 Wildrose	Flagstaff	AZ	86001	$ 10

A Data in this worksheet will be merged with a Word form letter.

To perform a merge using the Mail Merge Wizard:

1. In Word, create a document similar to the one below **B**.

   Leave space for the mail merge fields.

2. Choose Mailings : Start Mail Merge : Start Mail Merge > Step by Step Mail Merge Wizard.

   The Mail Merge task pane appears on the right side of the window **C**.

3. Click the Letters radio button and then click Next: Starting document (at the bottom of the task pane).

   Step 2 of 6 appears in the task pane.

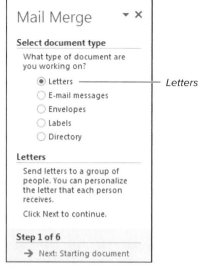

Letters

C Mail Merge Wizard: Step 1.

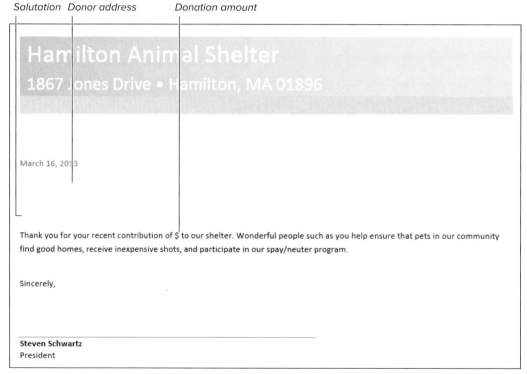

Salutation   *Donor address*   *Donation amount*

B The merge letter can be based on an existing document like this one or created from a template.

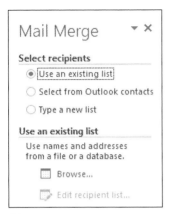

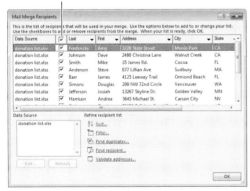

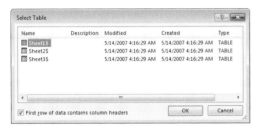

D Step 3 of 6: Select recipients.

E Select the first sheet in the workbook. Because the first row of the sheet contains the merge field names, ensure that the check box is checked.

Include/exclude check boxes

F Review the data, ensure that it looks correct, and specify the records to include.

4. *Select one of the following:*

▸ **Use the current document.** If the merge document is open and active, select this option.

▸ **Start from a template.** If you haven't created the document, select this option. Click the Select template text that appears and then pick a template, such as the Origin Letter.

▸ **Start from existing document.** If you have already created the document but it isn't open, select this option, select the document from the list that appears, and click the Open button.

5. At the bottom of the task pane, click Next: Select recipients.

Step 3 of 6 appears in the task pane **D**.

6. Select Use an existing list and then click Browse.

The Select Data Source dialog box appears.

7. Navigate to the drive/folder in which you saved the Excel data file, select the file, and click Open.

The Select Table dialog box appears **E**.

8. Select the first sheet (Sheet1$), ensure that First row of data contains column headers is checked, and click OK.

The Mail Merge Recipients dialog box appears **F**.

9. *Optional:* You can omit a recipient by removing the check mark before his or her name. Click OK when you're ready to continue.

TIP **You can sort the data by clicking the sort field's name and choosing Sort Ascending or Sort Descending from the menu that appears.**

continues on next page

10. At the bottom of the task pane, click Next: Write your letter.

11. In Step 4 of 6, you'll add the merge fields. To select the spot for the recipient's address, set the text insertion mark in the form letter at the start of the line below the date. Click the Address block... text in the task pane.

The Insert Address Block dialog box appears **Ⓖ**.

12. Ensure that Insert recipient's name in this format and Insert postal address are both checked. Select a format for displaying names. Click the arrows above the preview area to ensure that the names and addresses display properly, and click OK.

The Address Block merge field is inserted into the letter **Ⓗ**.

13. Set the text insertion mark where the greeting line ("Dear ...") will appear—below the Address Block field. Click the Greeting line... text in the task pane.

The Insert Greeting Line dialog box appears **Ⓘ**.

14. Format the greeting line by selecting options from the drop-down lists. Click the arrows above the preview area to see how the greeting line looks when filled with your data. Click OK.

15. Finally, you'll add a merge field for the donation amount. In the first line of the letter, set the text insertion mark after "...contribution of $". Then click More items... in the task pane.

The Insert Merge field dialog box appears **Ⓙ**.

Name format   *Preview*

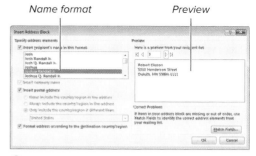

Ⓖ Select a format for the recipient's name in the address block.

Ⓗ Each inserted merge field is surrounded by « and » characters.

Ⓘ The Insert Greeting Line dialog box.

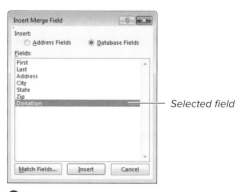

Selected field

Ⓙ Select a merge field to add at the text insertion mark.

K If necessary, edit the text immediately surrounding the merge field to ensure that it will display correctly.

Address   *Donation*

March 16, 2013

Josh Kimes
2171 Skipper Lane
Lake Havasu City, AZ 86403

Dear Josh:

Thank you for your recent contribution of $100 to our shelter. community find good homes, receive inexpensive shots, and p

Salutation

L The form letter now includes the Excel data.

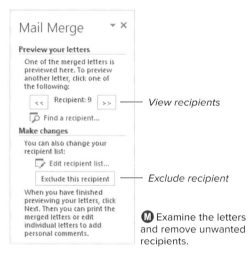

—— *View recipients*

—— *Exclude recipient*

M Examine the letters and remove unwanted recipients.

N The Preview Results group provides additional options, such as searching for recipients and error checking.

16. Select the Donation field. Click Insert.

The merge field is added to the letter.

TIP You can format merge fields. Be sure to select the entire field, including the surrounding bracket characters.

17. Close the dialog box by clicking Close.

18. The Donation merge field must be preceded by a dollar sign (**$**) and followed by a space. If either is missing **K**, add it to the letter now.

19. At the bottom of the task pane, click Next: Preview your letters.

Step 5 of 6 appears, displaying a merge letter **L**.

20. Click buttons to examine the recipient letters **M**. If you see a person whom you don't want to include in the merge, click Exclude this recipient.

TIP Navigation buttons are also provided in the Mailings: Preview Results group **N**.

continues on next page

21. At the bottom of the task pane, click Next: Complete the merge.

22. In Step 6 of 6, *do one of the following:*

- ▸ Click Print... to merge directly to the printer. A separate letter will be printed for each recipient.

- ▸ Click Edit individual letters... to produce a new Word document as the merge output.

A Merge to Printer or Merge to New Document dialog box appears ❶.

23. Specify the records to include in the merge and click OK.

TIP In the final task pane, the option to Edit individual letters... serves several important functions. First, it allows you to edit—or delete—individual letters. Second, because it produces an ordinary Word document, you can save it as documentation of the mailing. Finally, after proofing the letters and making any necessary edits, printing this document is the same as choosing the Print option. A letter is produced for each merged recipient.

❶ Specify which records to include in the printout or the Word output document.

Working with Tabs

The ability to set indents and create tables in Word has virtually eliminated the need to use tabs in most documents. However, if you need them to create a column of numbers aligned on the decimal point, for example, here's what you should know:

- By default, you can press Tab at the start of or within a paragraph to space to the next 0.5" increment on the horizontal ruler.

- To set a left tab for selected paragraphs, click the desired spot on the horizontal ruler.

- To create other types of tab stops (right, center, decimal, or bar), modify existing tab stops, or specify a *leader character* (such as a string of periods), double-click a tab marker on the ruler. Then make the necessary changes in the Tabs dialog box.

- Change a tab stop position by dragging its marker or by entering a new position in the Tabs dialog box.

- You can remove a tab stop by dragging its marker from the ruler onto the document page.

6

Creating Outlines

If you remember high school or college, you probably remember *outlines* (lists of key points organized into headings and subheadings), too. To demonstrate that you had a thorough plan, some teachers required that you create an outline before starting a paper or report.

Even after you've left school, you may find that writing an outline is an excellent way to get organized. Whether you're about to write an important report, preparing to give a presentation or lecture, or planning a complicated home renovation, you can create an outline to ensure that you've hit the important points in the proper order. Although dedicated outlining applications may be easier to use or have more features, many users will find Word's Outline view sufficient for handling basic outlining tasks.

Note that Outline view isn't only for outlines. Because it has some unique tools, such as the ability to collapse sections and easily reorganize paragraphs, it's sometimes helpful to use Outline view to polish a normal document.

In This Chapter

Entering and Exiting Outline View

As far as Word is concerned, a document is a document. Nothing distinguishes an outline from any other Word document. Outline is merely a *view* you can work in—just like Print Layout view. The only real difference is that Outline view provides special tools for working with outlines.

To enter or exit Outline view:

1. Click the View : Views : Outline icon Ⓐ.

   The document is displayed in Outline view Ⓑ (bottom). The Outlining tab appears and is automatically selected.

2. To exit from Outline view, click Outlining : Close : Close Outline View Ⓒ.

TIP You can also exit Outline view by simply switching to another view. Click a view icon in the View : Views group or on the status bar.

TIP While working in Outline view, you can freely switch Ribbon tabs to apply formatting, insert objects, and so on.

Outline view

Ⓐ Click the Outline icon to enter Outline view.

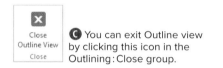

Ⓒ You can exit Outline view by clicking this icon in the Outlining : Close group.

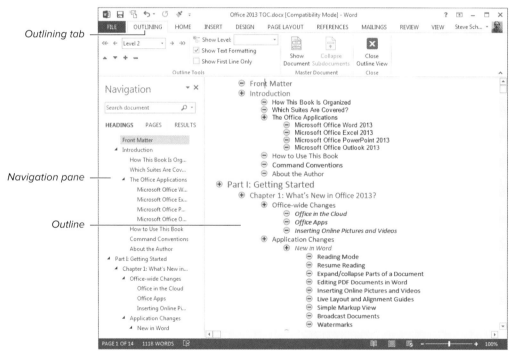

Outlining tab

Navigation pane

Outline

Ⓑ Outline view provides all the tools needed to create and edit outlines.

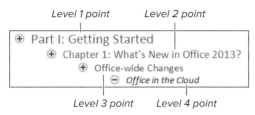

Level 1 point Level 2 point

Level 3 point Level 4 point

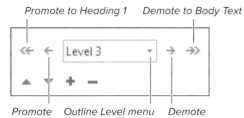

A The level of each point is indicated by its indentation and (typically) its formatting. Each paragraph is considered a separate point.

Promote to Heading 1 Demote to Body Text

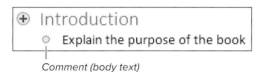

Promote Outline Level menu Demote

B To set or change a point's level, you can use these tools.

C A comment is preceded by a bullet symbol, rather than a plus (+) or minus (–).

Point Symbols

A point that has one or more subordinate points is preceded by a plus (+) symbol. A point that has no subordinate points is preceded by a minus (–) symbol.

Starting an Outline

A Word outline consists of outline points and, optionally, comments. Each point is assigned a *level* **A**; the higher the level, the more important the point. For example, the outline for this book consists of parts, chapters, main headings, and secondary headings—assigned levels 1, 2, 3, and 4.

To create an outline:

1. In a new document, click the View:Views:Outline icon (see **A** in "Entering and Exiting Outline View").

   A minus (–) symbol appears, ready for you to enter the first point.

2. Type the first point and press Enter.

   The cursor moves to a new line.

3. *Do one of the following:*

   ▸ To treat the new point as Level 1, type the text for the point and press Enter.

   ▸ Use tools in the Outline Tools group **B** to demote this to a Level 2 point by choosing Level 2 from the Outline Level menu, clicking the Demote icon, or pressing Alt-Shift-right arrow.

   ▸ To treat the new text as a *comment* **C** rather than a point, choose Body Text from the Outline Level menu or click the Demote to Body Text icon **B**.

4. Continue entering outline points. By default, when you press Enter to create a new point, the level of the point matches that of the one immediately above it.

TIP You can *promote* a selected point by choosing a higher level from the Outline Level menu, clicking Promote to Heading 1, or clicking Promote (or pressing Alt-Shift-left arrow) to raise the level by one.

Reorganizing an Outline

Creating an outline involves a certain amount of reorganizing: changing point levels, adding and deleting points, and moving points and sections to new spots. The first step in reorganizing is to select the point or points that you want to manipulate.

To select outline points:

- *Do one of the following:*

  - ▸ **Single point or comment.** Click to the left of the point or comment.

  - ▸ **Point and its subordinates.** Double-click to the left of the main point **A**.

  - ▸ **Contiguous points.** Click to the left of the first point and drag down.

  - ▸ **Noncontiguous points.** Ctrl-click to the left of each point.

TIP Selecting a collapsed point also selects its subordinate points.

To insert a new point:

1. Click at the end of the point immediately before where you want to insert the new point and then press Enter.

   A line for the new point appears **B**, set to the same level as the point above it.

2. *Optional:* You can change the new point's level by using a tool in the Outline Tools group (see **B** in "Starting an Outline").

To delete one or more points:

- Select the point or points, and press Del, Delete, or Backspace.

CAUTION Deleting a collapsed point also deletes its subordinate points.

A Double-click to the left of a point to select the point and its subordinate points, if any.

B To make room for this new point, I clicked to the right of Template and pressed Enter.

Level Formatting

If you don't care for the fonts, color, or other aspects of the default level formatting applied to your outline, you're free to change it.

- *To change the formatting of selected words or entire points,* use normal formatting techniques. You can set options on the Home tab or the Mini toolbar. (The Mini toolbar automatically appears whenever you select text.)

- *To change the formatting for a level throughout the outline,* format a single point for that level and update its style. (The style names for Levels 1–6 are Heading 1–6; comments use Normal style.) For information on modifying styles, see "Working with Styles" in Chapter 5.

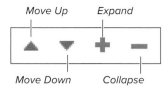

Move Up   Expand

Move Down   Collapse

C Click a Move icon to move the selected point(s) one line at a time.

Destination indicator

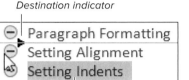

Selected point

D You can drag selected points up or down in the outline.

Expand/collapse icon

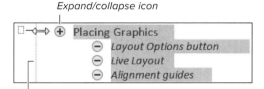

Level indicator

E You can promote or demote selected points by dragging to the left or right.

Undo icon

Outline Move Up
Outline Move Up
Grammar Ignore Error
Grammar Ignore Error

F You can undo one or multiple actions and edits using the Undo icon on the Quick Access Toolbar.

To move points up or down:

- *Do one of the following:*
    - ‣ Click the Move Up or Move Down icon in the Outline Tools group **C**. Each click moves the selected point(s) up or down one line in the outline.
    - ‣ Cut the selected point(s) by pressing Ctrl-X, click to set the text insertion mark where you want to insert the point(s), and then paste by pressing Ctrl-V.
    - ‣ Click the symbol that precedes the point or group of points you want to move, and then drag up or down to the destination **D**. When you release the mouse button, the dragged point(s) are moved to the new location.

To promote or demote points:

- To change the level of points, *do one of the following:*
    - ‣ Use the tools in the Outline Tools group (see **B** in "Starting an Outline") to demote (Alt-Shift-right arrow) or promote (Alt-Shift-left arrow) the selected point(s).

TIP You can also press **Tab** and **Shift-Tab** to demote and promote points, respectively.

- ‣ Drag the symbol that precedes a point (and its subordinates, if any) to the left or right **E**. Release the mouse button to set the new level.

TIP When moving, promoting, or demoting points, mistakes are commonplace. To correct a move that goes awry, click the Undo icon on the Quick Access Toolbar or press **Ctrl-Z**. To undo *multiple* actions, click the Undo icon's down arrow and choose the last action that you want to correct **F**. The selected action and all actions above it in the list will be undone.

Changing Display Settings

Word provides viewing features and tools to make it easier to work with outlines 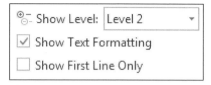. You can collapse sections to focus on the rest of the outline; hide lower-level, less significant levels so only important details are visible; or remove level formatting to make it easier to read the outline.

To change display settings:

- *Do any of the following:*

  ► **Collapse sections.** To collapse a section, double-click the + symbol that precedes the section's main point. Or with the section's main point selected, click the Collapse icon in the Outline Tools group (see ● in "Reorganizing an Outline") or press Alt-Shift-minus (–). The section and all its subordinate sections and points collapse ●.

  ► **Expand sections.** To expand a collapsed section, double-click the + symbol that precedes the section's main point. Or with the section's main point selected, click the Expand icon in the Outline Tools group (see ● in "Reorganizing an Outline") or press Alt-Shift-plus (+). The section and its subordinate sections expand.

  ► **Show Level.** To focus on higher-level points, you can choose a level number from the Show Level drop-down menu ●. Only points at that level or higher are then displayed; lower-level points are collapsed. To view the full outline again, choose All Levels from the drop-down menu.

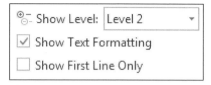

Ⓐ View options are set in this section of the Outline Tools group.

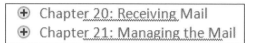

Ⓑ Collapsed sections are denoted by a squiggly underline. To expand collapsed points, double-click the symbol beside their section heading.

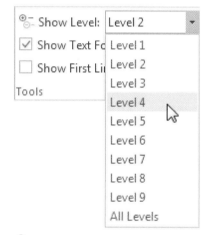

Ⓒ Choose the lowest level to display from the Show Level menu.

Using the Navigation Pane

Although it isn't required, you can use the Navigation Pane to help create, revise, and navigate an outline. You can click a heading in the Navigation Pane to jump to that point in the outline, for instance. And by right-clicking entries in the pane, you can promote, demote, add, and delete points.

To display the Navigation Pane on the left side of the document window (see Ⓑ in "Entering and Exiting Outline View"), click the View:Show:Navigation Pane check box.

▸ **Hide formatting.** Remove the check mark from Show Text Formatting Ⓐ to display the entire outline in a single default font, size, and style.

▸ **Show First Line Only.** Click this check box Ⓐ to hide additional lines of text beyond the first line for each outline point.

TIP To print an outline, choose File > Print, and then click the Print button. Note that collapsed points will not print. If Show Text Formatting isn't checked Ⓐ, a single default font will be used for the entire printout.

Sharing Word Documents

Some Word documents are destined never to leave your hard disk. You might mail printouts of selected documents as letters, but the actual *files* are meant for your use only.

Other Word documents, however, are meant to make the rounds. You might intend to email them to a friend, share them on the company network, put them out for review by members of a workgroup, or post them on the web. In this chapter, you'll learn about tools for sharing such documents.

Note: See Chapter 2 for information on protecting documents by marking them as final or password-protecting them.

In This Chapter

Choosing a File Format

The most straightforward way to share Word documents is to provide the file—on disk, by email, or via a download link on your web site. However, the decision concerning which *file format* to use 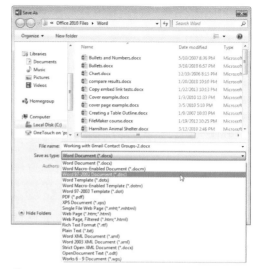 depends on the recipient's software and whether the document needs to be editable. The most commonly used Save As file formats include:

- **Word Document (.docx).** These native Word 2007–2013 files can be read and edited only by owners of Word 2007–2013 or by users of earlier versions who have installed the converter software.

> **TIP** Users of Office XP, 2000, or 2003 can download the free Microsoft Office Compatibility Pack from http://microsoft.com to enable their version of Office to read native Word, Excel, and PowerPoint 2007–2013 documents.

- **Word 97–2003 Document (.doc).** This binary file format is used by Word 97–2003 documents. Recipients with Word 97 or newer can read and edit .doc files.

- **Rich Text Format (.rtf) and Plain Text (.txt).** Rich Text Format is a good choice for files that must retain their formatting and be readable by other word-processing applications. Plain Text files can be read and edited by *all* word-processing programs and text editors, but character and paragraph formatting are removed.

- **PDF (.pdf).** This is the most common format for distribution of read-only documents that remain true to their original formatting. These Adobe Acrobat files can be opened with Adobe Reader, Apple's Preview, and similar utilities.

> **TIP** Word can now open PDF files.

 To save a copy of a Word document in a different format, click the File tab, click Save As, select a format from the Save as type drop-down list, name the file, and click Save.

Emailing a Document as the Message Body

In addition to emailing Word documents as attachments, you can send them as the *body* of a message. Click the Send to Mail Recipient icon in the Quick Access Toolbar, enter recipients, and click the Send a Copy toolbar icon.

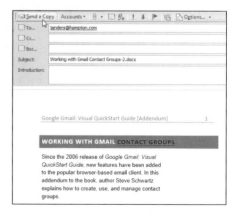

A To email a document from within Word, click the File tab, select Share, click Email, and select an option by clicking its icon.

Attached document

B You can enclose the current document in an email message without leaving Word.

Viewing XPS Files

XPS files can be opened only by certain programs, such as Internet Explorer and XPS Viewer. Be certain that the recipient has a program that can display XPS and that he or she actually wants this format.

Emailing Word Documents

As explained in Chapter 18, *any* kind of document—including Word files—can be sent as an email attachment. In addition to attaching the file within Outlook or another email program, you can attach Word documents to messages from within Word.

To send a Word document as a message attachment:

1. In Word, open the document you want to send via email. Ensure that any recent changes have been saved.

2. *Optional:* To send the document as Word 97–2003, Rich Text Format, or Plain Text format, click the File tab, select Save As, and save a copy of the document in the desired format.

   The document in the new format becomes the active document.

3. Select the File tab, click Share, and then click Email **A**. *Click one of these icons:*

   ▶ **Send as Attachment.** A message window opens with the current document attached as a Word file **B**. Enter recipients, type the message text, and click Send.

   ▶ **Send as PDF, Send as XPS.** A message window opens with the current document attached as an Adobe Acrobat (PDF) or XML Paper Specification (XPS) file. Enter recipients, type the message text, and click Send.

   ▶ **Send as Internet Fax.** The document is sent as a fax using an Internet Fax service. If you don't have a fax service provider, you can enroll with one after choosing this option.

Change Tracking

When multiple people will be working on, reviewing, or commenting on a document, you can use Word's *change tracking* features to simplify and coordinate the process. When change tracking is enabled, you can see every modification made to a document: deletions, insertions, and formatting changes. If multiple people edit the document, each person's changes are differentiated from everyone else's. During the writing and editing or at the end of the process, the document's author can finalize the document by accepting or rejecting each suggested change.

To enable/disable change tracking:

- Choose Review : Tracking : Track Changes > Track Changes (Ctrl-Shift-E).

  When enabled, the Track Changes icon is blue **A**.

To set tracking options:

1. In the Review : Tracking group, click the Change Tracking Options dialog box launcher **A**.

   The Track Changes Options dialog box appears **B**.

2. Make any desired changes and click OK.

> **TIP** Click Advanced Options **B** to set the color and formatting of various edits **C**. Click Change User Name **B** to specify the name or text that will identify your edits.

Track Changes on   Display for Review menu

Change Tracking Options dialog box launcher

A Change tracking and its options are set in the Review : Tracking group.

B Specify the types of changes to display.

C Set more specific change-tracking options.

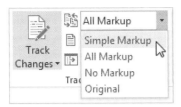

Reviewing Pane

D Choose a display option for the document from this menu.

E Edits can be explained in the margin.

F The Reviewing Pane presents all edits in a scrolling list. Double-click any entry to scroll the document directly to that edit.

G Process revisions by clicking these icons.

To set the view for change tracking:

1. Choose an option from the Review: Tracking: Display for Review menu **D**.

   ▸ *Original* displays the original document, prior to edits.

   ▸ *No Markup* displays the document as if all changes have been accepted.

   ▸ *All Markup* shows the current state of the document with all markup visible.

   ▸ *Simple Markup* displays the document as if all changes have been accepted. All edits are denoted by red change bars in the left margin.

TIP You can toggle between All Markup and Simple Markup by clicking any change bar.

2. When All Markup is active, edit details can be shown inline or in the right margin. Choose an option from the Review: Tracking: Show Markup > Balloons submenu **E**.

To process document revisions:

1. *Optional:* Open the Reviewing Pane **F** by choosing Review: Tracking: Reviewing Pane > Reviewing Vertical or Reviewing Horizontal.

2. Click in the document at the point where you want to start and, using the icons in the Review: Changes group **G**, *do the following for each revision:*

   ▸ To accept the revision, click Accept or choose an option from its menu. (Accepting incorporates the edit into the text.)

   ▸ To reject the revision, click Reject or choose an option from its menu. (Rejecting removes the edit.)

   ▸ Temporarily ignore a revision by clicking the Next or Previous icon.

TIP You don't have to share a document to use change tracking. You can use it to track and manage your own edits, too.

TIP Another way to view the content of edits and comments is to move the cursor over them in the body of the document. A pop-up box appears **H**.

TIP You can close the Reviewing Pane by clicking its Ribbon icon or the pane's close box.

TIP Any reviewer can insert comments into the text. Comments can be used for any purpose, such as explaining the reason for an edit or pointing out material that needs to be rewritten or added. To insert a comment, set the insertion mark or select the text to which the comment refers, click Review : Comments : New Comment, and type the comment.

TIP To accept or reject *all* edits, choose Accept All Changes in Document or Reject All Changes in Document from the Review : Changes : Accept or Reject icon's menu **I**.

TIP If you mistakenly accept or reject an edit, you can reverse your action by immediately clicking the Undo icon on the Quick Access Toolbar or by pressing Ctrl-Z.

TIP Excel has change tracking, too. When it's enabled in the Review : Changes group, users can hover the cursor over any changed cell to see the change details. PowerPoint, on the other hand, only allows you to add comments.

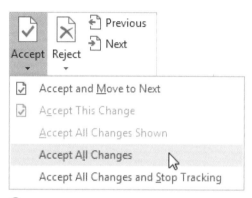

H Hover the cursor over an edit or comment to view its details.

I If desired, you can simultaneously accept or reject all edits.

Other Office Sharing Tools

If you need to share your Office 2013 documents with users of earlier versions of Office, the Document Inspector and Compatibility Checker are helpful utilities. Both can be found in the Info section of the Backstage by opening the Check for Issues menu and are discussed in Chapter 2.

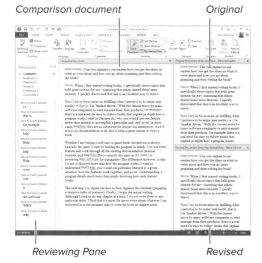

Show/hide options Browse Browse

A Select the original and revised documents, set options, and click OK.

Comparison document   Original

Reviewing Pane   Revised

B You can customize the display by choosing commands from the drop-down menus in the Review : Tracking group and the Track Changes Options dialog box (see **B** in "Change Tracking").

Comparing Documents

Whether you're working alone on an important document or with others, it can be helpful to compare two versions to see what's been changed. (This assumes, of course, that you've saved multiple versions of the document or, at least, an original and a current version.)

To compare two document versions:

1. Choose Review : Compare : Compare > Compare.

   The Compare Documents dialog box appears **A**.

2. Select the original and revised documents from the drop-down lists.

   If a document isn't listed, click its Browse icon to locate the document on disk.

   TIP You can compare *any* two versions of a document—not just the first and last or the previous and current versions.

   TIP If a document has undergone multiple revisions, you'll find it more manageable to compare the last two versions than to compare the original and final.

3. If the bottom half of the dialog box is hidden, click the More button to reveal the document-comparison options.

4. Review and set options, and then click OK.

   The comparison document is generated and displayed **B**.

   TIP Each pane in the comparison document has its own close box (X).

   TIP Compare Documents can also be used to compare the last saved version with an auto-saved version. See Chapter 2 for information about autosaved documents.

Combining Documents

If multiple reviewers are independently reviewing the same document, you can use the Combine command to merge their edits and comments—two documents at a time—into a single master document. Then the author or group leader can process the revisions, as explained in "Change Tracking."

To merge two documents:

1. Choose Review : Compare : Compare > Combine. The Combine Documents dialog box appears **A**.

2. Select the two documents from the drop-down lists.

   If a document isn't listed, click its Browse icon to locate the document.

3. If the bottom half of the dialog box is hidden, click the More button to reveal the procedure settings and options.

4. At the bottom of the dialog box, select Show changes in: New document. Review the other options, and click OK.

   The combined document is generated and displayed **B**.

5. Save the combined document by clicking the File tab, followed by Save As.

6. If more documents need to be merged with the new, combined document, repeat Steps 1–5, but specify the combined document saved in Step 5 as one of the documents.

7. *Optional:* To process the revisions, open the Reviewing Pane by choosing an option from the Review : Tracking : Reviewing Pane menu.

> **TIP** You can customize the display by choosing commands from the Review : Tracking group and the Track Changes Options dialog box.

Show/hide options

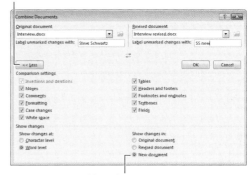

New document

A Select the two documents to combine, specify options, and click OK.

Combined document   *Original document*

Reviewing Pane   *Revised document*

B The combined document appears in a new window. You can open the Reviewing Pane to process revisions.

A Select your blogging service. Click Next.

B To enable Word to transmit blog posts to your account, enter your user name and password.

C Select the blog's picture-hosting service from the drop-down list.

Publishing Blog Entries

Another way to share written information is to publish it to a web log (*blog*). Blog journals can be viewed in any browser. To create your own blog, you must register with a blog service provider, such as Blogger (http://www.blogger.com) or WordPress (http://wordpress.org). Many providers host blogs without charge.

To configure Word for blog work:

1. If you haven't registered with a blog service, do so before proceeding.

2. The first time you issue a blog-related command in Word, the Register a Blog Account dialog box appears. Click Register Now.

3. In the New Blog Account dialog box **A**, select your blogging service from the drop-down list, and click Next.

4. In the New *service* Account dialog box **B**, enter the user name and password for your blog account. Click the Remember Password check box.

5. Click the Picture Options button.

   The Picture Options dialog box **C** appears.

6. Select your blogging service from the Picture provider drop-down list and click OK.

   If your blogging service isn't listed or your blog posts won't contain images, select None - Don't upload pictures.

   TIP You may still be able to upload pictures to an unlisted blogging service. For instructions, see the service's Help pages.

7. Click OK to close the New *service* Account dialog box **B**.

To create and publish a blog entry from scratch:

1. Click the File tab to go to the Backstage, select New, click the Blog post thumbnail, and click Create.

   A blog post template appears. The Ribbon tabs and icons provide the tools to write, format, and post your blog entry.

2. Create the new blog entry by typing the entry text and replacing the title placeholder with a title **D**.

3. When you're satisfied with the entry, choose Blog Post:Blog:Publish > Publish.

   The new entry is posted to your blog.

4. To view your blog **E**, click the Blog Post:Blog:Home Page icon.

To create and publish a blog entry from an existing Word document:

1. Click the File tab to go to the Backstage, select Share, click Publish as Blog Post, and click the Publish as Blog Post icon.

   The document is reformatted as a blog entry. The Ribbon tabs and icons provide the tools to edit, format, and post your blog entry.

2. Replace the title placeholder with a title for the entry **D**.

3. To publish and view your entry, perform Steps 3 and 4 of the previous task list.

TIP To edit a previously published blog entry, click Blog Post:Blog:Open Existing **F**. In the Open Existing Post dialog box, select the entry to edit and click OK. Make the necessary changes, and then publish it as you did before.

TIP To delete a blog post, use the tools provided by the blog service.

TIP To add, change, or delete blog accounts, click Blog Post:Blog:Manage Accounts.

Entry title   *Entry text*

D Enter a title for the entry and write the text.

E Here's how the blog entry looks when viewed in a browser.

F Tools for publishing posts, editing previous posts, and managing blog accounts can be found in the Blog Post:Blog group.

A Click the Present Online icon to prepare the document for presentation.

B Click an option to copy the presentation URL or communicate it via email.

Broadcasting a Word Document

Using the free Office Presentation Service, you can broadcast a Word document over the Internet. After connecting to a special web address, attendees can read along in their browsers as you scroll through the document.

To present a document online:

1. Open the Word document that you want to present.

2. Click the File tab.

3. In the Backstage, select Share, select Present Online, and click the Present Online icon **A**.

   Word prepares the document for online presentation.

4. The Present Online dialog box **B** appears, showing the presentation URL.

5. *Do one of the following:*

   ▸ To email the presentation information to attendees, click Send in Email. A pre-written Outlook message appears. Enter recipients in the To, Cc, and/or Bcc boxes, and click Send.

   ▸ If you want to paste the URL into an instant message or email message, click Copy Link. Then paste the URL wherever you wish by pressing Ctrl-V.

6. When the attendees have their browser open to the presentation URL, click the Start Presentation button **B**.

   As you scroll the document, it scrolls in the attendee's browsers, too.

   continues on next page

7. *Optional:* You can pause the presentation to make edits by clicking the Present Online:Edit icon 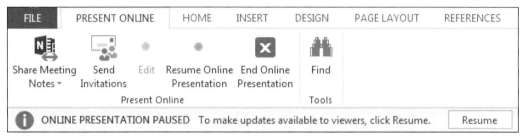. When you're ready to continue, click the Resume button or Present Online:Resume Online Presentation.

8. To end the presentation and disconnect the attendees, click Present Online:End Online Presentation . Confirm by clicking End Online Presentation in the dialog box that appears.

C To make changes to the document that you want attendees to see, click the Edit icon. Click Resume when you're ready to continue the presentation.

Getting Started with Excel 2013

Excel is Office 2013's spreadsheet application. You use Excel to create, analyze, and manage documents called *workbooks* that contain text and numeric data. Workbooks can consist of simple lists (address books, club rosters, and collections) or complex calculations (bookkeeping systems, sales and expense tracking, engineering computations, and manufacturing measurements).

To get you started, this chapter introduces you to the application interface and presents basic—but essential—Excel topics.

In This Chapter

The Excel Interface

Before we jump into how to use Excel, take a moment to examine the Excel interface 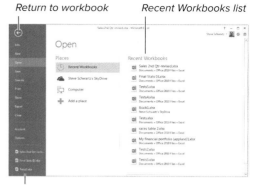 (below). You'll notice that some elements, such as the Ribbon, Quick Access Toolbar, and Backstage, can also be found in Word, PowerPoint, and Outlook.

Backstage. Click the File tab to switch to the Backstage **B** to perform file-related activities, such as creating, opening, saving, and printing documents. Click Options to set Excel preferences. To open a workbook you've recently viewed or edited, click Open and then click its filename. You can also open a recent workbook by clicking its name at the bottom of the Backstage category list.

Return to workbook   *Recent Workbooks list*

Most recent workbooks

B The Backstage.

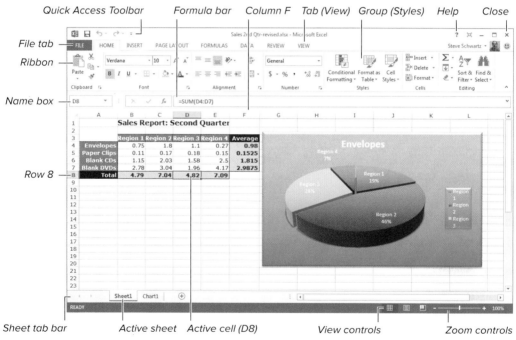

A Elements of the Excel 2013 interface.

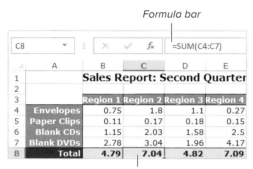

C Use the Sheet tab bar to switch among worksheets in a workbook.

Formula bar

	A	B	C	D	E
1			Sales Report: Second Quarter		
2					
3		Region 1	Region 2	Region 3	Region 4
4	Envelopes	0.75	1.8	1.1	0.27
5	Paper Clips	0.11	0.17	0.18	0.15
6	Blank CDs	1.15	2.03	1.58	2.5
7	Blank DVDs	2.78	3.04	1.96	4.17
8	Total	4.79	7.04	4.82	7.09

Active cell

D In addition to using the formula bar to enter or edit data and formulas, it always displays the contents of the *active cell*.

Quick Access Toolbar. Common commands are found here, such as Save, Undo, and Redo.

Ribbon. The Ribbon is what Office 2013 uses rather than menus. Similar commands and procedures are listed together on a *tab*, such as Insert or View. Within a tab, procedures are further divided into *groups*, based on similarity of function. To perform a command, you switch to the appropriate tab by clicking its name and then click the command's icon.

Sheet tab bar. A workbook can contain multiple worksheets (or *sheets*). This area **C** of the document window shows the names of all worksheets in the current workbook. To switch worksheets, click the sheet's name.

Active sheet. This is the sheet you're currently viewing and/or editing.

Columns and rows. A worksheet is a grid of columns and rows. Columns are designated by letter and rows are numbered. A *column* consists of all cells beneath a column letter. A *row* is the string of cells to the right of a row number.

Active cell. This is the currently selected cell (indicated by a heavy black border), named by combining the intersection of a column and row. For example, **D8** is in column D, row 8. The active cell name is shown in the name box, and the cell's column letter and row number are highlighted.

Name box. The name box performs a variety of functions, including displaying the name of the active cell and creating *names* (a descriptive name for a cell or range, such as **SalesTax**). Names are also referred to as *range names* and *named ranges*.

Formula bar. Data and formulas can be entered in the formula bar or directly into the active cell. The formula bar displays any formula or data in the active cell **D**.

View controls. Click an icon to switch views **E**. You can also change views by clicking an icon in the View:Workbook Views group. Use Normal or Page Layout view to work with or view your data. Before you print, you can switch to Page Break Preview to examine and manually adjust page breaks.

Zoom controls. You can change the current magnification by dragging the slider, clicking – (decrease) or + (increase), or clicking the zoom percentage number **F**.

Close. Each workbook has a close box that you can click to close the file or—if only one workbook is open—to quit Excel.

Normal   *Page Layout*   *Page Break Preview*

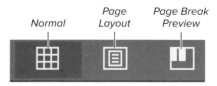

E Click a View control icon to switch views.

F Use the zoom controls to change the worksheet magnification. Click the – or + to decrease or increase the magnification by 10 percent.

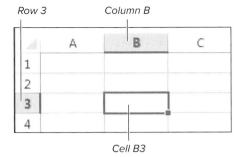

Row 3 *Column B*

Cell B3

A A worksheet is a grid of columns and rows. A cell address is the intersection of a column and row.

Sheets per workbook

B To set Excel preferences (such as the number of sheets for a new workbook), click the File tab to go to the Backstage and then click Options.

Workbooks and Worksheets

An Excel document consists of a single workbook containing one or more worksheets. A *worksheet* (or sheet) has numbered rows and lettered columns that form a grid. The intersection of a row and column is called a *cell* **A**. You can enter text data, numeric data, or formulas into the cells. Unlike in other programs you may have used, data doesn't have to be entered from the top down, left to right. You can use any cells that you want, leaving blank rows and columns as best suits the data.

A setting in the General section of Excel Options **B** determines the initial number of worksheets in a new workbook. Depending on the data you're entering and analyzing, you can ignore all worksheets but the first or use the others for related data or a completely different type of data. Because Excel lets you perform calculations across worksheets within a workbook, you can also use one sheet to consolidate the data from other sheets. For example, in a bookkeeping workbook, you might collect each month's data in a separate sheet and use another sheet to calculate running figures, combining the data from the monthly sheets.

Worksheets are managed using the *Sheet tab bar*, found in the bottom-left corner of every workbook window **C**. To make a different worksheet active, you click its tab. You can add, delete, and change the order of the sheets. You can also rename a sheet to make it easier to identify.

Prev. *Next*   *Active sheet*   *Scroll right*   *New sheet*

C You use the Sheet tab bar to make a worksheet active and to manage your worksheets.

To rename a worksheet:

- Right-click the tab of the worksheet you want to rename and choose Rename from the context menu 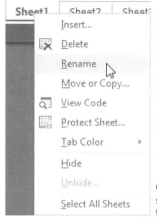. Type a new name and press Enter.

TIP Another way to rename a sheet is to double-click its tab, selecting the current name for editing.

To delete a worksheet:

- *Do either of the following:*
  - ▸ Right-click the tab of the worksheet you want to delete and choose Delete from the context menu **D**.
  - ▸ Make the worksheet active and choose Home : Cells : Delete > Delete Sheet.

If the worksheet contains data, a warning dialog box appears. Otherwise, the worksheet is immediately deleted.

To insert a new worksheet:

- *Do one of the following:*
  - ▸ Click the New Sheet icon in the Sheet tab bar **C** or press Shft-F11.
  - ▸ Right-click a worksheet name in the Sheet tab bar and choose Insert from the context menu **D**. On the General tab of the Insert dialog box **E**, select Worksheet, and click OK.
  - ▸ Choose Home : Cells : Insert > Insert Sheet.

The new worksheet is appended to the end of the sheet list or inserted to the right of the currently selected sheet.

To change the order of worksheets:

- Drag the sheet name to the left or right in the Sheet tab bar **C**. Release the mouse button to set the new position.

D Right-click a sheet tab to reveal this context menu.

E To insert a new worksheet, ensure that the Worksheet icon is selected and click OK.

Creating New Workbooks

Although you can continue to add sheets to a workbook, you'll typically want to create a *new* workbook whenever you begin a project.

- To immediately create a new standard workbook, press Ctrl-N.
- To create a specific type of workbook, click the File tab and click New. Select Blank workbook or a template, and then click the Create button.

A To specify a destination, enter an address, range, or name in the Reference text box or select a recently visited address, range, or name.

Name box

B Type an address, range, or name in the name box.

C You can use the Find and Replace dialog box to search for a cell based on its contents.

Anchor (A1)   Last cell in selection (D5)

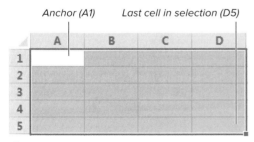

D To select a range, click a cell in one corner of the range and drag to the opposite corner.

Cell and Range Selection

Whether you're preparing to enter, edit, or format data, the first step is to select a cell or cell range. The following are some cell-selection techniques.

To select cells:

- **Single cell.** *Do one of the following:*
  - ▸ Scroll to bring the cell into view and then click the cell.
  - ▸ Press a navigation key (such as an arrow key, Tab, Shift-Tab, Enter, or Shift-Enter) to move into the cell.
  - ▸ Choose Home:Editing:Find & Select > Go To or press Ctrl-G. In the Go To dialog box **A**, select or type the cell address or name (if a name has been assigned to the cell). Click OK.
  - ▸ Type the cell address, range, or name in the name box **B** and press Enter.
  - ▸ To find a cell based on its contents **C**, choose Home:Editing:Find & Select > Find (Ctrl-F). Enter the text, number, date, or time contained in the cell and click Find Next. When the desired cell is selected, click Close. See "Finding and Replacing Data," later in this chapter, for additional options.

- **Contiguous cell range.** *Do one of the following:*
  - ▸ Click a cell in any corner of the range (called the *anchor*) and drag to the opposite corner to select the additional cells **D**.

continues on next page

- ► To select an entire column or row, click its letter or number **E**.
- ► To select the entire worksheet, click the intersection of the column and row headings **E**.
- ► Choose Home : Editing : Find & Select > Go To or press Ctrl-G. In the Go To dialog box **A**, enter the cell range in the form

    start cell : end cell

    such as **a1:d4**. If you've named the range (see "Naming Cells and Ranges," later in this chapter), you can enter its name rather than the range. Click OK.
- ► Enter the cell range or its name in the name box **B** and press Enter.

- ■ **Noncontiguous cells and ranges.** While pressing Ctrl, click or click-and-drag to select the cells, ranges, columns, and/or rows **F**. You can also enter noncontiguous selections in the name box, separated by commas, such as **a13,d6:d9**.

TIP If you need to regularly return to a cell or range, naming it will enable you to easily navigate to it using the Go To command or the name box (see "Naming Cells and Ranges," later in this chapter).

TIP You can speed the entry of new data by preselecting the destination range. After each entry, press Tab or Enter to move through the range in left-to-right or top-to-bottom fashion, respectively.

TIP Press Ctrl-End to select the last cell in the active area of the worksheet, press Home to move to the first cell in the current row, or press Ctrl-Home to move to cell A1.

TIP Press Ctrl and an arrow key to move to the next filled cell in the specified direction. If there are no other filled cells, the first or last cell in the row or column will be selected.

Click to select worksheet   *Selected column (B)*

E To select a column or row, click its letter or number.

F You can also select any combination of cells, ranges, rows, and columns (marked with grey highlighting).

A You can format any data as text by choosing Text from the Number Format menu.

Number Format menu

Using Entry AutoComplete

When you enter text or a combination of text and numbers into a cell, Excel checks the current column for matching entries. If one is found, Excel proposes it. To accept the AutoComplete entry, press Enter. To ignore it, continue typing.

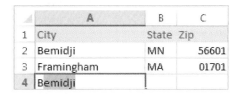

	A	B	C
1	City	State	Zip
2	Bemidji	MN	56601
3	Framingham	MA	01701
4	Bemidji		

Entering Data

A cell can contain one or more lines of text, a number, a date, a time, or a formula that results in one of these data types. To enter data into a cell, follow the instructions below. (Formulas are discussed in Chapter 10.)

To enter data into a cell:

1. Select the cell into which you want to enter data, making it the active cell.

   You can select a cell by clicking in it. For other cell-selection methods, see the previous section.

2. *Do one of the following:*

   ▸ **Text.** Type or paste the text.

   ▸ **Number.** Type or paste the number.

   TIP If the cell shows a string of # characters (#####), it means that the number in the cell is too large to display. To display the complete number, widen the column (see Chapter 9).

   TIP If you enter a number that begins with one or more zeros, Excel discards the zeros. This presents a problem with some ZIP codes, for example. To force Excel to retain the leading zeros, choose Text from the drop-down menu in the Home:Number group **A** before entering the data.

   ▸ **Date.** Type a date in a recognizable format, such as **9-20-13**, **09/20/2013**, or **20-Sep-13**. Date components must be separated by a slash (**/**) or hyphen (**–**) character.

   TIP To enter today's date, press Ctrl-; (semicolon).

continues on next page

- ▸ **Time.** Type a time in a recognizable format, such as **4:**, **4:07**, **4:07:53**, **4:07 p**, **4 pm**, or **16:07**. Time components must be separated by a colon (**:**).

TIP When a 12-hour time is entered, such as **10:43, it is assumed to be AM. To indicate PM, you must enter the time in military (24-hour) format or follow the time with p or pm, such as 6:15 p or 6:15 pm. Morning times can** *optionally* **be followed by an a or am, such as 7:15 a or 7:15 am.**

TIP To enter the current time, press Ctrl-Shit-; (semicolon).

3. To complete the entry, click another cell or press a navigation key, such as Enter or Tab. See **Table 8.1** for options.

TIP To enter multiple lines of text, numbers, dates, or times into a cell **ⓑ**, press Alt-Enter to insert a line break between each pair of lines.

TIP If you want the data to display differently, apply formatting to the cell (see Chapter 9). The current formatting for the active cell is shown in the Home : Number : Number Format box **ⓐ**.

TIP Excel distinguishes between data *display* (determined by formatting) and what is *stored*. When performing calculations, Excel uses the stored data, regardless of what's shown in the cells. For example, when calculating a sales tax of 7.75% on a $12.50 purchase, the result is 0.9675. When formatted as Currency, the number displays as $0.97—the result rounded to two decimal places. If you create a formula in another cell that adds the sale amount ($12.48) to the sales tax, the result is 13.46875—*not* $13.47.

1723 Ashford Ln.
Apt. 43B
Jonesville, NH 01236

ⓑ You can force line breaks within a cell.

TABLE 8.1 Keystrokes to Complete a Cell Entry

Keystroke	Direction
Tab, right arrow	Right
Shift-Tab, left arrow	Left
Enter, down arrow	Down
Shift-Enter, up arrow	Up

Changing the Behavior of Enter

Normally, pressing Enter when you finish entering data into a cell causes the cursor to move down, selecting the cell directly beneath the current cell. However, if you like, you can change the behavior of the Enter key:

1. Click the File tab. Click Options in the Backstage.

2. In the Excel Options dialog box, select the Advanced category.

3. Select a cursor-movement direction from the Direction drop-down list.

4. Click OK.

Editing options

☑ After pressing Enter, move selection

Direction: Down ▼

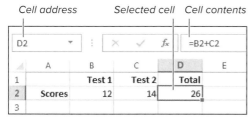

Cell address   Selected cell   Cell contents

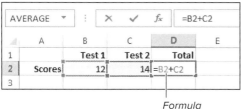

Formula

A When you select a cell (top), its contents are shown in the formula bar. When you set the text insertion mark for editing (bottom), the result is replaced in the cell by the actual formula.

Editing Data

As you create and work with a worksheet, you can correct errors, update data with new values, and revise formulas.

To edit the contents of a cell:

1. Select the cell whose contents you want to change.

2. You can edit in the formula bar or in the cell itself. To set the text insertion mark and begin editing, click in the formula bar or double-click in the cell.

   If the cell contains a formula, the formula appears **A**. Otherwise, the data is shown.

3. Make the desired changes.

4. To complete the edits, *do one of the following:*

   ▸ Press a navigation key, such as Enter, to move to another cell (see Table 8.1).

   ▸ Click another cell.

   ▸ Click the check mark (√) icon in the formula bar **A**.

TIP You can use the same editing techniques you use when modifying other kinds of Windows documents. For example, press Backspace to delete the character to the left, press Del or Delete to delete the character to the right, or press any of these keys to delete selected text. To replace a string, select it and type the replacement or delete the string and then type.

TIP The cursor keys are active while editing. Press left arrow or right arrow to move one character in the desired direction; press Ctrl-left arrow or Ctrl-right arrow to move one string at a time.

TIP To rearrange data within a cell, you can cut (Ctrl-X) selected data, set the text insertion mark where you want to move the data, and then paste (Ctrl-V).

Reorganizing a Worksheet

In addition to editing cell contents, you can rearrange the data. You can move cells to other locations, add or delete cells (automatically shifting the affected surrounding cells), and insert or delete rows and columns.

To move cells to another location:

1. Select the cell or range you want to move.

2. *Do one of the following:*

   ▸ Cut the cell/range by pressing Ctrl-X or by clicking the Home:Clipboard:Cut icon **A**. Select the destination cell or the cell in the upper-left corner of the destination range. Press Enter, press Ctrl-V, or click the Home:Clipboard:Paste icon **A**.

   ▸ Move the cursor over the border of the selected cell or range **B**. Drag the selected cell to the destination cell or the selected range to the cell that will serve as the upper-left corner of the destination range. Release the mouse button to complete the move.

   Neither procedure *deletes* the original cells. Their data is simply moved to the new location.

CAUTION Whether performed by cut-and-paste or drag-and-drop, cell/range moves are *destructive*. That is, if you select a destination that already contains data, the old data will be replaced by the moved data. If this happens unintentionally, immediately click the Undo icon in the Quick Access Toolbar **C** or press Ctrl-Z.

TIP To move data between *worksheets*, use cut-and-paste.

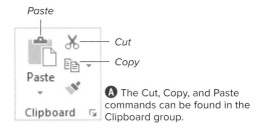

Paste

Cut

Copy

A The Cut, Copy, and Paste commands can be found in the Clipboard group.

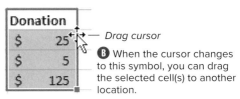

Drag cursor

B When the cursor changes to this symbol, you can drag the selected cell(s) to another location.

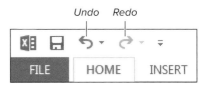

Undo   *Redo*

C To undo your last action, click the Undo icon. To undo multiple actions, choose an action from the Undo icon's drop-down menu.

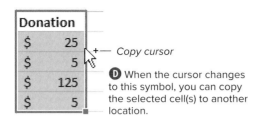

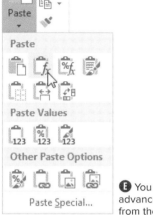

D When the cursor changes to this symbol, you can copy the selected cell(s) to another location.

E You can choose advanced Paste options from the Paste gallery.

F When inserting new cells, you must specify how surrounding cells will be affected.

To copy cells to another location:

1. Select the cell or range you want to copy.

2. *Do one of the following:*

   ▸ Copy the cell/range by pressing Ctrl-C or by clicking the Home:Clipboard: Copy icon **A**. Select the destination cell or the cell in the upper-left corner of the destination range. Press Enter, press Ctrl-V, or click the Home:Clipboard:Paste icon **A**.

   ▸ While pressing Ctrl, move the cursor over the border of the selected cell or range. A tiny plus symbol is added to the cursor **D**. Drag the cell/range to the destination cell or to the cell in the upper-left corner of the destination range.

TIP Rather than just clicking Paste, you can click the arrow beneath Paste to reveal a gallery of Paste options **E**. If you rest the cursor on an option, a ScreenTip explains the option and a preview is shown on the worksheet.

To insert cells:

1. Select the cell or range where you want to insert new, blank cells.

2. *Do one of the following:*

   ▸ Choose Home:Cells:Insert > Insert Cells.

   ▸ Right-click the cell or cell range and choose Insert from the context menu.

3. In the Insert dialog box **F**, select Shift cells right or Shift cells down, and then click OK.

   Cells affected by the insertion are shifted to make room for the inserted cell(s).

To delete cells:

1. Select the cell or range you want to delete.

2. *Do one of the following:*

   ▸ Choose Home : Cells : Delete > Delete Cells.

   ▸ Right-click the cell or range and choose Delete from the context menu 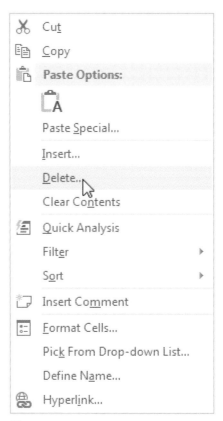.

3. In the Delete dialog box Ⓗ, select Shift cells left or Shift cells up, and click OK.

   Surrounding cells affected by the deletion are shifted to close the space left by the deleted cell(s).

To insert a row:

1. Select the row where you want to insert a new row by clicking its row number.

2. *Do one of the following:*

   ▸ Click the Home : Cells : Insert icon.

   ▸ Right-click any cell in the selected row and choose Insert from the context menu Ⓖ.

   The new row appears. The selected row and all those beneath it shift down one.

TIP You can also select a single cell in the row where you want to insert a new row. However, you must choose Home : Cells : Insert > Insert Sheet Rows or select Entire row in the Insert dialog box Ⓕ.

TIP To insert multiple rows, select as many rows as you want and click the Insert icon. You can also right-click any cell in the selected rows and choose Insert from the context menu Ⓖ.

Ⓖ Right-click a selected cell or range, and then choose Delete.

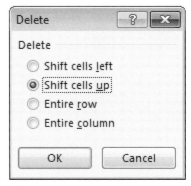

Ⓗ Specify how neighboring cells should shift in response to the cell or range deletion.

Original worksheet

Selected column

	A	B	C	D	E	F
1		Test 1	Test 2	Test 3	Average	
2	Michelle	12	14	16	14.00	
3	Thomas	18	16	19	17.67	
4	Adrian	14	9	11	11.33	
5	Anthony	17	14	18	16.33	
6	Jonas	20	20	18	19.33	
7	Heidi	13	15	16	14.67	
8						

Modified worksheet

Inserted column

	A	B	C	D	E	F
1		Test 1	Test 2	Test 3		Average
2	Michelle	12	14	16		14.00
3	Thomas	18	16	19		17.67
4	Adrian	14	9	11		11.33
5	Anthony	17	14	18		16.33
6	Jonas	20	20	18		19.33
7	Heidi	13	15	16		14.67
8						

I Suppose that you need to record a fourth test. When you select column E and issue the Insert command, the original column E shifts to the right to become column F.

Selected cells in columns C and D

	A	B	C	D	E
1		Test 1	Test 2	Test 3	Average
2	Michelle	12	14	16	14.00
3	Thomas	18	16	19	17.67
4	Adrian	14	9	11	11.33
5	Anthony	17	14	18	16.33
6	Jonas	20	20	18	19.33
7	Heidi	13	15	16	14.67

J You can also begin a column or row insertion by selecting single cells or a range. In this example, to insert new columns in C and D, it's sufficient to select any pair of cells that spans both columns.

To insert a column:

1. Select the column where you want to insert a new column by clicking its column letter **I** (top).

2. *Do either of the following:*

   ▸ Click Home:Cells:Insert.

   ▸ Right-click any cell in the selected column and choose Insert from the context menu **G**.

   The new column appears **I** (bottom). Other columns affected by the insertion shift to the right.

TIP You can also select a single cell in the column where you want to insert the new column. However, you must then choose Home:Cells:Insert > Insert Sheet Columns or select Entire column in the Insert dialog box **F**.

TIP You can insert multiple columns by selecting the columns (or a cell in each column) where you want to add the new columns **J**.

To delete a row:

1. Select the row that you want to delete by clicking its row number.

2. *Do one of the following:*

   ▸ Click Home:Cells:Delete.

   ▸ Right-click any cell in the selected row and choose Delete **G**.

   The row is deleted. Other rows that are affected by the deletion shift up to close the space.

TIP You can also select a cell in the row that you want to delete. However, you must then choose Home:Cells:Delete > Delete Sheet Rows or select Entire row in the Delete dialog box **H**.

TIP To delete multiple rows, select the rows (or a cell in each row) that you want to delete in Step 1.

To delete a column:

1. Select the column that you want to delete by clicking its letter ❶ (top).

2. *Do one of the following:*

   ▸ Click Home:Cells:Delete.

   ▸ Right-click any cell in the selected column and choose Delete from the context menu ❻.

   The column is deleted, and all columns to its right shift to the left.

> **TIP** You can also select a single cell in the column you want to delete. However, you must then choose Home:Cells:Delete > Delete Sheet Columns or select Entire column in the Delete dialog box ❶.

> **TIP** To delete multiple columns, select the columns (or a cell in each column) that you want to delete in Step 1.

> **TIP** Deleting cells, rows, or columns isn't the same as clearing their contents. To clear selected cells, choose a command from the Home:Editing:Clear icon's menu. Depending upon the command chosen, you can clear a selected cell of its data (Contents). formatting (Formats), or both (All).

> **CAUTION** Deleting cells, rows, and columns are destructive processes. Because every row and column extends to the end or bottom of the worksheet, make sure you aren't accidentally deleting data that isn't in view.

Insertion and Deletion Considerations

When inserting or deleting cells, rows, or columns, you must consider the impact on your worksheet. Insertions and deletions often cause other data to move.

- When you insert a cell, the current cell must either move to the right or down. Other cells to the right or below the inserted cell will also shift to the right or down.

- When you delete a cell, all cells directly below or to the right of the deleted cell must shift up or left to fill the hole created by the deletion.

- When you insert a new row, the current row automatically moves down to make room for the new row. Rows below the current row also move down one row.

- When you insert a column, the current column and all columns to its right shift one column to the right.

The impact of an insertion or deletion on data *elsewhere* in the worksheet must be considered. For instance, if a worksheet contains a single data array or table, such as an address book, inserting or deleting a row or column will have little impact. And if you discover that you entered the same data in two cells in a row (causing the row to have an extra entry), deleting a duplicate and choosing Shift cells left quickly fixes the problem.

But when a worksheet is complex and has multiple data arrays, an insertion or deletion is liable to create problems elsewhere in the sheet. If this is the case, the safer approach may be to manually rearrange the data rather than make insertions or deletions.

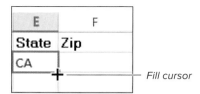

Fill cursor

Ⓐ You can fill cells by dragging.

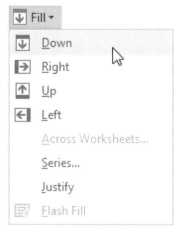

Fill handle

Selected cells

Fill preview

Ⓑ Drag to select the cells you want to fill.

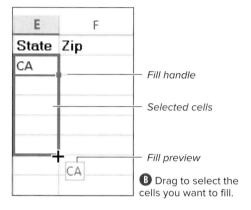

Ⓒ You can also perform a fill by choosing a direction from the Fill menu.

Filling Cells

Three situations occur in worksheet creation that can be simplified using Fill or Flash Fill (an Excel 2013 fill variation):

- **Fill.** You have a text constant, numeric constant, or formula that you want to repeat many times in the current row or column.

- **Fill.** You have or are creating a series of cell entries in the current row or column that you want to extend.

- **Flash fill.** You have a column of data that you want to parse into two or more columns.

To fill adjacent cells with a constant:

- *Do either of the following:*

  ▸ Select the cell that contains the text or numeric constant. Move the cursor over the lower-right corner of the cell (*fill handle*) **Ⓐ**. Click and drag in the direction that you want to fill **Ⓑ**.

  TIP You can perform a drag fill in any direction: right, left, down, or up.

  ▸ Select the cell with the text or numeric constant and the cells you want to fill. Choose the fill direction from the Home:Editing:Fill menu **Ⓒ**.

  The cells fill with the constant.

TIP To *duplicate* a cell regardless of the type of data it contains (text, number, date, or time), select the cell immediately to the right or below it and press Ctrl-R or Ctrl-D, respectively.

To fill adjacent cells with a formula:

- *Do either of the following:*
  - ▸ Select the cell with the formula. Click the fill handle and drag in the direction that you want to fill 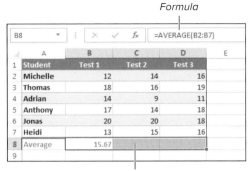.
  - ▸ Select the cell with the formula, as well as the cells you want to fill **D**. Choose a fill direction from the Home : Editing : Fill drop-down menu **C**.

  The cells fill with the formula. Note that *relative cell references* in the formula (see Chapter 10) are automatically adjusted in the filled cells.

To continue a series into adjacent cells:

1. If the series doesn't already exist, start it by typing at least two adjacent entries in a row or column.

   For example, for invoice numbers starting with 1050, you would enter **1050** and **1051**. For company divisions, you could type **Div1** and **Div2**, **Div. 1** and **Div. 2**, or **Division 1** and **Division 2**. For days of the week, you could enter **Sunday** and **Monday** or **Sun** and **Mon**.

2. Select two or more adjacent cells containing members of the series. Drag the fill handle of the rightmost or lowest cell in the direction you want to fill. As you drag, Excel shows the data each cell will contain. Release the mouse button to complete the fill **E**.

   TIP When expanding certain series such as dates, an Auto Fill Options icon appears **F**. Click it to set a fill specification for the series. If you drag-extend the series using the *right* mouse button, similar options appear in a context menu.

Formula

Selected cells (B2:D2)

D Select the cell that contains the formula (B2), as well as the cells you want to fill (C2:D2).

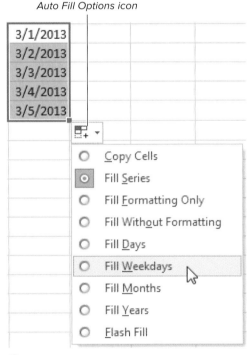

E As defined by the dates in the first two cells, this series will expand in 14-day increments.

F The Auto Fill Options menu.

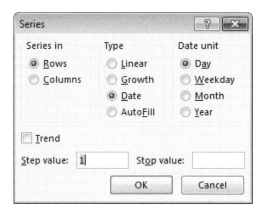

G You can also create a series by selecting the data and the fill range, and then setting options in the Series dialog box.

Full Name	Last Name	First Name
John Simpson		
Marcie Abrams		
Janice Henderson		
Marcus James		

H Flash Fill can parse a column of full names into first and last names.

Full Name	Last Name	First Name
John Simpson	Simpson	
Marcie Abrams	Abrams	
Janice Henderson	Henderson	
Marcus James	James	

I If Excel can match the reentered data with a component of the data in the first column, it offers to perform a Flash Fill.

Flash Fill options

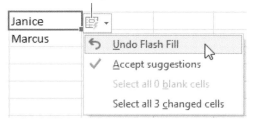

J After reviewing the results of a Flash Fill, you can reverse the process by clicking the Flash Fill Options icon and choosing Undo Flash Fill.

TIP When continuing a series, select enough data to enable Excel to discern the nature of the series. In some cases, such as a day name, month name, or numbered text (Quarter 1, Score 1, or Team 1, for example), one item may be sufficient.

TIP For more complex series (especially numerical ones), you can choose Home : Editing : Fill > Series and set options in the Series dialog box G. In general, however, you'll be happier if one of the previously described methods works. The Series dialog box can be seriously confusing.

To parse data using Flash Fill:

1. In a column, enter or arrange the data that you want to parse H.

2. In the column to the right, begin the parsing process by reentering the appropriate data from the first column.

   When Excel recognizes the parsed data, it offers to fill in the remaining data for the current column I.

3. To accept the Flash Fill suggestions, press Enter.

   The remaining data for the column is filled in for you.

TIP After accepting a Flash Fill, a Flash Fill icon appears J. Click it for additional options.

4. If there are additional columns to be filled with parsed data (such as First Name, in this example), repeat Steps 2–3 in the next column.

Importing Data

You don't have to manually enter the data in every worksheet. If the data exists elsewhere, such as in a table on the web, in another program, or in a properly formatted text file, you can import the data into a new or existing worksheet. Following are examples of common importing scenarios.

To import data from a web table:

1. Select a blank cell on the sheet. Choose Data : Get External Data > From Web.

   A New Web Query dialog box appears **Ⓐ**.

2. In the Address box, type or paste the URL for the web page that contains the data, and click Go. (If you recently viewed the page, you may be able to select its URL from the Address box's drop-down menu.)

   The web page is fetched and displayed.

URL Select this data table Recent URL list Go button Options

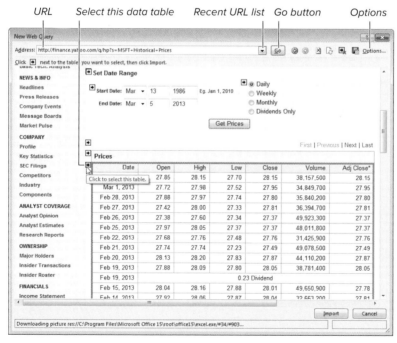

Ⓐ Type, paste, or select the URL of the web page that contains the data.

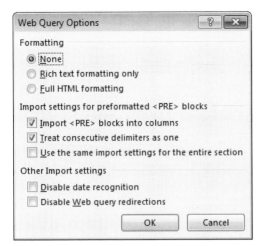

B To retain formatting, select a Formatting option in the Web Query Options dialog box.

C Specify a destination for the imported data and click OK.

D This is the data imported into cell A1 of an existing blank worksheet.

TIP After entering a URL in the Address box, you can interact with the fetched page. You can follow links by clicking them; enter your user name and password (for sites that require a login); and click buttons at the top of the dialog box to go backward or forward, refresh the page, or stop.

TIP To import data and retain its original formatting, click the Options button at the top of the dialog box. In the Formatting section of the Web Query Options dialog box **B**, select Rich text formatting only or Full HTML formatting, and then click OK.

3. Each table on the page is marked with an arrow enclosed in a yellow box. Click the box for each table that you want to import **A**, and click the Import button.

   The Import Data dialog box appears **C**, asking where you want to import the data. By default, the active cell on the current worksheet is proposed.

4. *Select one of the following:*

   ▸ **Existing worksheet.** Specify the starting cell to receive the imported data by typing its address in the box or by clicking the cell on the worksheet.

   ▸ **New worksheet.** Excel will create a new worksheet in the current workbook and import the data into a range beginning with cell A1.

   TIP Additional options for a web import can be viewed by clicking the Properties button.

5. Click OK.

   Each table selected in Step 3 is imported **D**.

   TIP Another way to retain a web table's formatting is to open the page in a browser, drag to select the table, and copy (Ctrl-C) the data. Select a destination cell in the worksheet and then paste (Ctrl-V).

To export data from another program as an Excel file:

1. Open the document in its creating application, such as a database, a spreadsheet, or an address book utility.

2. *Optional:* Select the records (or portion of the document) that you want to use in Excel. If possible, rearrange the data fields to match the order in which you want them to appear in the worksheet.

3. Use the program's Export, Save As, or equivalent command to save a copy of the data as an Excel (*.xls* or *.xlsx*) worksheet file 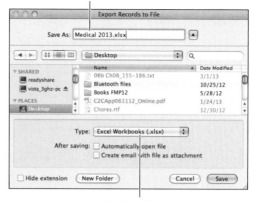.

   Note, however, that not all programs have this capability.

4. In Excel, click the File tab to go to the Backstage, click Open, and open the exported data file .

   As an alternative, you may be able to open the exported file by simply clicking or double-clicking its file icon.

TIP The exported data may require cleanup in Excel. For instance, you may need to add or edit column heads, rearrange the columns and change their widths, and add appropriate number and date formatting.

TIP Most Export and Save As procedures do not export formulas. In general, the *results* of such calculations are exported. If you intend to work with and extend the data in Excel, you'll probably want to recreate the formulas. On the other hand, if the reason you exported the data was so you could use Excel to analyze or chart it, working with the export as-is may suffice.

Export filename

Excel as file type

E In FileMaker Pro (Mac version shown), any database can be exported as an Excel file.

F Here's the exported FileMaker database opened in Excel 2013.

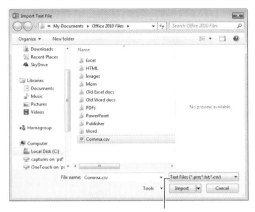

List these file types

G Select the exported data file in the Import Text File dialog box.

Field-type description

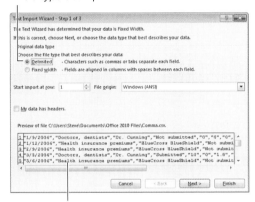

Data preview

H Examine the data in the preview area and ensure that the correct field-export description is selected.

To export data from another program as a text file:

1. Open the document in its creating application, such as a database, spreadsheet, or address book utility.

2. *Optional:* Select the records (or portion of the document) that you want to use in Excel. If possible, rearrange the data fields to match the order in which you want them to appear in the worksheet.

3. Use the program's Export, Save As, or equivalent command to save a copy of the data as a *tab-delimited* or a *comma-delimited text file*.

   The program may refer to these file types as *tab-* and *comma-separated*.

4. In Excel, choose Data : Get External Data > From Text.

   The Import Text File dialog box **G** appears.

5. Navigate to the drive and folder that contains the exported data file.

6. *Do one of the following:*

   ▸ If the exported data file appears in the file list, select it and click Import (or Open).

   ▸ If the export file is *not* present in the file list, select All Files from the file-type list. Select the export file in the file list and click Import (or Open).

7. In Step 1 of the Text Import Wizard **H**, ensure that Delimited is selected. Examine the data preview in the bottom of the window, verifying that it is the correct file and displays properly. Click Next to continue.

   continues on next page

8. In Step 2 of the wizard , ensure that the correct delimiter type is checked. (Data in the Data preview section will be properly divided into fields when the correct delimiter is selected.) Click Next to continue.

9. *Optional:* In Step 3 of the wizard 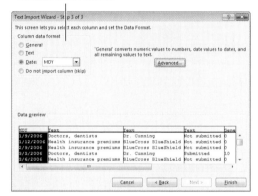, you can specify a format for the data in each field. Select the field in the Data preview and click the appropriate Column data format radio button.

Note that General format is appropriate for most types of data, including dates.

10. *Optional:* If you decide not to import certain fields, select those fields in the Data preview and click the Do not import column (skip) radio button.

11. Click Finish.

The Import Data dialog box appears **C**.

12. *Do one of the following:*

 ▸ To open the file in the current worksheet, select Existing worksheet and specify the starting cell in which to receive the data.

 ▸ To open the file in a new sheet in the workbook, select New worksheet.

13. Click OK to import the data into Excel.

TIP Excel can also import data from files with *fixed-width fields* **H**. Some programs, especially very old database applications, store data in fixed-width fields. When originally creating the file, you had to specify the maximum number of characters for each field. When you entered data but failed to use the allotted characters for a field, the program simply padded the field with spaces.

TIP Excel can also open comma-separated value (CSV) files directly, bypassing the Text Import Wizard. In Step 4, click the File tab, click Open, set the file type to Text Files, and then open the .csv file.

Select the delimiter character

I Select the delimiter character that was used to separate fields in the export file.

Column data formats

J Click each column in the Data preview area to ensure that an appropriate format is assigned.

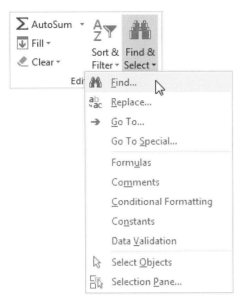

A Find, Replace, Go To, and selection commands can be chosen from the Find & Select menu.

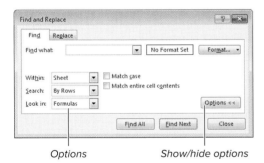

Options   *Show/hide options*

B The Find and Replace dialog box (with options displayed).

Finding and Replacing Data

Although you can scroll through a sheet to find a particular string (such as a label, data, a cell reference, or a formula element), you may be able to use the Find feature to quickly locate the item. You can optionally replace any found string with another string.

To perform a Find:

1. To restrict the search to a range, select the range. Otherwise, click the cell in which you'd like to begin the search.

TIP You can also limit the scope of a Find by first choosing a selection command **A**.

2. Choose Home : Editing : Find & Select > Find **A** (Ctrl-F).

The Find and Replace dialog box appears **B**.

3. Enter a search string in the Find what box.

4. *Optional:* If the additional search options aren't visible, click the Options button to display them. You can set any combination of the following options:

- ▸ **Within.** Indicate whether you want to search within the current worksheet or all sheets in the workbook.

- ▸ **Search.** Specify whether the search will proceed across rows and down (By Rows) or down columns and across (By Columns).

- ▸ **Look in.** Specify the cells to search. Choose *Formulas* to consider all cells, *Values* to search all cells except those containing a formula, or *Comments* to search only within comments.

continues on next page

▸ **Match case.** When this option is enabled, capitalization within a cell must match that of the search string.

▸ **Match entire cell contents.** Cell contents must match the search string *exactly*. For instance, searching for `Microsoft` will find cells that contain `Microsoft` but ignore those containing `Microsoft Corporation`.

TIP If you don't check this option, a match can be found *anywhere* within a cell. For example, searching for 3 would match 3, 7.23, 1:37, 5/3/2005, and =B7-G23.

▸ **Format.** To include formatting in the Find criteria, click the Format button and choose one of these options from the drop-down menu **C**:

Format. Specify format settings in the Find Format dialog box.

Choose Format From Cell. Using the eyedropper cursor, click a cell whose formatting will serve as the criterion.

Clear Find Format. Choose this option to remove previously specified formatting as a search criterion.

5. *Do one of the following:*

▸ Click Find Next to go to the first match (if any are present). Continue clicking Find Next to step through the matches.

▸ Click Find All to display a list of all matches in the bottom of the dialog box **D**. Click any match to go to that cell.

6. When you're finished, click the Close button.

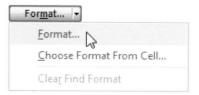

C To add or remove formatting as a match criterion, click the Format button and choose a command.

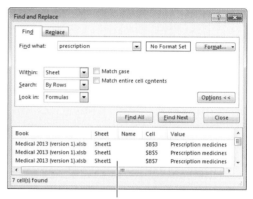

Find All results

D When you click Find All, matching cells are presented in a scrolling list.

Tips for Faster and Targeted Finds

To perform a simple search, hide the options in the Find and Replace dialog box by clicking the Options button, and then click Close. Reissue the Find command, enter a search string in the Find and Replace dialog box, and click Find Next or Find All. The search is performed by rows, identifies partial matches, and searches every cell.

Find and Replace procedures support the use of *wildcards* as criteria. Use the **?** wildcard to replace a single character and ***** to replace multiple (or no) characters. For example, you could enter `ba?k` to find `back`, `balk`, `bank`, `bark`, and `bask`. Enter `John*` to find `John`, `Johnny`, `Johnson`, and `Johnston`.

Show/hide options

E The Find and Replace dialog box (with options displayed).

Find/Replace Tips

You may find the following tips helpful when performing Replace operations.

- When the Find and Replace dialog box is open, you can switch freely between its modes by clicking the Find or the Replace tab. In fact, a Replace is frequently preceded by a Find, allowing you to first determine if there is anything to replace.

- When making a replacement without checking Match entire cell contents, you will only replace the matching portion of a cell's contents. For instance, if you search for **corp** with the intent of replacing it with **corporation**, **scorpio** will be replaced by **scorporationio**.

- You can also use the Find and Replace dialog box to replace formatting without changing cell contents. Leave the Find what and Replace with boxes empty, and set Format options for both.

To perform a Find/Replace:

1. To restrict the Find/Replace to a range, select the range. Otherwise, click the cell in which you'd like to start the search.

2. Open the Find and Replace dialog box by doing one of the following:

   ▸ Choose Home:Editing:Find & Select > Replace **A** or press Ctrl-H.

   ▸ Choose Home:Editing:Find & Select > Find **A** or press Ctrl-F. In the Find and Replace dialog box, click the Replace tab.

   The Find and Replace dialog box opens, ready to receive the search criteria **E**.

3. Enter a search string and set criteria by performing Steps 3–4 of the previous procedure. Enter a replacement string in the Replace with box.

TIP **Format can be set separately for the Find and Replace strings.**

4. *Do one of the following:*

   ▸ To make the replacement decision individually for each match, click Find Next. Excel moves to the first match, if one is found.

   To replace the matching contents with the Replace with string, click Replace. Or to ignore the current match, click Find Next. Excel selects the next matching cell. Repeat for each additional match.

   ▸ To simultaneously perform all replacements, click Find All. Review the matches in the bottom of the dialog box and click Replace All (if all matches are correct). Click OK to close the dialog box and examine the results of the Replace All.

5. Click Close.

Sorting Data

You can sort data to maintain it in a particular order—arranging entries in an address list by last name, phone number, or ZIP code, for example. You can sort any column in ascending or descending order, based on the contents of that column. If surrounding data is related to the data in the selected column (created as *records*), data in the adjacent columns can also be reorganized to match that of the sorted column.

To sort a column or data array:

1. Select the column you want to sort or by which you want to sort all surrounding data 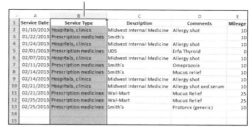.

2. Choose a sort order from the Home: Editing: Sort & Filter menu **B**, such as Sort A to Z, Sort Smallest to Largest, or Sort Oldest to Newest.

   The options presented vary with the type of data in the selected column. If there are no adjacent columns on either side of the selected column, the column is sorted as specified.

3. Otherwise, if columns *are* adjacent to the selected column, the Sort Warning dialog box appears **C**. *Select one of these options:*

   ▸ **Expand the selection.** Treat all contiguous columns (on both sides of the selected column) as a data array.

   ▸ **Continue with the current selection.** Sort only the selected column, leaving any surrounding columns unchanged.

4. Click Sort to sort the data as specified.

Selected column

A Start by selecting the column to sort.

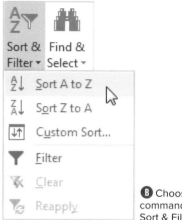

B Choose a sort command from the Sort & Filter menu.

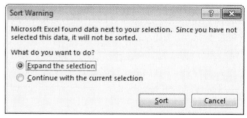

C To clarify your selection, indicate whether you want to sort the entire data array or only the selected column.

D Choose Custom Sort to sort on multiple fields. In this example, a medical expenses data array is sorted on Description (provider) and then—within Description—by Grand Total (service cost).

E Set additional options in the Sort Options dialog box.

Ascending sort

Descending sort

F You can also sort by clicking an icon in the Data:Sort & Filter group.

TIP To perform a more complex sort, choose Custom Sort from the Sort & Filter menu **B**, and then set options in the Sort dialog box **D**. Options include sorting on multiple columns (last name *and* first name, for example) and performing sorts based on cell or font color.

To sort by rows (rather than by columns) or to use letter case in a sort, click the Options button in the Sort dialog box. Set options in the Sort Options dialog box **E** and then click OK to return to the Sort dialog box.

TIP A sort can also be initiated using other cell and range selections. If you select only a cell in the column you want to sort or by which you want to sort all surrounding data, the sort is performed immediately. If there are no adjacent columns, the column is sorted as specified. If there *are* adjacent columns, they are treated as an array. The entire array is sorted based on the data in the sort column.

TIP If you select a range that contains multiple columns prior to choosing a Sort command, only the selected range will be sorted. The first column is automatically treated as the sort-by column. Other adjacent columns and cells outside the selected range are left unchanged.

TIP You can also sort using commands on the Data tab. To sort an array, select any cell within the column by which you want to sort. Then click the ascending or descending sort icon in the Data:Sort & Filter group **F**. For a more complex sort (such as sorting by multiple fields), click the Data:Sort & Filter:Sort icon to open the Sort dialog box **D**.

TIP Another way to analyze a data array is to *filter* it by hiding selected rows (*records*) or showing only records that satisfy a criterion, such as `after 3/1/13`. See Chapter 11 for more information about applying and using filters.

TIP To really simplify the process of working with a data array that regularly needs to be sorted or filtered, consider defining the array as a *table* (see Chapter 11).

Naming Cells and Ranges

In addition to referencing cells and ranges by their addresses (such as G17 and A1:D8), you can assign *names* to them. There are two reasons to name certain cells and ranges:

- It's easier to find important data in the Go To dialog box (see 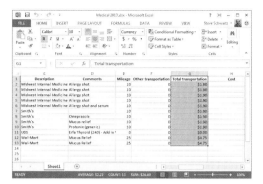 in "Cell and Range Selection") using a name because you don't have to memorize addresses.

- A name can be used in formulas (see Chapter 10) as a substitute for an address or range, making the formula easier to create and understand, such as **=Total*Tax_Pct**.

A name can contain 255 characters: letters, numbers, periods, and underscores (_). The first character must be a letter, underscore, or backslash (****). Although names can't contain spaces, you can represent a space with a period or underscore, such as **Div_1** or **Div.1**. Names aren't case-sensitive, so **Budget**, **BUDGET**, and **budget** are considered to be the same name.

To name a cell or range:

1. Select the cell or range that you want to name .

2. *Do either of the following:*

   ▸ Enter the name in the name box  and press Enter.

   ▸ Click the Formulas : Defined Names : Define Name icon or choose Formulas : Defined Names : Define Name > Define Name. Complete the information in the New Name dialog box  and click OK.

Ⓐ Select the cell or range to be named. (In this example, data in column G is selected.)

Ⓑ Enter a name for the selected cell or range in the name box.

Ⓒ Creating a name in the New Name dialog box allows you to set a *scope* for the name (worksheet or workbook), add an optional comment, and edit the cell or range reference.

Filter the name list

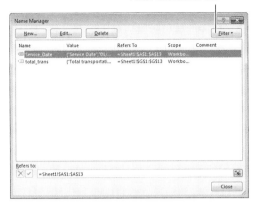

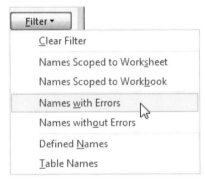

D You can create, rename, edit, or delete names in the Name Manager dialog box.

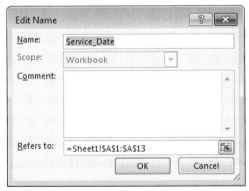

E If you've defined many names, you can filter the list to show certain ones.

F Use the Edit Name dialog box to rename a name, add a comment, or change the address or range to which the name refers.

TIP In previous versions of Excel and in other spreadsheets, a name was often referred to as a *range name* or *named range*.

TIP If Excel can associate a row or column label with the selected range, it will propose the label as the name in the New Name dialog box.

TIP Every created name has a *scope*; it can be a specific worksheet or all worksheets in the current workbook. When a name is created in the name box, its scope is automatically set to the workbook. If you create the name in the New Name dialog box **C**, you can set either as the scope.

TIP Tables can also be named. In fact, when you create a table, a default name is assigned to it, based on the number of tables already in the worksheet (Table1, Table2, and so on).

To rename, delete, or modify a name:

1. Click the Formulas : Defined Names : Name Manager icon.

   The Name Manager dialog box **D** appears.

   TIP To limit the names listed in the Name Manager dialog box to defined names, table names, names scoped to the sheet or workbook, or ones with or without errors, click the Filter button **D** and choose an option from the drop-down menu that appears **E**.

2. Select a name in the Name list, and click one of these buttons:

   ▸ **Delete.** Delete the name. To confirm the deletion, click OK in the dialog box that appears.

   ▸ **Edit.** Change the name, add or edit a comment, or change the cell or range to which the name refers **F**. Click OK to close the dialog box, saving your changes.

3. Click Close to dismiss the Name Manager dialog box.

Password-Protecting Workbooks

Excel provides a variety of tools for protecting data. One that you are likely to use is that of adding *password protection* to a workbook (requiring a password to open and/or modify its contents).

To password-protect a workbook:

1. Click the File tab to go to the Backstage.

2. In the Info section of the Backstage, click the Protect Workbook icon and choose Encrypt with Password 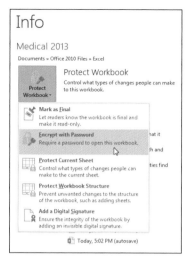.

   The Encrypt Document dialog box appears ⓑ.

3. Type a password and click OK.

   The Confirm Password dialog box opens.

4. Reenter the password and click OK.

   Note that letter case counts; that is, **Newt7**, **newt7**, and **NEWT7** are different.

> **TIP** You can also set a password while saving a workbook with the Save As command. Open the Tools menu at the bottom of the Save As dialog box and choose General Options. In the General Options dialog box ⓒ, there are two protection options for you to consider. First, you can prevent unauthorized users from opening the workbook by entering a password in the Password to open box (*open protection*). Excel encrypts the workbook when saving it.

> Second, to prevent unauthorized users from modifying the workbook but still let them view it, enter a password in the Password to modify box (*modify protection*). No encryption is added. Users who cannot supply the password will only be allowed to view the workbook.

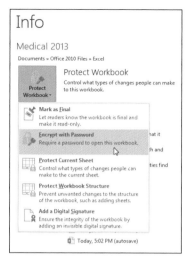

ⓐ You can encrypt and password-protect the current workbook.

ⓑ Type a password and click OK.

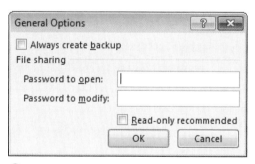

ⓒ Enter a password in the appropriate text box and click OK.

D This dialog box appears when a password to open has been set for a workbook.

E This dialog box appears when a password to modify has been set for a workbook.

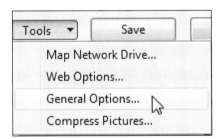

F To access password settings, choose General Options from the Tools menu at the bottom of the dialog box.

To open a protected workbook:

1. Open the workbook file.

2. Depending on the type(s) of password protection assigned to the file, one of the following occurs:

   ▸ **Open protection.** A Password dialog box appears **D**. Enter the password and click OK. If the password is incorrect or Cancel is clicked, the workbook doesn't open.

   ▸ **Modify protection.** A Password dialog box appears **E**. Enter the password for permission to modify the workbook or click Read Only for permission to only view the workbook.

To remove or change a password:

1. Open the workbook by supplying the password. The following occurs:

   ▸ **Open protection.** A Password dialog box appears **D**. Enter the password and click OK. If the password is incorrect or Cancel is clicked, the workbook doesn't open.

   ▸ **Modify protection.** A Password dialog box appears **E**. Enter the password for permission to modify the workbook.

2. Click the File tab, followed by Save As. Choose a folder or click Browse.

3. Open the Tools drop-down menu at the bottom of the Save As dialog box and choose General Options **F**.

4. In the General Options dialog box **C**, *do any of the following:*

   ▸ To eliminate a password, delete it from the appropriate Password text box.

   ▸ To change a password, delete the old password, type a new one, and then confirm the change.

continues on next page

5. Click OK to close the General Options dialog box.

6. *Optional:* In the Save As dialog box, you can change the file's name and/or its location on disk.

7. Click Save.

Any edits made to passwords, as well as password deletions, are recorded in the saved file. The edits and deletions will be in effect the next time you open the file.

CAUTION **Save an unprotected, archival copy of the workbook—just in case you forget the password(s).**

TIP **Use the Password to modify option when one or more users need to view a workbook but not change it. Restrict access to that password to those few users (or only yourself) who have permission to change the data.**

TIP **If you assign *both* types of password to a workbook, be sure to use two *different* passwords.**

Worksheet and Data Formatting

Although you're free to accept the default formatting for any worksheet by using the preset column widths, row heights, font, and font size, you're unlikely to do so very often. Simply put, properly formatted worksheets are easier to read and understand than those that use the default settings.

If you apply Excel's *attractive* formatting features (such as shading and border styles for cells, as well as fonts, styles, colors, and alignments for data), you can transform a run-of-the-mill worksheet into something worthy of being published in a corporate report.

For information on formatting tables, see Chapter 11.

In This Chapter

Setting Column Width and Row Height

Unless you've set a specific width for a column or height for a row, each row and column automatically adjusts to fit the data it contains, as follows:

- *Row height* adjusts to the largest font size in any cell within the row.

- *Column width* adjusts to the longest number in any cell within the column.

On the other hand, a lengthy text string in a cell 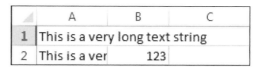 does *not* result in a column-width adjustment. If adjacent cells are empty, the extra text spills into them. If adjacent cells contain data, only the text that fits within the current cell's width is displayed.

To set a column width:

1. To select the column(s), *do one or a combination of the following:*

   - **Single column.** Click its letter or select a cell within the column.

   - **Multiple contiguous columns.** Drag-select the column letters.

   - **Multiple noncontiguous columns.** Ctrl-click each column letter.

2. Click Home:Cells:Format, and *do one of the following:*

   - To set one width for all selected columns, choose Column Width **B**. In the Column Width dialog box **C**, enter a number (representing the approximate number of characters), and click OK.

   - Choose AutoFit Column Width **B**. Excel will continually adjust the width to that of the longest number or text string in each of the columns.

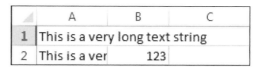

A Cells A1 and A2 contain the same text string. Because cells B1 and C1 are empty, A1's text spills into them. But because B2 contains data, the text string in cell A2 is truncated.

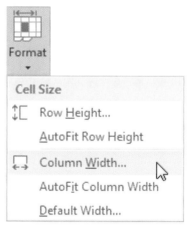

B Both column width and row height can be set using the Format menu.

C Enter a new column width (in characters) and click OK.

Back to Normal

After adjusting widths, you can quickly restore columns to the standard width by selecting them and choosing Home: Cells:Format > Default Width **B**.

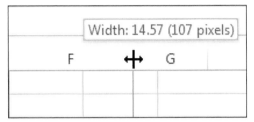

D Enter a new row height (in points) and click OK.

E Click and drag between column letters to resize the column on the left (in this case, column F).

To set a row height:

1. To select the row(s), *do one or a combination of the following:*

   ▸ **Single row.** Click the row number or select a single cell within the row.

   ▸ **Multiple contiguous rows.** Drag-select the row numbers.

   ▸ **Multiple noncontiguous rows.** Ctrl-click each row number.

2. Click Home : Cells : Format, and *do one of the following:*

   ▸ To set a single height for all selected rows, choose Row Height **B**. In the Row Height dialog box **D**, enter a height in *points* (72 points per inch), and click OK.

   ▸ Choose AutoFit Row Height **B**. Excel will continually adjust the row height to accommodate the largest font or text wrap in each of the selected rows.

   TIP You can *manually* adjust column widths and row heights: To adjust a column's width, click the right border of the column's letter and drag to the left or right **E**. To adjust a row's height, click the bottom border of the row's number and drag up or down.

   TIP You can simultaneously set a width or height for *multiple* columns or rows. Select the columns or rows, and then manually adjust the width or height of any one of them.

   TIP To instantly make a column wide enough to accommodate the longest number or text string in the column, double-click the column letter's right border. To adjust a row height in the same manner, double-click the row number's bottom border.

About Data and Cell Formatting

If you start a new worksheet by simply entering data, it will all have the same formatting. Every text and number entry will use the same font, size, style, and color. Numbers will be displayed using the General format (as typed, unless the column isn't wide enough to show the entire number). Cells will have no background color or borders.

However, Excel offers many data- and cell-formatting options. To make any worksheet more attractive and easier to interpret, you can do the following:

- Apply different fonts, styles, sizes, and colors to data within selected cells.

- Set paragraph alignment for individual cells (left-, center-, or right-aligned).

- Wrap text within cells or shrink it to fit, rather than let it spill into adjacent cells.

- Apply a variety of Number formats to cells that contain numeric data, such as setting the number of decimal places and formatting as currency.

- Fill cells with color and add *borders* (lines) around cell edges.

- Use *conditional formatting* to make certain numbers stand out, such as values below the average or values that correspond to a rule of your creation.

> **TIP** If you don't care for the default font used to format worksheets, you can change it. Click File and then click Options. In the General section of the Excel Options dialog box **A**, choose a new font and/or size, and click OK.

> **TIP** Displaying gridlines on any worksheet is traditional—*but optional.* To hide them, click the View:Show:Gridlines check box **B**.

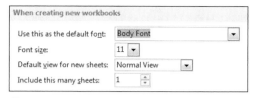

A You can change the default font and/or font size for all new worksheets in the Excel Options dialog box.

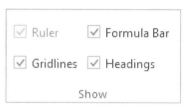

B You can click check boxes in the View:Show group to enable or disable display options.

A Character-formatting commands can be selected from the Font group.

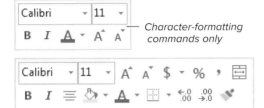

Character-formatting commands only

B The Mini toolbar displays different formatting commands when text within a cell is selected (top) or the cell itself is selected (bottom).

C Choose a style from the Cell Styles gallery to format headings, titles, totals, and good/bad data.

D Choose paragraph-formatting commands from the Home:Alignment group.

Character and Paragraph Formatting

By choosing commands from the Home: Font group or from the Mini toolbar, you can specify a font for selected text within a cell or the entire cell, as well as change the paragraph alignment.

To set character or paragraph formatting:

1. *Do one of the following:*

   ▸ To format all text within a cell, select the cell.

   ▸ To format only certain text within a cell, select the text that you want to format within a particular cell.

2. To apply character formatting, *do any of the following:*

   ▸ Choose character-formatting commands from the Home:Font group **A**.

   ▸ Right-click the cell or selected text, and choose formatting commands from the Mini toolbar **B**.

   TIP When you select text within a cell, the Mini toolbar automatically appears.

   ▸ Choose a style from the Home:Styles: Cell Styles gallery **C**. Note that cell styles can only be applied to an entire cell—not to selected text within a cell.

3. To apply paragraph formatting, choose commands from the Home:Alignment group **D**.

   TIP Character and paragraph formatting can also be applied simultaneously to multiple selected cells. Use any of the selection techniques described in "Cell and Range Selection" in Chapter 8 prior to applying formatting.

Fitting Text Within a Cell

Occasionally, a cell can contain more text than will fit. To fully display the text, you can allow the additional characters to overflow into adjacent cells, widen the column in which the cell is located, or use one of the methods described below.

To enable text wrap for cells:

1. Select the cell or cells in which you want the text to wrap.

2. Click Home:Alignment:Wrap Text.

   Text within the selected cells wraps. The row height increases as needed to accommodate present and future text in the row 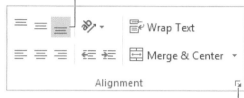.

> **TIP** To eliminate text wrap from selected cells, click the Wrap Text icon again.

> **TIP** If you set a specific height for a row, its height will no longer increase to accommodate text wrap.

> **TIP** If you've enabled text wrap, you may also want to set a vertical alignment for the entire row or selected cells within the row **B**.

To shrink text to fit within a cell:

1. Select the cell or cells containing text you want to shrink to fit the cell width.

2. Choose Home:Cells:Format > Format Cells.

> **TIP** You can also open the Format Cells dialog box by clicking the dialog box launcher in the Font, Alignment, or Number group **B**.

3. On the Alignment tab of the Format Cells dialog box **C**, click the Shrink to fit check box and then click OK. The text size is reduced to fit the cell width(s).

	A	B	C
1	Departmental Budget Worksheet - 2013	Jan	Feb

A Long text, such as the string in cell A1, can be wrapped within its cell.

Top, Middle, and Bottom Align icons

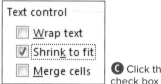

Format Cells dialog box launcher

B In figure **A** (above), Bottom Align was set for the column heads in cells A1–C1.

Text control
- ☐ Wrap text
- ☑ Shrink to fit
- ☐ Merge cells

C Click the Shrink to fit check box and click OK.

Mutually Exclusive Settings

Wrap Text and Shrink to Fit are mutually exclusive settings. To enable Shrink to Fit or Wrap Text in the Format Cells dialog box, you must first remove the check mark (if present) from the other setting.

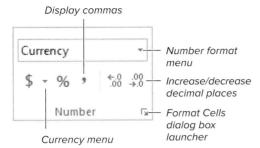

Display commas

Currency — Number format menu

$ ▾ % , ←.0 .00 .00 →.0 — Increase/decrease decimal places

Number ⌐ᵥ — Format Cells dialog box launcher

Currency menu

A Choose common number-formatting options from the Home : Number group.

Categories   Options

B For more complex formatting, as well as date and time formats, use the Format Cells dialog box.

Number Formatting

Like any modern spreadsheet application, Excel 2013 offers many formats that you can apply to numeric, date, and time data. You can format numbers as currency, per-centages, fractions, or scientific notation, for example. You can optionally display numbers with commas and a fixed number of decimal places.

Note that the display options set for a given cell do *not* affect the way its num-ber is stored or used in calculations. For example, if you apply a currency format to a cell containing 28.1225, $28.12 will display. The remaining .0025 isn't gone; it simply isn't shown.

To apply a Number format:

1. Select the cell or cells to which you want to apply a Number format.

2. *Do one of the following:*

   ▶ Choose formatting options from the Home : Number group **A**.

   ▶ Right-click any selected cell and choose format options from the Mini toolbar (see **B** in "Character and Paragraph Formatting").

   ▶ Click the Format Cells dialog box launcher **A**. Choose formatting options on the Number tab **B**. Click OK to apply the options to the selected cells.

TIP Be sure to thoroughly explore the Num-ber tab of the Format Cells dialog box. It also includes date and time formatting options. And if you choose the Special category, you'll find formats for ZIP codes, phone numbers, and Social Security numbers.

Conditional Formatting

By specifying *conditional formatting* (formatting that's applied only when certain criteria are met), you can make important data stand out from other elements in a data set. You can do any of the following:

- Overlay every member of the data set with a data bar, color, or icon that shows its position in the distribution.

- Apply a color highlight to a specific number of items that are highest, lowest, above average, or below average.

- Apply a color highlight to items identified by a *rule*, such as bowling averages greater than 200.

Unlike manually applied formatting, conditional formatting updates itself as required. That is, if the data that has been conditionally formatted changes, items formatted in this manner (highlighted in green, for example) will automatically change, too.

To apply data bars, color scales, or icon sets to data:

1. Select the cell range to which you want to apply conditional formatting.

2. Click the Home : Styles : Conditional Formatting icon.

    A drop-down menu appears 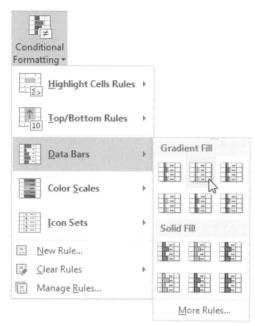Ⓐ.

3. Choose an option from the Data Bars, Color Scales, or Icon Sets submenu Ⓑ.

    A live preview is provided for each conditional formatting option.

Ⓐ Choose conditional formatting from this drop-down menu in the Home : Styles group.

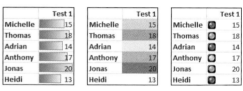

Data Bars   *Color Scales*   *Icon Sets*

Ⓑ You can show the relative size of each item in a data distribution by formatting with data bars, a color scale, or an icon set.

Custom Conditional Formatting

While you can quickly apply conditional formatting to a range by simply choosing an option from a Conditional Formatting submenu, you can customize the settings for a conditional formatting rule to show only particular values in a specified way. Choose More Rules from the appropriate Conditional Formatting submenu).

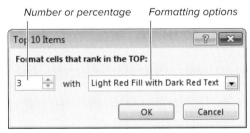

C Choose an option from the Top/Bottom Rules submenu to select the highest/lowest items or those above/below the average for the data set.

Number or percentage   *Formatting options*

D Set options for the rule and click OK.

E The Highlight Cells Rules submenu.

To apply a Top/Bottom Rule to data:

1. Select the cell range to which you want to apply a Top/Bottom Rule.

2. Click the Home:Styles:Conditional Formatting icon.

3. From the drop-down menu that appears, choose an option from the Top/Bottom Rules submenu C.

4. Set options in the dialog box that appears D. A live preview is shown.
   - For Average rules, the dialog box allows you to select fill and text colors.
   - For Top and Bottom rules, you can also set the cutoff point (as a number or percentage), highlighting only the lowest five scores, for example.

5. Click OK to apply the rule to the selected cell range.

To apply Highlight Cells Rules to data:

1. Select the cell range to which you want to apply a Highlight Cells Rule.

2. Click the Home:Styles:Conditional Formatting icon.

3. From the drop-down menu, choose an option from the Highlight Cells Rules submenu E.

4. In the dialog box that appears, set options and click OK to apply the rule.

TIP You can apply multiple types of conditional formatting to a range.

TIP Applying a different type of conditional formatting to a range does *not* clear the original formatting. To remove conditional formatting, select the range, open the Conditional Formatting drop-down menu, and choose **Clear Rules > Clear Rules from Selected Cells.**

Cell Backgrounds and Borders

In addition to formatting cell content, you can apply formatting to cell borders and backgrounds. For example, you can create a double-line border beneath a row to visually separate data from a totals row. Or you can make critical cells stand out by applying a colored fill to them.

To fill cells with color:

1. Select the cells to which you want to apply a background color.

2. On the Home tab, open the Format Cells dialog box by *doing one of the following:*

   - Choose Home : Cells : Format > Format Cells.

   - Click the Format Cells dialog box launcher in the corner of the Font, Alignment, or Number group (see Ⓑ in "Fitting Text within a Cell").

   - Right-click one of the selected cells and choose Format Cells from the context menu.

3. In the Format Cells dialog box, select the Fill tab ⒶA.

4. *Do one of the following:*

   - **Fill cells with a solid color.** Select a color in the Background Color section.

   - **Fill cells with a pattern.** Choose a pattern color and style from the drop-down menus.

   - **Fill cells with a gradient.** Click the Fill Effects button. Set options in the Fill Effects dialog box ⒷB and click OK.

5. Click OK to close the Format Cells dialog box.

Color fills   Pattern fill settings

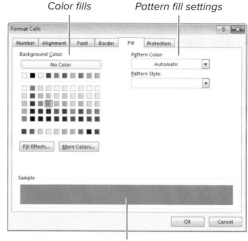

Preview of color, pattern, or gradient fill

ⒶA Set cell fill options on the Fill tab of the Format Cells dialog box.

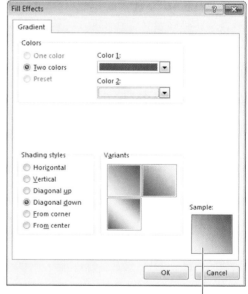

Preview

ⒷB You can apply a custom gradient to cells. Doing so frequently results in a 3D-like effect.

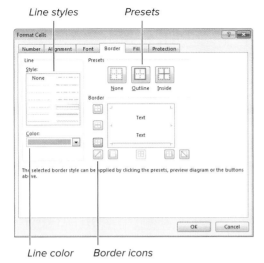

Line styles   Presets

Line color   Border icons

C You can add, remove, or modify borders for the currently selected cells.

Conditional Formatting with Quick Analysis

Using the new Quick Analysis feature, you can easily apply conditional formatting to any selected range.

1. Select the range to format.

2. Click the Quick Analysis icon.

3. On the Formatting tab, move the cursor over the icons for a live preview of each conditional formatting option.

4. Click an icon to apply its formatting.

Quick Analysis icon

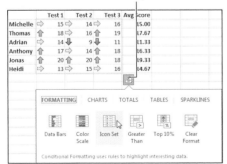

To add cell borders:

1. Select the cells to which you want to add one or more border lines.

2. On the Home tab, open the Format Cells dialog box by *doing one of the following:*

   ▸ Choose Home : Cells : Format > Format Cells.

   ▸ Click the Format Cells dialog box launcher in the corner of the Font, Alignment, or Number group (see **B** in "Fitting Text within a Cell").

   ▸ Right-click one of the selected cells and choose Format Cells from the context menu that appears.

3. In the Format Cells dialog box, select the Border tab **C**.

4. *Do any of the following:*

   ▸ **Add border lines.** Select a line style and color. To use one of the presets (such as Outline), click its icon. To add a single border line of the selected style and color, click its border icon or the spot in the sample where you want to add the line.

   ▸ **Remove border lines.** To remove *all* border lines from the selected cells, click the None preset. To remove a single border, click its border icon or the spot in the sample from which you want to remove the line.

   ▸ **Change border line properties.** To change the style or color of borders, select a new style and/or color, and click the preset or border icon that you want to reformat.

5. Click OK to close the dialog box.

TIP Border styles can also be chosen from the drop-down menu in the Home : Font group.

Removing, Replacing, and Reusing Formats

Whether you've applied character, paragraph, number, or conditional formatting, the formatting can be removed or replaced. And to simplify the process of applying existing formatting to other cells or ranges, you can *reuse* formatting.

To remove formatting:

1. Select the cell range from which you want to remove formatting, and switch to the Home tab.

2. *Do any of the following:*

   ▸ To remove all character, paragraph, and number formatting, choose Home : Editing : Clear > Clear Formats 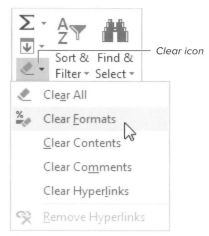.

   ▸ To selectively remove character style formatting (bold, italic, underline, or double underline) from selected cells or selected characters within a cell, reapply the same formatting.

   ▸ To remove conditional formatting from the selected cells, choose Home : Styles : Conditional Formatting > Clear Rules > Clear Rules from Selected Cells ⓑ.

   ▸ To remove all conditional formatting from the current worksheet, choose Home : Styles : Conditional Formatting > Clear Rules > Clear Rules from Entire Sheet ⓑ.

> **TIP** Applying Clear Formats also causes cell data to revert to the default font and size.

> **TIP** The Clear Formats command can also be used to remove conditional formatting.

Clear icon

ⓐ Choose Clear Formats to remove all formatting from the selected cells.

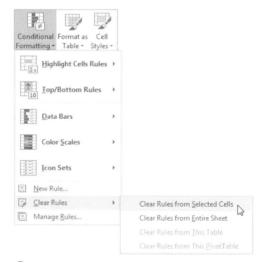

ⓑ You can remove conditional formatting from a selected range or from the entire worksheet.

C Use the Format Painter tool to copy cell formatting to another cell or range.

Format Painter icon

Formatting

D To perform a normal paste, click the Paste icon. To paste anything other than copied data (such as formatting), click an icon in the Paste drop-down menu.

To replace formatting:

1. Select the cell range for which you want to replace or modify the current format-ting. Switch to the Home tab.
2. *Do any of the following:*
   ▸ To set a new font or size, select options from the Home : Font group or the Mini toolbar (see **A** and **B** in "Character and Paragraph Formatting").
   ▸ To alter paragraph formatting, choose options from the Home : Alignment group (see **D** in "Character and Para-graph Formatting").
   ▸ To replace or modify Number format-ting, select options from the Home : Number group or the Number tab of the Format Cells dialog box (see **A** and **B** in "Number Formatting").

To reuse existing formatting:

1. Select a cell that contains the formatting that you want to duplicate.
2. Click the Home : Clipboard : Format Painter icon **C**.
3. *Do either of the following:*
   ▸ Click the cell to which you want to apply the formatting.
   ▸ Drag-select the cell range to which you want to apply the formatting.

TIP You can also reapply existing formatting using copy-and-paste. First, copy (Ctrl-C) the cell whose formatting you want to reuse. Next, select the target cells, open the Home : Clip-board : Paste menu and click the Formatting icon **D**. You can also specify copied properties that you want to paste by choosing Paste Spe-cial from the Paste icon's drop-down menu.

Worksheet Formatting

In addition to turning off the display of gridlines and specifying a new default font and size, you may want to try some of the following worksheet-formatting options:

- **Background.** You can use any image as a background for the current sheet . Click Page Layout:Page Setup:Background. In the Insert Pictures dialog box, pick an image source (such as From a file), select an image, and click Open.

> **TIP** A sheet background can be a file from your hard disk, a Flickr photo, Office.com clip art, an image stored on SkyDrive, or an image found as a result of a Bing web search Ⓑ.

> **TIP** To remove a sheet background, click the Page Layout:Page Setup:Delete Background icon.

- **Themes.** If you don't feel like manually selecting fonts, colors, and effects, you can choose a pre-designed *theme* from the Page Layout:Themes:Themes gallery. Each theme contains a complementary set of fonts, colors, and effects. When you insert a new chart or SmartArt graphic, for example, theme formatting is automatically applied. Similarly, when you select a color for text or an object, the color set will display only variations of theme colors.

- **Tab Color.** You may find it helpful to color-code the sheet tabs in a workbook to make them easier to identify. Right-click a sheet tab and choose a color from the Tab Color gallery Ⓒ.

Ⓐ As long as you apply contrasting font colors, a photo or graphic can serve as an interesting sheet background.

Flickr

Ⓑ Select an image source in the Insert Pictures dialog box.

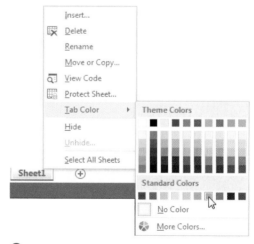

Ⓒ Choose a color for the current tab. Choose No Color to remove a previously applied color.

Formulas and Functions

After familiarizing yourself with Excel's list management features (using it to record mailing lists and membership rosters, for example), you'll want to explore its extensive calculation capabilities. By combining the contents of specific cells with each other or with constants, you can create *formulas*. For example, you can add two cells' contents, divide the contents of one cell by that of another, or multiply a cell's contents by a constant, such as a sales tax percentage or a commission rate.

You can also use Excel *functions* in your formulas. For instance, rather than laboriously adding the contents of several dozen cells, you can use the **SUM** function to generate a total for the range. In support of your calculation needs, Excel provides hundreds of built-in functions.

In this chapter, you'll learn the basics of combining cell references, constants, and functions into useful formulas. Techniques for troubleshooting formulas are also presented.

In This Chapter

About Cell References

Although a formula can be composed solely of constants, such as **=12+5**, you'll seldom use Excel to perform such calculations. Almost all formulas include *cell references*, such as **=A2+5**. This formula is interpreted by Excel as: "Take the current contents of cell A2 and add 5 to it."

A1 Reference Style

By default, Excel worksheets use *A1 reference style* in which columns are lettered and rows are numbered Ⓐ. Each *cell address* is named for the intersection of the column and row in which the cell is located. For example, C4 is the cell found at the intersection of column C and row 4 Ⓐ. A *range* is represented by a pair of addresses separated by a colon (:). For example, **B3:B6** means all cells between cells B3 and B6 inclusive—that is, B3, B4, B5, and B6. Refer to **Table 10.1** for some additional examples.

3-D Reference Style

Excel also provides a *3-D reference style* that enables you to include cells and ranges from other workbook sheets in formulas, as well as perform calculations across sheets:

- To include a cell or range from another sheet in a formula, precede the cell address or range with the sheet's name followed by an exclamation point:

  =Sheet2!a7-8

  In this example, 8 is subtracted from the contents of cell A7 on Sheet2.

- To consolidate data across multiple sheets, precede the cell or range address with the sheet range:

  =SUM(Sales1:Sales12!G50)

Columns (letters)

Rows (numbers)   *Cell C4*

Ⓐ A1 reference style has lettered columns and numbered rows.

TABLE 10.1 A1 Reference Style Examples

Example	Explanation
R5	Cell in column R, row 5
B3:E3	Cells B, C, D, and E in row 3
3:3	Row 3
F:F	Column F
5:8	Rows 5, 6, 7, and 8
A:C	Columns A, B, and C
A1:B3	All cells between cells A1 and B3 inclusive (A1, B1, A2, B2, A3, and B3)

	A	B	C	D	E
1	Student	Test 1	Test 2	Test 3	Total
2	Michelle	15	14	16	45
3	Thomas	18	16	19	53
4	Adrian	14	9	11	34
5	Anthony	17	14	18	49
6	Jonas	20	20	18	58
7	Heidi	13	15	16	44
8	Average	16.17	14.67	16.33	47.17

```
=SUM(Table1[@[Test 1]:[Test 3]])
```

B In Table 1 (top), Total (column E) is a calculated column. When the formula is expressed in structured reference style (bottom), it's identical in every cell in the column.

	1	2	3
1	Item	Due Date	Amount
2	Nissan	1/23/2013	$460.00
3	Sprint	1/24/2013	$19.00
4	Lake Havasu City	1/28/2013	$79.00
5	AAA Insurance	2/1/2013	$347.00

C In R1C1 reference style, both rows and columns are numbered.

TABLE 10.2 3-D Reference Style Functions

Function	Description
AVERAGE	Calculates the average (arithmetic mean)
COUNT	Counts the cells that contain numbers
MAX	Returns the largest value in the referenced cells
MIN	Returns the smallest value in the referenced cells
PRODUCT	Multiplies numbers in the referenced cells
STDEV.P, STDEV.S	Calculates the population or sample standard deviation
SUM	Adds numbers in the referenced cells
VAR.P, VAR.S	Calculates the population or sample variance

In this example, monthly sales are recorded in the first 12 sheets, each of which is named Sales, followed by the month number. Consolidating data this way assumes you've laid out the data in the sheets (Sales1–Sales12) in identical fashion; that is, cell G50 contains the appropriate number in each sheet, such as total monthly sales or Janice's monthly commissions.

TIP In 3-D reference style, only certain functions can be used to consolidate data across sheets. For a list of these functions, see Table 10.2. Supported variants of these functions that can be applied to text and logical values include AVERAGEA, COUNTA, MAXA, MINA, STDEVA, STDEVPA, VARA, and VARPA. Refer to "Excel functions (by category)" in Excel Help for descriptions of these and other built-in functions.

Structured Reference Style

Excel 2007 introduced *structured reference style*, a simplified means of addressing table data. When you create a formula in a table (a calculated column, for example), table-based structured references are automatically used rather than specific cell addresses **B**.

TIP When referring to a table cell in a formula, you can use structured or A1 reference style. If you point to the cell to add it to the formula, structured reference style is used.

TIP If you prefer, you can use *R1C1 reference style*, in which both rows and columns are numbered **C**. This style is generally used in Excel scripts (called *macros*). To enable R1C1, click File:Options. In the Excel Options dialog box, select the Formulas category, click the R1C1 reference style check box in the Working with formulas section, and then click OK.

Formula Essentials

This section presents the background information you'll need to create formulas.

Anatomy of a Formula

A basic formula Ⓐ consists of a combination of cell references, constants, and operators. (A *constant* is any data entered in a cell, such as text or a number, date, or time.) To distinguish a formula from data, every formula always begins with an equal (=) symbol.

Operators

Operators are used to specify the type of calculation to perform, such as addition or multiplication. Operators can be divided into four categories: arithmetic, comparison, text concatenation, and reference.

- **Arithmetic operators.** Used to perform mathematical calculations, producing a numerical result.

- **Comparison operators.** Used to perform logical comparisons between two values, resulting in either **True** or **False**.

- **Text concatenation operator.** Used to combine two text values, producing a single text string.

- **Reference operators.** Used to specify cell ranges.

See **Tables 10.3–10.6** for lists of supported operators.

Cell reference (A3)

=A3+18

Operator (+)   *Constant (18)*

Ⓐ In this simple formula, 18 is added to the data in cell A3. As is the case with all formulas, the result is displayed in the cell that contains the formula.

TABLE 10.3 Arithmetic Operators

Operator	Description	Example
+	Addition	A3+5
−	Subtraction	18−B7
−	Negation	−17
*	Multiplication	A6*B6
/	Division	G4/3
%	Percent	35%
^	Exponentiation (raise to a power)	A4^2

TABLE 10.4 Comparison Operators

Operator	Description	Example
=	Equal	A3=B5
>	Greater than	D2>12
<	Less than	E3<E4
>=	Greater than or equal to	A6>=15
<=	Less than or equal to	G4<=3
<>	Not equal to	B7<>5

TABLE 10.5 Text Concatenation Operator

Operator	Description	Example
&	Concatenation	"Phone: "&B5

TABLE 10.6 Reference Operators

Operator	Description	Example
:	Range	A3:A8 [all cells from A3 to A8]
,	Union	D2,F2:F5 [cells D2 and F2:F5]
[space]	Intersection	C4:D7 D6:D8 [cells D6 and D7]

TABLE 10.7 Operator Precedence

Operator	Precedence
:	Colon (range)
,	Comma (union)
[space]	Space (intersection)
–	Negation
%	Percent
^	Exponentiation
*, /	Multiplication and division
+, –	Addition and subtraction
&	Concatenation
=, <>, <=, >=	Comparison operators

Precedence

When calculating the result of a formula, Excel evaluates the elements from left to right. However, this holds true only when all operators are of the same importance (called *precedence*). Every operator has a precedence, as shown in **Table 10.7**. The higher in the table an operator appears, the higher its precedence. Thus, when a formula contains operators of differing precedence, the calculations are performed from highest to lowest precedence. Here are some examples:

4+2+3   [=9]

Explanation: All operators have the same precedence, so the formula is evaluated from left to right.

4*2+3   [=11]

Explanation: Multiplication has a higher precedence than addition. But because the multiplication occurs first in the formula, the left-to-right order is still followed (**8+3**).

4+2*3   [=10]

Explanation: Multiplication has a higher precedence, so **2*3** is evaluated first (**4+6**).

Note that you can change the order of evaluation by enclosing terms in parentheses. Such items are always evaluated first. When multiple sets of parentheses are used, items in the innermost sets are evaluated first.

4*(2+3) [=20]

Explanation: Because parentheses surround the last two terms, they are evaluated first—resulting in **5**. Without the parentheses, the formula would have been evaluated in left-to-right order: **4*2** (or **8**), plus **3**, for a result of **11**.

Relative, Absolute, and Mixed

Cell references in formulas can be relative, absolute, or mixed. When you enter a reference by typing an address (such as entering **=(B2+C2+D2)/3** in cell E2), the references to cells B2, C2, and D2 are *relative* to the location of the formula cell (E2). If the formula is moved or copied to another cell, Excel adjusts the cell references to point to the correct cells. For example, copying the formula to cells E3:E7 results in the correct formula in each new cell **B**.

You use an *absolute reference* (preceding both the column and row with dollar signs) for a cell address that must not change when copied or moved. For example, in a business mileage worksheet **C**, you could create a formula to calculate Mileage Amount: the trip's total mileage multiplied by a fixed mileage rate (found in cell I2). The initial formula in row 2 would be **=F2*$I$2** and then repeated in every cell in column G (for example, **=F3*$I$2**). Unlike relative references, absolute references never change, no matter where on the worksheet the formula is copied or moved.

Finally, Excel also supports *mixed references* in which the column or the row is absolute and the other is relative, such as **$A1** (column A is absolute, row 1 is relative) and **A$1** (column A is relative, row 1 is absolute).

TIP When a formula is copied or moved **D**, cell references change as shown in Table 10.8. Relative references change to match the formula's new location, relative to the original location; this also applies to the relative part of a mixed reference. Absolute references do not change; the absolute portion of a mixed reference also remains unchanged.

Formula copied to E3

B When the formula **=(B2+C2+D2)/3** in E2 is copied to cells E3:E7, the relative cell references in the formula automatically adjust to refer to the correct cells.

C The formula in column G uses an absolute reference to the fixed mileage rate in cell I2.

D If a formula in C1 is copied or moved to cell D3, it changes as described in Table 10.8.

TABLE 10.8 Result of Copying or Moving a Formula

Formula in C1	Copied or Moved to D3	Reference Type
=A1	=B3	Relative
=$A$1	=$A$1	Absolute
=$A1	=$A3	Mixed (absolute column)
=A$1	=B$1	Mixed (absolute row)

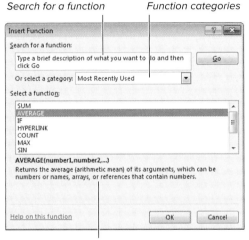

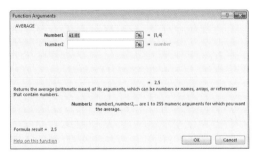

Functions

Functions are formula helpers—built-in computational routines that you can include in formulas to simplify the creation of complex and special-purpose calculations. For instance, rather than laboriously totaling a string of cells with the formula **=A1+A2+A3+A4+A5**, you can use the **SUM** function to total the range: **=SUM(A1:A5)**.

All but a few functions require *arguments,* the data on which the function operates. Arguments are enclosed in parentheses and—if there are multiple arguments—separated by commas. The argument to the **SUM** function above is the range **A1:A5**. In addition to operating on a single range, **SUM** can be used to total individual cells and constants, as seen in this formula:

> **=SUM(A1:A5,B7,23)**

In this example, the total of cells A1, A2, A3, A4, A5, B7, and 23 is calculated.

When the text insertion mark is at the desired spot in a formula you're creating, you can insert a function in these ways:

- Functions for which you know the spelling and syntax can be typed directly into the formula.

- On the Formulas tab, you can choose a function by clicking a menu icon in the Function Library group ⓔ.

- For guidance in selecting a function, click Insert Function in the Function Library group. In the Insert Function dialog box ⓕ, select a function and then click OK.

In the latter two function-insertion methods, the Function Arguments dialog box appears ⓖ. Using the guidance provided, enter the argument(s) and click OK to insert the function into your formula.

ⓔ The Function Library group organizes Excel functions by category.

Search for a function   Function categories

ⓕ Select a function and click OK.

Description of selected function

ⓖ You can enter arguments by typing, clicking a cell, or drag-selecting a range.

TIP You can also open the Insert Function dialog box by clicking the *f*x icon in the formula bar or by pressing Shift-F3.

Creating Formulas

Formulas can be created from any combination of cell contents, constants, and functions. Many common formulas, such as sums or averages of a column or row, can quickly be created using the AutoSum tool.

To create a formula without functions:

1. Select the cell that will contain the formula and type an equal sign (=).

2. Construct the formula by typing constants, cell references, and operators 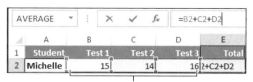. Press Enter or click the check mark in the formula bar to complete the formula.

   The formula is replaced in the cell by the calculated result .

To create a formula with functions:

1. Select the cell that will contain the formula and type an equal sign (=).

2. Insert constants and cell references as needed. To insert a function at the text insertion mark, *do one of the following:*

   ▸ Type the function name, a left parenthesis, the argument(s), and a right parenthesis.

   ▸ Choose a function from the Formulas:Function Library group. In the Function Arguments dialog box , enter the argument(s) and click OK.

   ▸ Click the Insert Function icon in the Function Library group or on the formula bar. In the Insert Function dialog box , select a function and click OK. In the Function Arguments dialog box , enter the argument(s) and click OK.

3. Press Enter or click the check mark in the formula bar to complete the formula. The formula is replaced in the cell by the calculated result.

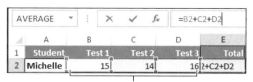
Referenced cells (B2:D2)

Ⓐ The formula in E2 totals Michelle's three test scores. As you select cells or type their addresses, Excel shows handles around each referenced cell.

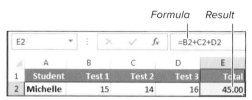

Ⓑ When you complete a formula, the result is displayed in the cell. Note that the formula is shown in the formula bar.

Ⓒ The Function Arguments dialog box.

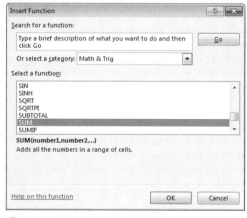

Ⓓ Select a function from the scrolling list.

⊿	A	B	C	D	SUM(number1, [number2], ...)
1	Student	Test 1	Test 2	Test 3	Total
2	Michelle	15	14	16	=SUM(B2:D2
3	Thomas	18	16	19	53.00

E To specify a range for this **SUM** function, type **=SUM(** and drag-select the range to be totaled. Type the closing parenthesis to complete the formula.

Formula in F2

=End_Mileage-Start_Mileage			
C	D	E	F
Destination	Start Mileage	End Mileage	Total Mileage
Post Office	3585	3595	10

F Columns D and E have been named **Start_ Mileage** and **End_Mileage**. To calculate total mileage for any cell in column F, the names can be substituted for the two cell references.

Formula cell   Formula AutoComplete list

	E	F	G	H	I
	Total				
	=Su				

- 𝑓ₓ SUBSTITUTE
- 𝑓ₓ SUBTOTAL
- 𝑓ₓ SUM — Adds all the numbers in a range of cells
- 𝑓ₓ SUMIF
- 𝑓ₓ SUMIFS
- 𝑓ₓ SUMPRODUCT
- 𝑓ₓ SUMSQ
- 𝑓ₓ SUMX2MY2
- 𝑓ₓ SUMX2PY2
- 𝑓ₓ SUMXMY2

G Double-click the desired function to insert it into the formula.

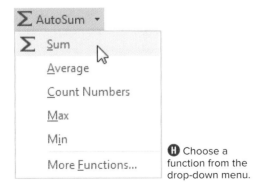

Σ AutoSum ▾

Σ Sum

Average

Count Numbers

Max

Min

More Functions...

H Choose a function from the drop-down menu.

TIP When you create a formula, a cell reference can be typed or added by clicking the cell you want to reference. You can type or drag-select a range **E** as an argument to a function.

TIP Typed cell references can be entered in uppercase or lowercase.

TIP As explained in Chapter 8, if you've named cells or ranges, you can substitute the names for the addresses and ranges in formulas **F**.

TIP If required, a formula can contain multiple functions, as well as functions within functions (called *nested functions*).

TIP If you can type the first few letters of a function's name when creating a formula, you can use Formula AutoComplete to insert the function **G**. Double-click the desired function name in the drop-down list.

TIP Functions don't ignore empty cells within the argument range(s).

To create an AutoSum formula:

1. Select the cell at the bottom of the column or end of the row that will contain the formula.

   The cells that will serve as the argument to the AutoSum function must be a contiguous string within a single column or row, such as **B2:B23** or **H7:R7**.

2. On the Formulas tab, click the AutoSum icon in the Function Library group **H**. Choose a function from the drop-down menu or choose More Functions to view all Excel functions.

3. Excel highlights the range it thinks you want to use as the argument to the function. Adjust the range, if necessary.

4. Press Enter or click the check mark in the formula bar to complete the formula.

Editing Formulas

You can edit existing formulas to correct errors and to change cell or range references. Many of the techniques described below are also applicable to editing data.

To edit a formula:

1. Select the cell that contains the formula you want to edit.

2. You can edit in the cell or the formula bar, whichever is most convenient. *Do one of the following:*

   ▸ Double-click the cell.

   ▸ Click in the formula bar to set the text insertion mark.

3. *Do any of the following:*

   ▸ Use normal text-editing techniques to add, delete, or change cell contents.

   ▸ To clear the cell, drag-select its contents and press Backspace, or select the cell and press Del or Delete.

   ▸ To change a cell reference from relative, absolute, or mixed to another reference type, select the address within the formula and repeatedly press F4.

   ▸ To replace a function, select its name in the formula. Begin typing the new function's name, and then choose it from the Formula AutoComplete list by double-clicking **A**. You can also replace a selected function name by choosing a new function from the Formulas:Function Library group **B**.

4. Press Enter to complete the formula.

TIP To make an entry in a cell in multiple worksheets, Ctrl-select the sheet names in the Sheet tab bar, select the cell, and then enter the data or formula.

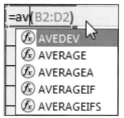

A All functions that begin with the typed letters are presented.

Selected function

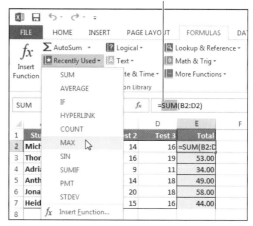

B Functions can be chosen from the Function Library group's icons. If you regularly use a function, you can often choose it from the Recently Used icon.

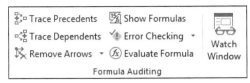

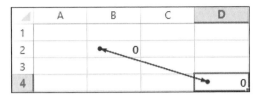

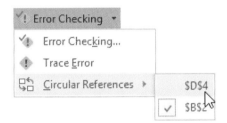

Troubleshooting Tips

Following are some techniques for finding and correcting errors in formulas. Start by switching to the Formulas tab to make the icons in the Formula Auditing group Ⓐ accessible:

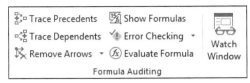

Ⓐ Troubleshooting tools can be found in the Formulas : Formula Auditing group.

Ⓑ This arrow connects two cells that reference each other. The formula in B2 is **=D4**; the formula in D4 is **=B2+8**.

Ⓒ You can go directly to a circular reference cell by choosing it from the Error Checking > Circular References submenu.

- **Formulas replaced by data.** To find cells in which you've accidentally replaced a formula with data, click the Show Formulas icon Ⓐ. Any cell containing a formula will now display the formula rather than the result. Click Show Formulas again to restore the worksheet to its normal state.

- **Circular references.** If the formulas in two cells rely on each other, Excel cannot perform the calculations. This is known as a *circular reference* and is denoted by an arrow connecting the cells Ⓑ. Only one cell can refer to the other cell, so you must edit one of them. You can go to a particular circular reference by clicking the Error Checking icon and choosing a cell listed in the Circular References submenu Ⓒ.

TIP To selectively display or hide the arrows, click the Trace Precedents or Trace Dependents icon. You can also choose commands from the Remove Arrows menu Ⓐ.

continues on next page

- **Incorrect result.** If a formula displays an unexpected result, select the cell and click Evaluate Formula 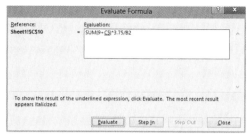. By repeatedly clicking the Evaluate button in the Evaluate Formula dialog box **D**, you can step through the elements in the formula, displaying the calculated result for each step. Evaluating a formula often makes it easy to find incorrect cell references and identify flaws in logic.

- **Is it an error?** Excel notifies you immediately if it detects a possible formula error—often by displaying a tiny triangle in the cell's upper-left corner. Select the cell **E** and choose a handling option from the alert icon's drop-down menu.

D Click the Evaluate button to replace the underlined formula element with its data. Click Close when you're finished.

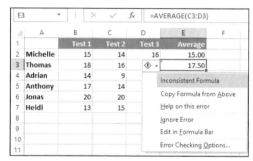

E Click the icon and choose an option.

Working with Tables

Although number-crunching is the purpose of the typical worksheet, many worksheets are used only to record lists of related data, such as addresses, club memberships, or a course roster. New users quickly discover that a worksheet's grid is better for handling lengthy lists than a word processing document. Such worksheets are essentially simple databases in which each row is a *record* and each column is a *field*.

In Excel 2007, lists were renamed *tables*. Any area of a worksheet can be designated a table, and a worksheet can contain as many tables as you need. Here are some advantages of formatting data as a table rather than using normal Excel formatting and tools to manage your list:

- Quickly sort the table by the contents of any field

- Filter the data to show only certain records or those that match a criterion

- Display a summary statistic for selected columns in an optional *total row*

- Simplify the process of performing a calculation on row data using *calculated columns*

In This Chapter

Creating a Table

You can create a table in any blank range or convert existing data to a table.

To create a table:

1. *Do one of the following:*

- ► Select a blank range in which to insert the table.

- ► Select a range containing data that you want to convert to a table.

2. *Do one of the following:*

- ► Click Insert : Tables : Table or press Ctrl-T.

- ► Click Home : Styles : Format as Table and choose a table format from the gallery **A**.

  The Create Table or Format As Table dialog box appears **B**.

3. If the proposed table range contains a header row, check My table has headers.

4. Click OK to create the table **C**.

TIP The icons (called *filter buttons*) in the header row can obscure the header labels. You may want to widen the columns, change the alignment, or apply text wrap to any lengthy headers.

TIP To quickly select a table, click in any table cell and then move the cursor over one of the table's top corners. Click when the cursor changes to a plus (+) with arrows.

TIP To delete a table, select the entire table and press Del or Delete.

TIP To change a table back to a normal range, select any table cell. Click Design : Tools : Convert to Range. Click Yes in the confirmation dialog box that appears.

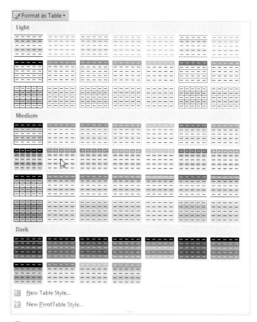

A One way to create a table is to simply format a cell range as a table.

B Edit the range (if necessary), indicate whether the range already contains a header row, and click OK.

C A new table created from a blank range.

Fill tab

A A color fill or gradient can be applied to selected table rows, columns, or cells. To display the Format Cells dialog box, choose Home: Cells: Format > Format Cells.

B Click check boxes in the Table Style Options group to hide, show, and format table components.

Formatting a Table

A table is just a worksheet range. As such, if you aren't thrilled with the default formatting, you can format individual cells, rows, columns, or the entire table as you like.

To format a table:

- **Format the entire table.** Select any cell in the table. Select a new style from the Design: Table Styles gallery.

- **Format a row, column, or range.** Select the row, column, or range within the table. Select a cell format from the Home: Styles: Cell Styles gallery. Alternatively, you can apply a fill color, gradient, or pattern to selected cells by selecting options on the Fill tab of the Format Cells dialog box **A**.

- **Format the first or last column.** The first column often contains record identifiers and the last column is frequently used to summarize each record's data. To apply distinctive formatting to these columns, click the check boxes for Design: Table Style Options: First Column and/or Last Column **B**.

- **Create alternating rows or columns.** Click the check box for Design: Table Style Options: Banded Rows or Banded Columns **B**.

> **TIP** The effect of selecting First Column and Last Column in the Table Style Options group depends on the table's current formatting. For example, only boldface is applied to the column's data for many table styles.

Creating Calculated Columns

Formulas in a table work differently from ones found elsewhere on the worksheet. If you insert a formula, it's automatically copied to all cells in the same column. And if you later add rows to the table, the formula is copied to the new cells in the column, too. Any table column that contains a formula is referred to as a *calculated column*.

To create a calculated column:

1. If necessary, insert a new column into the table in which to place the formula.

    To be treated as a calculated column, the column must be empty when you create the formula. If the column contains any data, the formula will be applied only to the current cell.

2. Select a cell in the empty column, and type or paste the formula into the cell.

    Many table formulas are automatically converted by Excel to equivalent *structured references* .

3. Complete the formula by pressing Enter or clicking the check mark in the formula bar .

    The formula is automatically copied to all other cells in the column .

TIP If you replace the formula with data in any cell in a calculated column, Excel marks that cell as an *exception*. You can correct an exception by clicking the alert icon beside the cell .

TIP As long as a calculated column contains no exceptions, you can replace the formula with a new one. Like the original formula, it will automatically copy itself to every cell in the column.

A Formulas within tables are often converted to structured references.

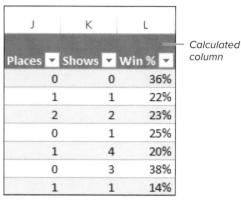

B The Win % calculated column is based on the formula `=Wins/Races`.

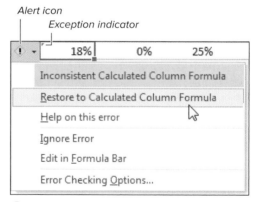

C An exception cell in a calculated column is denoted by a tiny triangle in the cell's upper-left corner. When you select the cell and click the alert icon to its left, you can choose an error-handling option.

Ⓐ Enable or disable the total row by clicking this check box.

Total row

Ⓑ When enabled, a total row appears at the bottom of the table.

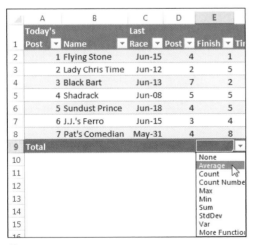

Ⓒ Each cell in the total row has a drop-down menu from which you can choose a statistical function.

Adding a Total Row

A table can optionally have a single *total row* at its bottom, enabling you to calculate a summary statistic across all records in the table. Each column can display a different statistic or none at all. For instance, in a donations table, you could compute the total of all donations, the average of the most recent donation (across all donors), or a count of the number of donor records.

To add a total row to a table:

1. Select a cell in the table to make the table active.

2. Click the Design : Table Style Options : Total Row check box **Ⓐ**.

   The total row appears at the bottom of the table **Ⓑ**.

3. *Optional:* Edit or delete the Total label in the first cell of the total row.

4. To display a summary statistic for a column, click the total row cell beneath the column. Click the icon that appears to the right of the cell and choose a statistic from the drop-down menu **Ⓒ**.

5. Repeat Step 4 for each additional column that you want to summarize.

6. Format the total row cells as desired.

TIP If the function you need isn't listed in the drop-down menu, choose More Functions **Ⓒ**.

TIP To eliminate the summary statistic for a column, choose None from the drop-down menu **Ⓒ**.

TIP You can disable and enable the total row as needed **Ⓐ**. When you re-enable the total row, any previously specified statistics reappear.

Sorting and Filtering

Excel provides two tools that simplify viewing and analyzing table data:

- **Sorting.** Sort an entire table based on the contents of one or more fields (columns).

- **Filtering.** Restrict visible records (rows) to those that match a criterion. If desired, criteria can be chosen from multiple columns. For instance, you might filter a business table to show June absences of only those employees who earn less than $10 per hour.

TIP You can optionally hide or reveal the filter buttons in the header row by clicking the Design : Table Style Options : Filter Button check box (see **A** in "Adding a Total Row").

To sort a table:

1. *Do one of the following:*

   ▸ In the header row, click the filter button of the column by which you want to sort **A**.

   ▸ Right-click in any cell of the column by which you want to sort and open the Sort submenu.

   ▸ Select any cell in the column by which you want to sort. Click the Home : Editing : Sort & Filter icon **B**.

2. Choose a sort order (ascending or descending) from the menu.

   The table is sorted as specified.

TIP You can perform a multi-field sort by choosing Custom Sort. In the Sort dialog box that appears, click the Add Level button to add more sort fields, such as sorting by Payee and then by Amount.

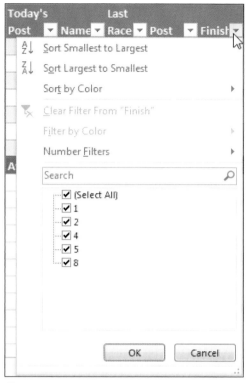

A Click the filter button for the column by which you want to sort the table.

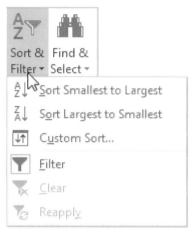

B You can also choose a Sort command from the Home : Editing : Sort & Filter menu.

Selected field

Last
Race	Post	Finish	Time	Odds	Races	Wins	Places	Sho

					11	4	0
					18	4	1
					13	3	2
					4	1	0
					10	2	1
					8	3	0

Sort Smallest to Largest
Sort Largest to Smallest
Sort by Color ▶
Clear Filter From "Odds"
Filter by Color ▶
Number Filters ▶

Search

- ☑ (Select All)
- ☑ 1.0
- ☑ 3.9
- ☑ 5.0
- ☑ 8.1
- ☑ 15.1
- ☑ 24.6
- ☑ 32.5

OK   Cancel

Equals...
Does Not Equal...
Greater Than...
Greater Than Or Equal To...
Less Than...
Less Than Or Equal To...
Between...
Top 10...
Above Average
Below Average
Custom Filter...

C Creating a custom filter (**Odds ≤ 5**).

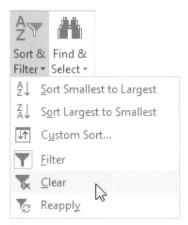

Quick Analysis
Sort ▶
Filter ▶
Table ▶
Insert Comment
Format Cells...
Pick From Drop-down List...
Hyperlink...

Clear Filter From "Wins"
Reapply
Filter by Selected Cell's Value
Filter by Selected Cell's Color
Filter by Selected Cell's Font Color
Filter by Selected Cell's Icon

D You can also filter the data based on the selected cell, but your options are limited.

A
Z ▼
Sort &
Filter ▼

Find &
Select ▼

Sort Smallest to Largest
Sort Largest to Smallest
Custom Sort...
Filter
Clear
Reapply

E Choose Clear to remove all filtering from the current table.

To filter a table:

1. In the header row, click the filter button of the column by which you want to filter the table.

2. Set a filter criterion by *doing either of the following:*

   ▸ Use the check boxes to specify the data elements that you want to show and click OK **A**.

   ▸ To filter using a formula (such as values greater than 7), open the Number, Text, Date, or Time Filters menu and choose an option **C**. If additional details are requested, enter them in the Custom AutoFilter dialog box and click OK.

   Records that do not match the filter criterion are hidden. If present, statistics in the total row are recalculated to reflect only the visible records.

TIP To filter based on a cell's contents or properties, right-click the cell in the column by which you want to filter the table and choose an option from the Filter submenu **D**.

TIP To remove all filtering effects from a table (restoring the full record set), select any cell in the table and choose Home:Editing: Sort & Filter > Clear **E**.

TIP To selectively remove a filter when multiple filters have been applied to a table, click the filter button in the column header whose filtering you want to remove and choose Clear Filter From "*field name*" **C**.

TIP If you've added records to a sorted or filtered table, you can reapply the current sort instructions and filter criteria to accommodate the new records. Choose Home:Editing:Sort & Filter > Reapply **E**.

Changing a Table's Size

Table contents can change over time. In addition to editing the data, you may want to add or delete fields (columns), as well as add or delete records (rows).

To change a table's size:

- **Insert records (rows) within a table.** Select a cell in the row beneath where you want to insert a new row. (To insert multiple rows in the same spot, begin by selecting that number of cells in adjacent rows.) Choose Home : Cells : Insert > Insert Table Rows Above 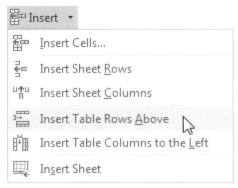.

- **Insert fields (columns) within a table.** Select a cell in the column to the right of where you want to insert a new column. (To insert multiple columns in one spot, begin by selecting that number of cells in adjacent columns.) Choose Home : Cells : Insert > Insert Table Columns to the Left .

- **Delete records (rows).** Select one or more cells in the row or rows you want to delete. Choose Home : Cells : Delete > Delete Table Rows 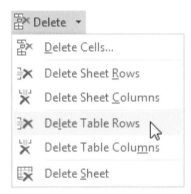.

- **Delete fields (columns).** Select one or more cells in the column or columns you want to delete. Choose Home : Cells : Delete > Delete Table Columns .

- **Increase a table's size by dragging.** Move the cursor over the lower-right corner of the table. When the cursor changes to a double-headed arrow , drag to the right to add columns or drag down to add rows.

A To insert table rows or columns, choose a command from the Insert icon's menu.

B You can delete table rows or columns by choosing a command from the Delete icon's menu.

C You can append rows or columns to a table by dragging the lower-right corner.

D Rather than manually resizing a table, you can enter a new range.

Selecting Tables, Table Rows, and Table Columns

To select a table column rather than an entire worksheet column, move the cursor over the top edge of the column header. When the cursor changes to a black down-pointing arrow, click to select the table column.

To select a table row, move the cursor over the left edge of the row. When the cursor changes to a black right-pointing arrow, click to select the table row.

To select an entire table, move the cursor over the table's upper-left corner and click when the cursor changes to an arrow. Or you can choose the table's name from the Name Box menu **E** (to the left of the formula bar).

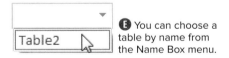

E You can choose a table by name from the Name Box menu.

TIP You can also resize a table by entering a new range. Select a cell in the table and click Design : Properties : Resize Table. Type a new range in the Resize Table dialog box **D** or manually select the range on the worksheet, and then click OK. Unlike resizing by dragging **C**, you can use the Resize Table dialog box to add new rows and columns at the same time.

TIP You can also use the Insert Sheet Rows, Insert Sheet Columns **A**, Delete Sheet Rows, and Delete Sheet Columns **B** commands to modify a table. However, unlike the equivalent Insert Table and Delete Table commands, the Insert Sheet and Delete Sheet commands also affect data *outside* of the table.

TIP You can move a selected table to a new location using cut-and-paste or drag-and-drop. To use cut-and-paste, press Ctrl-X or click Home : Clipboard : Cut. In the destination location, click the cell that will serve as the table's new upper-left corner, and press Enter to perform the paste. To use drag-and-drop, select any cell in the table, and then move the cursor over any corner or edge. When the cursor changes to a plus symbol with arrowheads, click and drag the table to the new location.

Printing Tables

You can print a table as part of the current worksheet. On the other hand, there may be instances when you prefer to print *only* the table—without printing any of the surrounding worksheet cells.

To print a table:

1. Select the table or a cell within the table.

2. Click the File tab.

3. Click Print.

   The Print screen appears.

4. In the Settings area, choose Print Selected Table from the top drop-down menu **A**.

   TIP You can also print a table by preselecting the table on the worksheet and then choosing Print Selection from the same drop-down menu.

5. Change other print settings as desired, such as the orientation and printer.

   As you select and change settings, the print preview changes to reflect the new settings **B**.

6. Click the Print button.

   The table is sent to the designated printer and the worksheet reappears.

Settings

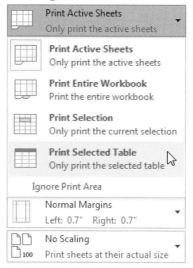

A To print only a selected table, choose Print Selected Table from the drop-down menu.

Print button   Print preview

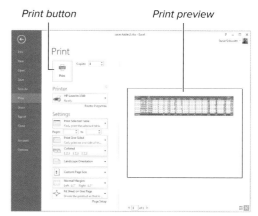

B The print preview reflects the current print settings—in this case, printing only a selected table in landscape mode, scaled to fit on one page.

Creating Charts

In Excel, you can create charts to display your data visually. Although many kinds of charts can be made from tiny data sets, charts are especially useful for presenting and summarizing large quantities of data.

A normal Excel chart is a *floating object*. As such, you can move a chart to any convenient location on the worksheet or change its size by dragging a corner. You can customize almost any part of a chart, such as its title, axis labels, legend, chart wall, or chart floor. You can choose which optional elements to display and which ones to hide, such as data labels, gridlines, or the data itself. Finally, if you aren't satisfied with the current chart style, you can replace it with a variation or a completely different kind of chart.

Excel's charting tools are also used to create charts in PowerPoint, Word, and Outlook. Charts in these non-Excel documents can be *embedded* (static objects that are unlinked from the worksheet data) or *linked* (objects that are linked with the data and automatically reflect changes to it). See Chapter 3 for information on creating charts in other Office applications.

In This Chapter

Chart Elements

Designing a chart is similar to creating art. You can freely add or remove elements, move them to new positions, and change their size, shape, and formatting. (Of course, you're free to accept the default elements and formatting used in a newly created chart, but you're unlikely to do so very often.)

Because you'll spend so much time working with chart elements, it's important that you be able to identify each element **A**. Note that many are optional.

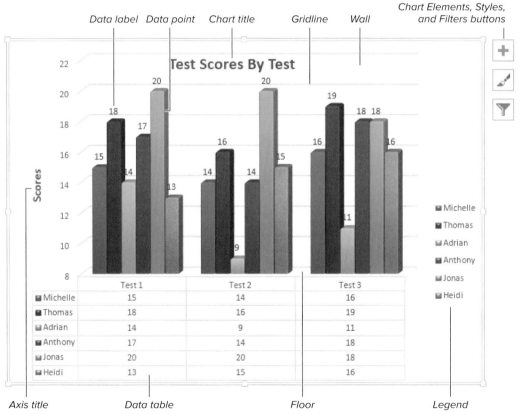

A A typical Excel chart and its elements.

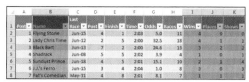

A In this example, column B (labels) and columns I, J, and K (data) have been selected.

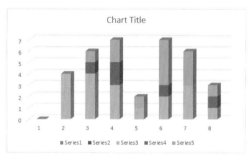

B Specify the chart type by clicking an icon in the Insert:Charts group and choosing a chart style from the drop-down menu that appears.

Chart Title

C Excel adds the chart as a floating object on the worksheet.

Creating a Chart

In many instances, creating a chart is as simple as selecting the labels and data on the worksheet and then picking a chart type. Your chart data can be arranged in columns or rows. However, the columns or rows must be in a specific order for some types of charts.

You can create charts as you did in previous versions of Excel, making all decisions concerning the chart type, elements, and formatting. But if you're new to charting, in a rush, or don't know what chart types are appropriate for your data, Excel 2013 can *recommend* some charts.

To create a chart:

1. If necessary, rearrange the data so it conforms to the chart's requirements.

   For example, to create one type of stock chart, the data must be in High, Low, Close order. For other chart requirements, search for "Available chart types" in Excel Help.

2. *Optional:* Sort the data to ensure that it will be in the desired order when charted.

3. On the worksheet, select the labels and data from which the chart will be created **A**.

   TIP As shown in **A**, the labels and data don't have to be a contiguous range.

4. Choose a chart from an Insert:Charts drop-down menu **B**. Hovering the cursor over a chart style displays a pop-up preview. When you see the type and style of chart you want, click to select it.

   The new chart appears on the sheet **C**.

5. Complete the chart by following the instructions in the rest of this chapter.

To create a recommended chart:

1. Perform Steps 1–3 of "To create a chart" (the previous task list).

2. Click the Insert : Charts : Recommended Charts icon **B**.

   The Insert Charts dialog box appears **D**.

3. *Do one of the following:*

   ▸ Select a chart from the Recommended Charts scrolling list (on the left). A preview appears.

   ▸ To view additional chart types other than the recommended ones, click the All Charts tab. Select a chart type and style, and click the thumbnail of the chart you want **E**.

TIP When the All Charts tab is selected, you can hover the cursor over any thumbnail to see a larger preview.

4. Click the OK button.

   The chart appears on the worksheet as a floating object.

5. As desired, move, modify, and embellish the chart by following the instructions in the rest of this chapter.

TIP To change a chart's type and/or style, select the chart, click Design : Type : Change Chart Type **F**.

TIP To delete a chart, select it and press Del, Delete, or Backspace.

TIP If you select a chart, the labels and data used to create the chart are highlighted in the worksheet. You can also select the data by clicking Design : Data : Select Data **E**.

TIP To change the location of a chart on the worksheet, click and drag.

Chart types   *Preview*

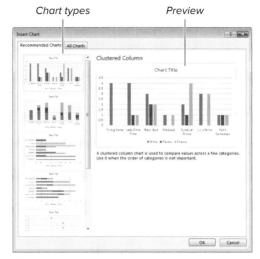

D The Insert Chart—Recommended Charts tab.

Chart types   *Chart Styles*   *Thumbnail*

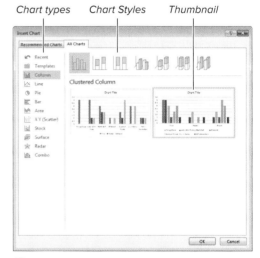

E The Insert Chart—All Charts tab.

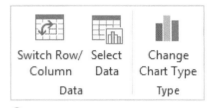

F You can click icons in the Design : Data and Type groups to reveal the chart data or change the chart's type and style.

Format Shape task pane launcher

A You can add an outline, fill, and effects to a selected chart component by selecting options from the Shape Styles group.

Categories   Close

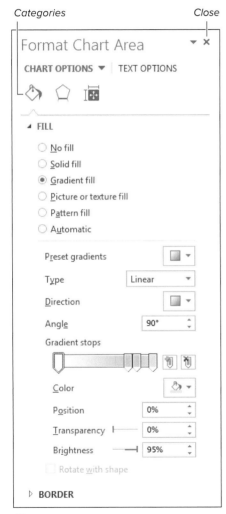

B Select a category and set options to format the currently selected chart component, such as the chart or plot area.

Changing the Background

If you aren't satisfied with the background formatting on a generated chart, you can change it. You can apply formatting to the entire chart, the plot area, or the legend, as well as to objects you've placed on the chart, such as a titles and text boxes.

To change the background for the chart or a component:

1. Select the chart or component that you want to format, such as the chart area, plot area, wall, floor, or legend.

2. *Do one of the following:*

    ▸ Choose formatting options from the Format:Shape Styles group **A**.

    ▸ On the Format or Page Layout tab, click Current Selection:Format Selection. Set formatting options in the Format *item* task pane **B**.

    ▸ Click the Format Shape task pane launcher **A**. Set formatting options in the Format *item* task pane **B**.

    ▸ Right-click the selected area and choose Format *item* from the context menu. Set formatting options in the Format *item* task pane **B**.

TIP To easily select a particular chart element, switch to the Format or Page Layout tab and choose the element from the menu at the top of the Current Selection group. Then click the Format Selection icon in the same group.

TIP You can click the Page Layout:Page Setup:Background icon to use an image as a chart background.

Adding and Formatting Text

Although primarily visual, charts can also include a prodigious amount of text. You can add a title, legend, grid division labels, axis labels, data labels, and text boxes.

To add a text item to a chart:

1. With the chart selected, click the Chart Tools : Design contextual tab.

2. *Do either of the following:*

   ▸ Click the Chart Elements button, and then click the check box of each text item that you want to add .

   ▸ Choose a text element from the Design : Chart Layouts : Add Chart Element submenus.

3. If the text item is represented by a placeholder (such as a chart or axis title), select it and edit the text.

   TIP Newly created charts often include a chart title placeholder that you can edit. See **C** in "Creating a Chart" for an example.

4. To add other text, click Insert : Text : Text Box. Click and drag to create a text box on the chart **B**, and then type or paste the text into the box.

To format chart text:

1. Select the text to be formatted: either the text object or specific text within the object. (Only certain chart objects allow the latter, such as a title, axis label, or text box.)

2. *Do any of the following:*

   ▸ Choose character- and paragraph-formatting commands from the Home : Font and Alignment groups **C**.

Chart Elements button

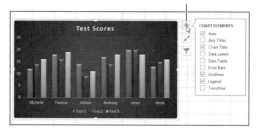

A You can easily add or remove chart elements by clicking check boxes. The chart buttons appear whenever you select the chart.

B After creating a text box, you can type or paste into it.

Font dialog box launcher

C The Home : Font and Home : Alignment groups.

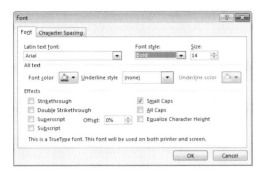

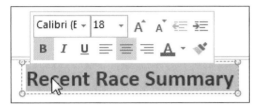

D For complex text-formatting, you may prefer to use the Font dialog box.

E When you select text, the Mini toolbar appears.

F You can apply a variety of text formatting options (including some esoteric ones) in the Format task pane.

‣ For more advanced font settings, click the Font dialog box launcher **C**, or right-click the selected object or text string and choose Font from the context menu. Select formatting options in the Font dialog box **D** and click OK.

‣ With text selected, you can move the cursor up and choose formatting commands from the Mini toolbar **E**.

‣ Choose options from the Format: WordArt Styles group.

TIP If you hover the cursor over a WordArt style in the gallery, a preview of the effect is applied to the currently selected text.

TIP Another way to format a text object is to choose Design:Chart Layouts:Add Chart Element > *text object* > More *text object* Options **A**. A Format *object* task pane **F** appears in which you can apply a background fill, specify a border style and color, add a shadow, format the text, and so on.

To select another text object to format, click the down-arrow beside the *object name* Options text at the top of the task pane.

TIP To remove a text object, select it and press Del, Delete, or Backspace; clear the object's Chart Elements check box **A**; or choose Design: Chart Layouts:Add Chart Element > *text object* > None. For example, to remove the chart title, choose None from the Chart Title submenu.

Rows or Columns

Regardless of how your data is organized on the worksheet, you can plot it by rows or by columns. With many types of charts, plotting it *both* ways can give you a new perspective on the data.

To switch rows and columns:

1. Select the chart.

2. Click Design : Data : Switch Row/Column.

   The chart updates to reflect the change.

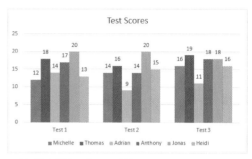

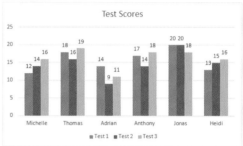 By switching rows and columns, you can see how students compared with one another on each test (top) or how each student scored over the three tests (bottom).

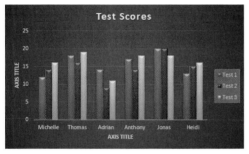

A Choose a new chart layout from the Quick Layout gallery.

B The chart changes to match the chosen layout.

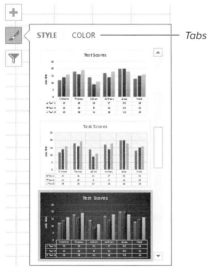

Tabs

C You can change the selected chart's style or color palette.

Changing Layout and Style

One of the simplest ways to modify a chart is to pick a new layout or style. *Layout* refers to the elements appearing on the chart and their positions. *Style* refers to the coloring of chart elements, including the data objects, plot walls, and background.

To specify a new layout:

1. Select the chart.

2. Click an icon in the Design : Chart Layouts : Quick Layout gallery **A**.

   The chart is modified to match the chosen layout **B**.

3. If previously undefined text elements appear in the chart (such as a title or axis titles), you can delete them or edit their placeholder text.

To change the chart style:

1. Select the chart.

2. Choose a different style from the Design : Chart Styles gallery or from the Chart Styles button's Style and Color tabs **C**.

   The chart is modified to match the selected style.

> **TIP** When choosing a new style from the Chart Styles gallery, you can scroll one line of options at a time by clicking the up and down scroll arrows. To view all options simultaneously as a gallery, click the bottom arrow. Hover the cursor over any style to display a preview on the chart.

> **CAUTION** Choosing a new chart style is a *destructive* process. Some elements that you've manually formatted may be replaced with the features specified in the new style.

Displaying the Data Set

If a chart is based on a small data set, it can be informative to show the data table on the chart.

To display the data table on a chart:

1. Select the chart.

2. *Do one of the following:*

   ▸ Click the Chart Elements button, and click the Data Table check box 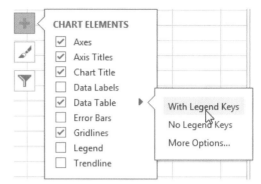. Choose a Legend Keys option from the pop-out menu.

   ▸ Choose a data display option from the Design:Chart Layouts:Add Chart Element > Data Table submenu **B**.

   ▸ From the Design:Chart Layouts:Quick Layout gallery, choose a layout that includes the data table (see **A** in "Changing Layout and Style").

   The data table is added to the chart **C**.

3. If necessary, resize the chart by dragging a corner handle.

> **TIP** To remove the data table, clear the Data Table check box **A**, choose None from the Data Table submenu **B**, or choose a layout from the Chart Layouts:Quick Layout gallery that doesn't include the data table.

> **TIP** Another way to show data is to place it directly on chart items, such as data bars and pie slices. Choose a placement option from the Design:Chart Layouts:Add Chart Element > Data Labels submenu.

A Click the Data Table check box, and then choose a display option from the pop-out menu.

B The same options can be chosen from the Data Table submenu.

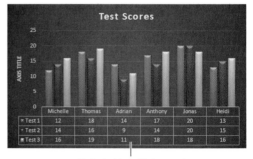

Data table with legend

C The data and legend can be combined (shown here) or displayed as separate chart items.

Test Scores

A Gridlines behind the data can make it easier to see or estimate the size of data points.

B The Gridlines submenu.

C To change the color or style of the major gridlines, you can open this task pane.

Working with Gridlines

To make it easier to estimate the size of data points, you can display horizontal and/ or vertical lines called *gridlines* **A** on many kinds of charts. You can modify gridlines by displaying major, minor, or both types for each axis; and selecting a new line color or style.

To add, remove, or modify gridlines:

1. Select the chart.

2. Choose gridline settings from the Design: Chart Layouts: Add Chart Element > Gridlines submenu **B** or from the Chart Elements button (see **B** in "Displaying the Data Set"). Options include:

   ▸ **Major Gridlines.** Display major data divisions on the chosen axis, such as 1–5 or integers divisible by 5, 10, or 25 (depending on the size and spread of the data).

   ▸ **Minor Gridlines.** Display subdivisions between major gridlines (regardless of whether major gridlines are visible).

   ▸ **More Options/More Gridline Options.** Open the Format Major Gridlines task pane **C** to set color, style, shadow, glow, or soft edges for horizontal or vertical primary gridlines.

> **TIP** Each major and minor gridline option works as a toggle. Choose it a second time to remove the gridline. You can also remove gridlines by selecting them on the chart and pressing Del, Delete, or Backspace.

> **TIP** To simultaneously remove *all* gridlines, click the Chart Elements button and clear the Gridlines check box (see **A** in "Displaying the Data Set").

Working with the Legend

If you select row or column labels when creating a chart, a *legend* (key to the data series) is generally added to the chart 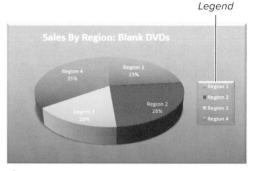. You can add or remove the legend, specify its placement in relation to the chart, change its properties (such as fill color and border style), and edit its labels.

To add, remove, or modify the legend:

1. Select the chart.
2. *Do any of the following:*

   ▸ To add or change the position of the legend, click the Chart Elements button, enable the Legend check box, and choose a position from the pop-out menu **B**. Or choose a position from the Design:Chart Layouts:Add Chart Element > Legend submenu **C**.

   ▸ To manually change the size or position of the legend, drag a handle or the center, respectively.

   ▸ To format the legend, open the Format Legend task pane by choosing More Options **B** or More Legend Options **C**.

> **TIP** You can also open the Legend task pane by double-clicking the legend; right-clicking the legend and choosing Format Legend from the context menu; or selecting the legend and clicking Format:Current Selection:Format Selection.

> **TIP** You don't have to close the Format task pane immediately. To format a *different* chart element, select that element on the chart. The Format task pane changes to one appropriate for the selected element.

Legend

A The legend serves as a key to the chart. Each element in the legend represents a data series.

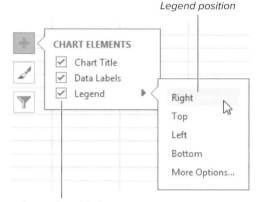

Legend position

Legend enabled

B You can add, remove, or change the placement of the legend by clicking the Chart Elements button.

C You can also add and position the legend by using this submenu.

Objects and Charts

You can embellish your worksheets and charts by inserting objects, such as shapes, pictures, SmartArt, clip art, and screen shots. For instructions on inserting, resizing, moving, and rotating objects, see Chapter 3.

▸ To change the properties (such as the color) of a single data series, select and right-click that element in the legend, choose Format Data Series or Format Legend Entry from the context menu, and make changes in the Format Data Series or Format Legend Entry task pane.

▸ To change the text used for legend entries, make the edits in the worksheet cells that you used as labels.

▸ To remove the legend, select and delete it; click the Chart Elements button and remove the Legend check mark Ⓑ; or choose Design:Chart Layouts:Add Chart Element > Legend > None ⒸC.

Adding Trendlines

If data is gathered over time, you can add lines called *trendlines* that summarize the data and predict future values. Depending on the data set, different trendline types may provide a better fit to the data.

To add a trendline:

1. Select the chart.

2. *Do one of the following:*

   ‣ Choose a trendline type from the Design : Chart Layouts : Add Chart Element > Trendline menu 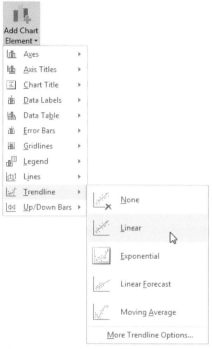.

   ‣ Click the Chart Elements button and click the Trendline check box. To specify a type of trendline other than linear, choose a specific type from the pop-out menu.

   If the chart includes multiple data series, an Add Trendline dialog box appears **B**. Select the data series to which the trendline will be applied and click OK.

   The trendline appears on the chart **C**.

   TIP Adding trendlines is cumulative. That is, you can plot multiple trendlines on the same chart.

A Choose a trendline type from the submenu.

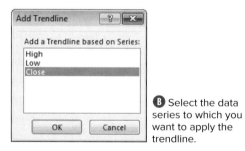

B Select the data series to which you want to apply the trendline.

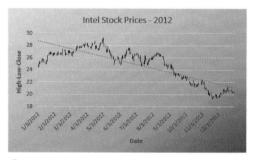

C A stock chart with a linear (straight) trendline.

D Set advanced trendline options in the Format Trendline task pane.

To modify a trendline's type, properties, or style:

1. Open the Format Trendline task pane **D** by doing one of the following:

   ▸ Double-click the trendline.

   ▸ Right-click the trendline and choose Format Trendline.

   ▸ Choose More Trendline Options from the Trendline submenu **A**.

   ▸ Click the Chart Elements button and choose More Options from the Trendline pop-out menu.

2. Make the desired changes. The new settings are reflected on the chart **E**.

TIP To remove all trendlines from a chart, choose **None** from the Trendline drop-down menu **A** or clear the Trendline check box in Chart Elements. To remove *one* trendline (when multiple trendlines are displayed), select the trendline on the chart and press **Del, Delete,** or **Backspace.**

TIP You may also want to explore lines and errors bars. *Lines* show high-low marks (especially useful for stock charts) and/or drop lines that extend up from the X axis to each data point. *Error bars* surround each data point with bars showing a confidence interval based on a percentage, standard deviation, or standard error.

TIP You can add error bars from the **Add Chart Element** menu **A** or the **Chart Elements** button. Lines are available only from the former **A**.

Trendline equation and R² value

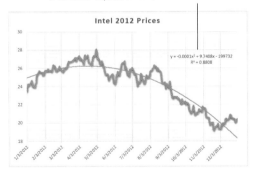

E The revised chart uses a polynomial rather than a linear trendline and displays the equation used to generate the trendline.

Modifying the Axes

Most charts have a horizontal (X) and a vertical (Y) axis. You can modify either axis by changing its labels or formatting.

To modify an axis:

1. Select the chart.

2. *Do any of the following:*

   ▸ To add or remove the major X or Y axis, choose an option from the Design : Chart Layouts : Add Chart Element > Axes submenu or from the Chart Elements button 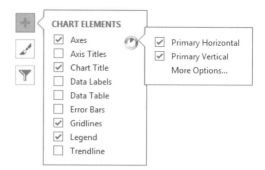.

   ▸ To change the formatting for an axis, double-click the X or Y axis labels on the chart. Make the desired changes in the Format Axis task pane .

   ▸ To change an axis label, edit the label's text in its worksheet cell. You can also modify axis labels in the Select Data Source dialog box. (Click the Design : Data : Select Data icon.)

   ▸ To add a title to the horizontal or vertical axis, choose Design : Chart Layouts : Add Chart Element > Axis Titles > Primary Horizontal or Primary Vertical. (You can also click the Axis Titles check box Ⓐ to enable one or both axis titles.) A title with place-holder text appears on the chart Ⓒ. Edit the placeholder and then change the formatting, if you wish.

Ⓐ You can enable the horizontal and/or vertical axes by clicking their check boxes.

Ⓑ Use the Format Axis task pane to change the maximum and minimum axis values and label positions.

Ⓒ This is a placeholder for the primary horizontal axis title.

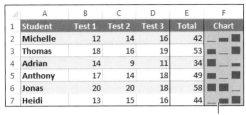

	A	B	C	D	E	F
1	Student	Test 1	Test 2	Test 3	Total	Chart
2	Michelle	12	14	16	42	
3	Thomas	18	16	19	53	
4	Adrian	14	9	11	34	
5	Anthony	17	14	18	49	
6	Jonas	20	20	18	58	
7	Heidi	13	15	16	44	

Sparklines

Ⓐ Column sparklines show the relative size of each student's three test scores.

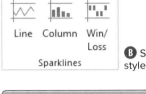

Line   Column   Win/ Loss

Sparklines

Ⓑ Select a sparkline style by clicking its icon.

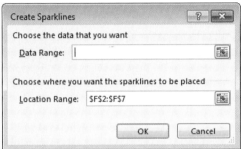

Ⓒ Specify the data range and location range for the sparklines. You can type the two ranges or select them on the worksheet.

Quick Analysis Sparklines

If there's a blank column beside your data range to receive the sparklines, you can create them using Quick Analysis.

1. Select the data range, and then click the Quick Analysis icon that appears beneath the right corner of the range.

2. Select the Sparklines category.

3. Click the sparklines style that you want to use.

Creating Sparklines

Sparklines Ⓐ are tiny charts that summarize data. Unlike normal charts that are floating, resizable objects, sparklines are presented in individual cells, visually linking them with their data.

To add sparklines:

1. Select the data or the target range into which you want to add the sparklines.

2. Click the Insert:Sparklines icon Ⓑ that represents the sparkline style you want to use.

   The Create Sparklines dialog box appears Ⓒ.

3. Fill in the two range text boxes by typing or selecting them on the worksheet.

   If you preselected a range in Step 1, it will already be specified in the dialog box. Edit it, if necessary.

   TIP **The target range does not have to be contiguous to the data. In Ⓐ, for example, it is separated by the Total column.**

4. Click OK.

   The sparklines appear in the designated location range.

TIP **As with other Excel charts, if you edit the data on which sparklines are based, the sparklines automatically update.**

TIP **To change their style, formatting, and other settings, select the sparklines and select options on the Sparkline Tools:Design contextual tab. You can change the formatting of an individual sparkline by selecting only its cell, rather than all sparkline cells.**

TIP **To remove all or selected sparklines, choose a command from the Design:Group: Clear menu.**

Changing the Chart Data

Even if you've created a chart and carefully formatted it exactly the way you wanted, a problem sometimes occurs. The data on which the chart is based changes! A column or row in the data source may need to be deleted, data in one or more cells may need to be edited, or you may want to add more rows or columns.

To modify the chart data:

1. Select the chart.

2. *Do any of the following:*

   ▸ **Edit existing data.** If you edit data in cells on which the chart is based, the chart automatically updates to reflect the revised data.

   ▸ **Delete rows or columns.** If you delete rows or columns within the range(s) used to create the chart, the data is automatically removed from the chart.

   ▸ **Add new rows or columns.** Adding rows or columns within the range of the original chart data triggers an update of the chart.

   To add rows or columns that are immediately *adjacent* to the existing rows, select the chart. This causes the original chart data to be selected on the worksheet. Drag a corner of the data selection rectangle to encompass the new rows or columns 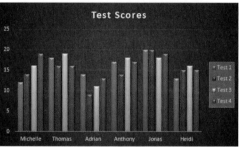.

TIP You can also add new data to a chart by selecting the chart and clicking the Design: Data: Select Data icon. The Select Data Source dialog box appears 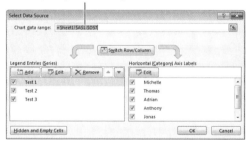. Edit the ranges in the dialog box or select new ones on the sheet, and then click OK.

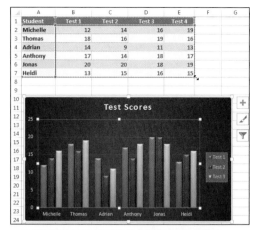

A With the chart selected (top), drag a corner handle of the data selection rectangle to select both the original (B1:D7) and new data (E1:E7). The revised chart and legend reflect the additional data (bottom).

B To change the data on which a chart is based, edit the range(s) in the Select Data Source dialog box or select new range(s) on the worksheet.

Getting Started with PowerPoint 2013

You can use PowerPoint to create presentations for almost any occasion, such as a business meeting, government forum, school project or lecture, church function, or club fund-raiser. A presentation is designed as a slide show and can be based on an included theme, use a company-provided theme, or be created from scratch.

Presentations can feature within-slide animations (such as flying text) and between-slide transitions (such as dissolves). Slides can include embedded movies and audio clips, as well as recorded narration. You can add notes on each slide to use when giving the presentation and to distribute as handouts.

The resulting slide show can be run on your computer, printed, output to transparencies for viewing on an overhead projector, converted to high-quality video, or saved as HTML for viewing in a browser on the web, an intranet, or a recipient's computer.

In This Chapter

PowerPoint Interface

The interface elements you'll use when creating presentations are shown below **A**. Many of them, such as the Ribbon and Quick Access Toolbar, can also be found in Word, Excel, and Outlook.

File tab. Click the File tab to perform file-related actions in the Backstage **B**, such as creating, opening, saving, and printing. Click Options to set PowerPoint preferences. To open a presentation on which you've recently worked, select it in the Open > Recent Presentations list.

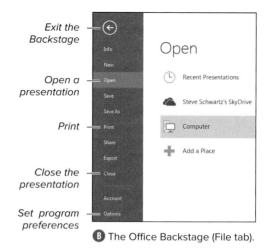

Exit the Backstage

Open a presentation

Print

Close the presentation

Set program preferences

B The Office Backstage (File tab).

File tab *Quick Access Toolbar* *Placeholder* *Tab (Review)* *Group (Drawing)* *Close*

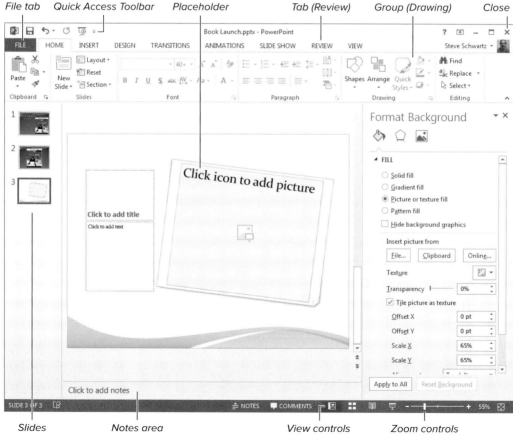

Slides *Notes area* *View controls* *Zoom controls*

A The PowerPoint 2013 interface (Normal view).

1 ☐ **STEVE SCHWARTZ**

Visual QuickStart and
QuickProject Guides
(Peachpit Press)

2 ☐ **Visual QuickProject Titles**

✓ Creating a Database in
FileMaker Pro 8.5
✓ Creating a Database in
FileMaker Pro 8
✓ Creating a Database in
FileMaker Pro
✓ Organizing and Editing
Your Photos with Picasa

3 ☐ **Creating a Database in
FileMaker Pro 8.5**

✓ For Macintosh and
Windows
✓ Available in Adobe PDF
format only

C Use Outline view to rearrange
slides and edit content.

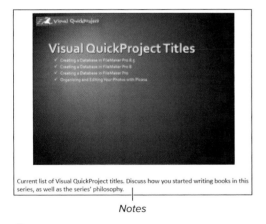

Current list of Visual QuickProject titles. Discuss how you started writing books in this
series, as well as the series' philosophy.

Notes

D When printed, you can use note pages to
assist you in the presentation or distribute them
as handouts. Here's a slide in Notes Page view.

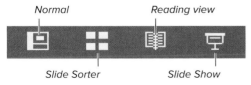

Normal *Reading view*

Slide Sorter *Slide Show*

E You can switch views by clicking an icon at the
bottom of the document window.

Quick Access Toolbar. Icons for performing
common commands, such as Save, Undo,
and Redo, can be found here.

Ribbon. As in Office 2007 and 2010, you
choose commands from the Ribbon rather
than from menus. Similar commands and
procedures are listed together on a *tab*,
such as Insert or View. Within each tab,
procedures are further divided into *groups*,
based on similarity of function. To perform
a command, you switch to the appropriate
tab by clicking its name and then click the
command's icon or control.

Slides. In Normal view **A**, thumbnails of
your slides (in their current order) are displayed. Click a thumbnail to work with that
slide. Click View:Presentation Views:Out-
line View to work with the presentation in
Outline view **C**.

Placeholders. Every PowerPoint theme
contains a predefined set of layouts.
In each slide layout, placeholders are
provided in which you can add your own
formatted text, photos, and so on.

Notes. To assist with a presentation, you
can type notes in this area and print them
out, along with a miniature version of the
slide to which the notes refer **D**.

View controls. Click an icon to switch
views **E**. You can also change views by
clicking an icon in the View:Presentation
Views group.

Zoom controls. Change the magnification by dragging the slider or by clicking +
(Zoom In), – (Zoom Out), the zoom percentage, or the Fit slide to current window icon.

Close. Click the close box to close an open
presentation or to quit PowerPoint. (When
the current presentation is the only one
open, clicking the close box quits Power-
Point.) You can also close a presentation by
clicking Close in the Backstage **B**.

Working in Different Views

Depending on what you want to do at the moment, you'll work in one of PowerPoint's many *views*. To switch views, you can click an icon in the View controls (see 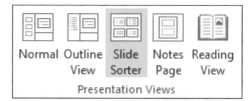 and E in "PowerPoint Interface") or in the View: Presentation Views group A. Because creating a presentation is an interactive process, you'll switch views frequently.

The PowerPoint views are as follows:

- **Normal** and **Outline.** Create, edit, and delete slides (see A and C in "Power-Point Interface").

- **Slide Sorter.** Rearrange, delete, and hide slides B.

- **Notes Page.** Add and edit notes for each slide in a convenient full-screen format (see D in "PowerPoint Interface").

- **Reading View.** Use Reading view to step through a presentation and its animations within the document window. Reading view is also useful when delivering a presentation to someone on their computer. To exit Reading view, press Esc or click a view icon at the bottom of the document window (see E in "PowerPoint Interface").

- **Slide Show.** View the presentation as a full-screen slide show as it will appear to your audience.

- **Slide, Handout, and Notes Masters.** Switch to a Master view to create or modify the underlying theme for slides, note pages, and handouts. For instance, changes made to a master slide (such as setting a different font, size, or color for heading text on a title slide) instantly affect all current and new title slides C.

A Change views by clicking an icon in the View: Presentation Views group.

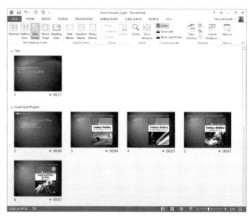

B In Slide Sorter view, a thumbnail of each slide is shown. Rearrange the slides by dragging them to new positions or into other sections.

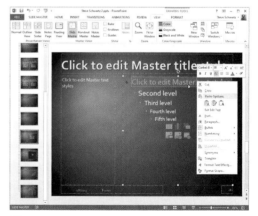

C If you don't care for a particular font, you can change it on its master slide.

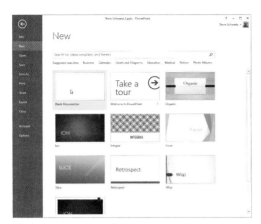

(A) When starting a new presentation, you can create one from scratch or use a template.

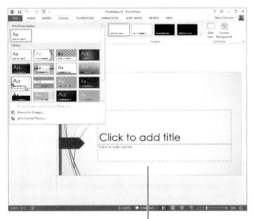

Live theme preview

(B) Pick a theme from the Design:Themes gallery.

Creating a Presentation

If you've never made a PowerPoint presentation, following are the basic steps in the process. Note that many steps, such as creating notes and handouts, are optional. In addition, because presentation design is seldom linear, you can change the step order as your creative flow dictates.

To create a presentation:

1. *Optional:* **Create an outline.** This step can help you decide what to present and the approximate order in which you intend to cover the material.

   You can use Word's Outline view (see Chapter 6) for this task.

2. **Create a new PowerPoint presentation.** *Do one of the following:*

   ▸ If you just launched PowerPoint, select Blank Presentation, select a different theme, or search for a theme or template at Office.com.

   ▸ Click the File tab and then click New in the Backstage. Select Blank Presentation, select a different theme, or search for a template at Office.com **(A)**.

3. **Select a theme.** If a theme wasn't set in Step 2, select a theme from the Design:Themes group **(B)**.

   A theme gives a consistent look to all slides in the presentation.

4. **Create the slides.** From the Home:Slides: New Slide gallery, select a slide style (such as Section Header or Picture with Caption) to add to the presentation. Replace placeholders with appropriate text and pictures.

continues on next page

5. **Add notes.** If you like, you can add comments to the slides to assist you when delivering the presentation. Notes can be entered in Normal or Notes Page view (see Ⓐ and Ⓓ in "Power-Point Interface").

6. **Organize the slides.** In Slide Sorter view (see Ⓑ in "Working in Different Views"), arrange the slides in the order in which you want to present them. Delete or hide unwanted slides.

TIP **PowerPoint allows you to divide lengthy presentations into** *sections*. **Like points in a Word outline, you can collapse selected sections to make it easier to concentrate on one part of the presentation at a time.**

7. **Add within-slide animations.** You can add motion (fly-in or spin, for example) to slide elements, such as text objects and pictures. With the object selected, select effects from the Animations : Animation group Ⓒ.

8. **Add between-slide transitions.** You can also specify visual and/or auditory transition effects that play when you move from one slide to the next. Common transitions include fades, dissolves, and wipes, for example. By choosing effects from the Transitions : Transition to This Slide group Ⓓ, you can set a different transition for each slide or apply the same transition to every slide.

Show gallery

Ⓒ Use the scroll arrows to find an effect or click the bottom arrow to reveal the entire gallery.

Show gallery

Ⓓ You can select a between-slide transition effect for the current slide from the Transition to This Slide gallery.

New Presentation Tips

- To quickly create a blank presentation without switching to the Backstage, press Ctrl-N.

- Regardless of the format intended for a presentation (such as HTML for display in a browser or on the web), you should save the working version in a native PowerPoint format: PowerPoint Presentation or PowerPoint 97-2003 Presentation.

9. **Play and rehearse the presentation.** To play the presentation, switch to Slide Show view or click an icon in the Slide Show: Start Slide Show group. As the show plays, rehearse what you'll say while each slide is onscreen. On the Transitions tab, you can specify that each slide will advance in response to a mouse click or be based on timing established during a rehearsal.

TIP You can also use Reading view to preview and fine tune a presentation.

10. **Print notes and handouts** (if any).

11. **Output the show in its final format.** In addition to playing the slide show on a computer, you can convert it to a movie, save it as a PDF, package it for distribution on CD, save it as a series of JPEG images, or output the show in HTML for viewing in a browser.

TIP When distributing a presentation, your audience doesn't need PowerPoint. They can use the PowerPoint web app to open and view presentations. (Note that a version of PowerPoint Viewer, a free utility for viewing older PowerPoint presentations, doesn't exist for PowerPoint 2013.)

Creating a Presentation

In this chapter, you'll learn the mechanics of creating a presentation and the tools used in the process:

- Starting a new presentation and choosing a theme
- Adding and deleting slides
- Replacing slide placeholders with text, images, charts, tables, and objects
- Adding other types of items to slides, such as shapes, text boxes, date/time stamps, and slide numbers
- Creating a photo album slide show
- Previewing a presentation onscreen as a slide show

For information on working with and formatting slide text and objects (such as pictures, clip art, tables, charts, and text boxes), see Chapter 3.

In This Chapter

Starting a Presentation

As explained in Chapter 13, there are several ways to begin a presentation.

To create a blank presentation (no theme):

■ *Do one of the following:*

  ▶ Launch PowerPoint 2013. On the opening screen **Ⓐ**, click the Blank Presentation thumbnail.

  ▶ With PowerPoint open, press Ctrl-N.

  ▶ Click the File tab. In the Backstage, click New and then click the Blank Presentation thumbnail.

To create a new presentation based on a theme or template:

1. Click the File tab to go to the Backstage, and click New.

2. *Do either of the following:*

  ▶ To base the presentation on a listed theme **Ⓑ**, click its thumbnail, examine the preview that appears, and click Create to generate the presentation.

TIP To view the layouts that a template or theme contains, you can also right-click its thumbnail and choose Preview from the context menu.

  ▶ To base the presentation on an online theme or template, click a category in Suggested searches or enter a search term in the box and click the Search icon (or press Enter).

  If you see a template or theme of interest, click its thumbnail, examine the preview that appears **Ⓒ**, and click Create to download and generate the new presentation.

  The presentation opens in a new window.

Blank Presentation

Ⓐ Click the Blank Presentation thumbnail to create a new presentation without a theme.

Suggested searches   *Search box* *Search icon*

Ⓑ Click a thumbnail, or search for a theme or template at Office.com.

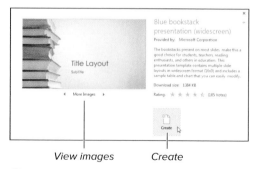

View images   *Create*

Ⓒ Click Create to download the template or theme and generate the presentation.

Save

D You can click the Quick Access Toolbar's Save icon to save the file.

Locations   *Recent Folders*

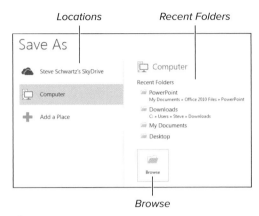

Browse

E Select a location (SkyDrive or Computer) in which to store the file, as well the folder to use.

Active folder

Filename   *File type*   *Save*

F Name the file, specify a file type (such as PowerPoint Presentation or PowerPoint 97-2003 Presentation), and click the Save button.

TIP Regardless of the presentation-creation method you choose, you can change the *theme* applied to the slides. See the next section for instructions on specifying a theme.

To save the new presentation:

1. Any time after generating the new presentation, you can save it to disk by *doing one of the following:*

    ▸ Click the Save icon in the Quick Access Toolbar **D**.

    ▸ Press Ctrl-S.

    ▸ Click the File tab to go to the Backstage, and then click Save or Save As.

    Because this is the file's initial save, the Save As area of the Backstage is automatically displayed **E**.

2. Select a location for the new file by *doing one of the following:*

    ▸ **Save to SkyDrive.** Select *your name* SkyDrive. Then click a recent folder or click Browse to select a different folder.

    ▸ **Save to your computer.** Select Computer. Then click a recent folder or click Browse to select a different folder.

3. In the Save As dialog box **F**, name the new file, select a file type from the Save as Type drop-down menu, and click Save.

TIP If you decide you don't want to keep the presentation, close it without saving.

TIP Periodically, you should save changes made to your presentation. Click the Save icon in the Quick Access Toolbar, click the File tab and select Save, or press Ctrl-S. In each case, the presentation's file is overwritten by the new version and brought up to date.

Setting the Theme

A *theme* provides a consistent background, fonts, colors, and effects for a presentation. If you started with the Blank Presentation (which has no theme) or you want to change the theme, you can select a new theme from the Themes gallery or options from the Variants group.

To apply a theme to a presentation:

- *Do any of the following:*
  - ‣ Select a theme from the Design: Themes gallery 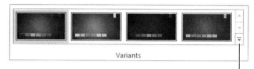.
  - ‣ Select a variant of the current theme by clicking its thumbnail in the Design: Variants group **B**.
  - ‣ Change elements of the current theme by choosing options from the Design: Variants menus (Colors, Fonts, Effects, Background Styles) **C**.

  Each theme and variant displays a *live preview* on the current slide when you hover the cursor over an option. Click a theme or variant to apply it to the presentation.

> **TIP** The sooner in the design process that you finalize your theme choices, the fewer modifications you'll have to make to existing slides.

> **TIP** Open the Format Background task pane if you want to make extensive changes to the theme. Click the Design: Customize: Format Background icon, or open the Design: Variants gallery and choose Background Styles > Format Background **C**. By default, changes made in the task pane apply only to the current slide. To apply them to every slide in the presentation, click the Apply to All button at the bottom of the task pane.

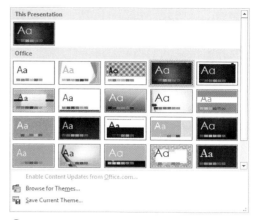

A You can select a new theme from the Themes gallery.

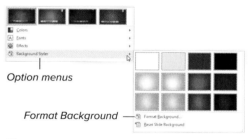

Open Variants gallery and menus

B Some themes also provide variants that you can apply.

Option menus

Format Background

C Open the Variants gallery to change certain theme settings. For greater control, open the Format Background task pane.

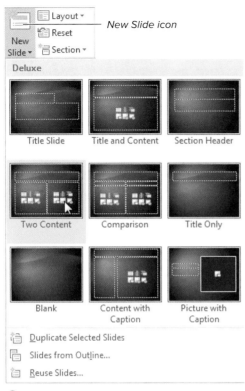

New Slide icon

A Select a layout for the slide you're adding to the presentation.

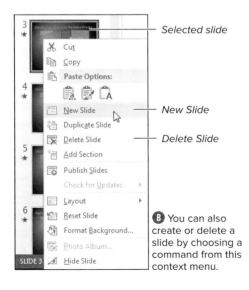

Selected slide

New Slide

Delete Slide

B You can also create or delete a slide by choosing a command from this context menu.

Adding and Deleting Slides

You can add new slides and delete ones that you decide not to use in the presentation.

To add a slide to a presentation:

1. Switch to Normal, Outline, Slide Sorter, or Notes Page view by clicking an icon in the View: Presentation Views group.

2. Select the slide after which you want the new slide to be added.

3. Choose a slide layout from the Home: Slides: New Slide gallery **A**.

   The slide appears after the current slide.

TIP To quickly create a new slide with the same layout as the current slide, press Ctrl-M or right-click the slide's thumbnail and choose New Slide from the context menu **B**.

TIP To modify a slide's layout (changing it from one style to another), switch to Normal, Outline, or Slide Sorter view and choose a layout from the Home: Slides: Layout gallery.

To delete a slide:

1. Switch to Normal, Outline, or Slide Sorter view by clicking an icon in the View: Presentation Views group.

2. *Do either of the following:*

   ▸ Select the slide's thumbnail and press Del.

   ▸ Right-click the slide's thumbnail and choose Delete Slide from the context menu **B**.

   The slide is immediately deleted.

Replacing Placeholders

Most slide layouts contain *placeholders* for text or graphics **A**. To use placeholders, you replace them with your material. Replacing placeholders and other design work is done in Normal or Outline view.

PowerPoint 2013 slides can contain images from your computer and online files. Sources for the latter can include clip art from Office.com, images from your SkyDrive and Flickr accounts, and photos found via a Bing web search.

TIP To remove an unneeded placeholder from a slide, select it and press Del.

TIP To alter the format, appearance, rotation, size, or position of placeholders and other elements (such as background graphics) throughout the presentation, make the changes on the master slides. Changes made to a master title slide, for example, will automatically be applied to all current and new title slides.

To replace a text placeholder:

1. Click a "Click to add title," "Click to add text," or similarly worded placeholder **B**.

   The placeholder text vanishes.

2. Type the text **C**. If additional paragraphs are needed, press Enter to begin each new paragraph.

To replace a picture placeholder:

1. Click the picture placeholder icon **A**.

   An Insert Picture dialog box appears **D**.

2. Navigate to the folder on your computer that contains the picture, select the file, and click Insert.

   The picture appears in the placeholder.

TIP If desired, you can resize or rotate the image by dragging its handles.

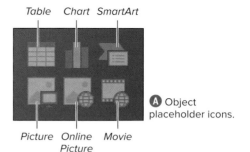

Table   *Chart*   *SmartArt*

Picture   *Online Picture*   *Movie*

A Object placeholder icons.

Subtitle text placeholder

Title text placeholder

B This title slide has two text placeholders.

Visual QuickStart Guides (Peachpit Press)

STEVE SCHWARTZ

C The replacement text adopts the character and paragraph formatting of the placeholder text.

D Select an image from your hard drive and click the Insert button.

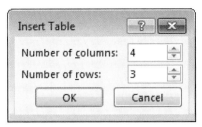

E Set the number of columns and rows.

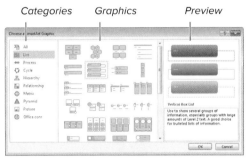

F A table with the specified number of columns and rows appears.

Categories   *Graphics*   *Preview*

G Select a SmartArt graphic from the center of the dialog box and click OK.

To replace a table placeholder:

1. Click the table placeholder icon **A**.

   The Insert Table dialog box appears **E**.

2. Enter the number of columns and rows for the table, and then click OK.

   The new table appears **F**.

3. Complete the table by entering labels and data.

To replace a SmartArt placeholder:

1. Click the SmartArt placeholder icon **A**.

   The Choose a SmartArt Graphic dialog box appears **G**.

2. Select a graphic category from the list on the left, select a graphic from the center of the dialog box, and click OK.

   The SmartArt graphic appears in the image placeholder.

3. Replace the text and image placeholders in the SmartArt graphic with your own text and images.

4. *Optional:* Choose options on the Smart-Art Tools : Design and Format contextual tabs **H** to change the style and colors of the SmartArt graphic.

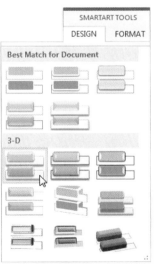

H You can alter the SmartArt by choosing a new style and colors.

To replace a chart placeholder:

1. Click the chart placeholder icon **A**.

   The Insert Chart dialog box appears **I**.

2. Select a chart category.

3. Click the icon that represents the style of chart that you want to create, and click OK.

   TIP You can get a larger preview of the selected chart style by hovering the cursor over its preview.

   An Excel worksheet containing sample data appears **J**.

4. Replace the chart labels and data with your information. To change the chart range (adding or removing columns and/or rows), drag the lower-right corner of the range. As you make edits, the changes are instantly reflected on the chart. Click the worksheet's close box (X) when you're done entering data.

5. *Optional:* With the chart or any part of it selected on the slide, Chart Tools contextual tabs (Design and Layout) appear. You can choose commands from these tabs (or from the Chart buttons **K**) to modify the chart type, layout, and formatting.

Categories   Styles   Preview

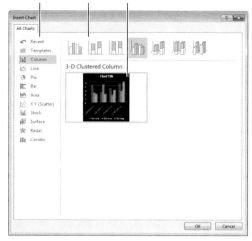

I Select a chart style from the Insert Chart dialog box. Click OK.

Close

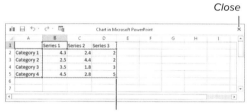

Drag to resize

J Replace the sample data and labels, and resize the range as necessary.

Buttons

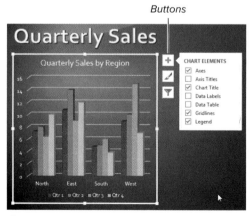

K You can fine-tune the chart's elements and appearance.

Flickr

L Specify an image source and select the image that you want to use.

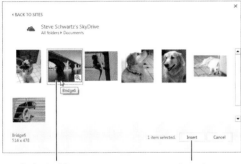

Selected image   *Insert*

M Select an image and click the Insert button.

N Video clips from a variety of sources can be inserted onto slides.

To replace an online picture placeholder:

1. Click the online picture placeholder icon **A**.

   The Insert Pictures dialog box appears **L**.

2. Search Office.com or the web by entering a search string in the appropriate text box and pressing Enter. To insert one of your own online images, click the SkyDrive or Flickr button.

3. Select the image and click Insert **M**.

   The image appears in the placeholder.

TIP If desired, you can resize or rotate the image by dragging its handles.

To replace a movie placeholder:

1. Click the movie placeholder icon **A**.

   The Insert Video dialog box appears **N**.

2. *Do one of the following:*

   ▸ **From a file.** To insert a video that's stored on your computer or network, click the Browse button. Navigate to the folder that contains the movie clip, select the file, and click Insert.

   ▸ **Bing Video Search or YouTube.** Type a search string in the text box and press Enter to search the web or YouTube for clips. In the results list, select a thumbnail and click Insert.

   ▸ **SkyDrive.** Click Browse, select a video clip from the ones stored on your SkyDrive, and click Insert.

   ▸ **From a Video Embed Code.** Paste the "embed code" for the video clip (provided by the web site) into the text box and press Enter. (Note that some embed code styles don't work.)

   The movie appears in the placeholder.

Inserting Other Items

In addition to replacing placeholders with objects or text, you can place items *any-where* on a given slide by choosing commands from the Insert tab  (below). To position an inserted item, click a location on the slide or drag the item into position.

To insert a table, picture, clip art, SmartArt, chart, or movie clip, see the instructions in "Replacing Placeholders." For instructions on inserting screen shots, see Chapter 3.

To insert a shape:

1. Choose a shape from the Insert:Illustrations:Shapes gallery **B**.

2. Click and drag to draw the shape on the slide.

3. *Optional:* To change the shape's color and formatting, choose settings from the Format:Shape Styles group **C**.

4. *Optional:* To add text inside the shape, *do either of the following:*

   ▸ Right-click the shape and choose Edit Text from the context menu.

   ▸ Click the Insert:Text:Text Box icon and then click inside the shape to set the text insertion mark.

   Type and format the text **D**.

B Choose a shape from the Shapes gallery.

C To change the formatting for a shape, you can choose options from the Shape Styles group.

D Many shapes can optionally contain text.

A You can add text and objects anywhere on a slide by choosing commands from the Insert tab.

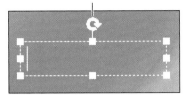

Rotation handle

E This new text box is ready to receive typed or pasted text.

Font dialog box launcher   *Paragraph dialog box launcher*

F Common character and paragraph formatting commands are available on the Home tab.

G To create stylized text (stand-alone or inside an object), you can choose options from the WordArt Styles group.

Replacing a Shape

Sometimes after carefully formatting and adding text to a shape, the shape just doesn't "work." Rather than create another shape and add the same text and formatting, you can replace the original shape with a new one—while retaining the original formatted text.

1. On the slide, select the shape that you want to replace.

2. Choose Format : Insert Shapes : Edit Shape > Change Shape, and select a replacement shape from the gallery.

To insert a text box:

1. Click the Insert : Text : Text Box icon.

   A text box insertion cursor appears.

2. Click where you want to add the text or drag to set the box's approximate dimensions **E**.

3. Type the text. Press Enter to begin each additional paragraph.

4. *Optional:* Change the text formatting by performing any of these actions:

   ▸ **Character/Paragraph Format.** Set new character and paragraph formatting by choosing commands from the Home : Font and Paragraph groups **F** or from the Mini toolbar.

   ▸ **Rotate.** Click the rotation handle **E** and drag to the left or right to change the text's angle.

   ▸ **Stylize.** Choose options from the Format : WordArt Styles group **G**.

   ▸ **Wrap.** Reduce or increase the width of the text box by dragging the center handle on either side. The text within the box will automatically rewrap as required.

5. *Optional:* Reposition the text by moving the cursor over any edge. When a plus cursor appears, you can drag the text box to a new location.

To add a slide number or date/time:

1. Click the Insert : Text : Header & Footer, Date & Time, or Slide Number icon .

   The Header and Footer dialog box appears ⓘ. Click the Slide tab.

2. To number the slides consecutively, click the Slide number check box.

3. To display the date, time, or both, click the Date and time check box, and *do one of the following:*

   ▸ To always display the current date and/or time, click Update automatically and select a date/time format from the drop-down list.

   ▸ To stamp the slide(s) with the current date/time, click Fixed and enter the text to display, such as **8/23/2013**.

4. *Optional:* To prevent the slide number and date information from being shown on title slides, click the Don't show on title slide check box.

5. *Do one of the following:*

   ▸ To add the specified information to all slides in the presentation, click Apply to All ⓘ.

   ▸ To add the specified information only to the current slide, click Apply ⓘ.

> **TIP** You can enter *any* text that you want in the Fixed text box. You aren't restricted to date and time information.

> **TIP** To add text that will be centered in the footer (between the date/time and slide number), click the Footer check box and type the text in the box.

Ⓗ Open the Header and Footer dialog box by clicking the Header & Footer, Date & Time, or Slide Number icon.

Placement preview

Ⓘ Set date/time and numbering options, and then click Apply or Apply to All.

References to External Media

If you embed online pictures, video, or other media in a presentation, a security warning will appear the next time you open the presentation. Click the Enable Content button to allow the online content to be fetched from the Internet.

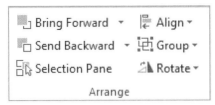

Selected object   *Selection task pane*

Ⓑ Use the Selection task pane to easily select objects on cluttered slides.

Matching Colors

If you'd like the color of a shape, photo, or other object to precisely match that of a shade of blue found in a photo or other item on the slide, you can use Power-Point's new eyedropper tool to "pick up" the color that you want to match.

1. Select the object or photo that you want to color.

2. Choose Format:Adjust:Color:More Variations > Eyedropper, Format: Shape Styles:Shape Fill > Eyedropper, or a similar command.

3. Move the eyedropper over the slide until the desired color is found and then select it by clicking the mouse.

    The color is transferred to the selected shape or photo.

Tips for Working with Objects

Here are a few tips that you may find help-ful when working with objects on slides:

■   Inserted objects can be laid over one another. For example, you can combine shapes to create an illustration. After combining objects in this manner, you can *group* them to prevent individual items from accidentally being moved.

Select the objects that you want to group. Then choose Format:Arrange: Group > Group Ⓐ or Home:Drawing: Arrange > Group.

■   To change the layering of objects, select an object and choose a command (such as Send to Back) from the Format: Arrange group menus Ⓐ. Layering commands are also available on the Home:Drawing:Arrange menu.

■   When moving an object, faint red guidelines appear whenever it's aligned with an edge or center of another object. You can also align selected objects by choosing a command from the Format: Arrange:Align menu Ⓐ.

■   For help selecting objects, open the Selection task pane Ⓑ by *doing one of the following:*

▶   Click the Format:Arrange:Selection Pane icon Ⓐ.

▶   Choose Home:Drawing:Arrange > Selection Pane.

▶   Choose Home:Editing:Select > Selection Pane.

Click an item in the task pane to select it on the slide, regardless of the item's layer and whether it's visible or buried under other items.

Creating a Photo Album

A *photo album* is a special presentation you can create to present a slide show of personal or business photos.

To create a photo album:

1. Choose Insert : Images : Photo Album > New Photo Album.

   The Photo Album dialog box appears **A**.

2. To add photos, click the File/Disk button.

   The Insert New Pictures dialog box appears.

3. Navigate to the folder that contains the photos. *Do one of the following:*

   ▸ To add a single photo, click its icon.

   ▸ To simultaneously add multiple photos from the folder, Ctrl-click each file.

   ▸ To simultaneously add all image files from the folder, select any photo and then press Ctrl-A to select them all.

4. If the Insert New Pictures dialog box is still present, click the Insert button.

   The selected photo(s) are added to the Pictures in album list **B**.

5. As necessary, repeat Steps 2–4 to add more photos. To remove a photo, select it in the Pictures in album list by clicking its check box and click Remove **C**.

6. *Optional:* The order of photos in the Pictures in album list will match the slide order. To change a photo's position in the list, click its check box, and click an arrow button beneath the list **C**.

7. *Optional:* You can modify the rotation, contrast, or brightness of a checked photo by clicking icons beneath the preview area **C**.

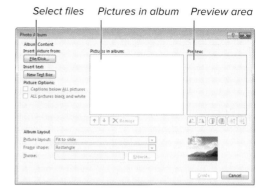

Select files   Pictures in album   Preview area

A The Photo Album dialog box.

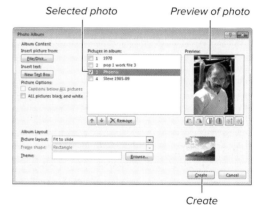

Selected photo   Preview of photo

Create

B Photos are added to Pictures in album in the order in which they're inserted.

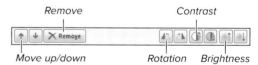

Remove   Contrast

Move up/down   Rotation   Brightness

C Click icons below the preview to change the position, rotation, contrast, and brightness of the selected photo.

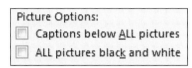

D Select a slide layout in the Album Layout section of the Photo Album dialog box.

Picture Options:
- ☐ Captions below ALL pictures
- ☐ ALL pictures black and white

E If desired, each slide can display a caption and the photos can be presented in black-and-white.

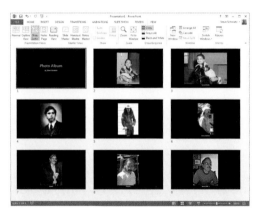

F The new photo album (in Slide Sorter view).

Duplicating Slides

After you've created several slides, one of the fastest ways to move the creation process along is to duplicate slides and then edit the duplicates—rather than designing each new slide from scratch.

To duplicate a slide, select its thumbnail in the current view, such as Normal, Outline, or Slide Sorter view. Then choose Home : Slides : New Slide > Duplicate Selected Slides.

8. In the Album Layout area of the dialog box **D**, select a layout from the Picture layout drop-down list.

If you select a "with title" layout, every slide will contain a text placeholder.

9. If you chose any layout other than Fit to slide in Step 8, you can select a frame from the Frame shape drop-down list.

A preview of the selected Picture layout and Frame shape settings is shown to the right.

10. *Optional:* To apply a theme to the slides, click the Browse button. Select a Power-Point theme in the Choose Theme dialog box and click Open.

11. *Optional:* In the Picture Options area of the dialog box **E**, click check boxes to add a caption and/or display the photos in black and white.

By default, the photo's filename is used as its caption. You can edit the captions after the slides have been generated.

12. Click the Create button **B**.

PowerPoint creates a presentation from the selected photos **F**.

13. *Optional:* Edit the album title on slide 1.

14. To save the presentation, click the Save icon on the Quick Access Toolbar, press Ctrl-S, or select the File tab and click Save or Save As in the Backstage.

TIP You can treat the photo album as a finished presentation or enliven it by adding PowerPoint features such as animations, transitions, and audio.

TIP After generating the presentation, you can change its settings or add new photos by choosing Insert : Images : Photo Album > Edit Photo Album. Make the desired changes in the Edit Photo Album dialog box and click Update.

Previewing a Slide Show

Every slide show is a work in progress. As such, you'll want to periodically preview it to check the effect of changes, the application of special effects, the addition of new slides, and so on.

To preview a slide show:

1. *Optional:* To begin the slide show with a particular slide (other than the first), select or switch to that slide.

   You can select a slide in Normal, Outline, Slide Sorter, or Notes Page view.

2. *Do one of the following:*

   ▸ To run the show starting with the first slide, press F5.

   ▸ To run the show starting with the current slide, press Shift-F5.

   ▸ Click Slide Show : Start Slide Show : From Beginning or From Current Slide .

   The show begins .

3. *Do any of the following:*

   ▸ To step forward through the slides and within-slide animations (if any), click the mouse or press n (for next), Enter, Page Down, Spacebar, right arrow, or down arrow.

   ▸ To move backward through the slides and within-slide animations (if any), press p (for previous), Page Up, Backspace, left arrow, or up arrow.

   ▸ To end the show, press Esc.

TIP You can also navigate by clicking the onscreen controls in the bottom-left corner ⓒ.

From Beginning   From Current Slide

ⓐ If you can't remember the keyboard shortcuts, you can start the show by clicking one of these icons.

ⓑ The slide show runs in full-screen mode.

Previous slide

Next slide

ⓒ If you move the cursor during the slide show, these controls appear.

Using Reading View

Another way to preview a slide show—but restrict its size to the PowerPoint window rather than use the entire screen—is to switch to Reading view. You can advance through slides and animations using the same keystrokes that apply to a normal slide show. To exit Reading view, press Esc or click the Normal or Slide Sorter view icon in the status bar.

Wrapping Up a Presentation

In this chapter, you'll learn about putting the finishing touches on a presentation:

- Add within-slide animations, between-slide transitions, and action buttons

- Make minor edits to movies that you've placed on slides

- Rearrange slides to match their final order, as well as delete and hide slides

- Rehearse the presentation while recording the time spent on each slide and on the total presentation

- Print notes, handouts, and other material you'll need for the presentation

- Save the presentation in other formats (such as PDF) and package its contents on a CD or DVD

- Present the slide show in person or broadcast it over the Internet

TIP To run a finished presentation, follow the steps in "Previewing a Slide Show" in Chapter 14.

Animating Objects and Text

To add motion to a presentation, you can animate any object on a slide, such as a text block, picture, chart, or SmartArt object. You can choose animation effects from the Animation or Add Animation gallery. You can fine-tune an effect by choosing commands from the Animations tab or the Animation Pane. A slide can contain multiple animated objects. You can even assign multiple animations to the same object.

To assign an animation to an object:

1. In Normal view, select the object on the current slide that you want to animate.

   TIP To set an effect for multiple objects that will all play simultaneously, select all of the objects and then choose the effect.

2. Choose an effect from the Animations : Animation gallery **Ⓐ** (bottom).

   The effect plays and a number appears beside the object that shows the order in which the effect will play **Ⓑ**.

   TIP To view additional effects, choose a More... command from the Animation gallery or Add Animation drop-down menu.

3. *Optional:* To add another effect to the object, choose it from the Animations : Advanced Animation : Add Animation gallery.

Animation number

Ⓑ Each animation is numbered to show the order in which it will play.

More

Ⓐ View different animation effects by clicking the scroll arrows or click More to see the entire gallery.

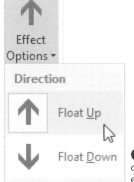

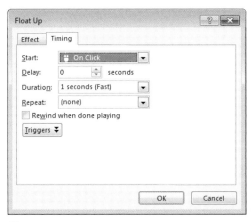

C When available, options differ for each effect.

D You set options for a selected effect in an effect-specific dialog box. You can associate a sound or timing with the effect, for example.

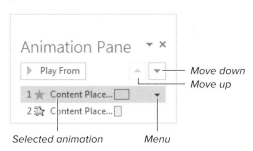

Selected animation   Menu

E Use the Animation Pane to select the animation that you want to modify, move, or remove.

To set options for an effect:

1. In Normal view, select the Animations tab. On the slide, select the number of the animation effect you want to modify.

2. *Do any of the following:*

   ▸ Choose an option from the Effect Options menu **C**.

   ▸ Click the dialog box launcher icon at the bottom of the Animation group and set options in the dialog box that appears **D**.

   ▸ Open the Animation Pane task pane **E** by clicking the Animations : Advanced Animation : Animation Pane icon. In the pane, select the animation that you want to modify. Then choose an option from the Effect Options menu, click the Effect Options dialog box launcher, or choose Effect Options from the drop-down menu to the right of the object name.

To change animation playback order:

1. Open the Animation Pane task pane **E** by clicking the Animations : Advanced Animation : Animation Pane icon.

2. In the pane, select the effect that you want to move, and then *do any of the following:*

   ▸ Drag the effect up or down to a new position in the list.

   ▸ Click a Move icon at the top of the pane **E**.

   ▸ Click Animations : Timing : Reorder Animation : Move Earlier or Move Later.

continues on next page

3. To remove an animation from a selected object, *do one of the following:*

   ▸ Click None in the Animation gallery 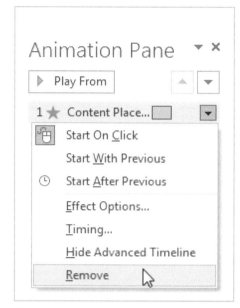.

   ▸ Choose Remove from the effect's drop-down menu in the Animation Pane **F**.

   ▸ Select the effect in the Animation Pane or select the effect's number on the slide, and then press Delete.

TIP Even information in the footer, such as the slide number, can be animated.

TIP To apply one object's animations to another object, select the object with the animation(s) that you want to copy, click the Animations:Advanced Animation:Animation Painter icon **G**, and click the target object.

TIP When animating a complex object composed of multiple elements, such as a SmartArt graphic or chart, you can animate it as though it were a single object, one element or item type at a time, and so on.

TIP To replace one animation with another, select the effect step for the object in the Animation Pane and choose a replacement effect from the Animation gallery **A**.

TIP You can view a slide's animations by clicking the Animations:Preview:Preview icon or by clicking the Play All/Play From button in the Animation Pane **F**. (Play All is available only when no animation is selected in the pane. Play From, on the other hand, appears when an animation is selected in the pane. It plays that animation, as well as all that follow.)

TIP Don't overuse animations. A few can draw attention to key elements on important slides; too many can turn a presentation into a carnival sideshow.

F To remove an effect, you can select it in the Animation Pane and choose Remove from the effect's drop-down menu.

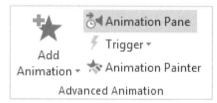

G Use the Animation Painter tool to copy animations from one object to another.

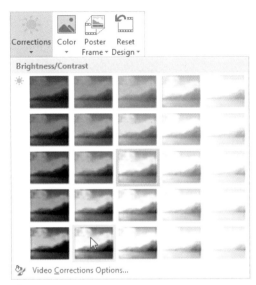

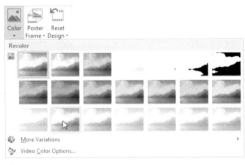

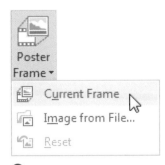

<A> You can alter the brightness/contrast of a movie by choosing a thumbnail from the Corrections gallery.

<B> Open the Color gallery to alter the color cast of the selected movie.

<C> You can set a poster frame for a video.

Editing Movies

Using tools introduced in Office 2010, you can edit videos. When you select a movie on the current slide, the Video Tools contextual tab appears. You can choose new settings from its Format and Playback tabs.

Format Contextual Tab Tools

Using commands on the Video Tools : Format tab, you can perform the following edits on a selected movie clip:

- **Correct brightness/contrast.** Choose a brightness/contrast thumbnail from the Adjust : Corrections gallery <A>. For more precise settings, choose Video Corrections Options from the bottom of the gallery menu.

- **Recolor movies.** To display the video in *grayscale* (shades of gray) or with an overall color cast, choose a thumbnail from the Adjust : Color gallery <B>. Choose More Variations if you want to use a color that isn't shown.

- **Set a poster frame.** A *poster frame* is an image used to represent the movie when it's not playing. Advance the movie to the desired frame and choose Adjust : Poster Frame > Current Frame <C>. (If you prefer, you can use a picture from your hard disk as the poster frame by choosing Image from File.)

- **Add a border or frame.** If you want to surround the movie with a border or stylized frame, you can select an option from the Video Styles gallery; choose settings from the Video Styles : Video Border menu; or click the Format Video task pane launcher (found at the bottom of the Video Styles group) and select settings from the first two categories: Fill & Line and Effects.

continues on next page

- **Resize movies.** You can resize the movie frame by *doing any of the following:*
  - ▸ Click a corner and drag.
  - ▸ Type new numbers or click the arrows in the Size: Video Height and Video Width boxes **D**.
  - ▸ Click the Format Video task pane launcher **D** and enter specific dimensions or scaling percentages.

- **Reset formatting.** To remove all applied formatting changes and/or reset the frame size, choose a command from the Adjust: Reset Design menu **A**.

TIP Other than selecting a poster frame to ensure that a consistent image appears when the slide is first presented, it's unlikely that you'll use many of the commands on the Format tab to modify the appearance of your movies.

Playback Tab Tools

Using commands on the Video Tools: Playback tab, you can specify how a selected movie clip will play during the presentation:

- **Trim videos.** Click Editing: Trim Video to remove unwanted frames from the start or end of a video clip. In the Trim Video dialog box **E**, drag the green start marker and/or the red end marker to new positions, and then click OK.

- **Add/remove bookmarks.** You can mark key points in a movie by assigning *bookmarks* to them. Bookmarks enable you to jump directly to a frame or can be used to trigger animations.
  - ▸ To add a bookmark, drag the movie slider to the desired spot and then click Bookmarks: Add Bookmark **F**.
  - ▸ To delete an unwanted bookmark, select its icon on the movie slider **G** and click Remove Bookmark **F**.

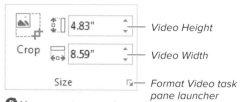

Video Height

Video Width

Format Video task pane launcher

D You can set a new size for a movie by entering dimensions in these boxes.

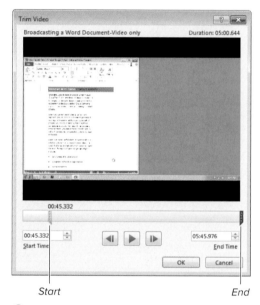

Start   *End*

E Drag the start and/or end markers to new positions to cut out unwanted frames. As you drag, a live preview of the movie is shown.

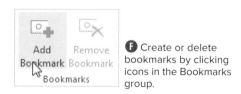

F Create or delete bookmarks by clicking icons in the Bookmarks group.

Selected bookmark

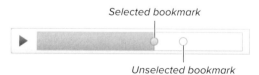

Unselected bookmark

G Each bookmark is a circle. A selected bookmark is yellow; unselected ones are empty.

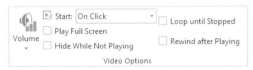

You can apply a Fade In or Fade Out to a movie clip.

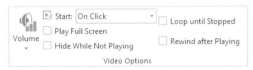 You can apply additional settings from the Video Options group.

Embedded vs. Linked Videos

Normally, inserted movies are embedded in the presentation. The video is saved with the PowerPoint file, ensuring that it will always be available whenever and wherever the show is presented. Another option is to *link* the movie to the presentation—using either a movie from a web site or a file on disk. To play such a movie, you must have access to the Internet or to the file's location, such as a flash drive or DVD.

To link a movie file, select a slide placeholder, and choose Insert:Media:Video > Online Video or Video on My PC. If you choose the former, you'll be asked to paste the "embed code" provided by the web site.

- **Fade In or Fade Out.** You can instruct a movie to smoothly fade in or out by entering numbers (in whole and fractional seconds) in the Editing:Fade Duration boxes ⒣.

- **Other playback options.** The self-explanatory tools in the Video Options group ⒤ are used to set key playback behaviors, such as audio volume, whether the clip will play automatically or wait for a mouse click, and so on.

TIP You can remove inserted videos that you no longer want. Select the video on the slide and press Delete or Del.

TIP To reduce the size of all embedded videos in a presentation, click the File tab. Select the Info category and choose a quality setting from the Compress Media drop-down menu. View the results by running the show. If you aren't satisfied, you can undo or change the compression by revisiting the Compress Media command.

Organizing the Slides

In Slide Sorter view , you can rearrange the slides to match their final order. You can also delete unwanted slides, as well as hide ones that you want to keep but won't be using in the current presentation.

To organize the slides:

1. Switch to Slide Sorter view by clicking its icon in the View:Presentation Views group or on the status bar.

2. Adjust the magnification to clearly display the slide thumbnails.

3. *Do any of the following:*

   ▸ To change a slide's order in the show, drag its thumbnail to a new position.

   ▸ To delete a slide, right-click its thumbnail and choose Delete Slide from the context menu **B**.

   ▸ To hide a slide, right-click its thumbnail and choose Hide Slide from the context menu **B**. The slide number shows a slide's hidden status **C**. In Normal and Slide Sorter view, hidden slides' thumbnails are fuzzy.

TIP If you need to modify a slide, double-click its thumbnail. The slide appears in Normal view, ready for editing.

TIP You can play a slide's animations in Slide Sorter view by clicking the animation indicator beneath the thumbnail.

TIP You can also organize slides in Normal view. To change a slide's position, drag its thumbnail to a new location in the list. To delete or hide a slide, right-click its thumbnail and choose Delete Slide or Hide Slide from the context menu.

Magnification controls

A Slide Sorter view.

B Right-click a thumbnail to delete or hide a slide.

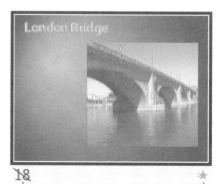

Hidden slide indicator   *Play animations*

C When a slide is hidden, its thumbnail is hazy and the slide number is slashed.

Effect Options

More

Ⓐ Select a transition effect from the gallery.

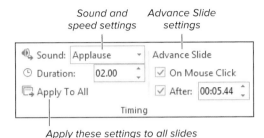

Sound and speed settings *Advance Slide settings*

Timing

Apply these settings to all slides

Ⓑ You can set other options in the Timing group.

What About Sections?

Although we've gotten along without them for 20+ years, PowerPoint 2010 and 2013 allow you to group your slides into logical *sections*. Because you can expand or collapse a section in Normal or Slide Sorter view, sections are especially useful for focusing on specific parts of a large presentation.

To insert a section, select the slide that will be the first one in the new section and choose Home : Slides : Section > Add Section. To name the section, right-click its current name (*Untitled Section*) and choose Rename Section from the context menu.

You can collapse or expand a section by clicking the triangle that precedes the section name. To simultaneously collapse or expand *all* sections, right-click any section name and choose Collapse All or Expand All from the context menu.

Adding Transitions

A *transition* is an effect that appears when switching to a new slide during a show. You can use the same transition for every slide change, different transitions for different slides, or no transitions at all. When setting transitions, note that they are applied to the current slide's *entrance*—not its exit.

To specify a transition:

1. In Normal or Slide Sorter view, select the slide thumbnail to which you want to add a transition.

2. Choose an effect from the Transitions : Transition to This Slide gallery **Ⓐ**. (Click the More icon to view the entire gallery or click the up and down arrows to scroll by row.)

   The transition effect plays.

3. *Optional:* To change the direction of the effect, choose an option from the Effect Options menu **Ⓐ**.

   Effect options differ for different effects.

4. *Optional:* To add a sound effect to the transition, choose one from the Transitions : Timing : Sound menu **Ⓑ**. To change the length of the transition effect, enter a new Duration (in seconds).

5. Select an Advance Slide option **Ⓑ** to determine whether the slide will advance manually (under presenter control) or automatically (based on time).

6. *Optional:* To apply the transition to every slide in the presentation, click Apply To All.

TIP To view transitions in Normal or Slide Sorter view, click the Transitions : Preview : Preview icon.

continues on next page

TIP Transitions can be skipped if you won't be presenting on a computer—when using physical slides or an overhead projector, for example.

TIP To change a transition effect and options for a slide, select the slide and select new settings from the Transitions tab (Ⓐ and Ⓑ).

TIP To remove a transition from a selected slide, select the None transition from the Transition to This Slide gallery. To remove transitions from *all* slides, set any slide's transition to None and then click Transitions : Timing : Apply to All. (Note that this also has the effect—good or bad—of applying the current slide's timing settings to all slides, too.)

TIP In addition to applying the same transition settings to every slide in a presentation, you can apply these settings to a selected group of slides. In Slide Sorter view, select the slides by Ctrl-clicking each one, and then set the transition settings. Only the selected slides will be affected.

Adding Action Buttons

An *action button* is a shape you can place on a slide that performs a function when clicked, such as returning to the first slide, playing a sound effect, or launching an application.

To add an action button to a slide, switch to Normal view. Choose a button from the Action Buttons section of the Home : Drawing gallery or the Insert : Illustrations : Shapes gallery. Click and drag to draw the button on the slide. (To keep the button proportional to its original dimensions, press Shift as you drag.) Like other objects, you can move, resize, or format an action button.

In the Action Settings dialog box Ⓒ, specify the action that you want the button to perform in response to a mouse click or *mouse over* (moving the mouse over the button). Close the Action Settings dialog box by clicking OK.

Ⓒ On the Mouse Click or Mouse Over tab, specify a button action and click OK.

Time for current slide   *Total time*

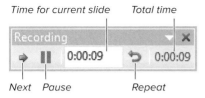

Next   Pause   Repeat

A Use the Recording toolbar to view slide timings, pause the show, or perform the next action.

B A Next button can also be found on the pop-up toolbar in the bottom-left corner of the screen.

Microsoft PowerPoint

The total time for your slide show was 0:01:45. Do you want to save the new slide timings?

Yes   No

C If the rehearsal went well, you can save the slide timings for use during the presentation.

Using the Saved Timings

To replay a presentation using the saved timings, click the Slide Show:Setup:Use Timings check box. Then click Slide Show: Start Slide Show:From Beginning. The slide show will play and automatically advance through the animations and slides using the saved timings.

Rehearsing a Presentation

You'll want to rehearse your presentation before giving it to an audience. In addition to helping prepare what you'll say for each slide, a rehearsal can record the time spent per slide and on the total presentation. This serves two purposes. First, by reviewing slide timings, you can determine if you're spending too much or too little time on some slides or the entire presentation. Second, if the presentation will run in kiosk mode, timings can be used to automatically advance slides.

To rehearse slide timings:

1. Click Slide Show:Set Up:Rehearse Timings.

   The slide show begins.

2. Present the show as you intend to give it to your audience, advancing through the animations and slides by clicking the mouse, pressing a keyboard short-cut (see "Previewing a Slide Show" in Chapter 14), or clicking Next (**A** or **B**).

   As you switch slides, PowerPoint notes the amount of time spent on each one.

3. During the rehearsal, you can also use the Recording toolbar as follows:

   ▸ Click Pause if you need to take a break. Click the button again when you're ready to continue.

   ▸ To restart the timing for the current slide, click the Repeat button.

4. When the show ends, a dialog box displays the total time and asks if you'd like to save the slide timings **C**. Click Yes to save or No if you prefer not to save the timings.

Printing Notes and Handouts

In preparation for the presentation, you can print your notes and audience handouts.

To print notes:

1. Click the File tab and select the Print category in the Backstage.

   A print preview **A** allows you to see the output prior to routing it to your printer.

2. Choose a printer from the Printer menu.

   If your printer isn't shown, choose Add Printer.

3. Using the following drop-down menus in the Settings section, enter these settings:

   ▸ **Menu 1.** Specify the slides you want to include in the printout, such as Print All Slides.

   ▸ **Menu 2.** Choose Notes Pages.

   ▸ **Menu 5.** Choose an orientation for the printout.

   ▸ **Menu 6.** Indicate whether the notes should be printed in shades of gray (grayscale), black-and-white, or color.

4. To review the slides and notes as they'll print, click the page controls beneath the preview **B**.

5. *Optional:* To edit the header or footer, click Edit Header & Footer. Make the necessary changes on the Notes and Handouts tab of the Header and Footer dialog box **C**.

6. At the top of the Print window **A**, specify the number of copies to print (Copies).

7. Click the Print button.

   The notes will print one slide per page.

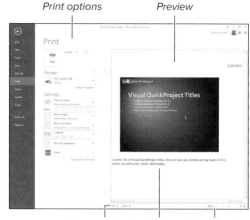

Print options   *Preview*

Page controls   Notes   Magnification

A All print settings can be chosen and their effects previewed in the Backstage.

Page controls   *Magnification controls*

B The page controls and magnification controls are located beneath the preview.

C By default, only the slide number is included as footer data on a notes page. However, you can customize the header and footer to include other information.

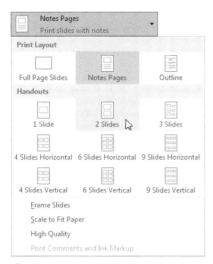

D Choose a Handouts layout from the second menu.

To print audience handouts:

- Perform the "To print notes" task list. In Step 3, however, choose a Handouts layout **D** from the second drop-down menu rather than choosing Notes Pages.

TIP Choose Full Page Slides **D** to print an enlarged version of each slide (one slide per page).

TIP In a printed handout, the 3 Slides **D** option provides lines on which the audience can write notes.

TIP It can be helpful to choose Outline **D**. The printout provides a slide-by-slide listing of the text contained on each slide **E**.

E Choose Outline to print slide text in outline form.

Saving a Presentation In Other Formats

If a slide show will be presented or needs to be delivered to recipients in a form other than as a PowerPoint 2013 presentation, you can generate an additional copy of it in the necessary format. In PowerPoint 2013, all of the essential commands can be found in the Export and Share areas of the Backstage. From these areas, you can save or convert the current presentation to a variety of popular formats.

In this section, you'll learn to save presentations in alternative PowerPoint formats, convert a presentation to a PDF file, package a presentation for distribution on CD, and generate a presentation video.

To save a presentation in an alternative PowerPoint format:

1. Click File tab, Export, Change File Type.

   A list of supported file types appears Ⓐ.

2. Select an output file type and click the Save As button.

   A Save As dialog box appears Ⓑ. The correct file type is preselected in the Save as type list.

3. Navigate to the drive and folder in which you will save the file, rename the file (optional), and click Save.

> **TIP** You can also save in an alternate format by selecting Save As in the Backstage. When the Save As dialog box appears, simply select the desired file type from the Save as type list.

> **TIP** If the intended recipient has an older version of PowerPoint, choose PowerPoint 97-2003 Presentation as the output file type.

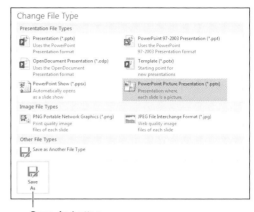

Save As button

Ⓐ Select an output file type and click the Save As button.

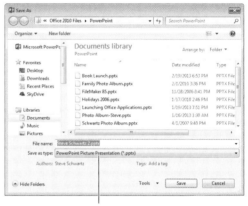

Save as type list

Ⓑ Select a location in which to save the new file and click Save.

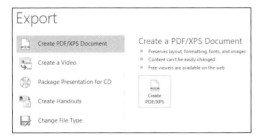

Export

Create PDF/XPS Document

Create a Video

Package Presentation for CD

Create Handouts

Change File Type

Create a PDF/XPS Document
- Preserves layout, formatting, fonts, and images
- Content can't be easily changed
- Free viewers are available on the web

Create PDF/XPS

C The Export section of the Backstage.

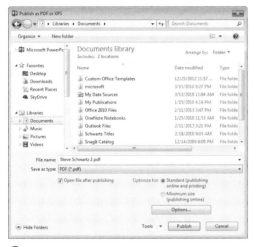

D Use this modified file output dialog box to specify a name, location, and quality for the PDF file.

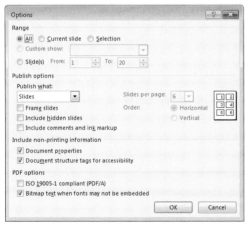

E Set options for the PDF export file.

To save a presentation as an Adobe Reader (PDF) file:

1. Click the File tab, Export, Create PDF/XPS Document **C**.

2. Click the Create PDF/XPS button.

   The Publish as PDF or XPS dialog box appears **D**.

3. *Optional:* If you want to specify a sub-set of slides to include or publish hand-outs, notes, or an outline view of the presentation, click the Options button and change the settings in the Options dialog box that appears **E**. Click OK.

4. At the bottom of the Publish as PDF or XPS dialog box **D**, specify whether to generate a Standard or Minimum size (compressed, lower resolution) file by clicking the appropriate radio button.

5. Navigate to the drive and folder in which you will save the file, rename the file (optional), and click the Publish button to create the PDF file.

   The resulting PDF file can be viewed in Adobe Reader, Apple's Preview, and similar utilities.

> **TIP** If you intend to email the PDF file, you can streamline the process by clicking the File tab, followed by Share, Email, Send as PDF. Similarly, if you want to share the actual presentation via email (enabling it to be edited and viewed by the recipient in a current ver-sion of PowerPoint), click Send as Attachment.

To package a presentation for distribution on CD or DVD:

1. In the Export section of the Backstage, select Package Presentation for CD and click the Package for CD button.

   The Package for CD dialog box  appears.

2. Type a short name for the CD/DVD in the Name the CD text box.

3. If you want to add other presentations to the same CD/DVD, click Add. Select the additional presentation filename(s) from the Add Files dialog box.

   The presentation names are added to the list in the Package for CD dialog box. You can change their order by selecting a filename and clicking the up- or down-arrow button.

4. *Optional:* If you want to password-protect a presentation or include fonts and linked files on the CD, click the Options button and make the necessary changes in the Options dialog box .

5. Click the appropriate Copy button  as described below. Note that if you intend to create a DVD rather than a CD, you must use Copy to Folder and then create the DVD using separate DVD burning software.

   ▶ **Copy to CD.** Insert a blank CD into your CD or DVD burner. In the dialog box that appears , click Yes or No to include linked files on the CD. Office burns the presentation(s) onto the CD.

TIP **A presentation CD contains normal copies of your PowerPoint files. If you don't want to allow these files to be opened or edited in PowerPoint, set password(s) in the Options dialog box** **.**

CD name   Presentations

F The current presentation is automatically included in the Files to be copied list. Add other presentations (if desired), set options, and copy the files to a CD or a folder.

G In the Options dialog box, you can add password-protection to the copied presentations.

H If your presentation(s) include linked files, click Yes to include them on the CD.

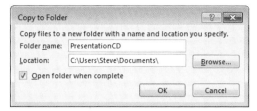

Create a Video options

Create Video button

J Set options and click the Create Video button.

▸ **Copy to Folder.** In the dialog box that appears **H**, click Yes or No to copy linked files. In the Copy to Folder dialog box **I**, specify an output location, name the folder, and click OK.

I Specify a disk location and new folder name, and then click OK.

TIP A recipient can view the presentations with PowerPoint or PowerPoint Viewer (2007 or higher). A link for downloading and installing PowerPoint Viewer is provided on the CD.

TIP If you want to avoid the requirement that recipients have PowerPoint or Power-Point Viewer on their computer, you might prefer to create a video of the presentation as described below.

To create a video from a presentation:

1. *Optional:* Record the slide timings (Slide Show:Set Up:Rehearse Timings) or timings and narrations (Record Slide Show). These elements can be incorporated into the video.

2. Click the File tab, Export, and Create a Video.

   Create a Video options appear **J**.

3. From the first menu, choose an output size/quality setting.

4. In the second menu, you can elect to use recorded timings and narrations or a default duration per slide.

5. In the Seconds to spend on each slide box, enter a default duration to use for displaying each slide.

   If you chose Don't Use Recorded Timings and Narrations in Step 4, this timing will be applied to all slides. If you chose Use Recorded Timings and Narrations, this timing will be applied to every slide for which no timing has been recorded.

   continues on next page

6. Click the Create Video button 🔘.

A Save As dialog box appears.

7. Name the output file, select a disk and folder in which to save it, select a video format (MPEG-4 or WMV) from the Save as type drop-down list, and click Save.

A progress bar appears in PowerPoint's status area, enabling you to track the video-generation process **K**. At its conclusion, the video file is saved to disk.

TIP As in a live PowerPoint slide show, hidden slides are not included in a video.

TIP Before running, saving, or exporting a presentation, it's a good idea to review the settings in the Set Up Show dialog box **L**. Included options enable you to create a self-running presentation (*kiosk mode*) and specify whether recorded timings will automatically advance slides. To open the dialog box, click Slide Show : Set Up : Set Up Slide Show.

TIP The recipient must have a media player that can play the resulting video. (The typical Mac user, for example, won't be able to play a WMV file.) You may want to ask if they have a preferred video file format.

Cancel

K A progress bar appears in the status area. If necessary, you can click the Cancel icon to halt the video-generation process.

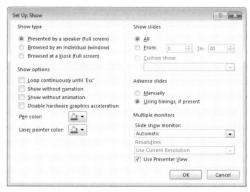

L Select slide show options in the Set Up Show dialog box.

Delivering the Presentation

Delivering the presentation is the ultimate goal of your work in PowerPoint. In this section, you'll learn how to present a show in person or broadcast it over the web.

Delivering an In-Person Slide Show

These steps show how the majority of slide shows are presented to an audience.

To deliver an in-person presentation:

1. *Optional:* To begin the show with a slide other than the first, select or switch to that slide.

2. Set options in the Slide Show : Set Up and Monitors Ⓐ groups as follows:

   ▸ **Hide Slide.** Select each slide that you want to skip and click Hide Slide.

   ▸ **Use Presenter View.** If you'll be using multiple monitors to present the show, enable this option in the Monitors group.

   ▸ **Set Up Slide Show.** Click this icon to open the Set Up Show dialog box (see Ⓛ on the previous page). You can set primary show options here or click check boxes in the Set Up and Monitors groups.

continues on next page

Ⓐ Before presenting the show, make sure these settings are correct.

3. *Do one of the following:*

- ▸ To run the show starting with the first slide, press F5.

- ▸ To run the show starting with the current slide, press Shift-F5.

- ▸ Click Slide Show: Start Slide Show: From Beginning or From Current Slide.

4. *Do any of the following:*

- ▸ If Use Timings is checked in the Set Up group Ⓐ, the show will play automatically from start to finish.

- ▸ To manually step forward through the slides and within-slide animations (if any), click the mouse or press n, Enter, Page Down, Spacebar, right arrow, or down arrow.

- ▸ To move backward through the slides and within-slide animations (if any), press p, Page Up, Backspace, left arrow, or up arrow.

TIP **You can also control the presentation with the toolbar in the screen's bottom-left corner Ⓑ.**

- ▸ To end the show, press Esc.

Broadcasting a Slide Show

You can broadcast a presentation over the Internet that invited audience members can view with a browser Ⓒ. PowerPoint provides two methods for broadcasting a presentation:

- ■ To broadcast over a network, the company must use SharePoint Services 4.

- ■ To broadcast over the Internet using the Office Presentation Service, all you need is a Windows Live or Hotmail account.

In this section, you'll learn how to perform a web broadcast. For information on broadcasting using SharePoint, contact your network administrator.

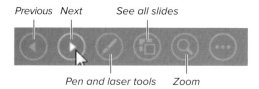

Previous   Next   See all slides

Pen and laser tools   Zoom

Ⓑ The presenter's toolbar.

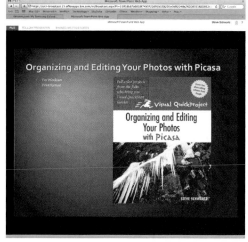

Ⓒ The audience views the broadcast in a browser. New slides and animations appear based on slide timings or the presenter's mouse clicks.

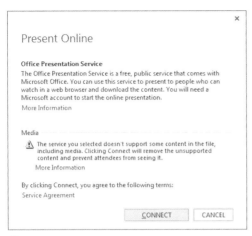

D The Present Online dialog box.

E Communicate the show's address to your audience.

To broadcast a slide show using the PowerPoint Broadcast Service:

1. Open the PowerPoint presentation that you want to broadcast.

2. In the Slide Show:Set Up and Monitors groups, set show options as explained in Step 2 of the previous task list.

3. Choose Slide Show:Start Slide Show: Present Online > Office Presentation Service.

   The Present Online dialog box appears **D**.

4. Click the Connect button.

   TIP If prompted, enter your Windows Live or Hotmail email address and password.

   Office connects to the Office Presentation Service and prepares the show for broadcast.

5. A link to the presentation appears **E**. *Do any of the following:*

   ▸ **Copy Link.** Click Copy Link or press Ctrl-C, and then paste (Ctrl-V) the URL into an email or instant message. Instruct recipients to click or paste the URL into their browser's address box.

   ▸ **Send in Email.** Click Send in Email to generate an email message that contains the link. Address the message, edit the message text as desired, and click Send.

   TIP When contacting the audience prior to the broadcast, you may want to ask them to confirm they're ready by clicking Reply in response to your email announcement.

continues on next page

6. When audience members have the presentation URL opened in their browser, click Start Presentation **E**.

The slide show begins **C**.

7. When the presentation is finished, click the mouse button or press Esc to return to the PowerPoint window.

8. Click Present Online:End Online Presentation **F**.

9. Confirm by clicking the End Online Presentation button in the dialog box that appears **G**.

"The presentation has ended" appears in attendees' browsers.

TIP If some attendees arrive late and you haven't ended the broadcast, you can restart the slide show by clicking Slide Show:Start Slide Show:From Beginning.

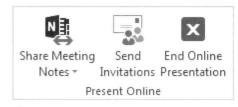

F When the show is finished, click End Online Presentation.

G Confirm that you want to end the presentation.

Getting Started with Outlook 2013

Even if you're new to the Internet, you've heard the term *email* bandied about. Short for *electronic mail*, email is a text message sent from one person's Internet account to another's. With most email accounts, you must have a computer program known as an *email client* to compose and send messages, as well as to receive and read email from others. In addition to serving as your mail client, Outlook can manage appointments, handle to-do lists, and receive Really Simple Syndication (*RSS*) feeds.

In this chapter, you'll set up your email accounts, learn how to subscribe to RSS feeds, and explore these essential topics:

- Understanding the Outlook interface
- Creating and using profiles
- Creating groups to schedule automatic send/receive operations
- Using the Outlook Social Connector
- Working online and offline
- Setting options to customize the way that Outlook works
- Getting help while running Outlook 2013

In This Chapter

Types of Email Accounts

Outlook supports four types of Internet mail accounts: Post Office Protocol (*POP3*), Internet Message Access Protocol (*IMAP*), Microsoft Exchange, and Microsoft Active-Sync (Windows Live/Hotmail). Outlook can send and retrieve mail from all such accounts. If you aren't certain what account type(s) you have, your Internet Service Provider (*ISP*), company, or school can tell you.

POP3 Accounts

The majority of ISP email accounts are POP3. When Outlook connects with the ISP to check for new mail, the mail is downloaded to your PC from a POP3 server. After you've received the new mail, it's automatically deleted from the server. Thus, POP3 mail servers normally act only as temporary repositories for outgoing and incoming mail.

IMAP Accounts

Unlike a POP3 account, an IMAP account is *not* a temporary repository for email. The email never actually leaves the IMAP server. Instead, the server acts like a node on a network to which you can connect. Rather than downloading new mail to your PC, you're simply *viewing* it on the server. IMAP is rapidly catching up with POP3 as the most common email account type.

Exchange Server Accounts

Exchange Server accounts are primarily used by individuals in large companies, educational institutions, and the like. With many Exchange-compatible clients, you must have an active connection to the server in order to read your current messages. However, you can enable Outlook's *Cached Exchange Mode* to store copies of messages on your PC, enabling you to view them even when you're offline.

Windows Live/Hotmail Accounts

Windows Live and Hotmail accounts are web-based. Normally, you interact with them using a browser rather than an email client. However, you can use Outlook 2013 to send and receive email from such accounts via Microsoft's POP3 or ActiveSync servers.

TIP A few ISPs require you to use their proprietary software to send/receive email. You cannot use Outlook for such accounts.

TIP Web-based accounts other than Hotmail may be supported by Outlook via POP3 or IMAP. For this to occur, the web-based email service must provide auxiliary mail servers to which email clients can connect. For example, Google's Gmail is handled this way. Yahoo! Mail provides similar support, but only for paying Yahoo! Mail Plus customers.

TIP Some email accounts can be accessed in multiple ways. For instance, many ISPs now offer both POP3 and IMAP support. You can configure Outlook to use either account type.

User name   @ symbol   Domain name

james47@ispworld.com

A Every email address consists of these three components.

Anders, James

James Anders
Anderson Plumbing Supply
1800 Highway 7
Bemidji, MN 56601
(218) 446-8842 Work

janders@yahoo.com
www.andersonplumbing.com

B In addition to a name and email address, an Outlook contact record can store mailing and telephone information, a web site, and a picture.

ISP Email from Anywhere

You don't have to restrict email activities to your home or work computer. In fact, odds are excellent that you can interact with your ISP's mail servers from anywhere you can get Internet access.

Simply create a new account in the current computer's email client using the same settings you used when adding the account in Outlook 2013. Then delete the account when you're done using the computer.

Note that many ISP email accounts can also be accessed with a browser. Contact your ISP or its web site for details.

About Email Addresses

Regardless of the type of email account you have, each one is identified by a unique address, such as **jpt417@msn.com** or **bobp@linetop.net**. An address consists of three parts: a user name, the @ (at) symbol, and a domain name **A**. When you create the account, you normally get to choose your user name. The *domain name* is the name of the company or organization that is providing email access. In many cases, the same entity also provides your Internet access.

When people want to send you a message, they address it to your email address. And when you want to send someone else a message, you send it to that person's email address. Because you may know dozens or even hundreds of people, there's little point in attempting to memorize email addresses. Programs such as Outlook generally provide an address book **B** in which you can record important email addresses. When you want to create a new message, you can select addresses from the address book rather than type them from memory. See Chapter 17 for instructions on using People, Outlook's address book.

TIP An email address can't include blank spaces. The underscore (_) and period (.) are commonly used to represent spaces, such as **bill_smith@link.com**.

TIP Letter case is ignored in an email address. Thus, the convention is to type email addresses using all lowercase letters.

TIP Domains in countries other than the United States often end in a country abbreviation, such as *.ca* (Canada), *.uk* (United Kingdom), or *.jp* (Japan).

The Outlook 2013 Interface

Whether you'll be using the Mail, Calendar, People, Tasks, or Notes component of Outlook 2013, it's important that you familiarize yourself with the parts of the interface 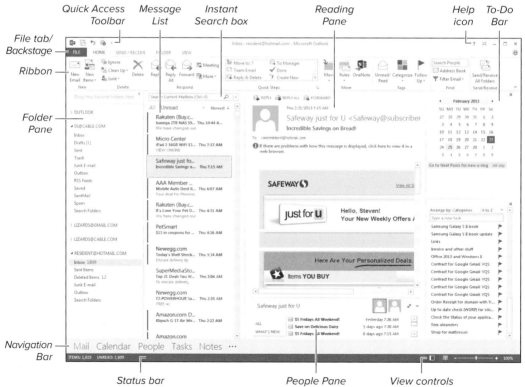 and what they do.

The Ribbon interface was introduced in Outlook 2010. If you're upgrading from an earlier version, your first challenge will be to learn where the former menu commands can be found in this new interface.

File tab/Backstage. Click the File tab to open the Backstage, where you can print, manage your accounts and RSS feeds, and set preferences.

Ribbon. Click Ribbon tabs to reveal important command groups. To learn more, see "Using the Ribbon" in Chapter 2.

Quick Access Toolbar. The Send/Receive All Folders and Undo commands can always be found here, regardless of the Ribbon tab that's currently selected.

The Outlook 2013 main window and important interface elements.

Mail Calendar People Tasks Notes ···

B Click the name of the Outlook component to which you want to switch. The active component has blue letters.

Customizing the Display

There are several simple things you can do to customize the appearance of the Outlook window:

- Drag the dividing line between any pair of panes to adjust the relative width or height of the two panes.

- Choose options from the View:Layout and View:People Pane groups to disable, minimize, or change the position of the Folder Pane, Reading Pane, To-Do Bar, and People Pane.

- Change the magnification by dragging the magnification slider on the status bar, clicking the plus (+) or minus (–) on either end of the control, or clicking the current percentage.

- Toggle between Normal and Reading view by clicking the appropriate icon beside the magnification control in the status bar.

Folder Pane. When Mail is selected in the Navigation Bar, all email accounts, RSS feeds, and their folders are shown in this pane. Messages from the selected folder are shown in the message list.

Navigation Bar. Click to select the component that you want to use, such as Mail or Calendar **B**.

Message list. Lists message headers from the folder that's selected in the Folder Pane. The name of the selected folder is shown in Outlook's title bar.

Instant Search box. Type here to search the current folder (or all folders) for matching text in a message or item.

Reading Pane. The text of the email message or RSS feed that's selected in the message list is presented here.

Help icon. Click the question mark (?) icon to open Outlook Help.

To-Do Bar. This optional pane can show to-do items, upcoming appointments and events, and/or contacts.

People Pane. The People Pane (also called the Outlook Social Connector) enables you to view other communications (email and social network feeds) that are related to the current message.

Status bar. This bar across the bottom of the window shows messages about Outlook's state (Working Offline, for example) and current activity, such as performing a send/receive.

View controls. Use these controls to change the magnification or switch between Normal and Reading view. In Reading View, the Folder Pane and Navigation Bar are collapsed, providing additional screen space for reading.

Adding Email Accounts

If a previous version of Outlook is on your PC, Outlook 2013 will automatically use the old version's data: all email accounts, messages, contacts, appointments, and so on. However, if no previous version of Outlook is found, you must add the email accounts that you want Outlook to manage.

New accounts can be added *automatically* with Outlook attempting to discern settings from the email address or *manually* by hand-entering the required information. (The manual approach is beneficial when the automatic method fails repeatedly or it chooses the wrong account type.)

To automatically add an account:

1. Click the File tab, and select the Info category in the Backstage.

2. Click the Add Account button, or click the account listed at the top of the Account Information pane and choose Add Account from the drop-down menu.

   The Add Account dialog box appears .

3. Enter the requested information. Click Next.

   Outlook contacts the domain's mail server, attempts to configure the account, and then sends a test message.

4. *Do one of the following:*

   ▶ If the test is successful, the final screen appears. Click Finish to add the new account .

   ▶ If Outlook can't contact the server, the user name and password aren't recognized, or the server can't handle encrypted messages, instructions for correcting the problem appear. Follow them to retry or click Cancel.

Ⓐ Enter your name as you want it to be shown in outgoing messages, the account's email address, and the account password.

Ⓑ If the automatic account setup and test are successful, this Congratulations screen appears.

Adding Hotmail, Windows Live, and Gmail Accounts

These accounts are readily handled by Outlook's automatic configuration. As a bonus, rather than defaulting to POP3 (as has been the case in the past), Gmail accounts are now automatically configured as IMAP. Hotmail/Live accounts are configured as Exchange ActiveSync.

TIP Try the automatic approach first. If it doesn't work, you can use the manual method as described in one of the following task lists.

Require Secure Password   More Settings
Authentication

D Enter the requested information, and choose POP3 or IMAP from the Account Type menu.

E Some ISPs require that you enable authentication for outgoing mail.

To manually add a POP3 or IMAP account:

1. Perform Steps 1 and 2 from the previous task list.

2. In the Add Account dialog box **A**, select the Manual setup or additional server types radio button. Click Next.

The Choose Service screen appears **C**.

3. Select the POP or IMAP radio button, and then click Next.

The POP and IMAP Account Settings screen appears **D**.

4. Enter the requested account information.

You'll need the names of the incoming and outgoing mail servers. You can obtain them from your ISP or from most web-based accounts' online help.

TIP Unless you are told by ISP or network personnel that your account uses Secure Password Authentication **D**, assume that it is neither required nor supported.

TIP If the outgoing mail server requires authentication, click More Settings. In the Internet E-mail Settings dialog box **E**, click the Outgoing Server tab. Enter your user name and password or select the first radio button (Use same settings as my incoming mail server). Click OK.

5. *Optional:* If adding a POP3 account, click the Test Account Settings button to send a test message using the provided settings.

A successful test ensures that the basic settings are correct and that you'll be able to send and receive mail.

6. Click Next, and then click Finish.

To manually add an Exchange Server account:

1. Quit Outlook if it's currently running. Open the Mail control panel.

   The Mail Setup - Outlook dialog box appears **F**.

2. Click the E-mail Accounts button.

   Outlook's Account Settings dialog box appears.

3. Click the New icon.

   The Choose Service dialog box appears.

4. Select E-mail Account. Click Next.

5. In the Auto Account Setup screen **A**, select Manual setup or additional server types. Click Next.

   The Choose Service screen appears **C**.

6. Select Microsoft Exchange Server or compatible service. Click Next.

   The Microsoft Exchange Settings screen appears **G**.

7. Enter the information provided to you by your Exchange Server administrator. Click Next to move to subsequent screens.

   TIP Messages in an Exchange Server account are normally readable only when you're online. To automatically download copies of all messages so they can also be read when you're offline, click the Use Cached Exchange Mode check box **G**.

8. When you're done creating the account, close the dialog boxes.

F To manually add an Exchange account, you must use the Mail control panel. Outlook cannot be running.

G Enter the Exchange server and your user name.

Why Configure Manually?

There are two important reasons you might want to configure a new account manually:

- First, although automatic configuration works better than it did in earlier versions of Outlook, it *can* fail.

- Second, some accounts can be configured as multiple types, such as POP3 and IMAP. Automatic configuration selects a type for you. To switch account types, you must delete the original account and then configure a new one manually.

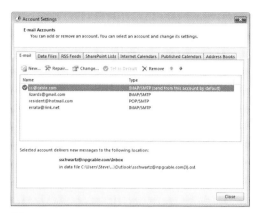

A In the Account Settings dialog box, select an account to modify.

The Case for Web Accounts

Why bother with web-based accounts if you already have an ISP or a company-provided email account? Here are three excellent reasons:

- If you travel, you can access a web-based account from anywhere in the world using a browser that's installed on your PC, Mac, tablet, or cell phone.

- Because web accounts are often free, you can use them to handle email that you'd rather not have cluttering up an ISP or corporate email account. When registering at web sites, for example, you are usually asked for an email address. To avoid receiving volumes of unwanted advertising mail (called *spam*) in your primary account, you can direct it to your web account.

- Many popular web-based services, such as Hotmail and Gmail, also provide POP3 or IMAP support that enables you to use them in Outlook and other email clients.

Changing Account Settings

After adding an email account automatically or working with any account for a while, you may want to modify the account's settings to make it behave in a different manner.

You can also specify a *default account* from which all outgoing mail will be sent unless another account is specified, change an account's position in the Account Settings list, test an account, or delete an account.

To edit an account's settings:

1. In the Backstage, select the Info category and choose Account Settings > Account Settings.

    The Account Settings dialog box appears **A**.

2. *Do either of the following:*

    ▸ Select the account and click Change.

    ▸ Double-click the account's name.

    A Change Account dialog box appears (similar to **D** in "Adding Email Accounts").

3. Make any desired changes to the settings, such as the name used to identify your outgoing messages or the mail server names.

continues on next page

4. *Optional:* To view other account-specific settings, click More Settings. The Internet E-mail Settings dialog box appears . Settings that you might want to change include the following:

   ▸ **General tab, Mail Account.** Enter a descriptive name for the account, such as Home or the ISP's name.

   ▸ **General tab, Reply E-mail.** When someone replies to a message from you, the reply is addressed to the account from which you sent the message. To direct replies to a *different* account (a work account, for example), enter that address here.

   ▸ **Advanced tab (POP3 accounts only), Leave a copy of messages on the server.** Normally, when you retrieve a message from a POP3 server, the message is simultaneously deleted from the server. If you're retrieving the account's mail from *multiple* computers (work and home, for example) or devices, enable this option on the secondary computers and devices . Doing so ensures that all messages retrieved on a secondary computer or device will also be downloaded to your main computer before being deleted from the server.

   Click OK to save all changes made in the Internet E-mail Settings dialog box or click Cancel to ignore the changes.

5. To save the changes to the account, click Next and then Finish. (Click Cancel if you don't want to save the changes.)

6. Close the Account Settings dialog box.

Name the account

B On the General tab, you can enter a new display name for the account that will be used to identify it in the Folder Pane.

C For POP3 accounts, you can specify the circumstances under which delivered messages are deleted from the mail server.

To change the default email account:

- In the Account Settings dialog box 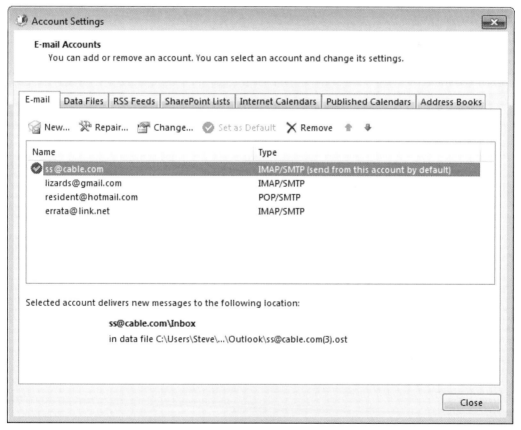, select an account and click Set as Default.

To change an account's position in the Account Settings list:

- In the Account Settings dialog box D, select the account and click the up- or down-arrow icon.

To check a malfunctioning account:

- In the Account Settings dialog box D, select the account and click Repair.

To delete an account:

- In the Account Settings dialog box D, select the account, click Remove, and confirm the deletion.

  The account is removed from the Folder Pane and its associated email messages, Calendar events, and other data are removed.

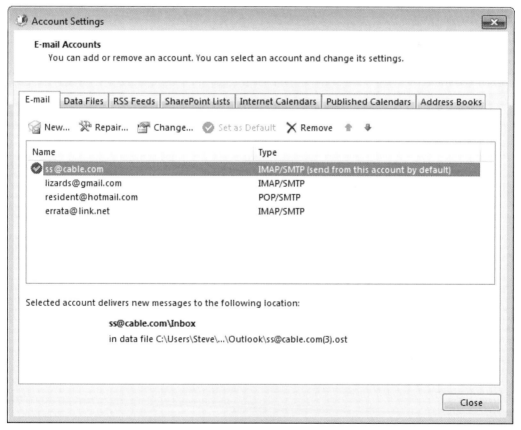

D Use the Account Settings dialog box to create new accounts and modify, repair, or remove current Outlook accounts. Choose commands by clicking icons in the toolbar beneath the tabs.

Working with Profiles

Outlook uses *profiles* to determine which mail accounts should be displayed in an Outlook session. When you install Outlook, a single profile is created for all your accounts. However, if several people use the PC, each user will need their own profile. Similarly, if you want to keep your work and home accounts separate, you can create another profile.

Note that on most single-user PCs, one profile will suffice. Even if you have multiple Exchange accounts, Outlook 2013 allows you to store them in a single profile.

To create a new profile:

1. Quit Outlook if it's currently running, and open the Mail Control Panel.

   The Mail Setup - Outlook dialog box appears (see **F** in "Adding Email Accounts").

2. Click the Show Profiles button.

   The Mail dialog box appears **A**.

3. Click Add.

   The New Profile dialog box appears **B**.

4. Name the new profile and click OK.

   The Add Account dialog box appears **C**.

5. *Do either of the following:*

   ‣ Add the first email account for the new profile (as described in "Adding Email Accounts," earlier in this chapter).

   ‣ Click Cancel to create the profile without specifying its first email account.

TIP Additional email accounts can be added to a profile at any time within Outlook or in the Mail control panel.

Current profiles

A You can create, delete, or set startup options for profiles in the Mail dialog box.

B Name the new profile and click OK.

C You can add accounts to the new profile using the automatic or manual methods described in "Adding Email Accounts."

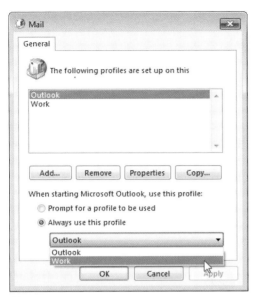

D You can specify a profile that will automatically be used whenever you launch Outlook or ask to be prompted to select a profile.

Switching Profiles

You can't switch profiles from within Outlook. If the wrong profile is active, quit Outlook, and *do one of the following:*

- If Outlook is set to Prompt for a profile, relaunch Outlook and select the correct profile.

- If Outlook is set to Always use this profile, open the Mail control panel, click Show Profiles, select the desired profile, and click OK.

To set a startup profile:

1. Perform Steps 1 and 2 of the previous task list.

2. *Do either of the following:*

   ▸ To automatically use a certain profile, select a profile from the drop-down list and click Always use this profile **D**.

   ▸ To be prompted to select a profile at the start of every Outlook session, select Prompt for a profile to be used.

3. Click OK.

CAUTION Outlook profiles aren't password protected. While profiles are convenient for keeping your mail, appointments, and contacts separate from those of other Outlook users, there's nothing to prevent one user from viewing another's material. If security and privacy are concerns, a better approach is to create a separate password-protected Windows user account for each person.

Working with Send/Receive Groups

Outlook automatically sends and receives email every so many minutes. By creating *send/receive groups* (each containing one or more email accounts), you can specify a different send/receive schedule for each group. (When you initially set up Outlook, it creates a default All Accounts group that consists of all defined email accounts and RSS feeds.)

To create a group:

1. Choose Send/Receive : Send & Receive : Send/Receive Groups > Define Send/ Receive Groups.

   The Send/Receive Groups dialog box appears .

2. Click the New button.

3. In the Send/Receive Group Name dialog box, type a name for the new group and click OK.

   The Send/Receive Settings dialog box for the new group appears .

4. In the Accounts list on the left, group member icons contain blue "refresh" arrows and non-member icons have a red *X*. To change an account's membership in the group, select its icon and click the Include the selected account in this group check box.

5. For each included account, select its icon in the Accounts list, and set options by clicking check boxes and radio buttons. Click OK when you're done examining the settings of all included accounts.

6. In the bottom of the Send/Receive Groups dialog box , set send/receive options for the new group and click Close.

Create new group

A Group creation, editing, and deletion begin in the Send/Receive Groups dialog box.

Include the selected account

B Change group membership and individual account settings in this dialog box.

Group-creation Tips

The easiest way to decide how many groups you need is to base the decision on *send/receive schedules*. Schedules often differ by account type.

- POP3 accounts offered by your ISP can usually support a send/receive every 1–2 minutes, allowing you to instantly receive most incoming messages.

- IMAP and Exchange accounts normally don't need to be included in *any* group because they are automatically checked and synced about once per minute.

- Web-based accounts and RSS feeds may have restrictions on how often you can perform scheduled send/receives, such as once every 5 or 15 minutes (although you can usually perform *manual* send/receives as often as you like). See the site's Help for details.

In addition, you may have some seldom-used accounts that you don't want to include in *any* group. For such accounts, it may suffice to do a manual send/receive now and then.

To modify a group's settings:

1. Choose Send/Receive : Send & Receive : Send/Receive Groups > Define Send/Receive Groups.

   The Send/Receive Groups dialog box appears **Ⓐ**.

2. Select the group name whose settings you want to modify.

3. Change any of the top three settings **Ⓒ**:

   ▸ **Include this group in send/receive.** When this option is enabled, all accounts and RSS feeds in the group will perform a send/receive when you press F9, click Send/Receive : Send & Receive : Send/Receive All Folders, or click the Send/Receive All Folders icon on the Quick Access Toolbar.

   ▸ **Schedule an automatic send/receive every *X* minutes.** When this option is enabled, all accounts and RSS feeds in the group will automatically perform a send/receive at the designated interval. To change the interval, type in the text box or click the arrows.

   ▸ **Perform an automatic send/receive when exiting.** When this option is enabled, a final send/receive will be performed for the accounts in the group whenever you quit Outlook.

4. Click Close.

continues on next page

Setting for group

☑ Include this group in send/receive (F9).

☑ Schedule an automatic send/receive every [30 ⬍] minutes.

☐ Perform an automatic send/receive when exiting.

Ⓒ These settings govern online send/receive behavior for the selected group.

TIP A group can contain only one account, if desired.

TIP All RSS feeds—regardless of whether they have one or many sources—are treated as a single account. You may want to lump them together into a separate group.

TIP Remove any account from the All Accounts group that needs to be checked on a different schedule. For instance, while POP3 accounts can be checked once per minute, it would be overkill to check web-based accounts or RSS feeds on the same schedule.

TIP To change a group's membership or edit an account's options within a group, select the group in the Send/Receive Groups dialog box 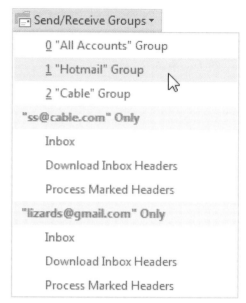 and click Edit.

TIP To change the name of a selected group, click Rename **A**. To delete an unneeded group, select it and click Remove.

TIP For a dial-up connection, you may want to set the group that includes your ISP account to perform a send/receive every few minutes. Doing so ensures regular line activity that can prevent disconnects.

TIP To perform a manual send/receive for a group, choose its name from the top of the Send/Receive Groups menu **D**. To check a single account for new messages, choose *account name* Only > Inbox.

TIP If people routinely send huge, unwanted attachments to your POP3 account, you can enable the option in the Send/Receive Settings dialog box to Download only headers for items larger than *X* **E**.

D To perform a manual send/receive, choose the group or an account's Inbox from this menu.

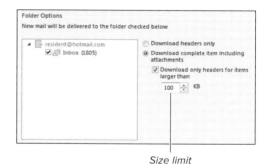

Size limit

E You can set this option for a POP3 account that regularly receives email with large, unwanted attachments.

RSS feed symbol

A Locate and click the site's RSS feed symbol or link.

The Pessimist
You are viewing a feed that contains frequently updated content. When you subscribe to a feed, it is added to the Common Feed List. Updated information from the feed is automatically downloaded to your computer and can be viewed in Internet Explorer and other programs. Learn more about feeds.

☆ Subscribe to this feed

Click to subscribe

B Click the Subscribe to this feed link.

Subscribe to this Feed

Subscribe to this Feed
When you subscribe to a feed, it is automatically added to the Favorites Center and kept up to date.

Name: The Pessimist

Create in: Feeds ▾ New folder

☐ Add to Favorites Bar

What is a Feed? Subscribe Cancel

C If desired, you can change the name of the feed and the folder in which it's stored. Then click the Subscribe button.

You've successfully subscribed to this feed!
Updated content can be viewed in Internet Explorer and other programs that use the Common Feed List.

☆ View my feeds

D This confirmation message appears when you've successfully subscribed to a feed in Internet Explorer.

Subscribing to RSS Feeds

Many web sites now offer to deliver their latest information to you via Really Simple Syndication (*RSS*) feeds. Subscribed-to feeds can be viewed in Outlook 2013, although most are designed to be viewed in a browser.

There are several ways that you can sign up for and track RSS feeds in Outlook:

- Subscribe to feeds in your browser and then sync them with Outlook (described below)

- Subscribe to a feed in your browser that is automatically linked to Outlook

- Manually add the feed on the RSS Feeds tab of the Account Settings dialog box

To subscribe to a feed and sync it with Outlook:

1. In your browser, find and click the site's RSS feed link. The feed may be represented by an RSS symbol **A**, a link, or a series of links.

2. Click the Subscribe to this feed link **B**.

3. A Subscribe to this Feed dialog box appears **C**.

4. *Optional:* Edit or rename the feed.

5. Specify a Create in folder or subfolder in which to store the feed.

6. Click the Subscribe button.

   The new feed will now be available for viewing in Internet Explorer **D**.

continues on next page

7. In Outlook, click the File tab. Select the Options category.

The Outlook Options dialog box opens.

8. Select Advanced and scroll to the RSS Feeds section .

9. Click the Synchronize RSS Feeds to the Common Feed List (CFL) in Windows check box, click OK, and restart Outlook.

Existing feeds and new ones will now go directly to Outlook.

TIP Feed subscriptions are listed in the Folder Pane in the RSS Feeds folder **F**.

TIP If you want to receive feeds on a schedule, make sure that the RSS account is in a send/receive group. You can also use the Send/Receive Settings dialog box to selectively include and exclude certain feeds (see **B** in "Working with Send/Receive Groups").

TIP To delete a feed, select it on the RSS Feeds tab of the Account Settings dialog box and click Remove.

TIP Feed publishers may set an *update limit* (a minimum time between updates). To check this limit, double-click the feed's name in the Account Settings dialog box to view its RSS Feed Options **G**.

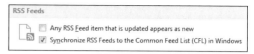

E Enable the Synchronize RSS Feeds setting in the Advanced section of Outlook Options.

◢ RSS Feeds
    Microsoft at Home (This c... 38
    Microsoft at Work (This co... 41
    MSNBC News (This comp... 22
    Office Next (This computer ... 9
    Popular Government Questi... 2
    The Pessimist (This comput... 8
    USA.gov Updates: News an... 2

F To read a feed, select its name in the Folder Pane. The number of unread messages is displayed following the feed name.

Update Limit

☑ Use the publisher update recommendation. Send/Receive groups do not update more frequently than the recommended limit to prevent your RSS Feed from being suspended by the content provider.

Current provider limit: 1 hour

Use provider limit   *Provider limit*

G You can learn a feed provider's recommended update limit. When this box is checked, Outlook automatically respects the specified limit when checking for feed updates.

The Outlook Social Connector

Beneath the Reading Pane, Outlook 2013 has an optional area called the People Pane . The People Pane has several purposes. First, it shows material related to the currently selected message or item, such as message headers. Second, if you belong to the same social networking sites (Facebook and LinkedIn are currently supported) as people in the selected item, you can view updates posted by them. Finally, if you're on the same SharePoint Server, updates such as changes to contact info also appear in the People Pane.

You can do the following with the pane:

- **Show/hide the pane.** To display the pane, choose View:People Pane:People Pane > Normal or Minimized. To hide the pane, choose Off.

- **Change the pane's height.** When the pane is displayed, drag the dividing line that separates it from the Reading Pane.

- **Collapse/expand the pane.** Click the arrow icon at the pane's top-right edge.

- **Display items.** Click an item in the scrolling list to open it in its own window.

- **Display an item class.** Click an icon to filter the list.

continues on next page

Item-class filters | People filters | Collapse/expand

FileMaker, Inc. | Toggle views

	FileMaker Unveils iOS Demo Solutions	5 days ago 7:32 AM
ALL	Introducing FileMaker iOS Demo Solutions – Inspiration for your iPad and iPhone!	6 days ago 10:00 AM
WHAT'S NEW	Bento eNews February 2013	11 days ago 8:23 AM
MAIL	FileMaker eNewsletter February 2013	12 days ago 11:48 AM
ATTACHMENTS	Encore FileMaker Web Seminar in February	14 days ago 12:06 PM
MEETINGS	FileMaker Webinar Recording Available	19 days ago 10:26 AM
	FileMaker Go 12 Tech Brief UPDATE	21 days ago 11:02 AM
	Bento eNews January 2013	1/25/2013 8:45 AM
	FileMaker Webinar in February	1/24/2013 8:36 AM
	Bento eNews December 2012	12/20/2012 8:59 AM

A The People Pane.

- **Display material for multiple people.** Some selected items, such as meetings and email messages, may be related to several people. To view items relevant to a specific person, click her or his icon at the top of the pane. Each icon has a ScreenTip that appears to identify the person when you hover the cursor over her or his icon. (You can click the Toggle views icon to see larger icons.)

TIP To configure the People Pane to include social networking material, choose View : People Pane : People Pane > **Account Settings** Ⓑ.

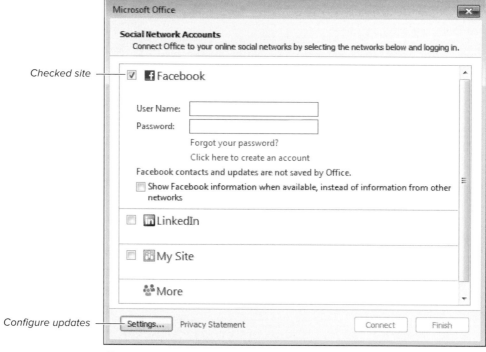

Checked site

Configure updates

Ⓑ To add a social networking site, click its check box and enter your user name and site password. Click Settings to specify an update method for the site.

Work Offline

Preferences

 When enabled, the Work Offline icon is blue.

Dial-up and Working Offline

If you have dial-up Internet, quitting Outlook or going offline does *not* disconnect you from the Internet. To do so and free up your phone line, you'll also have to disconnect.

Working Online and Offline

In addition to working with Outlook interactively by reading and replying to email messages while online, you can work while you're *offline* (not connected to the Internet).

Why would you want to work offline? Here are a few common reasons:

- If you have a dial-up account and use your phone line for both voice calls and Internet access, you can work offline to free up the phone line.

- When traveling with a laptop, you can read previously received email messages and compose new messages that will be sent the next time you connect to the Internet.

- If the Internet account you're currently using (such as one at an Internet cafe) doesn't provide unlimited access, you can save on time-based connect charges by doing much of your work offline.

To go offline, click the Send/Receive:Preferences:Work Offline icon or click the same icon in the Quick Access Toolbar. When you're working offline, the icon is colored blue and the status bar shows *Working Offline.*

While offline, you can read previously downloaded email and RSS feeds. You can also compose new messages. When you click the Send button, Outlook stores them in the Outbox until the next time you're online.

To resume working online, click the Work Offline icon again. If you've also disconnected from the Internet (using a dial-up connection), you'll need to reconnect.

Setting Preferences

You can customize the way Outlook works by setting preferences in the Outlook Options dialog box **Ⓐ**. To open the dialog box, click the File tab and select Options in the Backstage. Make any desired changes and click OK.

The default Options settings are initially fine for most users. However, after using Outlook for a bit, it's worth exploring them. Here are some of the more useful ones listed in *category, section* order:

General

- **Start up options.** Set Outlook as your default email, contact, and calendar program.

Mail

- **Compose messages (Spelling).** Specify whether an automatic spell check occurs before you send each message and whether quoted text is also checked **Ⓑ**.

- **Compose messages (Signatures).** Create *signatures* to append to outgoing messages. A signature can be your full name, a web address, or additional contact information, for example.

- **Outlook panes.** Specify how messages are automatically marked as read **Ⓒ**.

- **Message arrival.** Specify how you're notified when new email arrives.

- **Replies and forwards.** Specify whether original text is quoted in replies and forwards, as well as how it's formatted.

Selected category

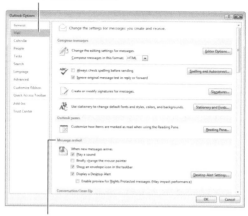

Section heading

Ⓐ Outlook preferences can be viewed and set in the Outlook Options dialog box.

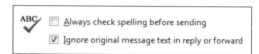

Ⓑ Set spell-checking options for outgoing messages in the Compose messages section of the Mail category.

Ⓒ Click one of the first two mutually exclusive check boxes to specify the manner in which messages are automatically marked as read.

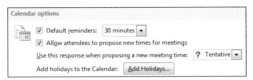

D When you set a reminder for a new appointment, Outlook proposes the time interval specified in Default reminders.

E Calendar appointments always reflect your time zone. When working out of town or to accommodate Daylight Saving Time, ensure that these preferences are correct. Changes here are used to automatically update appointment times.

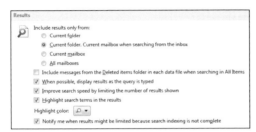

F Use Search preferences to set a default scope for searches, as well as indicate whether matching text within found items will be highlighted and using what color.

More Preferences

As you'll learn in subsequent chapters, not all preferences are set in the Outlook Options dialog box. For example, junk mail preferences are set by choosing Home:Delete:Junk > Junk E-Mail Options. To set IMAP folder purge options, choose Folder:Clean Up:Purge > Purge Options.

Calendar

- **Work time.** Specify your work hours and the days of your work week.
- **Calendar options.** Specify a default reminder period and add holidays to the Calendar **D**.
- **Display options.** Change the Calendar's color.
- **Time zones.** Set or change your time zone **E**.
- **Weather.** Hide or display the current weather at the top of the Calendar.

People

- **Names and filing.** Set the default order for displaying and filing contacts.

Tasks

- **Task options.** Set display colors for overdue and completed tasks. Specify the default reminder time for tasks.

Search

- **Results.** Specify how Instant Search will work and present its results **F**.

Advanced

- **Outlook Panes (Navigation).** Specify the components shown in the Navigation Bar.
- **Outlook start and exit.** Set Outlook's startup folder and indicate whether the Deleted Items folders will automatically be emptied at the end of each session.
- **AutoArchive.** Set options for archiving or deleting old mail.
- **Reminders.** Change the sound that plays when a reminder occurs.
- **Other.** Indicate whether you want to be prompted to confirm deletions.

Getting Help

Help with commands and procedures is only a click away. Help is presented in the resizable Outlook Help window .

To view help information:

- To open Outlook Help, click the Help (?) icon in the upper-right corner of the Outlook window or press F1. To dismiss Outlook Help, click its close box.

- To view help text for a dialog box, click the ? button in the upper-right corner of the dialog box.

To use the Outlook Help window:

- To view Outlook Help's start page, click the Home icon **B**.

- To view a help topic, select it on the Home page or click the blue text.

- To go back or forward through previously viewed help pages, click the arrow icons.

- To search for help on a subject, enter search text and click the Search icon.

- To print the current help page or selected text on the page, click the Print icon.

- You can view help from the file stored on your hard disk or from Office.com. The latter requires an active Internet connection. Choose a help source by clicking the down arrow to the right of the Outlook Help text **C**.

A The Outlook Help window.

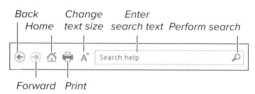

B The Outlook Help toolbar.

C Select a help source.

Managing Your Contacts

People (formerly called Contacts) is where you store contact information for people, companies, institutions, and mailing lists. After you create a record for a contact, you can address email to him or her simply by typing part of their name.

In addition to standard address information (such as name, home and work addresses, phone numbers, and email addresses), a contact can store other information, such as a web page address, photo, and notes.

You can do any of the following in the People window:

- Record multiple email addresses, mailing addresses, and phone numbers for each contact

- Browse through and search for contacts

- Import contact information from older Outlook versions, as well as other email, database, and address applications

- Create an Electronic Business Card, enabling you to easily share your contact information with others

- Create contact groups to simplify mass mailings

In This Chapter

The People Window

To view or work with your contacts, click People in the Navigation Bar at the bottom of the window or press Ctrl-3. In the People window **Ⓐ**, you can change views; view and edit contacts; and find specific contacts by scrolling, clicking alphabetical index icons, or searching.

> **TIP** To quickly find an email address without switching to the People window, click Home : Find : Address Book or press Ctrl-Shift-B. You can address a new message to a selected contact in Address Book by pressing Ctrl-N.

Hotmail/Windows Live Contacts

Although the typical home user will have only one Contacts database, Outlook 2013 supports multiple databases. For example, if you add a Hotmail or Windows Live account to Outlook, its associated address book will automatically be added as a new Outlook folder. To view or work with that account's contact records, select its folder (such as **Contacts - steve79@ Hotmail.com**) in the folder pane.

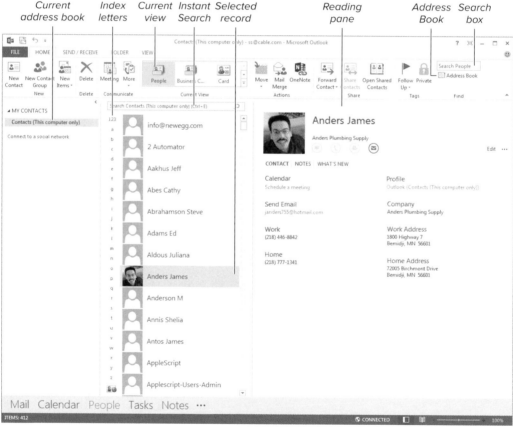

Ⓐ The People window.

General   Details   Close box

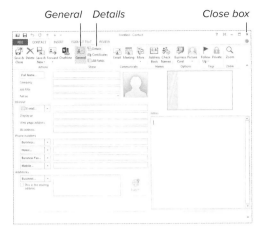

A An Outlook contact record can store a wealth of data In addition to a name and email address.

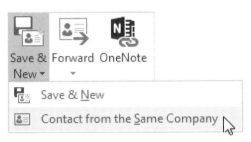

B If you want to create several contact records for the same company, choose this command to avoid some repetitive typing.

Creating Contact Records

There are several ways to create contact records. You can do any of the following:

- Manually create records from scratch

- Create a contact record from a received email message

- Import contact records from another copy of Outlook 2013, an earlier version of Outlook, or another email program or database

To manually create a new contact:

1. *Do either of the following:*

   ▸ In any Outlook component, choose Home:New:New Items > Contact (Ctrl-Shift-C).

   ▸ In People, click Home:New:New Contact (Ctrl-N).

   An Untitled - Contact window appears **A**.

2. Fill in as much information as desired.

3. *Do one of the following:*

   ▸ To save the record and close its window, click Contact:Actions:Save & Close.

   ▸ To save the record and immediately create another, click Contact:Actions:Save & New.

   ▸ To save the record and immediately create another using the same company information, choose Contact:Actions:Save & New > Contact from the Same Company **B**.

   ▸ If you decide not to save the record, click its close box (X) or click Contact:Actions:Delete and then confirm the deletion.

   continues on next page

TIP To display a photo for a contact, click the picture placeholder or choose Contact:Options: Picture > Add Picture.

TIP Although many contacts will contain information only on their General page, you can click Contact:Show:Details  to enter secondary information, such as data about the person's family.

TIP The File as field **C** on the General tab is critical because records are sorted by it in most views. Use a consistent naming convention so you can easily browse your contacts. For corporate contacts, I ensure that File as displays as *company (person),* for example.

C The File as choice for each record determines how it will be sorted in the Contacts database.

To create a new contact record from a received email message:

1. While viewing the message in the reading pane or its own window, right-click the sender's name/address and choose Add to Outlook Contacts from the context menu **D**.

    A partially completed contact record for the person or organization appears **E**.

TIP You can also create the record by hovering the cursor over the email address, clicking the down-arrow in the pop-up window that appears, and then clicking Add.

2. *Optional:* Enter additional information for the new contact. Click plus (+) icons to expose additional fields.

3. Click Save to save the record.

    The record is saved and its window closes.

TIP If you attempt to create a new contact record for an email address that's already in People, the Add to Outlook Contacts command is presented as Edit Contact. Use this option to make changes to the existing record.

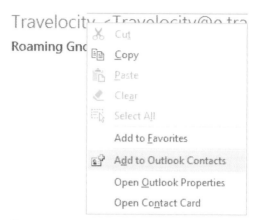

D Choose Add to Outlook Contacts.

Save

E Fill in as much information as you want for the person, company, or institution.

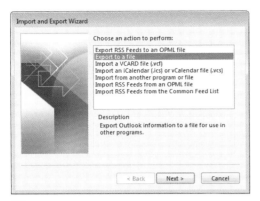

F Use the Import and Export Wizard to export contact data from any version of Outlook.

G If you're worried that someone else might open the file, you can optionally assign a password to it.

To import contact data from another copy of Outlook 2013 or a prior version:

1. **Exporting the contact data from the Outlook copy.** To export from Outlook 2013 or 2010, click the File tab, select Open & Export, and click Import/Export.

   To export from an earlier version of Outlook, choose File > Import or Export.

2. In the Import and Export Wizard, *do the following (in order):*

   ▸ Select Export to a file **F**.

   ▸ In Outlook 2013 and 2010, select Outlook Data File (.pst) as the output format. In Outlook 2007 or earlier, select Personal Folder File (.pst).

   ▸ Select Outlook\Contacts as the folder from which to export the data.

   ▸ Set a location for the export file by clicking the Browse button. Select Do not export duplicate items.

   ▸ Click Finish to create the export file.

   ▸ In Office 2013, a final dialog box appears in which you can assign an optional password for the file **G**. Fill in or leave the text boxes blank, and then click OK.

   The file is created. Move it to the target computer over the network or using removable media, such as a flash drive.

3. **Importing the data into Outlook 2013.** Click the File tab, select Open & Export, and click Import/Export.

4. In the Import and Export Wizard **F**, select Import from another program or file. Click Next.

5. On the Import a File screen, select Outlook Data File (.pst). Click Next.

   continues on next page

6. On the new screen 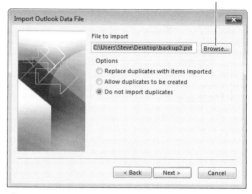, click Browse to locate the export file created in Steps 1–2. Specify how duplicates are to be handled and click Next.

7. On the final screen ⓘ, select Contacts as the import folder, select the folder that will receive the imported data, and click Finish.

   The records are imported into the selected Contacts database.

TIP **Outlook 2013 can also import contact data from other email programs and databases. The process is similar to the one in this task list. Export the contact data to an Outlook-compatible file format, such as Outlook Data File, tab-delimited, or Excel. Then import the data into Outlook. (You may have to instruct Outlook on the manner in which fields from the export file should map to Outlook fields.)**

Browse

Ⓗ Locate the export file that you created and indicate how duplicate records will be handled.

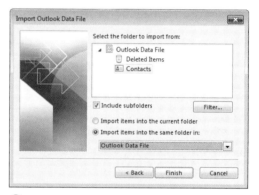

ⓘ Select the Contacts folder and direct the data into the appropriate Outlook folder.

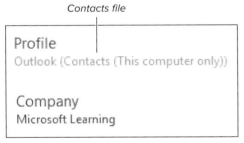

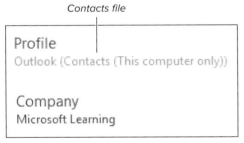

Save

 After opening a record, you can edit it or select and copy text (such as an email, web, or mailing address) for pasting elsewhere.

Contacts file

Profile
Outlook (Contacts (This computer only))

Company
Microsoft Learning

 Click the appropriate Contacts file to open the record for editing.

Editing Contact Records

After creating contact records, you can edit or delete records as needed.

To edit a contact (basic details):

1. To perform simple edits to a contact record, switch to People view. Double-click the record or click Edit in the reading pane.

   The record opens for editing in a separate window **A** or the reading pane, respectively.

2. Make the necessary changes.

3. Click the Save button.

To edit a contact (advanced details):

1. To make more extensive changes to a record or edit additional details, *do one of the following:*

   ▸ Select the record in People view. In the reading pane beneath the Profile heading, click the name of the Contacts file **B**. (More than one Contacts file may be listed.)

   ▸ In any other view, double-click the contact.

   The complete record opens for editing (see **A** in "Creating Contact Records").

2. Make the necessary changes.

3. Click Contact : Actions : Save & Close.

To delete a contact record:

1. *Do either of the following:*

   ▸ Select the record in the current view and click Home:Delete:Delete, press Ctrl-D, or press Del.

   ▸ Right-click the record in the current view and choose Delete from the context menu 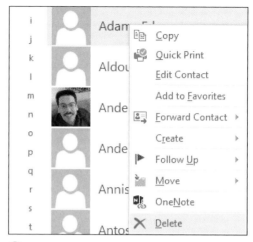 **C**.

2. If this is a *linked contact* (combining data from multiple sources), click Delete Contact in the warning dialog box **D**. Otherwise, the deletion is immediate.

> **TIP** If you delete a record by mistake, you can restore it by immediately pressing Ctrl-Z. Otherwise, you can retrieve it from the appropriate Deleted Items or Trash folder and drag it onto People in the Navigation Bar.

C You can right-click a record in any view and choose Delete.

D If a record is linked to multiple sources, a warning appears when you attempt to delete it.

Current View

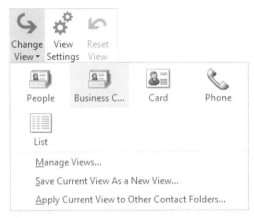

Ⓐ When the Home tab is selected, the quickest way to change views is to click an icon.

Ⓑ To switch views, you can also click an icon in the Change View menu.

The View:Arrangement Group

The View:Arrangement group has useful commands for modifying the current view. However, with the exception of Reverse Sort, they apply only to a columnar list view.

- **Reverse Sort.** Re-sort the records in reverse of their current order.
- **Add Columns.** Add or remove columns from the view.
- **Group By fields.** To group records by a field, select its field name (such as Company or Location) and choose Show in Groups from the drop-down menu.

Viewing Contact Records

Rather than searching for a specific record using the Instant Search box (described later in this chapter), you'll often find yourself simply flipping through contacts to find the one you want. There are four built-in *views* that you can use when browsing contacts; each can easily be customized.

To browse contact records:

1. Select a view by *doing either of the following:*

   ▸ Click an icon in the Home : Current View group **Ⓐ**.

   ▸ Choose a view from the View : Current View : Change View menu **Ⓑ**.

   TIP Outlook remembers the most recent view used—even between computing sessions.

2. In the contact list, *do any of the following:*

   ▸ Click the scroll arrows, click in the scroll bar, or drag the scroll box to a new position. Depending on the current view, the scroll bar will be on the right or bottom of the screen.

   ▸ In People, Business Cards, or Card view, click an index letter (see **Ⓐ** in "The Contacts Window") to view contacts beginning with that letter.

3. *Optional:* To view a complete contact record (in any view except People), double-click the record or select the record and press Ctrl-O.

   The record opens in a new window.

   TIP When working in a columnar list view (such as Phone or List), you can change the sort order by clicking a column heading. Click the heading again to reverse the sort order.

To customize a view:

1. Select a view to customize from the View: Current View: Change View menu **B**.

2. Click View: Current View: View Settings.

   The Advanced View Settings: *view name* dialog box appears **C**.

3. Click buttons to change their properties.

4. Click OK to close the Advanced View Settings dialog box.

   The view changes to reflect the new settings.

5. *Optional:* Choose View: Current View: Change View > Save Current View As a New View **B**, name the view in the Copy View dialog box, and click OK.

   The new view is added to the View: Current View: Change View and Home: Current View lists, enabling you to switch to the view whenever you like.

> **TIP** When working in a columnar list view, you can right-click a column heading to quickly change the sort field(s), apply a grouping, edit the field list, or remove the column **D**.

> **TIP** To add or remove fields in a columnar view, click View: Current View: View Settings and click Columns **C**. To change the column order, drag fields in the Show Columns dialog box, or you can select a field and click Move Up or Move Down. Click OK when you're done.

> **TIP** When a Group By field is specified, the records are organized in the view according to their membership in the group. You can collapse or expand a subgroup by clicking the triangle icon that precedes the group's name in the list.

> **TIP** To restore the active view to its original state (field list, field order, and so on), click View: Current View: Reset View.

> **TIP** To delete a custom view, right-click it in the View: Current View: Change View menu and choose Delete from the context menu.

Properties

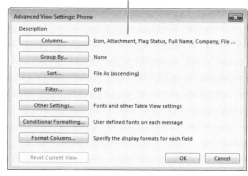

C Click buttons to change the properties of the current view.

D For simple changes to a list view, right-click a column heading.

Custom View Properties

Different views have various properties **C** you can change, such as the following:

Columns. Change the fields shown and their display order.

Group By. Set record-grouping fields.

Sort. Set a default sort order for the view. If you specify multiple sort fields, records will be sorted by the first field and—within that sort order—sorted by subsequent fields. For example, you could specify Company as the primary sort field, followed by Last Name and then First Name.

Filter. Apply a filter to generate a list of only those records that meet certain criteria. For example, by specifying that the Company field must contain **Microsoft**, you can create a Microsoft-only view.

Search string — *Results*

5 results.

Ⓐ You can perform a contact search by typing search text in the box in the Home:Find group.

Search string

Ⓑ Enter part of the name you're seeking and then click OK.

Searching for a Contact

If you want to quickly find a contact without browsing through records, Outlook provides search tools for you to use.

To search using the Find group box:

1. On the Home tab in any Outlook component, enter a search string in the box in the Find group Ⓐ.

   As you type, matching contacts appear in a scrolling list.

2. If the desired contact is shown, click the match to open the condensed, People-view record in its own window.

TIP After finding and opening a contact, you can create a new email message to the person or company by clicking the Send Email Message icon.

To perform a search in Address Book:

1. On the Home tab of any Outlook component, click the Find:Address Book icon.

   The Address Book window appears.

2. Choose Tools > Find (Ctrl-Shift-F).

   The Find window appears Ⓑ.

3. Enter search text and click OK.

   All matching records are displayed.

4. Double-click an entry to open its complete Outlook contact record.

TIP After finding and opening a contact, you can create a new email message to the person or company by clicking the Contact:Communicate:Email icon.

To perform an Instant Search:

1. Click in the Instant Search box above the contact record list (see Ⓐ in "The People Window").

   The Search Tools contextual tab appears Ⓒ.

2. *Do either of the following:*

   ‣ Type a search string in the top box Ⓓ.

   ‣ Type a search string in a content-specific box, such as State or E-mail.

   Potential matches appear as you type.

   TIP **The search string can be any part of a contact record, such as the name, company, area code, and so on.**

3. *Do any of the following:*

   ‣ Double-click a found record to open it for viewing or editing.

   ‣ Choose a recent search to repeat from the Search : Options : Recent Searches menu.

   ‣ To perform a more complex or specific search, add criteria by choosing options from the Refine group menus.

   TIP **Criteria chosen from the Refine group build the query text. Choices made from the Categorized, Has Phone Number, or Has Address menus** Ⓒ **are added directly to the query text. Any field chosen from the More menu (such as City and Company) displays a new text box in which you can type a criterion.**

   ‣ To remove a criterion Ⓓ, click its close box (X) or delete its reference in the main search text.

4. To resume viewing all contact records, click the X in the main Instant Search box Ⓓ or the Close Search icon Ⓒ.

Close Search

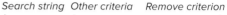

Ⓒ When you perform an Instant Search, the Search Tools contextual tab appears. Use its tools to refine the current search by adding criteria or to repeat a recent search.

Search string   Other criteria   Remove criterion

Matches   End search

Ⓓ Enter a search string. Matches appear as you type.

A Outlook displays the default fields and layout for a new business card. (If a card already exists, the current version is shown.)

B You can increase the size of the photo or logo. However, be sure that the longest text lines still fully display.

Using Business Cards

If people often ask for your contact information, Outlook provides a way for you to email your contact record as an *Electronic Business Card* (EBC) or *vCard*. If the recipient is an Outlook user, he or she can use it to create a contact record for you.

To create or edit a business card:

1. Open your complete contact record (or anyone else's) as explained in "To edit a contact (advanced details)," earlier in this chapter.

   Create the record if it doesn't exist.

2. If you want to display additional elements on the card, add those fields now.

3. Click Contact : Options : Business Card.

   The Edit Business Card window opens **A**.

4. *Do any of the following:*

   ▸ To change the business card layout, choose an option from the Layout drop-down menu.

   ▸ To use a different image, click the Image (Change) button. To change the image placement, choose an option from the Image Align menu. To change the image size **B**, enter a percentage in the Image Area box.

   ▸ To remove a field, select it and click Remove. To add a field, click Add and choose the field to add.

   ▸ To change a field's placement, select the field in the Fields list and click the up or down arrow.

   ▸ To change a field's formatting, select the field in the Fields list and pick formatting options from the Edit toolbar.

   continues on next page

- ▸ To add or remove a field label, select a field and specify the label and its position (relative to the field).

5. Click OK to save the business card.

   The finished business card appears above the record's Notes area Ⓑ.

6. Click Contact:Actions:Save & Close.

To email a business card:

1. Create a new email message.

2. Click Insert:Include:Business Card Ⓒ, and *do one of the following:*

   - ▸ Choose the card from the menu.
   - ▸ If the card isn't listed, choose Other Business Cards and select the desired contact record.

   The card is inserted into the message as a graphic and attached as a .vcf file.

To save a received business card as an Outlook contact record:

1. Display the received email message in the reading pane or open it in its own window. If you like, you can view the card fields by clicking the attachment tab above the message body Ⓓ.

2. In the message body, right-click the business card image and choose Add to Outlook Contacts Ⓔ.

   A contact record for the business card opens.

Ⓒ Choose a business card to attach to the current email message.

View the email message

View the business card

Ⓓ When you receive email with an attached business card, you can view the message or the card information by clicking these tabs.

Ⓔ You can create a contact record for the received vCard file.

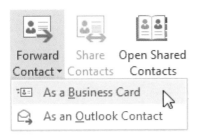

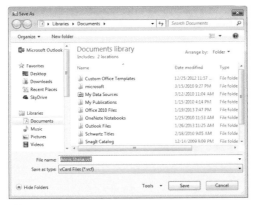

F You can forward any Outlook record as a business card.

G You can manually create a vCard file from a contact record, enabling you to email it as an attachment or import the data into another program or copy of Outlook.

3. *Do either of the following:*

▸ To save the record, click the Contact: Actions:Save & Close icon. (If you want, you can edit the information.)

▸ If you decide not to save the contact or believe it's a duplicate, click the close box (X) or click the Contact: Actions:Delete icon.

TIP You can forward *any* contact record as a business card by selecting the record in a contact list and choosing Home:Share:Forward Contact > As a Business Card **F**. Prior to doing so, you may want to modify the card's Fields list as explained in Step 4 of "To create or edit a business card."

TIP You can also save any record as a .vcf file. Open the full contact record for the person, click the File tab, and click Save As. In the Save As dialog box that appears **G**, the Save as type is automatically set to vCard Files (*.vcf).

Creating Contact Groups

Do you ever find yourself repeatedly addressing email to the same group of people? A project manager, for example, might email a weekly update to all group members. When you need to regularly send messages to a clearly defined group, you can create a *contact group* (called a distribution list in earlier Outlook versions).

To create a contact group:

1. *Do one of the following:*

   ▶ In People, click Home: New: New Contact Group.

   ▶ In any other Outlook component, choose Home: New: New Items > More Items > Contact Group.

   ▶ Press Shift-Ctrl-L.

   An Untitled - Contact Group window appears **Ⓐ**.

2. Enter a name for the contact group in the Name box.

   Choose a descriptive name. It's how the group will be identified in your contact list.

3. To add members with contact records to the group, choose Contact Group: Members: Add Members > From Outlook Contacts or From Address Book **Ⓑ**.

   The Address Book window opens. To add a person to the group, select their name and click the Members button **Ⓒ**. Repeat for each additional member and then click OK. The new members are added to the contact group **Ⓐ**.

Name box

Ⓐ Create and edit contact groups in this window.

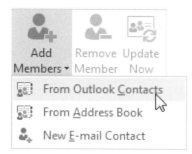

Ⓑ To add existing contacts to a group, start by choosing the source.

Members button *New members*

Ⓒ The email addresses of the chosen members are added to the box at the bottom of the Address Book window.

D You can also add members who aren't in your Address Book. Click the Add to Contacts check box if you'd also like to create a contact record for the person.

Group name

E If you address an email message to the group, a copy is sent to each group member.

4. To add a member to the contact group who does not have a contact record, choose Contact Group : Members : Add Members > New E-mail Contact **B**.

The Add New Member dialog box appears **D**. Enter the person's name, email address, and email options. Click OK.

5. To save the contact group and create a record for it using the group name, click Contact Group : Actions : Save & Close.

To modify a contact group:

1. Open the contact group record, and *do any of the following:*

- ▸ To remove a member, select the member, and click Contact Group : Members : Remove Member.

- ▸ To add new members, perform Step 3 or 4 from the previous task list.

- ▸ If any list member's data has changed (a new email address, company name, or display name, for example), click Contact Group : Members : Update Now to update their contact data with the current information.

2. To save your changes, click Contact Group : Actions : Save & Close.

TIP To address a message to a contact group, enter the group name in the email message's To, Cc, or Bcc box **E**. To selectively exclude certain members from this mailing, double-click the group name in the To, Cc, or Bcc box, click OK, and then delete the unnecessary names or email addresses.

TIP To delete a contact group, select its record in any list and click Home : Delete : Delete; right-click the record and choose Delete; or press Ctrl-D, Del, or Delete. If the group's contact record is open, click Contact Group : Actions : Delete Group.

Composing and Sending Mail

While much of a new user's email experi-
ence will consist of receiving and reading
messages from supervisors, mailing lists,
unwanted ads, and jokes from friends, most
will eventually participate in the other part
of the process: sending mail to others. You
can create new messages, reply to incoming
messages, and forward received messages
to others.

Whether you are composing a new message, writing a reply, or forwarding email to
a co-worker, the process of composing and
sending a message consists of these steps:

1. Open a window for the new message,
   reply, or message to be forwarded.

2. Specify recipients and enter a Subject.

3. Select a message format.

4. Compose the message.

5. Add optional attachments, such as a
   photo, text document, or worksheet.

6. Send the message.

In this chapter, you'll learn to create new
messages, reply to and forward received
mail, and use Outlook tools to ensure that
your messages are correct and attractive.

In This Chapter

The Message Window

You can create three types of email messages in Outlook:

- **New messages.** Messages you compose from scratch.

- **Replies.** Responses to received messages.

- **Forwarded messages.** Received messages you are sending to someone else.

Messages are composed in a window 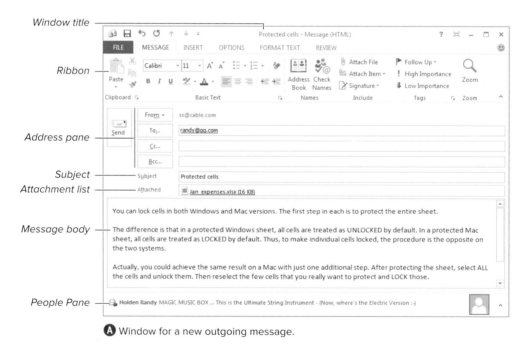 or the Reading Pane. The main sections include the message header or address pane (the To, Cc, Bcc, and Subject boxes), the attachment list, and the message body (the text of the message).

When you compose a message in a window, the Ribbon is displayed across its top. When composing replies or forwarded messages in the Reading Pane, commands are selected from the normal Ribbon and the Compose Tools : Message contextual tab.

Using Click-and-Type

Click-and-type, a feature introduced several years ago in Word, is also supported in Outlook 2013. You can type *anywhere* in the message window; that is, there's no requirement that you begin typing in the top-left corner. If you want to enter text somewhere else, simply double-click to position the text insertion mark where you want the new text to begin.

Composing Messages in the Reading Pane

New in Outlook 2013, you can elect to compose replies and forwarded messages in the Reading Pane. In Outlook Options, select the Mail category and scroll to the Replies and forwards section. If Open replies and forwards in a new window is unchecked, each Reply, Reply All, or Forward is composed in the Reading Pane.

Window title —

Ribbon —

Address pane —

Subject —
Attachment list —

Message body —

People Pane —

Ⓐ Window for a new outgoing message.

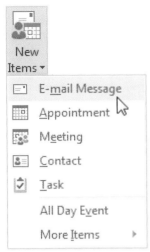

A You can also create a new message by choosing Home: New Items > E-mail Message.

Proposed account

B You can send the message from the proposed account or from another in the From list.

C You can type a few letters of a contact's name or email address and then select from a list of potential matches.

Creating Messages

To let a relative know what's new, send a web link or photo to a friend, or inform your supervisor how a project is progressing, you start by creating a new message. You can also create email by replying to or forwarding a received message. And you can resend any previously sent message—either to the same person or someone else.

To create a new message:

1. *Do one of the following:*

   ▶ When working in Mail, click Home: New: New Email (Ctrl-N).

   ▶ When working in *any* component (Mail, Calendar, People, Tasks, or Notes), choose Home: New: New Items > E-mail Message **A** (Ctrl-Shift-M).

   A message window opens (see **A** in "The Message Window"). The cursor is positioned in the To box, ready for you to enter recipients. The message will be sent from the active account in the Folder Pane or, when another Outlook component is active, from your default account (see Chapter 16). If you like, you can select a different account from the From list **B**.

2. Enter primary recipients in the To box. Specify the first To email address by *doing one of the following:*

   ▶ Start typing the person's name or email address. As you type, matching recipients drawn from addresses you previously typed in the address pane appear **C**. Select a recipient or continue typing.

   continues on next page

- Click the To button, click the Message:Names:Address Book icon , or press Ctrl-Shift-B. To add a person from the Address Book, select them and click the To button or double-click their name. Click OK.

D When entering message recipients, it can be helpful to consult your Address Book.

3. *Optional:* Repeat Step 2 to enter more To addresses. Note that each address pair must be separated by a semicolon (;).

4. *Optional:* Persons in the Cc (*carbon copy*) box represent secondary recipients. To add Cc recipients, click in the Cc box and follow Steps 2–3.

5. *Optional:* A message can also have Bcc (*blind carbon copy*) recipients. Addresses in the Bcc box are hidden from all recipients. To add Bcc recipients, click in the Bcc box and follow Steps 2–3.

E Click the Bcc icon to reveal the normally hidden Bcc box.

TIP If the Bcc box isn't visible, click the Options:Show Fields:Bcc icon **E**. Outlook remembers and uses the most recent Bcc setting in subsequent sessions.

6. Click or tab into the Subject box. Enter a subject to identify the message.

7. Click or tab into the message area and type the message text.

8. Click Send to send the message.

TIP You can also paste a copied email address into the To, Cc, or Bcc box. Click the Message:Clipboard:Paste icon or press Ctrl-V.

TIP You can drag addresses between the To, Cc, and Bcc boxes.

TIP The AutoComplete drop-down list **C** doesn't suggest contacts from the Address Book. However, if you type a contact's full name, Outlook will mail the message to the correct address.

Sending Messages from Different Accounts

If you just click the Send icon to send a new message, it is sent from the currently selected account or, if you're working in a non-Mail part of Outlook, from your default account. When you click the Send icon to send a reply or forwarded message, it is sent from your account that received the original message.

To send any message from a *different* account, click the From button and select the account you'd like to use.

Drafts: Works in Progress

You aren't required to immediately send each message. If you're still working on a message, you can save it as a *draft*. To save a message in progress, click the Save icon in the Quick Access Toolbar, click Save in the Backstage, press Ctrl-S, or close the message and elect to save it when prompted. Saved messages are stored in an account's Drafts folder, where you can continue working on them and send at your convenience.

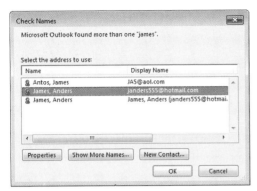

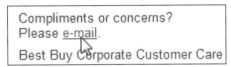

F Select the desired contact and click OK. If you can't find the person, click Cancel.

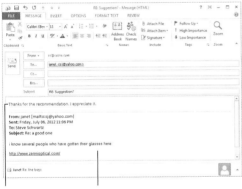

G Some web pages contain *mailto:* links, such as this one. Click the link to create a new pre-addressed message in Outlook.

Reply text   Quoted text from
original message

H When replying to email, you normally type your reply above the author's quoted text.

TIP If you enter only a partial name in an address box and click Send, the Check Names dialog box appears **F**. Select the correct person and click OK.

TIP You can create a pre-addressed message by clicking an email address or *mailto:* link in a received email message or on a web page **G**.

To create a reply:

1. In the message list, select the header of the message to which you are replying or open the message in its own window.

2. Click the Home:Respond:Reply icon or press Ctrl-R.

   A copy of the message appears in a new window or the Reading Pane, addressed to the original author. The author's text is *quoted* (repeated) at the bottom of the message **H**. The Subject becomes RE: *original Subject* and the text insertion mark is positioned above the quoted text.

3. *Optional:* You can add more recipients in the address pane boxes.

4. Type your reply to the message.

5. Edit the quoted text, if desired (removing extraneous material, for example).

6. Click the Send icon.

   Replies are automatically sent from the account to which the original message was addressed.

TIP When writing a reply, you should resist editing the automatically generated Subject. The RE: *original Subject* shows the recipient the message to which you're responding.

TIP To reply to everyone in the To and Cc lines of a received message, click Home: Respond:Reply All (Ctrl-Shift-R).

TIP Be sure to read the "Replying with Inline Comments" sidebar, later in this chapter.

To forward a received message:

1. Select the header of the message you want to forward or open the message in its own window.

2. Click the Home:Respond:Forward icon or press Ctrl-F.

   The author's text is *quoted* (repeated) at the bottom of the message. The Subject is automatically changed to FW: *original Subject* 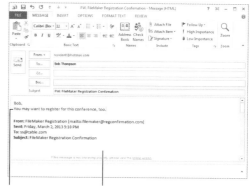.

3. In the address pane, specify recipients for the forwarded message.

4. *Optional:* You can edit the original text, as well as insert your own comments.

5. Click the Send icon.

   Forwarded messages are sent from the account to which the original message was addressed.

TIP In addition to forwarding a message as quoted text, you can forward it as an attachment. With the header selected or the message open in its own window, choose Home:Respond: More > Forward as Attachment.

To resend a previously sent message:

1. In a Sent or Sent Items folder, locate the previously sent message and open it in its own window.

2. Choose Message:Move:Actions > Resend This Message **J**.

   A copy of the original message appears.

3. *Optional:* Change the message recipient(s) or add others.

4. Click the Send icon.

TIP You can use the Resend This Message command to send the same message to multiple people, one at a time. Just change the recipient each time.

New text   *Forwarded message*

I When forwarding email, you can add your own comments, as well as edit the forwarded text.

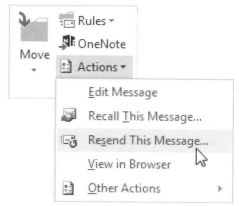

J Choose Resend This Message from the drop-down menu.

Recalling a Sent Message

If a message recipient has an Exchange Server account, you can optionally *recall* a message you've mistakenly sent to them or one that contains errors.

1. Open the previously sent message.

2. Choose Message:Move:Actions > Recall This Message **J**.

3. Select an option in the Recall This Message dialog box.

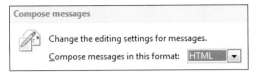

A By default, all new messages will use the chosen format.

B Select a format for the message. The current format is highlighted in blue.

Replying with Inline Comments

Rather than separate reply text from the quoted material to which you're replying, some prefer to write their comments—usually in a different color—embedded in the original message text. In Outlook 2013, a new *inline comments* feature makes this more convenient.

1. Open the Outlook Options dialog box and select the Mail category.

2. Check Preface comments with: and enter preface text, such as your name. To use colored text without preface text (such as [Steve]), leave the option unchecked.

3. Click OK to close the dialog box.

When replying to or forwarding email, you can now click anywhere in the body of the original message and type your comments. (If desired, you can still enter reply text *above* the quoted message.)

About Message Formats

Every message you create must be in Plain Text, HTML, or Rich Text format.

- *Plain Text* is a universally readable, single-font format. It doesn't support character formatting (such as boldface, italic, or color) or paragraph formatting.

- *HTML* is meant for messages that must contain formatting. You can format text with specific fonts and colors, create bulleted and numbered lists, embed pictures in the message body, insert links, and use stationery backgrounds.

- *Rich Text* messages can only be read by Microsoft email clients. When sent over the Internet, they're automatically converted to HTML. They are sent unaltered only to other Exchange Server accounts within your network.

You can set a default format to be used for new messages, as well as change the format of the message you're currently writing.

To set a default message format:

1. Click the File tab. In the Backstage, click Options.

   The Outlook Options dialog box appears.

2. Select the Mail category and choose a default format in the Compose messages section **A**.

3. Click OK to save your changes and close the Outlook Options dialog box.

To set a format for the current message:

- On the Format Text tab of the message you're composing, click an icon in the Format group **B**.

Formatting Message Text

When creating an HTML or Rich Text format message, you can selectively apply character and paragraph formatting. Outlook 2013 provides the Format Painter tool for quickly duplicating character formatting.

To apply character formatting:

1. *Do either of the following:*

   ▸ Select the text that you want to format.

   TIP You can make multiple noncontiguous selections by holding down Ctrl as you make each selection.

   ▸ Position the text insertion mark where you want the new character formatting to begin.

2. *Do any of the following:*

   ▸ Select character-formatting options from the Message:Basic Text group 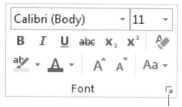.

   ▸ Select character-formatting options from the Format Text:Font group **B**.

   ▸ Select the text to be formatted, and then select formatting commands from the Mini toolbar **C** that appears.

   ▸ Click the Font dialog box launcher at the bottom of the Font or Basic Text group. In the Font dialog box, select character-formatting options and click OK to apply the formatting. (For more information on working with the Font dialog box, see "Character Formatting" in Chapter 5.)

   ▸ Press a formatting command's keyboard shortcut, such as Ctrl-B for Bold. To view the keyboard shortcut for a command, rest the cursor on its icon in the Basic Text or Font group. **Table 18.1** lists many of the shortcuts.

Font dialog box launcher

A The left side of the Basic Text group presents a subset of the most common character-formatting commands.

Font dialog box launcher

B The Format Text:Font group provides the most complete array of character-formatting commands.

Do you have any idea what I should buy for dinner?

C The pop-up Mini toolbar has frequently used character- and paragraph-formatting commands.

TABLE 18.1 Character-formatting Keyboard Shortcuts

Keypress	Definition
Ctrl-B	Boldface
Ctrl-I	Italic
Ctrl-U	Underline (single)
Ctrl-Shift-K	Small capital letters (small caps)
Ctrl-Shift-=	Subscript
Ctrl-Shift-+	Superscript
Ctrl-Shift-<	Decrease font size
Ctrl-Shift->	Increase font size

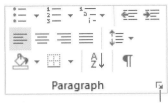

Paragraph dialog box launcher

D The Paragraph group contains general paragraph-formatting commands.

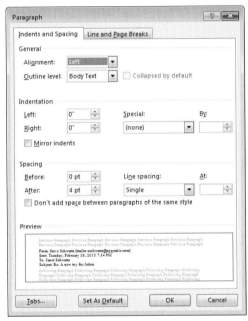

E Use the Paragraph dialog box when you have more extensive paragraph-formatting needs.

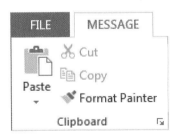

F You can select the Format Painter tool in the Clipboard group or on the Mini toolbar.

To apply paragraph formatting:

1. Position the text insertion mark in the paragraph that you want to format.

   You can also preselect multiple paragraphs or select some text within the paragraph.

2. *Do any of the following:*

   ▸ Select paragraph-formatting commands from the Format Text:Paragraph group **D**.

   ▸ Select paragraph-formatting commands from the Message:Basic Text group **A**.

   ▸ Click the Paragraph dialog box launcher at the bottom of the Format Text:Paragraph group, choose settings from the Paragraph dialog box **E**, and click OK.

   ▸ Enter a paragraph-formatting command's keyboard shortcut, such as Ctrl-J for Justify. (To see a command's shortcut, rest the cursor on its icon in the Paragraph or Basic Text group.)

To apply character formatting with the Format Painter tool:

1. Select specific text or a paragraph that contains the formatting you want to copy.

2. Select the Format Painter tool in the Message:Clipboard group **F**, the Format Text:Clipboard group, or the Mini toolbar.

3. Drag to select the text you want to format.

   When you stop dragging, the copied formatting is applied to the selected text.

   TIP When using the Format Painter tool, you can apply the copied format to a word by double-clicking the word.

To apply a Quick Style to text:

1. Select the text to be formatted or position the text insertion mark in the paragraph to be formatted.

2. Open the Quick Styles gallery in the Format Text:Styles group 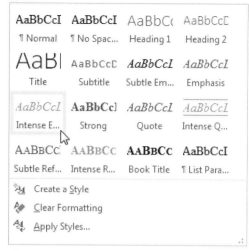.

3. As you move the cursor over a style in the gallery, a preview of the style is shown on the selected text or paragraph. Click a style to apply it.

   If you decide not to apply any of the styles, click outside the gallery.

To remove character formatting:

1. Select the text from which you want to remove previously applied formatting.

2. *Do one of the following:*

   ▸ If your most recent action was to apply the character formatting, press Ctrl-Z or click the Undo icon on the Quick Access Toolbar ◯.

   ▸ Select the same formatting command on the Ribbon or Mini toolbar.

   ▸ Click the Format Text:Font:Clear Formatting icon ◯ to remove *all* previously applied formatting from the selected text.

> **TIP** You can't reverse the Text Highlight Color or the Font Color of selected text by clicking the same icon again. Select the original color or click Clear Formatting ◯.

> **TIP** Most paragraph formatting can't be reversed by clicking the icon again. To restore the original formatting, click the appropriate icon in the Paragraph group. (However, you *can* eliminate Bullets and Numbering formatted paragraphs by clicking their icons again.)

G To easily apply complex, attractive character or paragraph formatting to selected text or paragraphs, select a style from the Quick Styles gallery.

H To reverse your most recent action, click the Undo icon on the Quick Access Toolbar.

I Click Clear Formatting to remove all applied character formatting from the selected text.

More Quick Styles

If you don't like the default Quick Styles, there are other style sets from which you can choose. You can also change the colors and fonts used. Click the Change Styles icon to explore these options. See "Working with Styles" in Chapter 5 for more information on using Quick Styles.

A Click the Attach File icon.

B Select one or more files and click the Insert button (Windows 7 shown).

C The Attached box shows the names and sizes of any attached files.

D The context menu contains a Remove command.

Adding Attachments

One popular use of email is to transmit documents and photos with your messages. These files are known as *attachments*.

To add an attachment to a message:

1. On the Message or Insert tab, click the Include:Attach File icon **A**.

   The Insert File dialog box appears **B**.

2. Navigate to the drive and folder in which the file is stored, select the file, and click Insert. (You can select multiple files within a folder by Ctrl-clicking them.)

   The file is added to the Attached list **C**. You can add other attachments by repeating these steps.

TIP You can also add attachments by dragging their file icons from the Desktop or any open folder onto the open message.

TIP To remove an attachment, select it in the Attached list and then press Backspace or Del. You can also right-click an attachment and choose Remove from the context menu **D**.

TIP Check the total size of the attachments before sending a message. First, ISPs have a maximum message size, and attachments tend to get larger when encoded for transmission. Second, not everyone has broadband Internet access. If you email a huge video or audio clip to a friend with a dial-up account, you'll tie them up for a very long time.

Inserting Items

The Insert tab provides tools for inserting items—such as tables, charts, horizontal lines, and clip art—directly into the body of HTML and Rich Text messages. In this section, you'll learn how to insert three common items: photos, business cards, and hyperlinks.

To insert a photo or other image:

1. Position the text insertion mark at the spot in the message body where you want to insert the image.

2. Click Insert : Illustrations : Pictures.

   The Insert Pictures dialog box appears.

3. Navigate to the drive/folder that contains the image, select the file, and click Insert.

   The image appears in the message body 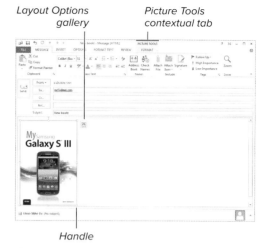.

4. *Optional:* With the image selected, you can resize it by dragging any corner handle. To rotate the image, drag the circle at the top. You can also perform image enhancement, editing, and formatting by selecting commands on the Picture Tools contextual tab.

To insert a business card image:

1. Position the text insertion mark at the spot in the message body where you want to insert the business card image.

2. Choose a card from those listed in the Insert : Include : Business Card menu **B**. To send contact info for someone whose name isn't listed, choose Other Business Cards.

   A graphic version of the business card is inserted into the message body and added as an attachment **C**.

Layout Options gallery   *Picture Tools contextual tab*

Handle

A When an inserted image is selected, image editing and enhancement commands appear.

B Choose a business card to insert.

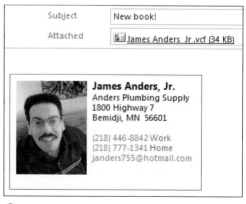

C The business card is added to the message as an image and as an attachment.

To insert a clickable web page link:

1. Position the text insertion mark at the spot in the message body where you want to insert the web link.

2. Click Insert:Links:Hyperlink (Ctrl-K).

   The Insert Hyperlink dialog box appears.

3. Select Existing File or Web Page in the Link to list and Browsed Pages in the inner list **D**.

4. Select a recently viewed page from the scrolling list or from the Address drop-down list. You can also type or paste an address (URL) into the Address box.

5. *Optional:* Edit the text in the Text to display box. This text will represent the link in the message.

6. Click OK.

   The link text is inserted into the message **E**. When the recipient clicks the link, the specified page will load in the person's default web browser.

> **TIP** You can also create a hyperlink by typing or pasting (Ctrl-V) a complete address into the message body. Outlook automatically converts the text to a hyperlink if the text is recognized as a proper link (such as `www.hotmail.com`).

Link text to display in message

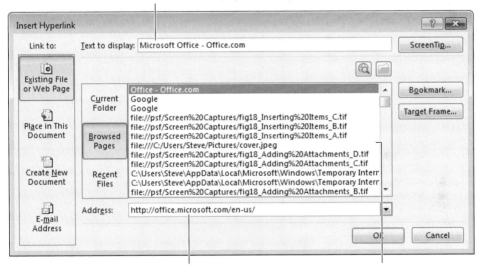

Page address   Recently viewed pages

D You can create a web page hyperlink by specifying the address and wording for the link text.

Microsoft Office - Office.com

E When inserted into a message, a web link looks and acts like one on a web page.

To insert a clickable email link:

1. Position the text insertion mark at the spot in the message body where you want to insert the email (*mailto:*) link.

2. Click Insert:Links:Hyperlink (Ctrl-K).

   The Insert Hyperlink dialog box **F** appears.

3. Select E-mail Address in the Link to list.

4. Type or paste the destination address into the E-mail address box.

   A *mailto:* prefix is automatically added to the address.

5. *Optional:* Edit the Text to display.

6. *Optional:* Enter a Subject for the message.

7. Click OK.

   The link text is inserted into the message **G**. When the recipient clicks the link, a new email message addressed to the specified recipient appears.

> **TIP** You can also convert existing message text to a hyperlink. In Step 1 of either task list, select the text rather than positioning the text insertion mark. The selected text is automatically treated as the Text to display.

> **TIP** To convert a hyperlink back to normal text, select the text, right-click it, and choose Remove Hyperlink from the context menu.

F You can also insert an email (*mailto:*) link that generates a new message to the specified address when clicked by the recipient.

Mailto: link

G When the recipient clicks the embedded mailto: link, a new pre-addressed message is generated.

Hyperlinks in Plain Text Messages

Hyperlinks work best in HTML or Rich Text messages. Although hyperlinks can also be used in Plain Text messages, the following restrictions apply:

- The Hyperlink command is unavailable, so you must enter links manually.

- Long URLs may be broken up, rendering them inoperable when clicked.

Correcting Spelling Errors

When correcting spelling in Outlook
☑ Check spelling as you type
☐ Mark grammar errors as you type
☑ Frequently confused words
☐ Check grammar with spelling
☐ Show readability statistics
Writing Style: Grammar Only ▼ Settings...
Recheck E-mail

A The top check box determines whether spelling errors are automatically flagged as you compose each message. Note that you can also check for errors in grammar, if you wish.

Suspect word

hedghbg for $5 that squeaks EV

hedgehog 🖰
Ignore All
Add to Dictionary
Who Is...
🌐 Hyperlink...

B To quickly correct an actual error, you may be able to select the correct spelling from the suggestions.

Unless you're both an exceptional speller and typist (or you trust that your recipients will simply *know* what you're trying to say, regardless of what you type), you should perform a spell check on each outgoing message. There are two options:

- Check for and flag errors as you type.
- Perform spell checks manually or automatically before each message is sent.

To check spelling as you type:

1. This option is enabled by default. If you've disabled it, click the File tab and then click Options in the Backstage.

2. In the Outlook Options dialog box, select the Mail category. In the Compose messages section, click the Spelling and Autocorrect button.

3. In the Editor Options dialog box, ensure that Check spelling as you type **A** is checked and click OK. Click OK again to close the Outlook Options dialog box.

4. As you type, Outlook checks each word. Suspect words are marked with a red underline. For each word, you can:
   - Ignore the error (because you believe the spelling is correct).
   - Edit the word to correct the error.
   - Right-click the word. From the context menu that appears **B**, choose the correct spelling, choose Ignore All to accept all instances of this spelling in the message, or choose Add to Dictionary to accept the spelling and add it to your spelling dictionary (so it will be recognized in future messages).

To perform a manual spelling check:

1. Click the Review : Proofing : Spelling & Grammar icon or press F7.

   If errors are found, the Spelling and Grammar dialog box appears 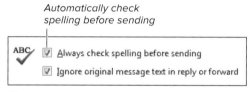. Otherwise, you're notified that the spelling check is complete.

2. Each suspect word is shown in boldface. *Do one of the following:*

   ▸ Select a replacement word from the Suggestions list and click Change to correct the error. (If you think you've made the same mistake elsewhere in the message, click Change All.)

   ▸ Edit the word in the Not in Dictionary text box and click Change.

   ▸ Click Ignore Once to ignore this instance of the spelling, leaving the current word unchanged.

   ▸ Click Ignore All to ignore all instances of this spelling, leaving all instances unchanged in this message.

   ▸ If the word is spelled correctly and you want it recognized in future spelling checks, click Add to Dictionary.

3. Repeat Step 2 for additional suspect words. The spelling check ends when all suspect words have been examined or you click Cancel.

TIP If you'd rather defer spelling checks until you're done writing each message, click **Always check spelling before sending** in the **Mail - Compose messages** section of the Outlook Options dialog box 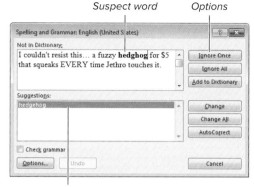. When this option is checked and you click Send for an outgoing message, a spell check will be performed.

Suspect word   Options

Possible replacements

C When you perform a spelling check, Outlook displays each suspect word in context.

Automatically check
spelling before sending

D Enable this option to automatically request a spelling check of every outgoing message.

Defined signatures

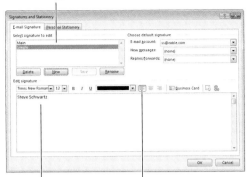

Create and   Formatting toolbar
edit signatures

A You create, edit, assign, and delete signatures in the Signatures and Stationery window.

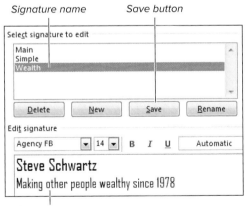

B Enter a name to identify this signature and click OK.

Signature name   Save button

Signature text

C This simple signature includes my name and a memorable quote.

Using Signatures

Optionally, an outgoing message can end with a *signature* (text or an image that provides your name and mailing address, web address, electronic business card, or a snappy quote). A signature can automatically be added to every outgoing message or manually added to only certain ones. You can create as many signatures as you need.

To create a signature:

1. Create a new mail message. Choose Message:Include:Signature > Signatures or Insert:Include:Signature > Signatures.

   The Signatures and Stationery dialog box appears **A**.

2. Click New to create a new signature.

   The New Signature dialog box appears.

3. Name the new signature **B** and click OK.

   The name is added to the list of defined signatures.

4. Enter one or multiple lines of signature text, formatted as you want them to appear when appended to a message. You can also *do the following:*

   ‣ Format selected text by applying fonts, sizes, and other options from the formatting toolbar **A**.

   ‣ Insert an image of your electronic business card, a photo, or a hyperlink (such as your web site address) by clicking formatting toolbar icons.

5. When you're done creating and formatting the signature **C**, click Save.

6. You can continue creating, editing, and deleting signatures or click OK to close the Signatures and Stationery window.

To set a default signature
for an email account:

1. In the Signatures and Stationery window, select the mail account to which a default signature will be added  **D**.

2. *Do any of the following:*

   ▸ To specify a default signature to be added to all new messages from the account, select a signature name from the New messages drop-down list.

   ▸ To specify a default signature to be added to all replies and to forwarded messages from the account, select a name from the Replies/forwards list.

3. Click OK to save your changes.

To manually add a signature
to a message:

1. Click to set the text insertion point in your message. Normally, this will be beneath the final message line.

2. On the Message or Insert tab, select a signature from the Include:Signature drop-down list **E**.

TIP You can also use a signature to store a complete message, such as one notifying people that you're out of the office.

TIP To edit a signature, select it in the Select signature to edit list **C**, make the desired changes, and click Save. To delete or rename a signature, select it in the same list and click the appropriate button.

TIP To replace a message's signature with a different one, select the other signature from the Signature icon's drop-down list.

TIP If you create a formatted signature and append it to a Plain Text message, an unformatted version of the signature is automatically used.

D You can specify a default signature to automatically be added to certain types of email from a given account. Choose None if you prefer no signature or intend to add one manually.

E Select a signature to include in the current message.

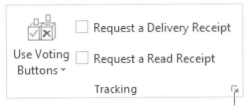

Properties dialog box launcher

A Click check boxes in the Tracking group to request receipts for the current message.

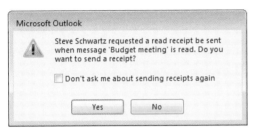

B In Outlook, this dialog box asks the recipient to verify that the message has been read. (Note that the recipient isn't required to respond and that few programs support this feature.)

C To help a message stand out, mark it as High Importance.

Properties dialog box launcher

TIP You can simultaneously set delivery, priority, and other options by clicking the Properties dialog box launcher at the bottom of the Options:Tracking **A**, Message:Tags **C**, or Options:More Options group.

Other Message Options

While not essential to most users (or most messages), this section explores some other Outlook message-creation options.

Requesting a Receipt

If a message is very important, you can request a delivery or read receipt. A *delivery receipt* is an email notification that the message has been delivered to the recipient. A *read receipt* indicates that the recipient has actually opened and read the message.

To request a delivery or read receipt:

- Prior to sending the message, click the appropriate check box(es) in the Options: Tracking group **A**.

  If a delivery receipt was requested, an email notification will be sent to you when the message is delivered. If a read receipt was requested and the recipient's email client supports this feature, they will be asked to confirm that they have read the message **B**.

Setting a Message Priority

You can set a *priority* for an outgoing message to indicate its relative level of importance. Setting a priority, however, has no impact on the manner in which it is delivered. Note that not all email programs recognize and display priorities.

To set a priority for a message:

- Prior to sending a message, click the Message:Tags:High Importance or Low Importance icon **C**.

  By default, all outgoing messages are sent Normal priority.

Applying a Background Color, Theme, or Stationery

In addition to allowing formatted text, HTML messages can have a *theme* (a coordinated set of fonts, bullets, colors, and effects) or be written on *stationery* (a colorful background). These elements can be applied on a message-by-message basis or to all new messages.

To apply a background color or theme to a message:

1. Create a new message. Click the Format Text:Format:HTML icon to set the message type to HTML.

2. *Optional:* Click in the message area and select a background color from the Options:Themes:Page Color palette 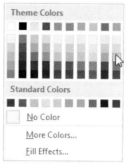 **D**.

3. *Optional:* To apply a theme, choose options from the other menus and palettes in the Themes group **E**.

To use stationery for a message:

1. Choose Home: New:New Items:E-mail Message Using > More Stationery.

   The Theme or Stationery dialog box appears **F**.

2. Select a stationery option from the Choose a Theme list. Click OK.

   A blank HTML message window appears, formatted to match the stationery.

3. Address and compose the message, and then click Send.

D You can select a color to serve as the message's background.

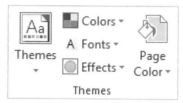

E You can apply colorful themes, fonts, and backgrounds to a message by choosing options from the Options:Themes group.

Themes   Preview

Options

F Select a theme from the Choose a Theme list. Set options for the selected theme by checking or clearing check boxes.

G If you want certain types of messages to use the same theme or stationery, you can set defaults. You can also specify a default font for different classes of messages.

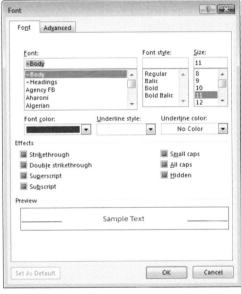

H Use the Font dialog box to select a default font, style, and color to use in new messages, replies, or forwards.

To set a default theme or stationery:

1. Click the File tab. In the Backstage, click Options to open the Outlook Options dialog box.

2. Select the Mail category. Click the Stationery and Fonts button in the Compose Messages section.

   The Signatures and Stationery dialog box appears, open to the Personal Stationery tab **G**.

3. Click the Theme button.

   The Theme or Stationery dialog box appears **F**.

4. Select a theme or stationery format.

5. Dismiss all open dialog boxes by clicking OK in each one.

   The theme or stationery will automatically be applied to every new HTML message you create.

TIP To remove a default theme, select (No Theme) from the Choose a Theme list in the Theme or Stationery dialog box **F**.

TIP Even if you don't want to designate a default theme, you can use the Signatures and Stationery dialog box to specify a default font to be used to compose new messages, reply to messages, or forward messages. Click a Font button **G** and select options in the Font dialog box **H**.

TIP You also may want to enable the option to Pick a new color when replying or forwarding **G**. This ensures that any text you add to a reply or forwarded message will always be in a different color from the original author's text.

19

Receiving Mail

In this chapter, you'll learn how to check for new email (manually and automatically); select and read messages; change your view and display message conversations; search for messages in a folder or in all mail folders; preview, open, and save attachments; and print messages or a list of message headers. Much of the information in this chapter applies not only to incoming mail but to sent messages, too.

For information on replying to and forwarding received messages, see Chapter 18. To learn about managing email (including deleting, copying, and moving messages, and managing conversations), refer to Chapter 20.

In This Chapter

Checking for New Mail

Outlook 2013 provides two ways to check for incoming mail:

- **Automatically.** Anytime Outlook is running and in online mode, all accounts in a given *send/receive group* (see Chapter 16) are automatically checked for new incoming messages every so many minutes, based on the group's schedule.

- **Manually.** To immediately check for new messages in an account or an entire send/receive group, you can perform a manual send/receive.

TIP Exchange and IMAP accounts are continuously synchronized with the server, so they don't need a schedule.

TIP The notification methods used to signal new mail are determined by the settings in Outlook Options:Mail:Message Arrival.

To perform a manual Send/Receive All Folders:

- *Do one of the following:*
  - ▸ Click the Send/Receive All Folders icon on the Quick Access Toolbar **A**.
  - ▸ Click Send/Receive:Send & Receive: Send/Receive All Folders **A**.
  - ▸ Press F9.

TIP By default, the All send/receive group contains every account group you've defined in Outlook. To change a group's inclusion in this group, see "Working with Send/Receive Groups" in Chapter 16.

Send/Receive All Folders

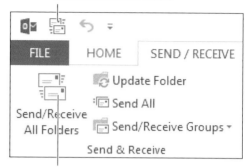

Send/Receive All Folders

A You can perform a manual Send/Receive All Folders by clicking the Quick Access Toolbar icon or the Send/Receive:Send & Receive:Send/Receive All Folders icon.

Send/Receive Groups ▾

   0 "All Accounts" Group

   1 "Hotmail" Group

B To initiate a manual send/receive for an Outlook group, choose the group from this menu.

To perform a manual send/receive for a specific group:

- Choose a group from the Send/Receive: Send & Receive: Send/Receive Groups menu **B**.

TIP Even if a given group is set for automatic send/receives, you can still perform manual send/receives whenever you like.

To perform a send/receive for a single account folder:

1. In the folder pane, select the account folder that you want to check.

2. Click Send/Receive: Send & Receive: Update Folder (Shift-F9) **A**.

TIP This procedure is available only for certain folders. If a selected folder is ineligible, Update Folder will be grayed out.

TIP The lower portion of the Send/Receive Groups menu **B** lists the Inbox for each of your Outlook accounts. You can select an Inbox from the list to check that account for new email.

Reading Messages

You can read any message that's displayed in Outlook—whether it's received mail, sent mail, or an RSS feed message. You can even read mail in a Deleted Items or Trash folder until the folder is emptied. And unless you have an uncached Microsoft Exchange account (see the sidebar on this page), you don't need an active connection with the mail server to read messages.

To read messages:

1. In the folder pane, select the account folder 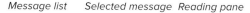 that contains the messages you want to read, such as the Inbox. If you can't see the account's folders, click the triangle that precedes the account name.

   Message headers for the selected folder are displayed in the message list. The name of the currently selected folder and its account are shown in Outlook's title bar.

2. *Do either of the following:*

   ▶ In the message list, select the header of the message that you want to read. The message is displayed in the reading pane **B**.

   ▶ To read a message in its own window, double-click its header in the message list. (You can also open a selected message by pressing Enter or Ctrl-O.)

   After you view a message, it's automatically marked as read; that is, the blue boldface is removed from the header.

3. If you're reading a message in its own window, close the window by clicking its close box.

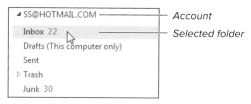

Ⓐ Select a message folder in the folder pane.

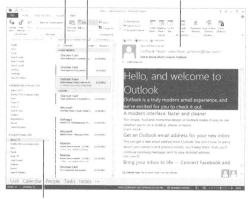

Ⓑ It's more convenient to read most messages in the reading pane than open them in a separate window.

Enabling Cached Exchange Mode

To determine whether your Exchange server messages are *cached* (copies are stored on your computer), *do the following:*

1. Click the File tab, select Info, and choose Account Settings > Account Settings.

2. On the E-mail tab of the Account Settings dialog box, select the Exchange account and click Change.

3. Under Offline Settings, ensure that Use Cached Exchange Mode is enabled.

Previous item   Next item

C Click these Quick Access Toolbar icons to read consecutive messages in an open message window.

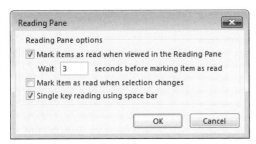

D Click the first or second check box to specify the manner in which messages are automatically marked as read.

E To change a message's read status, choose Mark as Read or Mark as Unread.

Missing Pictures?

By default, Outlook doesn't download linked graphics in messages, representing each by a boxed red X. Such graphics are sometimes used by spammers to verify email addresses. If a message is from a trusted source, right-click any instance of "Right-click here to download…" text and choose Download Pictures from the context menu.

TIP If a folder in the folder pane contains at least one unread message, the folder name is followed by the number of unread messages, such as "Inbox 8" **A**.

TIP Whether a message is in the reading pane or open in its own window, you can navigate within the message by using the vertical scroll bar. Drag the scroll box, click in a blank area of the scroll bar, or click the scroll arrow at either end.

TIP You can press Spacebar and Shift-Spacebar to move forward and backward, respectively, through any lengthy message in the reading pane.

TIP With a message open in its own window, you can also use normal navigation keys to move through the message, such as Page Up, Page Down, up arrow, and down arrow. You can use these keys in the reading pane, too, if you first click in the message body.

TIP If you open a message in its own window, you can read additional messages in the same window. Just click the Next Item or Previous Item icon in the Quick Access Toolbar **C** to read the next or previous message in the message list. (Note that if you go past either end of the message list, the message window will automatically close.)

TIP Read/unread message status is automatically determined by rules. To change the current behavior, choose View:Layout:Reading Pane > Options **D**.

TIP You can manually change a message from unread to read (or vice versa) by right-clicking the message header and choosing the appropriate command **E**, as well as by clicking the Home:Tags:Unread/Read icon.

Changing the View

To make it easier to read mail, you can set or change the view whenever you wish.

To change the current view:

- *Do any of the following:*
  - ▸ To change pane size, drag the line that separates a pair of panes.
  - ▸ Choose a special view from the View : Current View : Change View menu.
  - ▸ Choose commands from the View : Layout and People Pane groups to add, remove, or position the various email panes. Note that if you disable the reading pane, you'll only be able to read messages by opening them in their own window.
  - ▸ To reorganize the active message list, choose an option from the View : Arrangement gallery  **A** (or the Arrange By menu), or from the menu above the message list **B**.

    For example, you can sort an Inbox by From to group and alphabetize received messages by sender.

> **TIP** To limit the display to only the message list and the current message, click the **Reading** icon at the bottom of the window.

> **TIP** When choosing an Arrangement option, it's often useful to check **Show in Groups**. Doing so creates separate display groups for each sort unit. For example, if **From** is the Arrangement field, a group will be created for each unique sender. You can expand or collapse a group by clicking the triangle icon that precedes its name.

> **TIP** Choose a command from the View : Arrangement : Message Preview menu **C** to specify the number of preview lines displayed in each message header.

A You can click an icon to change the arrangement method for the current message list...

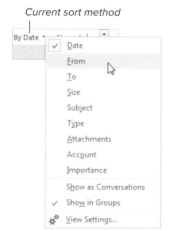

Current sort method

B ...or choose an option from the menu above the list.

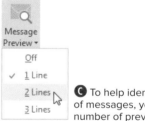

C To help identify the content of messages, you can specify the number of preview lines to display.

Changing the Magnification

To make it easier to view the current message in the reading pane, you can use the zoom controls at the bottom of the window to change the magnification. The new zoom setting affects only the current message. When you switch messages or folders, zoom resets to 100%. (If your mouse has a scroll wheel, you can also change the magnification by pressing Ctrl as you spin the scroll wheel.)

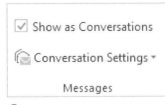

A Enable or disable the display of messages as conversations by clicking the Show as Conversations check box.

B Whenever you change the setting for Show as Conversations, you can apply the change to the current folder or to all mail folders in every account.

Viewing Conversations

Optionally, you can display related messages in any account folder as a *conversation* (similar to a web forum message thread). A conversation consists of two or more messages that share the same Subject. To enable conversation view for a folder, the Arrangement/Arrange By setting must be Date and View:Messages:Show as Conversations must be checked **A**.

The advantage of displaying messages as conversations is that related messages can be found and read in a single convenient location. You'll no longer need to flip between multiple account folders or scan for messages that may be scattered throughout the Inbox to follow a multi-message email exchange. To learn more about conversations, see "Managing Conversations" in Chapter 20.

To enable conversations for a folder:

1. Select the folder in the folder pane.

2. Click View:Arrangement:Date (or choose View:Arrangement:Arrange By > Date), or choose Date from the menu above the message list.

   TIP If View:Messages:Show as Conversations is currently checked, you can choose Date (Conversations) from any of these sources and go to Step 5.

3. Ensure that View:Messages:Show as Conversations is checked **A**.

4. A dialog box appears **B** whenever you change the state of the Show as Conversations check box. Click This folder to apply the change to only the current folder; click All mailboxes to apply it to every account and folder.

continues on next page

5. Set display options for conversations in the current folder by choosing commands from the View:Messages:Conversation Settings menu **C**.

TIP When you select a message header that represents a conversation and Always Expand Selected Conversation is enabled **C**, related messages are automatically shown. Otherwise, click the triangle icon to the left of the conversation header to view the conversation.

C You can specify different conversation settings for each folder.

office 2013 | ✕ | Current Mailbox ▾

All   Unread   ▾   Newest ↓

◢ **LAST WEEK**

Steve Schwartz
Office 2013 videos TOC   Wed 1/23
Pretty good. Submitted

Colby, Cliff   ☁
Office 2013 videos TOC   Wed 1/23
Hi, Steve, How is it going?

Highlighted match

A As you type the search text, Outlook scans for and displays matching messages.

Current Mailbox ▾

Current Folder
Subfolders
Current Mailbox
All Mailboxes
All Outlook Items

B Choose an option to change the search's scope. For example, All Outlook Items considers items other than email in the search.

Search by Domain

To find a message from someone whose name you've forgotten but whose company or ISP you remember, search for their domain or ISP. For example, enter **microsoft.com** to view messages from Microsoft employees or **earthlink.net** to find messages from Earthlink users.

Searching for Messages

In many cases, the simplest way to find a particular message in a folder is to sort the message list by choosing an Arrangement method (as explained in "Changing the View"). For example, to find all messages you received from a given person, you could sort your Inbox by From.

But if you can't find a message by sorting or manually hunting, Outlook also provides an Instant Search box that you can use to quickly find messages that contain a given text string.

To perform an Instant Search:

1. In Mail, select the account folder in the folder pane that you want to search.

   The message list for the folder appears.

2. Type a search string in the Instant Search box above the message list (Ctrl-E).

   As you type, Outlook filters the message list to show only matches **A**. Matches can be anywhere within a message: addresses, subject, message body, or attachments. The matching text is highlighted in each message.

3. To restore the message list, click the Search:Close:Close Search icon or the X in the Instant Search box.

> **TIP** To narrow a search's focus and show fewer—but more exact—matches, continue typing. For instance, type **microsoft** rather than **micro**.

> **TIP** To change the scope of the search, click the scope menu at the right end of the Instant Search box and choose a new setting **B**.

> **TIP** See Chapters 17 and 21 for additional help with building complex search queries.

Receiving Attachments

Attachments (images, documents, and other file types) can accompany any email message. In the message list, a message with an attachment is marked with a paper clip icon **Ⓐ**. When viewed in the reading pane or in its own window, such messages display the names of the attached files beneath the address information **Ⓑ**.

Depending on an attachment's file type and the programs installed on your computer, options for handling an attachment can include previewing it in the reading pane or message window, opening it in an appropriate program, and saving it to disk so it can later be opened without Outlook.

Previewing Attachments

You can view many attachments in the reading pane or message window. Whether or not this is possible depends on the file type and whether the necessary *attachment previewer* is installed. (Office 2013 installs and enables several previewers that rely on other Office applications to display various types of attachments.)

To preview an attachment:

- Click the attachment file icon, or right-click it and choose Preview from the context menu. If the file can be viewed in Outlook, *one of the following will occur:*

  ▸ Office files and common graphic file types will open and display.

  ▸ Other file types for which you have a previewer installed, such as PDF files, will present a Preview file button that you can click to view the file **Ⓒ**.

Attachment icon

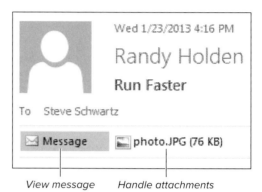

Ⓐ In a message list, attachments are denoted by a paper clip to the right of the sender or recipient.

View message   Handle attachments

Ⓑ Attached files, if any, are shown beneath the addresses. To resume viewing the message after previewing an attachment, click the Message icon.

Preview file

Ⓒ Click the Preview file button to display the attachment in the current window.

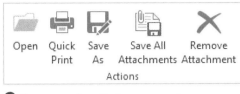

D Common actions that you can perform on an attachment can be executed by clicking one of these icons in the Attachments:Actions group.

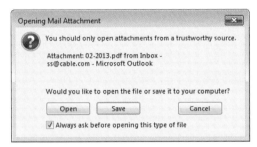

E If you have the appropriate program installed, you can open the attachment.

F If Windows can't identify an installed program that can open the selected attachment, this dialog box appears.

Opening Attachments

Rather than previewing an attachment in Outlook, you may prefer to open it in an appropriate program that's installed on your computer. Doing so will enable you to use the program's tools to view, edit, and save the file.

To open an attachment in another application:

1. Double-click the attachment's file icon **B**, right-click the icon and choose Open from the context menu, or select the icon and click Attachments:Actions: Open **D**.

2. Depending on the type of file, *one of the following will occur:*

   ▸ If a compatible program is installed, it launches and opens the file.

   ▸ The Opening Mail Attachment dialog box appears **E**. Assuming that you trust the file's source, click Open.

   ▸ If no compatible program is installed, a dialog box appears **F**. You can search the web for a program or select one from among your installed applications.

Saving Attachments

To avoid having to scour Outlook for the message that contains a critical attachment whenever you want to view, work with, or print it, you can save the attachment to disk.

To save an attachment:

1. *Do one of the following:*

   ▸ Drag the attachment icon(s) from the message window **B** onto the Desktop or into a folder.

continues on next page

- Select an attachment and click Attachments:Actions:Save As .

- Right-click the attachment icon and choose Save As from the context menu .

- Select the message header, click the File tab, and click Save Attachments.

  A Save Attachment or Save Attachments file dialog box appears .

2. Navigate to the drive and folder in which you want to save the file and click Save.

  The file is saved to disk.

TIP If a message has several attachments, you can elect to save them all with a single command. Select one of their file icons and click Attachments:Actions:Save All Attachments or choose this command from the context menu . Select the particular attachments that you want to save, click OK, and then specify a destination folder in which to store them.

TIP Unless you delete a message, any attachments it contains will continue to take up space on your hard disk. If the message is important but you don't need the attachment, click the attachment's icon, click Attachments:Actions:Remove Attachment , and confirm the deletion in the dialog box that appears.

TIP To periodically rid yourself of unwanted attachments, you need a way to find all messages with attachments. Select a mail folder in the folder pane, choose Attachments from the Arrangement menu (see in "Changing the View"), and set With as the sort order. All messages containing attachments will be shown at the top of the message list. (As an alternative, click in the Instant Search box and then click the Search:Refine:Has Attachments icon .)

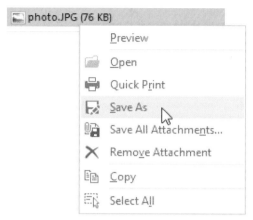

G Attachment-handling commands can be conveniently chosen from this context menu.

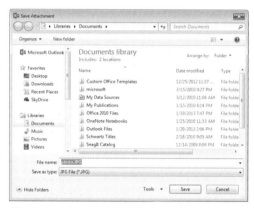

H Select a location on disk in which to save the attachment and optionally rename it.

I One way to easily identify all messages that contain attachments is to search for them by clicking the Has Attachments icon.

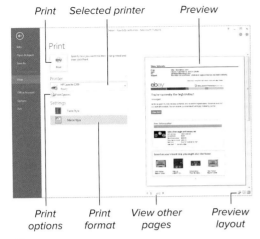

Print *Selected printer* *Preview*

Print *Print* *View other* *Preview*
options *format* *pages* *layout*

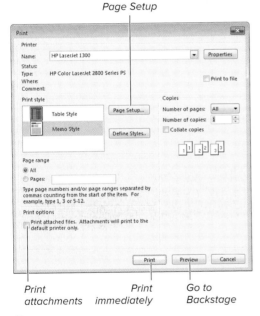

A In the Print area of the Backstage, you can set options and see their effects in the print preview.

Page Setup

Print *Print* *Go to*
attachments *immediately* *Backstage*

B Set options (such as number of copies and the page range) in the Print dialog box.

Printing Messages

You can print the contents (and attachments) of selected messages, as well as a list of message headers from the current view.

To print a message:

1. Select the message to print in the message list or open it in its own window.

2. *Do either of the following:*

   ▸ Click the File tab, and then select Print.

   ▸ Press Ctrl-P.

   The Print area of Backstage appears **A**. A print preview is shown, based on the current print settings.

3. Ensure that the correct printer is selected.

4. Select Memo Style in the Settings area.

5. *Optional:* To set print options, click the Print Options button. In the Print dialog box **B**, set options as desired. To view or change Page Setup settings, such as the page size, orientation, or margins, click the Page Setup button.

   Click Print to print immediately using the current settings or click Preview to return to the Backstage to examine the effects of the new settings prior to printing.

6. Click the Print button **A**.

TIP You can also print several messages at once. In Step 1, select contiguous messages by clicking the first header and then Shift-clicking the last one. To select noncontiguous messages, Ctrl-click each header. In the Print area, click the Preview icon to generate the preview pages.

TIP To immediately print a message using the default settings, right-click its header and choose Quick Print from the context menu.

To print a message list:

1. In the folder pane, select the message folder whose headers you want to print.

2. *Optional:* To print only certain headers from the list, select the ones to be printed.

   To select multiple contiguous headers, click the first header and Shift-click the last one. To select noncontiguous headers, Ctrl-click each one.

3. Click the File tab to go to the Backstage and select Print (or press Ctrl-P).

   The Print area of the Backstage appears Ⓐ.

4. Ensure that the correct printer is selected. Select Table Style in the Settings area.

5. Click the Print Options button.

   The Print dialog box appears Ⓑ.

6. Select an option from the Print range area Ⓒ:

   ▸ To print all message headers from the selected folder, click All rows.

   ▸ To print only the currently selected headers, click Only selected rows.

7. *Optional:* To set a paper size, fonts, or margins, click Page Setup.

8. *Do one of the following:*

   ▸ Click Print to print immediately using the current settings.

   ▸ Click Preview to return to the Backstage to preview the effects of the new settings prior to printing.

9. Click the Print button Ⓐ to print the message header list.

TIP Prior to printing a list of headers, you may want to perform an Instant Search to restrict the list's contents, as well as arrange the message list by sorting and grouping the messages.

Print range

○ All rows

◉ Only selected rows

Ⓒ Print all headers or only selected ones.

Managing the Mail

In addition to sending, receiving, and reading messages, you'll want to spend time organizing and managing your email.

To that end, Outlook provides commands and procedures that enable you to manually set the read status of messages, delete unneeded email, move and copy messages to other folders, set junk mail options, create message rules to automate the handling of incoming mail, and create Quick Steps.

In This Chapter

Marking Messages as Read

One of the simplest ways to manage email is to change a message's *read status* to read or unread. Unread messages (shown in bold blue in the message list) stand out and demand attention; read messages (shown in normal type) can be ignored or handled at your leisure.

A message's read status can be changed whenever you like. For example, to ensure that a previously viewed message will receive additional attention, you can reset it to unread. Similarly, messages you want to ignore can immediately be set to read—even though you've never viewed them. You can change a message's read status *automatically* (via a setting in Reading Pane options or in response to a message rule) or *manually* (by choosing a new status).

To set an automatic read option:

1. Choose View:Layout:Reading Pane > Options.

   The Reading Pane dialog box appears 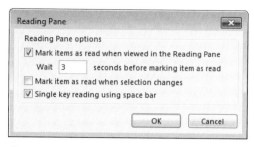.

2. To automatically mark new messages as read, click the first or second check box:

   ▸ **Mark items as read when viewed in the Reading Pane.** Any message header that is selected longer than the specified number of seconds will be treated as read.

   ▸ **Mark item as read when selection changes.** Whenever you select a different message, the currently selected message will be marked as read.

3. Click OK to close the Reading Pane dialog box.

Ⓐ Select one of the first two mutually exclusive options to indicate when messages will automatically be marked as read.

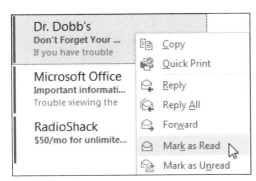

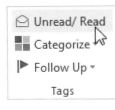

B You can manually change the read status of a message by right-clicking its header in the message list.

C You can also click this icon to toggle a selected message's read status.

D To simultaneously mark all messages in the current folder as read, click the Mark All as Read icon.

To manually change a message's read status:

- *Do one of the following:*
  - ‣ Right-click the message header in the message list. In the context menu that appears **B**, choose Mark as Read or Mark as Unread.
  - ‣ Select a header in the message list. Click the Home:Tags:Unread/Read icon **C** to toggle the message's status.
  - ‣ Select a message header in the message list. Press Ctrl-U to mark it as unread or Ctrl-Q to mark it as read.

TIP You can simultaneously change the status of *multiple* selected messages. Note that you can set only one read status for all selected messages, even if they are a mixture of read and unread.

TIP You can mark all messages in a folder as having been read. This is especially useful for quickly catching up on seldom-read RSS feeds or mailing lists. Start by selecting the folder in the folder pane. Click the Folder:Clean Up:Mark All as Read icon **D**.

TIP To automatically set certain incoming messages as read, include the Mark it as read action in a message rule. I use such rules to mark incoming mailing list messages as read. To learn how to create message rules, see "Creating Rules," later in this chapter.

TIP You can also mark a message as important by flagging it for follow-up. For instructions, see "Flagging Messages," later in this chapter.

Deleting Messages

To reduce message-list clutter and the size of your email account databases, you can delete unwanted messages.

To delete email or RSS messages:

1. Select one or more message headers in the message list.

2. *Do one of the following:*

   ▸ Click Home : Delete : Delete .

   ▸ Press Del, Delete, or Ctrl-D.

   ▸ Right-click one of the selected messages and choose Delete from the context menu.

   The message(s) are deleted or marked for deletion, depending on the account type, settings, and current view.

> **TIP** To delete a single message, you can also click the Delete icon **B** that appears in the header when you hover the cursor over it.

To restore deleted email or RSS messages:

▪ *Do any of the following:*

   ▸ Drag the item from the account's Deleted Items or Trash folder into the original message folder, such as the Inbox or Sent Items.

   ▸ Right-click the item in the Deleted Items or Trash folder and choose a destination folder from the Move submenu.

   If the folder isn't listed, choose Move > Other Folder. In the Move Items dialog box **C**, select the destination folder and click OK.

A Click the Delete icon to delete all selected messages.

B Every message header in Outlook 2013 has this handy Delete icon.

C To move selected messages from the Trash or Deleted Items folder, select a destination folder in the Move Items dialog box and click OK.

 When you empty a folder (top), select items for removal (middle), or purge a folder (bottom), you'll be asked to confirm the action.

Archiving vs. Deleting

If there's a chance you might eventually need an older message, you can *archive* it rather than delete it. The AutoArchive procedure executes at regular intervals, archiving all messages older than a certain age by moving them into Archive Folders in the folder pane.

To set AutoArchive options for the current folder, click Folder:Properties:Auto-Archive Settings. To perform a manual archive, click the File tab, select the Info category, and choose Cleanup Tools > Archive.

- *Exchange accounts only:* Select the account's Deleted Items folder or the folder in which the message was originally stored, such as the Inbox. Click the Folder:Clean Up:Recover Deleted Items icon. In the Recover Deleted Items dialog box, select one or more deleted messages and click Recover Selected Items.

To remove (empty) deleted items from a folder:

1. In the folder pane, select the folder that contains the deleted messages.

   Folders that you might want to empty include Deleted Items, Trash, and Junk E-mail, for example.

2. Depending on the account type and its settings, *you can do the following:*

   - Click Folder:Clean Up:Empty Folder.

   - Right-click the folder in the folder pane and choose Empty Folder from the context menu.

   - Select the previously deleted items. Press Del, Delete, or Ctrl-D; click the Home:Delete:Delete icon; right-click one of the selected items and choose Delete from the context menu; or click the Delete icon in the message header.

   - *IMAP accounts with Mark messages for deletion enabled:* Choose a command from the Folder:Clean Up: Purge menu.

   A confirmation dialog box appears .

3. Click Yes to confirm or click No to cancel the folder empty action, item deletion, or purge.

continues on next page

TIP To delete a message that's open in its own window, click the Message:Delete:Delete icon or press Ctrl-D.

TIP Most POP3, Hotmail, and RSS feed messages are moved to the Deleted Items folder where they remain until the folder is emptied or the individual messages are selected and deleted.

TIP Be sure to explore the deleted item settings for every account you have. For example, on the Advanced tab for a POP account, messages you delete in Outlook can automatically be deleted from the server at the same time.

TIP Deleted Items folders can be emptied automatically at the end of each Outlook session. Click the Advanced tab in the Outlook Options dialog box to see this setting **E**.

E You can automate the emptying of all Deleted Items folders at the end of each Outlook session.

IMAP Message Purging

Optionally, if you have an IMAP account, you can elect to *mark messages for deletion* rather than deleting them. A deleted message remains in its original folder in the folder pane (Inbox or Sent Items, for example), but the header is formatted with strike-through text. To permanently delete such messages and remove them from the mail server, choose a command from the Folder: Clean Up:Purge menu.

To specify that an IMAP account employ purging, *do the following:*

1. Click the File tab, select Info, and choose Account Settings > Account Settings.

2. In the Account Settings dialog box, select the IMAP account and click the Change button.

3. In the Change Account dialog box, click More Settings.

4. On the Advanced tab of the Internet E-mail Settings dialog box, enable the option to Mark items for deletion but do not move them automatically.

A You can instruct Outlook to delete redundant messages in the selected conversation.

B Specify conversation cleanup criteria in the Mail category of the Outlook Options dialog box.

Managing Conversations

In addition to deleting messages, Outlook provides two methods of managing conversations. You can clean up a conversation by removing redundant messages, and you can elect to ignore future email pertaining to a particular conversation.

To clean up a conversation:

1. In the message list, select the header of any message in the conversation.

2. Choose Home : Delete : Clean Up > Clean Up Conversation.

   The Clean Up Conversation dialog box appears **A**.

3. *Optional:* Click Settings to review the Conversation Clean Up preferences in the Mail category of Outlook Options **B**. If you make any changes, click OK to save them; otherwise, click Cancel.

4. Click Clean Up **A**.

   If no qualifying messages are identified by Outlook, a dialog box informs you. Otherwise, the redundant messages (as defined in the Conversation Clean Up settings **B**) are moved to the account's Deleted Items or Trash folder.

TIP To rid an entire folder of redundant messages, select the folder in the folder pane and choose Home : Delete : Clean Up > Clean Up Folder or Clean Up Folder & Subfolders.

To ignore a conversation:

1. In the message list, select the header of any message in the conversation.

2. Click the Home:Delete:Ignore icon or press Ctrl-Del.

   The Ignore Conversation dialog box  appears.

3. Click the Ignore Conversation button.

   The conversation and all future messages that would be part of it are moved to the account's Deleted Items or Trash folder.

C If you no longer want to participate in or read mail for a particular conversation, you can ignore it.

Destination folder

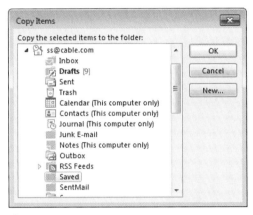

A You can copy or move a selected message into a folder by choosing a context command.

B Select a destination folder and click OK.

Copying and Moving Mail

Another way to organize your messages is to move or copy them to other folders. You've already seen how you can move mail out of the Deleted Items folder and back into your Inbox, for example. Similar procedures are used to copy or move messages between almost any pair of folders—including folders in different accounts.

To copy a message to another folder:

1. In the message list, select the header of the message you want to copy.

2. *Do either of the following:*

   ▸ Right-click and drag the message header onto the destination folder in the folder pane. When you release the mouse button, select Copy from the context menu **A**.

   ▸ Choose Home:Move:Move > Copy to Folder. In the Copy Items dialog box **B**, select a destination folder and click OK.

   A copy of the selected message is stored in the designated folder.

To move a message to another folder:

1. In the message list, select the header of the message you want to copy.

2. *Do one of the following:*

   ▸ Drag the message header onto the destination folder in the folder pane.

   ▸ Right-click and drag the message header onto the destination folder in the folder pane. When you release the mouse button, select Move from the context menu **A**.

continues on next page

- Choose a listed destination folder from the Home:Move:Move menu.

- Choose Home:Move:Move > Other Folder (or press Ctrl-Shift-V). In the Move Items dialog box **C**, select a destination folder and click OK.

The message is moved to the designated folder and deleted from the source folder.

TIP You can also move or copy *multiple* selected messages using these techniques.

TIP To reverse an incorrect move or copy, immediately click the Undo icon in the Quick Access Toolbar or press Ctrl-Z.

TIP In the Copy Items **B** or Move Items **C** dialog box, you can create a new folder to receive the copied or moved message(s) by clicking the New button.

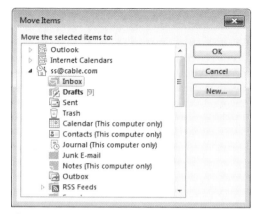

C The Move Items dialog box works the same as the Copy Items dialog box. Select a destination folder for the message and click OK.

Name the folder

A New folders are created in the Create New Folder dialog box.

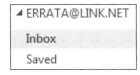

B The account now has a user-created Saved folder.

Creating Message Folders

Although deleting, copying, and moving messages are all essential to managing email, one of the best ways to organize messages is to create additional folders for them. For instance, you can create a folder to store project-related messages, save web and software registrations, or store copies of critical email. You can use these folders as targets of message moves and copies. As you'll learn later in this chapter, you can also create *rules* to automatically route incoming messages to specific folders.

To create a new message folder:

1. *Do one of the following:*

   ▸ Click Folder : New : New Folder.

   ▸ Right-click an account folder in the folder pane and choose New Folder from the context menu.

   ▸ Press Ctrl-Shift-E.

   The Create New Folder dialog box appears **A**.

2. Enter a name for the new folder.

3. Choose Mail and Post Items from the Folder contains drop-down menu.

4. Select a *parent* (containing) folder from the list in the dialog box. The new folder will be a subfolder of the selected folder.

   TIP By default, the folder that's selected or right-clicked when you issue the New Folder command is assumed to be the parent folder. Of course, you're still free to choose any other folder as the parent.

5. Click OK to create the new folder.

   The folder is added to the folder pane **B**.

continues on next page

TIP Folders can be nested within folders. For example, to handle book-related correspondence, I could create a Peachpit folder within the account folder or Inbox. Within that folder, I can create additional folders—one per book.

TIP To rename a folder, click its name twice in the folder pane and edit the name **C**. You can also select the folder and click Folder: Actions:Rename Folder **D**.

TIP You can move one folder inside another by dragging it onto the destination folder in the folder pane. You can also right-click the folder and choose Move Folder from the context menu.

TIP You can delete any user-created folder that you no longer need. Select the folder in the folder pane and click Folder:Actions:Delete Folder **D**. Click Yes in the confirmation dialog box. The folder and its messages are moved into the account's Deleted Items or Trash folder.

If you change your mind about deleting the folder and haven't emptied the Deleted Items or Trash, you can move the folder back into the folder list.

TIP For obvious reasons, you can't delete most of the automatically created folders, such as Inbox and Sent Items.

TIP To make it easy to access an important folder, drag it into the Favorites section at the top of the folder pane **E**. You might want to add each account's Inbox as a favorite, for example. You can also add a selected folder by clicking Folder:Favorites:Show in Favorites **F**. To remove a folder from Favorites, select it and click Show in Favorites again.

C This is an example of a folder name selected for editing.

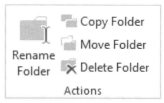

D You can rename, copy, move, or delete a selected user-created folder by clicking a command in the Folder:Actions group.

E You can drag an account folder into this area at the top of the folder pane.

F The Show in Favorites command acts as a toggle to add or remove a folder from the Favorites section of the folder pane.

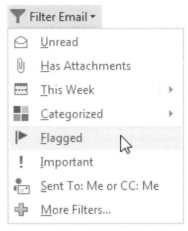

A You can flag a message by choosing this command on the Home tab.

B You can filter a message list to display only flagged messages.

Flagging Messages

If you need to *do* something about a message (such as respond to it at a later date or schedule a meeting regarding it), you can *flag* the message for follow-up. Flagged messages are denoted by a red flag in the message header.

To set a follow-up flag for an item:

- *Do one of the following:*
  - ▸ Click the white flag icon in any message header.
  - ▸ Select a message header and choose Home:Tags:Follow Up > Flag Message **A**.
  - ▸ Right-click the message header and choose Follow Up > Flag Message.

To clear a follow-up flag for an item:

- *Do one of the following:*
  - ▸ Click the red flag icon in any message header.
  - ▸ Select a message header and choose Home:Tags:Follow Up > Clear Flag **A**.
  - ▸ Right-click the message header and choose Follow Up > Clear Flag.

TIP Flags can also be assigned to tasks and contact records.

TIP To view all flagged messages in the current account folder, choose Home:Find:Filter Email > Flagged **B**. To restore the normal message list, click the close button (X) in the Instant Search box or click the Search:Close: Close Search icon.

Handling Junk Mail and Phishing Attempts

Everyone receives *junk mail* and *spam*—generally consisting of unwanted ads for mortgages, weight loss products, and the like. If you use your regular email address to register on web sites or if you send email to corporations, newsgroups, or mailing lists, your volume of received junk mail is liable to increase. Using the Junk E-mail Options feature, you can filter out much of this time-wasting, annoying email.

Outlook also provides protection against *phishing* (attempts via email to trick you into providing personal data such as bank account numbers, credit card information, and web site passwords).

To set junk mail and phishing options:

1. Select an account in the folder pane. Choose Home : Delete : Junk > Junk E-mail Options.

2. On the Options tab of the Junk E-mail Options dialog box **A**, click a radio button to set the desired protection level.

3. To enable phishing protection, check Disable links and other functionality in phishing messages.

4. *Optional:* To automatically delete potential junk mail, check Permanently delete suspected junk e-mail instead of moving it to the Junk E-mail folder.

5. Click OK to save the new settings.

   When received in this account, suspected junk mail is automatically moved to the Junk E-mail folder or deleted, depending on the settings on this tab.

6. Repeat Steps 1–5 for your other accounts.

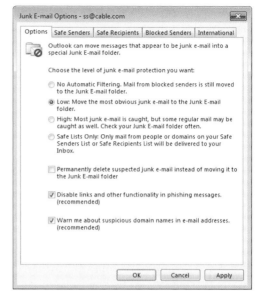

A Set junk mail and phishing options on the tabs of the Junk E-mail Options dialog box.

B You can block future messages from specific users, companies, or domains by adding them to the Blocked Senders list.

C You can add an address or domain to the Safe Senders list by selecting a message from them and choosing a Never Block Sender command.

D Certain countries are notorious for generating junk mail. To ignore all email from the country, add it to the list on the International tab.

TIP Outlook maintains a Blocked Senders list for each account that you can use to automatically classify new mail from certain addresses as junk. To add someone to the list, click the Blocked Senders tab **B** of the Junk E-mail Options dialog box, click Add, enter the person or company's email address, and click OK. To add someone to the list based on a received message, select the message and choose Home : Delete : Junk > Block Sender.

You can also block all mail from a given *domain*. Doing so is useful when you notice that you're receiving many junk messages from a domain, but each has a different user name. For instance, to block all email from krypton.net, add `krypton.net` or `@krypton.net` to the Blocked Senders list.

TIP To prevent Outlook from classifying mail from certain senders as junk, create contact records for them and add their email addresses to the list on the Safe Senders tab.

You can also accomplish this using a received message. Select the message header and choose a Never Block Sender command from the Home : Delete : Junk menu **C**.

TIP Using the International tab of the Junk E-mail Options dialog box, you can classify all email from certain *countries* as junk. Click the Blocked Top-Level Domain List button, select countries to block **D**, and click OK.

TIP Outlook will occasionally mark a received message as junk that is actually legitimate mail. To reclassify a selected or open message, choose Not Junk or Never Block Sender from the Junk icon's menu **C**.

TIP You can specify other actions for junk mail by creating *rules* (discussed in the next section).

TIP Junk E-mail Options are account-specific. Remember to set them for each email account that you've added to Outlook.

Creating Rules

By defining *rules*, you can instruct Outlook to automatically perform actions on new incoming or outgoing mail. A rule can store all incoming email from Peachpit.com in a Peachpit folder rather than the Inbox, for example. A rule can be based on a template or created from scratch. You can also create a rule based on a received message.

To create a rule from a template or from scratch:

1. *Do one of the following:*

    ▸ Choose Home:Move:Rules > Manage Rules and Alerts.

    ▸ Click the File tab, select Info, and click the Manage Rules & Alerts button.

    The Rules and Alerts dialog box **Ⓐ** opens.

2. Select the account and folder to which the rule will be applied from the Apply changes to this folder drop-down list.

3. Click the New Rule icon.

4. In the Rules Wizard **Ⓑ**, select a template on which to base the rule. If an appropriate template isn't listed, you can create the rule from scratch by selecting a blank rule. Click Next.

5. Add or remove *conditions* for the rule by clicking check boxes. Condition placeholders are displayed as blue underlined text in the Step 2 area of the wizard. Click each placeholder and replace it with appropriate data. Click Next.

6. Add or remove *actions* to be performed by the rule by clicking check boxes. Action placeholders are displayed as blue underlined text in the Step 2 area of the wizard. Click each placeholder and replace it with appropriate data. Click Next to continue.

Defined rules are listed here   Apply to folder(s)

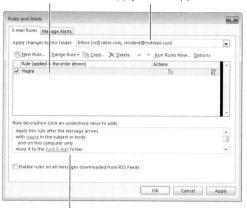

Description of selected rule

Ⓐ Rules are created and maintained in the Rules and Alerts dialog box.

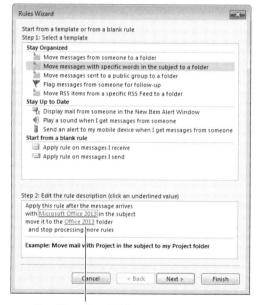

Condition placeholder

Ⓑ Select a template on which to base the rule. On the screens that follow, you can add, remove, and specify rule conditions, actions, and exceptions.

C To complete a rule definition, name and specify setup options for the rule.

D To test a new or revised rule, you can run it on the messages in a selected folder. Click Browse to select the folder.

7. Specify *exceptions* to the rule by clicking check boxes. Placeholders for exceptions are displayed as blue underlined text in the Step 2 area of the wizard. Click each placeholder and replace it with appropriate data. Click Next to continue.

8. On the final wizard screen **C**, name the rule and set rule options by clicking check boxes.

9. Click Finish to save the rule. Click OK to close the Rules and Alerts dialog box.

CAUTION Until a message-deletion rule has been successfully tested, do not use the Permanently delete it action. Instead, use the Delete action, which merely moves the item(s) into the Deleted Items folder.

TIP You can temporarily disable a rule by clearing its check mark in the Rules and Alerts dialog box **A**. To permanently eliminate a rule, select it and click the Delete icon.

TIP To edit a rule, double-click it in the Rules and Alerts dialog box **A**. Or you can select it and choose Change Rule > Edit Rule Settings.

TIP To alter only a rule's conditions, actions, or exceptions, it isn't necessary to edit the rule. Just select it in the Rules and Alerts dialog box and click the Rule description placeholder that you want to change.

TIP Rules are executed in the order in which they're listed in the Rules and Alerts dialog box. To change the order, select a rule and click the Move Up or Move Down icon.

TIP To test a rule, click Run Rules Now in the Rules and Alerts dialog box. In the Run Rules Now dialog box **D**, select the rule(s) to test, specify the folder to check, and click Run Now.

To create a rule based on a message:

1. Select the header of the message on which you want to base the rule.

   For example, you might want to route all messages from the sender directly into the Deleted Items or Trash folder. Or you may want to save them all in a custom folder you've created.

2. Choose Home:Move:Rules > Create Rule.

   The Create Rule dialog box appears 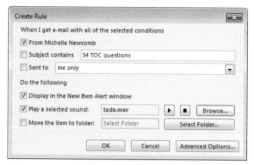.

3. Set options in the dialog box by clicking check boxes, editing text, and clicking buttons. When you're satisfied, click OK.

> **TIP** If the options in the Create Rule dialog box aren't sufficient to completely define the rule, click Advanced Options. The Rules Wizard dialog box appears **B**. Any options that you specified in the Create Rule dialog box will also be set in the Rules Wizard.

> **TIP** Because rules created in this manner are automatically named, you may want to open the rule for editing so you can rename it.

E In many cases, you can quickly create a rule from a received message without using the Rules Wizard.

Backing Up Outlook Folders

To safeguard your email and contacts, you may want to occasionally back up your Outlook data. Using the following procedure, you can export one account folder at a time.

1. Click the File tab, select the Open & Export category, and click the Import/Export icon.

2. In the Import and Export Wizard, select Export to a file. Click Next.

3. Select Outlook Data File (.pst) as the file type. Click Next.

4. Select an account folder to export, such as Inbox or Contacts.

5. Specify a location for the exported data file. Click Finish.

6. Repeat for other folders that you want to back up.

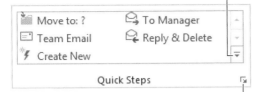

Expand gallery and open the menu

Manage Quick Steps dialog box launcher

A The Quick Steps gallery.

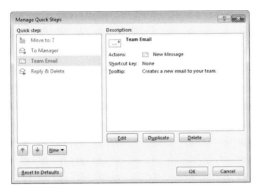

B The Manage Quick Steps dialog box.

Delete action

C The Edit Quick Step dialog box.

Working with Quick Steps

Quick Steps are single- or multiple-action scripts that you can use to help manage your email. In the Home : Quick Steps group **A**, Outlook provides default Quick Steps that you can use as-is or customize. You can also create Quick Steps from scratch.

To modify an existing Quick Step:

1. In the folder pane, select the account to which the Quick Step will apply.

2. *Do one of the following:*
   - Right-click the Quick Step's icon in the Quick Steps group **A** and choose Edit *name* from the context menu.
   - Click the Manage Quick Steps dialog box launcher or choose Manage Quick Steps from the Quick Steps menu. Select the Quick Step in the Manage Quick Steps dialog box **B** and click Edit.

   The Edit Quick Step dialog box opens **C**.

3. If the Quick Step contains an unwanted action, click its X to remove it.

4. To add other actions, click the Add Action button and select an action from the drop-down menu.

5. *Optional:* Up to nine Quick Steps can have a shortcut key (Ctrl-Shift, plus a digit between 1–9). To assign one to this Quick Step, choose it from the Shortcut key menu.

6. *Optional:* Edit the ToolTip text.

   The ToolTip will appear whenever you rest the cursor over this Quick Step.

continues on next page

7. *Optional:* Edit the Quick Step name in the Name box.

The new name will be displayed in the Quick Steps gallery.

8. Click Save to replace the original Quick Step with this edited version.

9. Click OK to dismiss the Manage Quick Steps dialog box.

To create a Quick Step from a template:

1. In the folder pane, select the account to which the Quick Step will apply.

2. Choose a template from the Home : Quick Steps : New Quick Step submenu 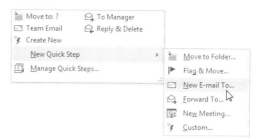.

A First Time Setup dialog box appears **E**.

3. *Do either of the following:*

▸ Fill in the requested information and click Finish.

▸ If you prefer to work with the full Edit Quick Step dialog box **C**, click Options. Fill in the necessary information and click Save.

The Quick Step is added to the gallery.

To create a Quick Step from scratch:

1. In the folder pane, select the account to which the Quick Step will apply.

2. Click the Create New icon **A** in the gallery or choose New Quick Step > Custom from the gallery's menu **D**.

The Edit Quick Step dialog box **C** appears.

3. Follow Steps 3–7 in "To modify an existing Quick Step." Name the Quick Step, add actions, and so on.

4. When you're done, click Finish.

D Open the gallery menu and choose a template from the New Quick Step submenu.

E To create a simple Quick Step, the First Time Setup dialog box will often suffice.

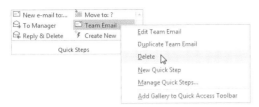

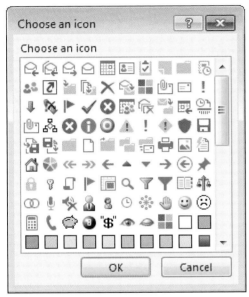

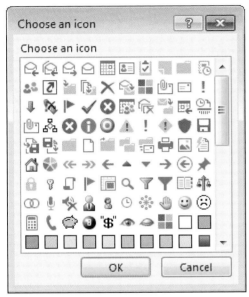 You can right-click a Quick Step in the gallery to choose common commands, such as Edit, Duplicate, and Delete.

 Feel free to change a Quick Step's icon.

To apply a Quick Step:

1. If appropriate (for a Move or Reply & Delete Quick Step, for example), select the message(s) to which you want to apply the Quick Step.

2. Click the Quick Step icon in the gallery or press its assigned keyboard shortcut (if any).

TIP Every Quick Step that you create is account-specific; that is, it will only be listed and accessible from the account that was active when it was created.

TIP To remove a Quick Step, right-click its icon and choose Delete .

TIP When creating or editing a Quick Step, you can select a new icon for it by clicking the icon to the left of the Name text box .

Appointments and Tasks

In addition to handling your email and Really Simple Syndication (RSS) feeds, Outlook has exceptional appointment, event, and task management capabilities.

You use Calendar to schedule one-time appointments (such as a project meeting or dinner with a friend), accompanied by a pop-up reminder before the event. You can also schedule recurring events, such as birthdays and weekly staff meetings.

You use Tasks to manage items on your to-do list, such as mowing the lawn, buying a bathrobe, or writing a proposal. Unlike Calendar appointments, a task isn't required to have a due date or a reminder, although it can optionally have either or both.

In This Chapter

Calendar Basics

To work with the Calendar **A** (below), click Calendar in the Navigation Bar and select a viewing option on the Home or View tab, such as Day, Week, or Month. In most views, *events* (all-day items) are shown at the top of each day, *appointments* (items with a particular start and end time) are listed by start time, and *tasks* appear at the bottom.

To change the details for an appointment or event, double-click it. To view an item's basic information, rest the cursor on it **B**.

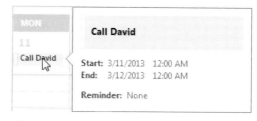

B Rest the cursor on an item to view its details.

Mini calendars Switch week View options Instant Search box Event Help

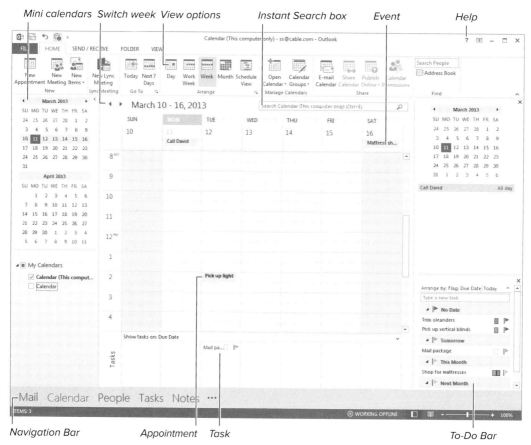

Navigation Bar Appointment Task To-Do Bar

A The Calendar component.

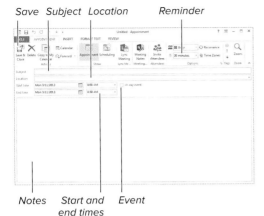

Save   Subject   Location   Reminder

Notes   Start and   Event
         end times

Ⓐ You can create a new appointment or event in a window.

8

Pick up light bulbs

9

Ⓑ Rather than open a window to create an item, it's often faster to select a date/time slot on a calendar and type the item's subject.

Deleting Appointments and Events

To delete a selected appointment or event, click Appointment:Actions:Delete, right-click the item and choose Delete from the context menu, or press Ctrl-D.

Creating an Appointment or Event

To track or be reminded of an appointment or event, you must first add it to the Calendar.

To create an appointment or event:

1. *Do one of the following:*
   - ▸ **From any component.** Choose Home: New:New Items > Appointment.
   - ▸ **From Calendar.** Click Home:New: New Appointment (Ctrl-N) or choose Home:New:New Items > All Day Event.

   An Untitled - Appointment or Untitled - Event window opens **Ⓐ**.

2. Enter a subject for the appointment or event. You can also specify a location.

3. *Do either of the following:*
   - ▸ To treat this item as an event, click the All day event check box.
   - ▸ To treat this item as an appointment, set start and end dates and times.

4. *Optional:* To set an alarm for this item, choose a time interval from the Appointment [Event]:Options:Reminder menu.

   A reminder will appear at the designated interval prior to the scheduled start.

5. Click the Appointment:Save & Close icon.

> **TIP** You can create an event or appointment in an Event or Appointment window. The state of the All day event check box is all that distinguishes an event from an appointment.

> **TIP** By clicking icons in the Tags group, you can mark the item as High or Low Importance.

> **TIP** You can quickly create an appointment or event by selecting a time or event slot on the Calendar and then typing the subject **Ⓑ**.

Creating Recurring Events

Not all appointments and events are one-time activities; many repeat at regular intervals. For example, you may attend weekly staff meetings or belong to a club that meets at 7 PM every third Tuesday of the month. Birthdays and anniversaries are also examples of recurring events.

To set a recurring schedule for an event or appointment:

1. *Do one of the following:*

   ▸ Create a new event or appointment by following Steps 1–4 of "To create an appointment or event."

   ▸ Choose Home : New : New Items > Recurring Event, Appointment, or Meeting 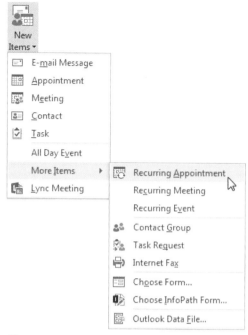.

   ▸ Select or open an existing event or appointment that you want to change into a recurring item.

2. If the Appointment Recurrence dialog box isn't open, *do the following:*

   ▸ If the item's window is open, click the Appointment [Event] : Options : Recurrence icon.

   ▸ If you've selected an appointment or event on the Calendar that you want to change into a recurring item, click the Appointment : Options : Recurrence icon.

Ⓐ You can create a recurring item directly by choosing a Recurring option. (However, it's just as easy to create an item normally and specify that it's recurring as part of the details.)

Recurrence pattern

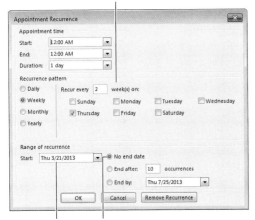

Start date   *End date*

 You set and change recurring schedules in this dialog box.

Working with Multiple Calendars

Although most users will have only one Calendar, you can create others for different purposes. Click Folder:New:New Calendar. Adding Hotmail accounts to Outlook will automatically add their associated calendars, too.

You can simultaneously show multiple calendars, either side-by-side or overlaid on a single calendar. To toggle between these two views, click the View:Arrangement:Overlay icon.

Whether a calendar is currently visible is determined by its check box in the folder pane. Checked calendars are visible; unchecked ones are hidden.

3. In the Appointment Recurrence dialog box ⑧, set a recurrence pattern. If the event or appointment has a known end date, indicate it in the Range of recurrence section.

TIP If a recurring appointment or event is scheduled for a specific time, you can enter a Start and End time. If it's an all-day event or one without a scheduled time, ignore the Start and End boxes.

4. Click OK to close the dialog box.

5. If the appointment or event window is open, click the Recurring Event:Actions: Save & Close icon.

TIP You can set a reminder for a recurring appointment or event.

TIP To change a recurring item to a one-time appointment or event (or end the recurrences), select it on the Calendar or open it in its own window. Open the Appointment Recurrence dialog box and then click the Remove Recurrence button ⑧. All recurrences from that date forward are deleted.

Responding to Reminders

Any event, appointment, or task can have a *reminder* (alarm) associated with it. If Outlook is running when a reminder is triggered, the Reminders window  appears. The window can also be opened by clicking View:Window:Reminders Window.

To respond to a reminder:

1. In the Reminders window, select the reminder to which you want to respond.

2. *Do one of the following:*

   ▸ Click the Dismiss button. This turns off the alarm associated with the item. (To disable the alarm for *every* listed item, click Dismiss All.)

   ▸ To repeat the reminder at a later date or time, choose a *snooze period* from the drop-down menu and then click the Snooze button.

   ▸ To view or edit the item, double-click it.

3. When you're done responding to this and other reminders, dismiss the Reminders window by clicking its close box (X).

TIP You can change the default appointment reminder period in the Calendar category of the Outlook Options dialog box **B**. This period is automatically used for each new appointment. However, you can assign a different period or disable the reminder for any item by choosing None from the Reminders drop-down menu.

TIP Although you won't receive additional reminders for a dismissed item, the item is *not* removed from the Calendar. You must delete an item to remove it from the Calendar. See the next section for item deletion methods.

Snooze menu

A Current and overdue reminders are shown as a scrolling list in the Reminders window.

B Choose the number of minutes, hours, or days ahead that you'll want to be reminded for most appointments and events.

Custom Calendar Color

If you don't care for a Calendar's color scheme, you can personalize it by choosing a new color from the View:Color:Color gallery.

You can also set the color in Outlook Options. Select the Calendar category and scroll down to the Display options section. If you have multiple calendars, each one can be a different color.

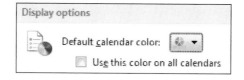

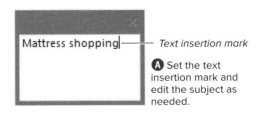

Text insertion mark

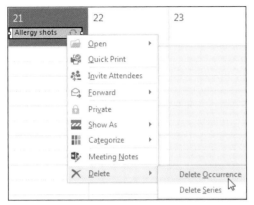

A Set the text insertion mark and edit the subject as needed.

B When deleting or editing a recurring item, the deletion or edits can be applied to the selected item only or to the entire series.

Modifying Events and Appointments

You can change the subject, date, start or end time, reminder period, and other elements of an existing event or appointment.

To change an event or appointment:

- *Do any of the following:*

  ‣ To edit only the subject, select the appointment or event on a Calendar page, set the text insertion mark in the subject **A**, and edit as desired.

  ‣ To delete a selected appointment or event on a Calendar page, click Appointment:Actions:Delete; right-click the item and choose Delete from the context menu; or press Delete or Ctrl-D.

  ‣ To change an item's start date or time, you can drag the item to a new Calendar time slot or date.

  ‣ To change *any* aspect of an event or appointment, double-click the item on a Calendar page, select the item, and click Appointment:Actions:Open, or press Ctrl-O. When you're done making changes, click the Save & Close icon.

TIP When deleting a *recurring* appointment or event, you can delete the current occurrence or all occurrences **B**.

TIP To change only the date while keeping the same start and end times, you can drag the item onto a new date on a mini calendar or a date in Month view.

Searching for an Event or Appointment

Flipping through Calendar pages or mini calendars isn't an efficient way to find an appointment or event—especially when you have only a vague idea of when the item will occur or has occurred. Use the Instant Search box to quickly find most items.

To perform a simple search:

1. To start a search, activate the Instant Search box **A** (bottom) by clicking in it or pressing Ctrl-E. Type the search text.

   The Search Tools:Search contextual tab appears, and the search box expands to show criterion boxes. Outlook lists matching items as you type.

2. If the appointment or event isn't found, you may want to change the search scope by *doing one of the following:*

   ► Select a different calendar or additional ones by clicking their check boxes in the folder pane **B**.

   ► Click icons in the Search:Scope group to indicate what you want to search **A**.

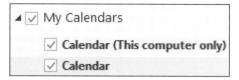

B If you have multiple calendars, you can select the ones you want to search.

Displaying a Date

Whether you're searching for an appointment, intend to create one, or just want to check your schedule, you can go to a date by doing any of the following:

- Click the scroll arrows in the upper-left corner of the Calendar.

- Click the date on a mini calendar or drag-select a range.

- Click Home:Go To:Today or Home:Go To:Next 7 Days.

- Click the Go To Date dialog box launcher beneath the Home:Go To group or press Ctrl-G. Specify the date in the Go To Date dialog box.

| Scope group | Found items | Search contextual tab | | Instant Search box | Close Search |

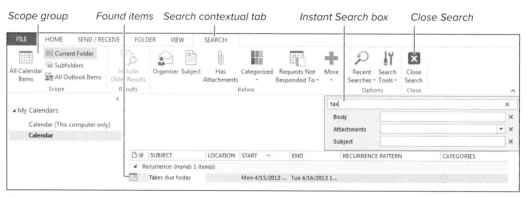

A To conduct a search that simultaneously searches all fields and item elements, type a search string in the Instant Search box. To build a multi-field query, see "To perform an advanced search."

C You can add query fields by choosing them from the More menu.

Query Building Tips

Combining criteria to perform a search can be a little confusing. Here are a couple of useful tips:

- By default, when you specify multiple criteria, you're performing an AND search; that is, *all* criteria must be satisfied to constitute a match. However, you can create an OR search (finding items that match this *or* that criterion) by typing **OR** to separate criteria, such as **Ken OR hasattachments:yes**. In this example, matches will contain the word **Ken** somewhere within the item *or* have an attached file.

- Added More criterion boxes are automatically displayed when you conduct new searches. You can remove any unwanted search field by clicking its close (X) box.

3. *Do any of the following with the search results list:*

- ▸ Double-click a found item to open it.

- ▸ To delete a found item from the Calendar, select it in the list and then press Del, press Delete, or click Search: Actions:Delete.

- ▸ To edit a found item (changing its Subject or Start, for example), click in that field in the search results list and make the changes.

4. To return to the Calendar, click the close icon (X) in the Instant Search box or the Search:Close:Close Search icon Ⓐ.

To perform an advanced search:

1. For a more specific or complex query, start by selecting the Instant Search box. Criterion boxes appear beneath it Ⓐ.

2. To build the query, type search text in any of the criterion boxes and choose values from the criterion drop-down menus.

    The criteria are combined in the Instant Search box, such as **subject:tax hasattachments:yes**.

3. To utilize the search results and complete the search, perform Steps 3–4 of the previous step list.

TIP You can add other criteria by selecting them from the Search:Refine group Ⓐ. If you aren't comfortable editing the query text generated by clicking Refine group icons, you can choose fields from the Search:Refine:More menu C. Each choice adds a field to the query that you can complete by typing text or choosing a value from the field's menu.

TIP To repeat a simple or advanced search, you may be able to select it from the Search: Options:Recent Searches list.

Sharing Calendars

While most of your work with the Calendar will be solitary, Outlook also provides ways to share your schedule with others. One of the simplest sharing methods is to email a date range of your appointments and events.

To email a calendar:

1. Create a new email message.

2. Set the text insertion mark in the message area, and *do either of the following:*

    ▸ Choose Message : Include : Attach Item > Calendar.

    ▸ Click the Insert : Include : Calendar icon.

    The Send a Calendar via E-mail dialog box appears Ⓐ.

3. If you have multiple calendars, choose one from the Calendar menu.

4. Specify dates to include by choosing an option from the Date Range menu.

    To set a different range or include past dates, choose Specify dates.

5. From the Detail menu, specify the amount of appointment information to include:

    ▸ **Availability only.** Show only whether you're free or busy (in general terms).

    ▸ **Limited details.** Show free times, plus the Subject for booked times.

    ▸ **Full details.** Show free times, plus full details for booked times.

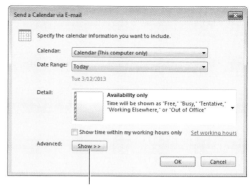

Display advanced options

Ⓐ Choose Calendar-sharing options in this dialog box and click OK.

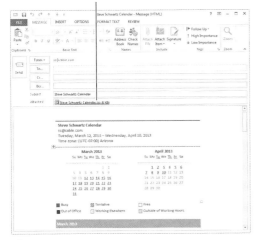

B You can customize the Calendar data that will be shared. Available options depend on the Detail setting **A**.

Calendar file attachment

C Information from the specified Calendar dates is added to the message.

6. *Optional:* Click the Show button to set Advanced options **B**:

   ▸ **Include details of items marked private.** Check to share private items; leave unchecked to omit these items. (This option is available only when you select Limited or Full details.)

   ▸ **Include attachments within calendar items.** If an appointment or event has an *attachment* (such as a picture or document) and this option is checked, the attachment will also be sent. (This option is available only when you select Full details.)

   ▸ **E-mail Layout.** *Daily schedule* is the standard layout, providing information on both free and booked times. *List of events* shows only booked times.

7. Click OK.

   The Calendar information is added to the message body **C** and included as an attachment that can be opened and viewed by another Outlook user.

8. Click Send to send the message.

   TIP When an Outlook user receives an emailed calendar, he or she can open the attached file in Outlook and view the two calendars side-by-side. Doing so makes it simple to see times when you're both free. Appointments from the received file can be dragged onto the recipient's calendar, if desired.

   TIP You can also share a calendar by clicking Home:Share:Share Calendar or publish it to a server by clicking Home:Share:Publish Online.

Task Basics

Click Tasks in the Navigation Bar to make the Tasks component active **A** (bottom). Use Tasks to view, create, and manage a to-do list. You can change the view, delete tasks, mark tasks as complete, or edit any aspect of a task.

TIP The distinction between appointments and tasks is up to you. Because a task can occur at a specific time and also have an alarm that appears in the Reminders window, such items can be recorded as tasks or as appointments.

TIP No matter which Outlook component is active, your tasks can be displayed in the To-Do Bar **B**. Choose View:Layout:To-Do Bar > Tasks. To remove Tasks from the To-Do Bar, choose the Tasks command again or click the Task pane's close (X) button.

Close pane

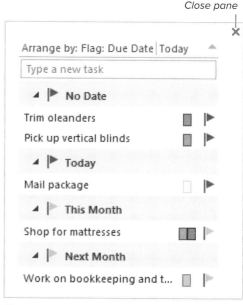

B Upcoming tasks can optionally be displayed in the To-Do Bar.

Change View   Folder Pane   Create task   Search To-Do List

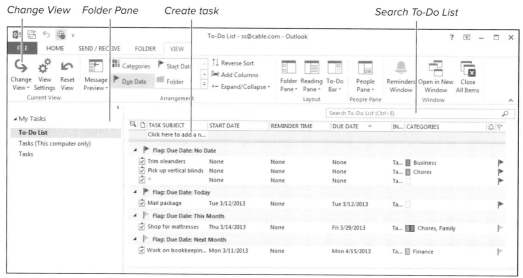

A The Tasks component.

A Like Calendar appointments and events, tasks are typically created in a special window.

Tasks vs. To-Do Items

You've undoubtedly noted and are wondering why the Tasks pane has at least two lists: Tasks and To-Do List. Don't feel bad. Whenever I write an Office book, I have to refresh my memory concerning the distinction between tasks and to-dos.

- **Tasks.** These are items you've created by clicking the New Task icon or issuing the New Task keyboard shortcut.

- **To-Do List items.** These items include all defined tasks *plus* any Outlook items you've flagged for follow-up.

Creating a Task

You can record as many new tasks as you like.

To create a task:

1. *Do either of the following:*

   ▸ **From any component.** Choose Home : New : New Items > Task (Ctrl-Shift-K).

   ▸ **From Tasks.** Click Home : New : New Task (Ctrl-N).

   An Untitled - Task window opens **A**.

2. Enter a Subject for the task.

3. *Optional:* For a time-sensitive task, enter a start and/or due date.

   For a task with no specific start and/or due date, leave the dates set to None.

4. *Optional:* To set an alarm for this task, click the Reminder check box and set a reminder date and time.

   At the appropriate time, the reminder will appear in the Reminders window (see **A** in "Responding to Reminders").

5. *Optional:* If the task will *recur* (repeat over time), open the Task Recurrence dialog box by clicking the Task : Recurrence : Recurrence icon. Set the recurrence pattern and range. See "Creating Recurring Events" for instructions.

6. *Optional:* Choose a progress setting from the Status drop-down menu.

   If you choose In Progress, you can also specify the % Complete.

continues on next page

7. *Optional:* Choose High or Low from the Priority drop-down menu (or click the Task:Tags:High Importance or Low Importance icon ⓑ). Otherwise, the default setting of Normal is assumed.

8. *Optional:* Categorize the task by choosing a category from the Task:Tags: Categorize menu ⓑ.

9. *Optional:* Enter task notes or details in the scrolling text area.

10. Click Task:Actions:Save & Close.

The new task is added to the To-Do List.

TIP You can also create a task by typing its subject directly into the text box above the To-Do List ⓒ, Tasks list, or the Tasks list area of the To-Do Bar.

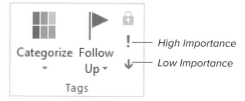

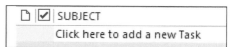
— High Importance
— Low Importance

ⓑ You can assign a priority or category tag to any task, enabling you to sort the list by the tag.

🗋	☑	SUBJECT
		Click here to add a new Task

ⓒ To quickly create a new task, type its subject in the text box. If you later need to add details, open the task and make the changes.

A Choose a view of the Tasks list.

Show group views

B In Details view, you can enter additional useful information.

Modifying Tasks

When a task is completed or you make progress on it, you can mark it as complete or change the % Complete setting. You can also delete tasks that you no longer need to track.

To modify a task:

1. In the folder pane, select the list that contains the item you want to edit.

2. On the Home or View tab, choose a view from the Current View:Change View gallery A that displays the fields you want to change.

3. *Optional:* You can change the sort order of most lists by clicking a column head. To change the groupings, click an icon in the View:Arrangement gallery.

4. *Optional:* To change the displayed fields, click View:Arrangement:Add Columns.

5. *Do either of the following:*

   ▸ Double-click the task to open it in its own window, make the changes, and click Task:Save & Close.

   ▸ Make changes by directly editing the task information in the list.

TIP When a task is open in its own window, icons in the Task:Show group determine the view. When Task is selected, the normal view is presented. In Details view B, you can record other information, such as mileage and hours worked.

TIP Views can be improved by enabling the Reading Pane. The Reading Pane lets you view the details of any selected task or flagged item. Choose a position (Bottom or Right) from the View:Layout:Reading Pane menu.

continues on next page

TIP To mark a task as complete, click the task's check box in the Tasks list **C**. Or you can select it in any list and click the Home:Manage Task:Mark Complete icon **D**. (To reverse the completion status, repeat the process).

TIP To delete a task you no longer want to track, select it in any list and click Home:Delete: Delete; click Home:Manage Task:Remove from List; or press Ctrl-D, Del, or Delete. (Note that most task deletions are carried out immediately—without a warning.)

Another way to delete a task or change its completion status is to right-click the task in the To-Do Bar or a Tasks list and choose a command from the context menu that appears **E**.

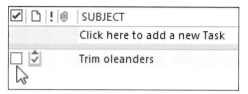

C When a Tasks list is selected in the folder pane, you can mark a task as completed by clicking its check box.

D Click an icon in the Home:Manage Task group to mark a task as complete or delete it.

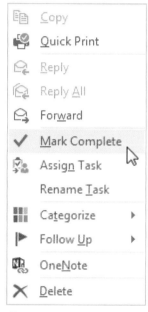

E If you prefer, you can right-click a task to change its completion status or delete it.

Combining Office Data

Separately, each Office 2013 application is impressive. But when combined, they form a powerful system for sharing information.

One simple way of combining information from different Office applications is by copying, embedding, or linking. You can copy a table of numeric data from Excel into a Word document to add some relevant numbers to a memo, for example. Or to ensure that later changes to the Excel data automatically flow to the table in the Word document, you can link the data between the documents.

In addition to explaining copying, linking, and embedding, this chapter provides several specific examples of ways to share data among Office applications.

Copying, Linking, and Embedding

Office lets you easily share information among its applications. The three methods are copying, embedding, and linking.

The simplest method is to copy and paste or drag and drop material between applications. For example, you can copy a range in Excel and paste it into a Word document. Or you can drag the range into Word. The data becomes part of the Word document as an editable table. Similarly, you can drag a copy of a PowerPoint slide into a Word document. Data added using the copy-and-paste or drag-and-drop method becomes a part of—and is saved with—the destination document. You can move the document to another machine or email it to someone secure in the knowledge that the copied or dropped data will be intact.

If you need to be able to edit the copied material using the source application (rather than the destination application), you can use embedding or linking. The difference between the two lies in where the material is stored.

- *Embedded* material (like copied material) becomes part of the destination document, making it transportable. Because no link is maintained with the source document, you can freely edit it without fearing that changes in either document will affect the other.

- *Linked* material, on the other hand, is stored only in the original document and is merely *referenced* by the destination document. Linking is an excellent choice when working with files on a network or combining data from workgroup members.

Adding Office Material to Email

In Outlook, HTML email messages can include Word tables, Excel charts and cell ranges, SmartArt, WordArt, and other objects.

1. Create a new HTML message. (Ensure that Format Text:Format:As HTML is selected.)

2. Select an Excel chart or data range, Word table, SmartArt layout, WordArt, or other object.

3. Click Home:Clipboard:Copy (Ctrl-C).

4. Set the text insertion mark in the email message body.

5. Click Message:Clipboard:Paste (Ctrl-V).

Note that you can also add material to HTML email messages using drag and drop.

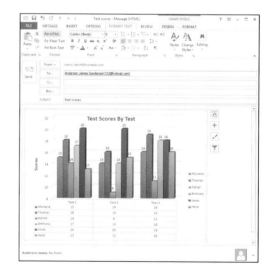

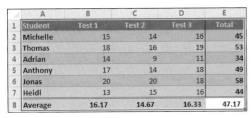

	A	B	C	D	E
1	Student	Test 1	Test 2	Test 3	Total
2	Michelle	15	14	16	45
3	Thomas	18	16	19	53
4	Adrian	14	9	11	34
5	Anthony	17	14	18	49
6	Jonas	20	20	18	58
7	Heidi	13	15	16	44
8	Average	16.17	14.67	16.33	47.17

A To duplicate this section of an Excel worksheet in a Word document, begin by selecting the data range to be copied—in this case, A1:E8.

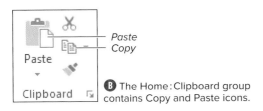

B The Home:Clipboard group contains Copy and Paste icons.

C When pasted into a Word document, the Excel range becomes a Word table.

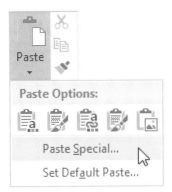

D The Paste drop-down menu.

Using Copy and Paste

Copy and paste and cut and paste are the simplest, most familiar methods of duplicating data between documents—even if the documents are from different applications. Pasted material maintains no link with the original data or its document.

To copy and paste between documents:

1. In the first document, select the material that you want to copy, such as a text block, cell range, slide, or one or more objects **A**.

2. Click Home:Clipboard:Copy **B**, press Ctrl-C, or right-click the object and choose Copy from the context menu.

   The material is copied to the *Clipboard*, a temporary area in memory that stores the most recent copied or cut item.

3. Switch to or open the target document.

   Note that the document must be capable of accepting the type of data you're about to paste. Office 2013 applications can accept most types of material created in other Office applications.

4. In the destination document, specify the location in which you'll paste by setting the text insertion mark, selecting a cell, or making a slide or slide placeholder active, for instance.

5. Click Home:Clipboard:Paste **B** or press Ctrl-V.

   The material is pasted from the Clipboard **C**.

TIP Every Office 2013 application also has a Home:Clipboard:Paste drop-down menu **D**. If you need to control the format when pasting material, be sure to examine the icons and commands in this menu.

Using Drag and Drop

Other than copy and paste (or cut and paste), the easiest way to move something from one application to another is to use drag and drop. The drag and drop process is the same whether it's between applications or within a single application. Arrange the document windows of the two applications so you can see them both. Then drag selected text or other material from one window to its destination in the other application's document window. **Table 22.1** lists some items that you can drag and drop between applications.

To drag and drop an object:

1. Arrange the applications' document windows so you can see both the source material and its intended destination .

2. Select the object or text, such as a worksheet range, chart, or table.

3. Drag the border of the object or text to its destination in the other window.

4. Release the mouse button.

   The object or text appears in the destination document 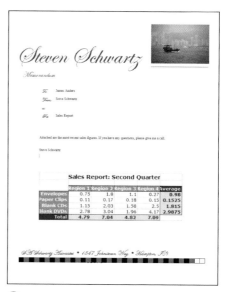. You are free to modify the dragged object or text in the destination document.

CAUTION Whether performed within a document or between documents, a drag and drop is the equivalent of a *cut and paste*—not a copy and paste. The material is deleted from the original document. However, if you right-click as you drag material between applications, a contextual menu enables you to either copy or move the material.

TIP When you drag and drop an item, it becomes part of the destination document. The item will not reflect changes made to the original material unless you establish a link. See "Linking objects," later in this section.

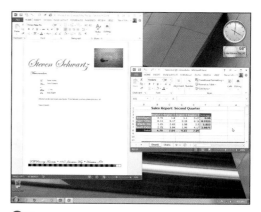

E You can drag and drop a cell range from Excel into a Word document.

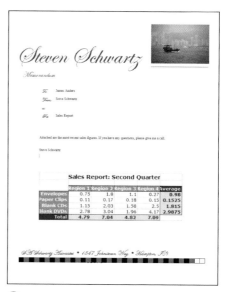

F Release the mouse button when the Excel range is correctly positioned in the Word document.

TABLE 22.1 Common Items to Drag and Drop

Source Application	Object
Word	Selected text or table cells
Excel	A cell, range, graphic, or table
PowerPoint	A slide from Slide Sorter view

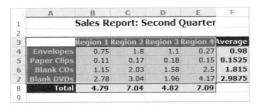

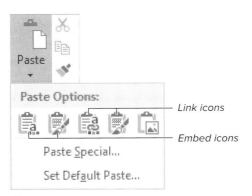

	A	B	C	D	E	F
1		Sales Report: Second Quarter				
2						
3		Region 1	Region 2	Region 3	Region 4	Average
4	Envelopes	0.75	1.8	1.1	0.27	0.98
5	Paper Clips	0.11	0.17	0.18	0.15	0.1525
6	Blank CDs	1.15	2.03	1.58	2.5	1.815
7	Blank DVDs	2.78	3.04	1.96	4.17	2.9875
8	Total	4.79	7.04	4.82	7.09	
9						

Ⓖ Select and copy the material that you want to embed, such as this Excel range (A3:E7).

Paste

Paste Options:

— Link icons

— Embed icons

Paste Special...

Set Default Paste...

Ⓗ Click an Embed icon to insert the copied material into the document.

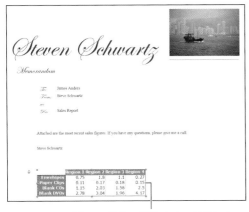

Microsoft Excel Worksheet Object

Ⓘ The embedded object appears in the Word document.

Embedding Objects

An *embedded object* is material that is copied in its source application and pasted into the target document as a Microsoft Object. The advantage to embedding rather than linking (see the next section) is that the material resides entirely in the target document, but is edited using the source application's tools. As a result, you can safely move the document to other computers.

Unlike a *linked object* (which is updated whenever the source data changes), an embedded object changes only when you edit it in the target document. This ensures that the object will change only when—or if—you want it to change.

You can embed an existing object in the target application or create an embedded object from scratch.

To embed an existing object:

1. Select the material in its source application Ⓖ.

2. Click Home : Clipboard : Copy Ⓗ, press Ctrl-C, or right-click the object and choose Copy from the context menu.

3. Switch to the target document and click to set the destination for the object.

4. *Do one of the following:*

   ▸ Choose Home : Clipboard : Paste > Paste Special. In the Paste Special dialog box, select the item (such as Microsoft Excel Worksheet Object), and click OK.

   ▸ In the target application, open the Home : Clipboard : Paste menu. Click an Embed icon (if one is available) in the Paste Options section Ⓗ.

   The embedded object appears in the destination document Ⓘ.

To create an embedded object:

1. In the target document, click to set the destination for the object.

2. Click Insert : Text : Object.

   The Object dialog box appears **J**.

3. Ensure that the Create New tab is selected, select the object type from the scrolling list, and click OK.

   The appropriate Office application opens in the current document window **K**.

4. Create the object.

5. When you're done creating the object, double-click anywhere else in the document window.

   The object appears and the normal Ribbon is restored.

To edit an embedded object:

1. Double-click the object **L**, such as a sheet embedded in a Word document.

   The source application's Ribbon and tools appear.

2. Make the desired changes to the object.

3. When you're done editing the object, double-click anywhere else in the document window.

   The normal Ribbon reappears.

Create New tab

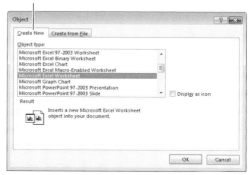

J Select the type of object you want to create.

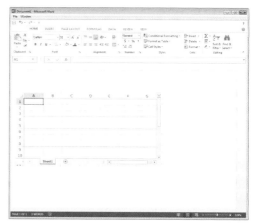

K Create the object. Note that the Ribbon takes on the attributes of the object's creating program—in this example, Excel.

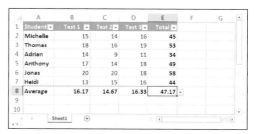

L Double-click the embedded object to open it for editing using the source application.

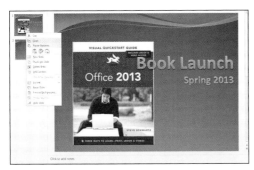

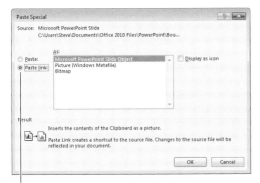

Paste link radio button

M Select and copy the data or material to which you want to link, such as this PowerPoint slide.

N Select the specific object type, click the Paste link radio button, and then click OK.

O The linked slide appears in the Word document.

Linking Objects

When you link rather than embed an object, the object remains in the original application's document. A *copy* of the object—linked to the original—is displayed in the destination application's document. Any changes made to the original object also appear in the linked copy.

You create linked objects using the Copy and Paste Special commands. The copied object is updated whenever you reopen the destination file, ensuring that the object is always current. Linking is ideal for any object whose data regularly changes or is being edited. In addition to—or rather than—updating a link automatically, you can update it manually.

To link an object:

1. Select the object in the source document that you want to link **M**.

2. Click Home : Clipboard : Copy **B**, press Ctrl-C, or right-click the object and choose Copy from the context menu.

3. Open the destination document and click where you want the linked object to appear.

4. *Do one of the following:*

   ▸ Choose Home : Clipboard : Paste > Paste Special. In the Paste Special dialog box **N**, select the object to link, click the Paste link radio button, and click OK.

   ▸ In the destination document, open the Home : Clipboard : Paste menu. Click a Link icon in the Paste Options area **H**.

   The linked object appears in the target document **O**.

TIP To edit the original object, double-click the linked object in the destination document.

TIP The linked object will appear in the destination document at its original size. You can resize it as necessary.

TIP When you open a document containing auto-updating links, a dialog box appears **P**. Click Yes to check the links for changes and update them in the current document; click No to ignore any changes. (To disable automatic updating for the document, remove the check mark from Update automatic links at open in File: Options: Advanced: General.)

To manually update a link:

■ Right-click the object in the destination document and choose Update Link from the context menu **Q**.

To change link settings:

1. Right-click the object in the destination document and choose Linked *object type* > Links from the context menu **Q**.

   The Links dialog box appears **R**.

2. Select the link that you want to examine, update, edit, or change.

3. *Do any of the following:*

   ▸ Specify whether the link is automatically checked for updates or will only be updated manually. Click the appropriate Update method for selected link radio button.

   ▸ To open the linked object's source document, click the Open Source button.

   ▸ To change the linked object into an embedded object, click the Break Link button.

   ▸ To force a manual update, click the Update Now button.

4. Click OK to close the dialog box and accept any changes you've made.

P To check for updates to linked objects in the document, click Yes.

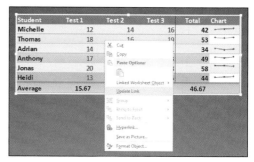

Q To manually check for changes to a linked object, right-click it and choose Update Links.

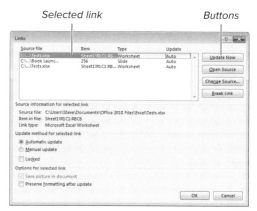

R You can change a link's settings.

Selection handle

A Select the entire table in the Word document.

B Specify the formatting for the pasted material.

Match Destination Formatting

Keep Source Formatting

	A	B	C	D	E	F
1		Qtr 1	Qtr 2	Qtr 3	Qtr 4	Totals
2	District 1	123	234	89	165	611
3	District 2	53	57	54	85	249
4	District 3	265	199	307	177	948
5	Totals	441	490	450	427	

C The formatted Word table appears in the Excel worksheet.

Word Table into Excel

Word and Excel work well together, especially when you're creating Word documents that display structured numeric data. The previous sections showed how to copy and link Excel data into Word documents. In this section, you'll learn to do the reverse: copy a Word table into an Excel worksheet. Later in this chapter, you'll learn to copy normal Word text into Excel and PowerPoint.

To copy a Word table into Excel:

1. In Word, move the cursor over the table that you want to copy and click the selection handle above the table's left corner **A**.

2. Click Home : Clipboard : Copy, press Ctrl-C, or right-click the table and choose Copy from the context menu.

3. Switch to Excel. Select the cell in which the Word table will begin.

4. *Do one of the following:*

   ▸ To retain the table's Word formatting, click Home : Clipboard : Paste or press Ctrl-V.

   ▸ To make the formatting of the pasted table match that of the target cells, click the Home : Clipboard : Paste > Match Destination Formatting icon **B**.

   The table appears in the worksheet **C**.

TIP A table copied in this manner can be edited in Excel. You can also change the formatting, if desired. The pasted data is not linked to the original Word document.

CAUTION Formulas in the Word table are *not* copied to Excel; only the results are transferred to the worksheet. If they're necessary, you'll have to recreate the formulas.

Sharing Outlines:
Word and PowerPoint

You can use Word and PowerPoint together, too. This section explains how to move an outline from one application to the other.

TIP **Starting a presentation in Word isn't outlandish. Most people find it easier to write and edit in Word rather than in PowerPoint.**

To use a Word outline file in a PowerPoint presentation:

1. Create a presentation outline in Word **A**. Each Level 1 paragraph will become the title of a new slide. Level 2 paragraphs will become first-level text.

2. Click the File tab. Select Save or Save As.

3. In the Save As pane, specify a location and folder for the file.

4. In the Save As dialog box, name the file, choose Word Document (*.docx) as the file type, and click Save.

5. Create a PowerPoint presentation or open an existing one to which you want to add the Word outline. (Note that no link is maintained between the presentation and the Word outline.)

6. In PowerPoint's navigation pane, select the slide after which the outline will be inserted.

7. Choose Home : Slides : New Slide > Slides from Outline.

   The Insert Outline dialog box appears.

8. Select the Word outline and click Open.

   The new slides are added to the presentation **B**.

A Open the Word outline. In this example, the outline is part of the table of contents for a book.

B The outline is incorporated into the new slides. Reformat the text and backgrounds as desired.

Tweaking the Word Outline

If the first line of the Word outline is its title, this will result in only one slide—because only the title is a Level 1 paragraph. To prepare such an outline for PowerPoint, select all outline text after the first line, click the Outlining : Outline Tools : Promote icon to raise every point by one level, and then delete the title line.

Outline view

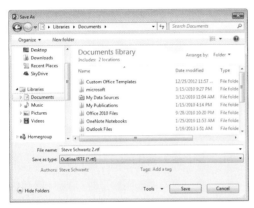

C A presentation in Outline view.

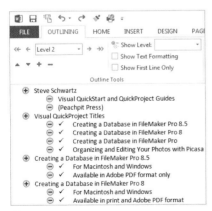

D Save the presentation in Outline/RTF format.

E This is the PowerPoint outline in Word with Show Text Formatting disabled.

To copy a PowerPoint presentation outline into a Word document:

1. In PowerPoint, switch to Outline view **C** by clicking View:Presentation Views: Outline View.

2. Click the File tab and select Save As.

3. Specify a location and folder for the file.

4. In the Save As dialog box **D**, name the file, choose Outline/RTF (.rtf) as the file type, and click Save.

5. Open the new outline file in Word.

6. In Word, switch to Outline View by clicking View:Views:Outline.

7. Reformat the text and edit the point levels as desired.

TIP To avoid reformatting the text in Word, remove the check mark from the Outlining: Outline Tools:Show Text Formatting check box. All text will be displayed in a single font and size **E**.

Word Text into Excel or PowerPoint

You can transfer text from Word into Excel or PowerPoint using copy and paste or drag and drop.

To copy text from Word:

1. Arrange the Word document window so you can also see the PowerPoint or Excel document window.

2. Select the text in Word.

3. *Do one of the following:*

   ▸ Click Home : Clipboard : Copy (Ctrl-C). Paste the text into an Excel cell **Ⓐ** or a PowerPoint slide **Ⓑ** by clicking Home : Clipboard : Paste (Ctrl-V).

   ▸ Right-click the text and drag it to the starting cell of the Excel range or onto a PowerPoint slide. When you release the mouse button, choose Copy Here from the context menu **Ⓒ**.

TIP Text formatting, such as font, size, and style, is also copied and will appear in Excel. In PowerPoint, however, the destination place-holder's text formatting and the amount of pasted text determine the initial font size.

TIP In Excel, pasted Word text frequently overflows the cells. If necessary, you can expand the column width or enable text wrap for the affected cells.

TIP Excel mimics the paragraph formatting of copied Word text. A tab within a paragraph is treated as an instruction to place the text in the next cell; a return is treated as an instruction to move down to the next row.

TIP The Paste icon in PowerPoint and Excel offers other paste options that you may want to explore. For example, you can paste text as a picture, unformatted text, or as a Word Document Object that you can continue to edit in Word.

	A	B	C	D	E
1	Lesson Outline				
2	1. What Is a Database?				
3	2. Introducing FileMaker Pro				
4	3. Working with Databases				
5	4. Creating a Simple Database				
6	5. Customizing a Database - Part 1				
7	6. Customizing a Database - Part 2				
8	7. Sorting and Searching				
9	8. Reports: Previewing and Printing				
10	9. Going Relational				
11	10. Automating with ScriptMaker				
12	11. Using FileMaker Pro in a Workgroup				
13	12. Publishing a Database on the Web				

Ⓐ Drag or paste the text into Excel. Each line of pasted text becomes a new row.

Lesson Outline
1. What Is a Database?
2. Introducing FileMaker Pro
3. Working with Databases
4. Creating a Simple Database
5. Customizing a Database - Part 1
6. Customizing a Database - Part 2
7. Sorting and Searching
8. Reports: Previewing and Printing
9. Going Relational
10. Automating with ScriptMaker
11. Using FileMaker Pro in a Workgroup
12. Publishing a Database on the Web

Ⓑ In PowerPoint, you can drag or paste text into a text placeholder or blank slide.

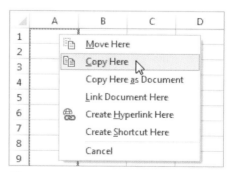

Ⓒ When using drag and drop between two documents, right-clicking enables you to either copy or move the data.

Index

Symbols

\+ (addition) operator, using in Excel, 208

& (concatenation) operator, using in Excel, 208

/ (division) operator, using in Excel, 208

= (equal) operator, using in Excel, 208

^ (exponentiation) operator, using in Excel, 208

\> (greater than) operator, using in Excel, 208

\>= (greater than or equal to) operator, using in Excel, 208

< (less than) operator, using in Excel, 208

<= (less than or equal to) operator, using in Excel, 208

* (multiplication) operator, using in Excel, 208

* wildcard, using in Excel finds, 181

– (negation) operator, using in Excel, 208

<> (not equal to) operator, using in Excel, 208

% (percent) operator, using in Excel, 208

: (range) operator, using in Excel, 209

– (subtraction) operator, using in Excel, 208

, (union) operator, using in Excel, 209

? wildcard, using in Excel finds, 181

A

action buttons, adding to slides, 278

addition (+) operator, using in Excel, 208

Address Book, searching for contacts in, 325

alarms, responding to, 396

aligning
    objects, 67
    paragraphs, 117

Animation Painter tool, using with presentations, 272

Animation Pane, 271

applications, launching, 10

Appointment Recurrence dialog box, 395

appointment reminders, responding to, 396

appointments in Outlook, 397.
        See also Calendar interface
    creating, 393
    deleting, 393
    searching, 398–399
    vs. tasks, 402

apps
    downloading from Office Store, 4, 39
    installing, 39
    launching, 39

artistic effects, adding, 71

artwork, resizing, 66

aspect ratio, cropping to, 73

attachments
    adding to messages, 343
    identifying, 366
    opening, 365
    previewing, 364
    purging, 366
    saving, 365–366

AutoCorrect feature
    using in Excel, 165
    using in Word, 92

AutoRecover feature
    enabled state, 14
    enabling, 33
    increasing interval, 33
    options, 32–33
    vs. saving, 33

AutoSum formula, creating in Excel, 213

AVERAGE function, 207

B

background color
    adding to pages, 104
    applying to table cells, 50

backgrounds
    applying watermarks, 105
    modifying, 104–106
    removing, 74
backing up Outlook folders, 386
Backstage
    closing, 11
    creating documents, 11
    opening, 11
Bcc box, displaying for messages, 336
black-and-white, converting color
        photo to, 70
blank documents, creating, 11
blank pages, inserting in Word documents, 110
Blocked Senders list, using for mail, 383
blog accounts
    adding, 154
    changing, 154
    deleting, 154
blog entries
    editing, 154
    publishing, 153–154
blog posts, deleting, 154
boldface keyboard shortcut, 126, 340
border properties, changing in
        tables, 49–50
borders, around pages in Word, 106
breaks, inserting in Word, 107–108
brightness, adjusting in images, 69
Broadcast Service, using with slide shows,
        289–290
broadcasting slide shows, 288–290
Bullet Library, accessing, 120
bulleted lists in Word
    changing formatting of, 121
    enabling, 119
    ending, 120
    selecting items at levels in, 122
    sorting, 121
bullets, creating, 122
business card images, inserting in
        messages, 344
business cards
    creating, 327–328
    editing, 327–328
    emailing, 328
    saving, 328
buttons, using, 3

C

cached Exchange mode, enabling for
        messages, 358
calculated columns, creating in tables, 220.
        See also columns
Calendar interface
    appointments, 392
    To-Do bar, 392
    events, 392
    help, 392
    Instant Search box, 392
    Mini calendars, 392
    Navigation Bar, 392
    switch week, 392
    tasks, 392
    view options, 392
Calendar preferences, setting in Outlook, 313
calendars
    customizing colors, 396
    emailing, 400–401
    sharing, 400–401
    using multiple, 395
CDs, packaging presentations for, 284–285
cell borders
    adding in Excel, 201
    removing from tables, 50
cell data, formatting in tables, 51
cell shading, applying in tables, 50
Cell Size group. *See also* tables
    Distribute Columns icon, 48
    Distribute Rows icon, 48
cells in tables
    alignment, setting, 51
    entering formulas into, 52
    merging, 49
    paragraph formatting, 51
    splitting, 49
cells in Excel
    copying, 169
    deleting, 170
    dragging and dropping, 410
    duplicating, 173
    editing contents of, 167
    entering data in, 165–166
    filling, 173–175
    filling with color, 200
    inserting, 169

formulas in Excel *(continued)*
    operator precedence, 209
    operators, 208
    reference operators, 209
    relative cell references, 210
    results of copying, 210
    results of moving, 210
    text concatenation operator, 208
forwarding received messages, 338
functions, copying into Formula box, 52
functions in Excel. *See also* Excel 2013
    entering arguments, 211
    inserting, 211
    organizing by category, 211
    selecting, 211, 213

G

Gmail accounts, adding, 296
grammar
    checking in Word, 90–92
    setting preferences in Word, 92
graphics, adding, 55. *See also* photos; SmartArt
greater than (>) operator, using in Excel, 208
greater than or equal to (>=) operator, using in Excel, 208
gridlines
    adding to charts, 237
    hiding in Excel, 194
    modifying in charts, 237
    removing from charts, 237
    showing and hiding in Word, 85
groups, Ribbon
    creating, 29
    moving, 29

H

handouts, printing for presentations, 281
header elements
    inserting, 114
    Page fields, 114
headers. *See also* footers
    adding, 111
    adding alignment tabs, 112
    adding page numbers to, 111
    adding pre-formatted, 112
    creating, 113

headers *(continued)*
    customizing, 113–114
    editing, 113, 115
    formatting text in, 115
    hiding body text, 115
    inserting date and time, 114
    Options group, 115
    positioning, 115
    repositioning, 115
headings in Word, going to, 98
help, getting, 40
help info, offline vs. online, 41
Help text, copying and pasting, 41
Help window
    floating, 41
    minimizing, 41
    in Outlook, 314
    working in, 40–41
Hotmail email accounts, 292, 296
hyperlinks
    adding to messages, 345–346
    converting message text to, 346
    converting to normal text, 346
    in Plain Text messages, 346

I

image editing. *See also* photos
    adding borders to photos, 71–72
    artistic effects, 71
    brightness, 69
    capabilities, 68
    color saturation, 70
    compressing pictures, 75
    contrast, 69
    cropping photos, 72
    removing backgrounds, 74
    replacing photos, 76
    resetting edits, 76
    sharpness, 69
    tips, 68
    tone, 70
images. *See also* graphics; photos; pictures
    adding, 55
    choosing for chart backgrounds, 231
    converting to SmartArt objects, 72
    embedding in documents, 56
    linking to files, 56

messages in Outlook *(continued)*
    stationery, 352–353
    themes, 352–353
    undoing actions, 378
    Unread/Read icon, 359
    viewing conversations, 361–362
Microsoft Excel 2013. *See also* formulas in
        Excel; functions in Excel; Office data;
        tables
    A1 reference style, 206
    3-D reference style, 206–207
    absolute cell references, 210
    accessing password settings, 189
    active cell, 158–159
    active sheet, 158–159
    adding cell borders, 201
    analyzing data arrays, 185
    arithmetic operators, 208
    Auto Fill Options menu, 174
    AutoComplete feature, 165
    AutoSum formula, 213
    AVERAGE function, 207
    Backstage, 158
    cell formatting, 194
    cell references, 206–207
    change tracking, 150
    changing font options, 194
    character formatting, 195
    charts, 5, 227–244
    choosing cell border styles, 201
    circular references, 215
    Clear Formats command, 202
    close box, 158, 160
    color scales, 198
    columns, 158–159
    comparison operators, 208
    conditional formatting, 194, 198–199, 201
    continuing series into cells, 174
    copying Word tables into, 415
    COUNT function, 207
    creating 3-D effect in cells, 200
    creating series, 175
    CSV (comma-separated value) files, 180
    custom gradients, 200
    data bars, 198
    data formatting, 194
    deleting cells, 172

Microsoft Excel 2013 *(continued)*
    deleting names, 187
    delimiter characters, 180
    display options, 194
    displaying and hiding gridlines, 194
    duplicating cells, 173
    Edit Name dialog box, 187
    eliminating text wrap, 196
    enabling text wrap, 196
    enhancements, 5
    entering data in cells, 165–166
    error alerts, 216
    Evaluate button, 216
    exporting data as text file, 179–180
    exporting from other programs, 178
    filling cells, 173–175
    filling cells with color, 200
    Find and Replace dialog box, 181, 183
    finding data, 181–182
    Find/Replace tips, 182
    Flash Fill, 5, 175
    Format Cells dialog box, 196
    Format Painter, 203
    formula bar, 158–159
    formulas, 208
    formulas replaced by data, 215
    Function Library group, 214
    Highlight Cells Rules, 199
    icon sets, 198
    importing data, 176–180
    importing fixed-width fields, 180
    improving finds, 181
    incorrect results, 216
    inserting cells, 172
    interface, 158–160
    MAX function, 207
    MIN function, 207
    mixed cell references, 210
    modifying names, 187
    name box, 158–159
    Name Manager dialog box, 187
    naming cells, 186–187
    naming ranges, 186–187
    navigating within cells, 167
    number formatting, 197
    operator precedence, 209
    operators, 208

WATCH
READ
CREATE